JOURNAL FOR THE STUDY OF THE OLD TESTAMENT
SUPPLEMENT SERIES
313

Sheffield Academic Press
A Continuum imprint

Borders, Boundaries and the Bible

edited by

Martin O'Kane

Journal for the Study of the Old Testament
Supplement Series 313

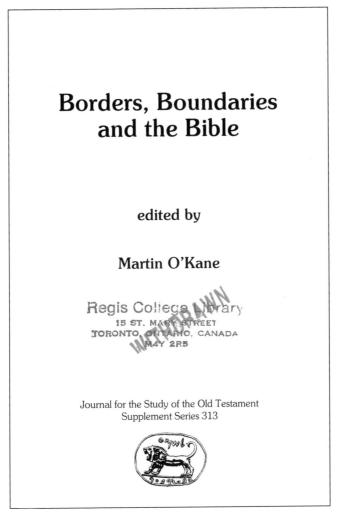

Published by
Sheffield Academic Press Ltd
The Tower Building, 11 York Road, London SE1 7NX
370 Lexington Avenue, New York, NY 10017-6550

www.SheffieldAcademicPress.com
www.continuumbooks.com

British Library Cataloguing-in-Publication Data

A catalogue record for this book is available from the British Library

Typeset by Sheffield Academic Press
Printed on acid-free paper in Great Britain by Bookcraft Ltd, Midsomer Norton, Bath

ISBN 1-84127-148-9

CONTENTS

Part I

LIST OF ILLUSTRATIONS AND TABLES

ABBREVIATIONS

ABD	David Noel Freedman (ed.), *The Anchor Bible Dictionary* (New York: Doubleday, 1992)
CBQ	*Catholic Biblical Quarterly*
HUCA	*Hebrew Union College Annual*
IDB	George Arthur Buttrick (ed.), *The Interpreter's Dictionary of the Bible* (4 vols.; Nashville: Abingdon Press, 1962)
JSJ	*Journal for the Study of Judaism*
JSNT	*Journal for the Study of the New Testament*
JSNTSup	Journal for the Study of the New Testament Supplement Series
JSOTSup	Journal for the Study of the Old Testament Supplement Series
JSS	*Journal of Semitic Studies*
JTS	Journal of Theological Studies
NTS	*New Testament Studies*
PG	*Patrologiae Graecae*
RB	*Revue Biblique*
SJSJ	Supplements to the Journal for the Study of Judaism
SOTS	Society for Old Testament Study
TNTC	Tyndale New Testament Commentaries
VC	*Vigiliae christianae*
ZPE	*Zeitschrift für Papyrologie und Epigraphik*

LIST OF CONTRIBUTORS

Anthony Axe, O.P., Ecole Biblique, Jerusalem and Blackfriars, Edinburgh

†Professor Robert Carroll, former Professor of Biblical Studies, University of Glasgow

Susan Docherty, Lecturer in Biblical Studies, Newman College of Higher Education, Birmingham

Professor Mary Douglas, University College, London

Professor J. Cheryl Exum, Professor of Biblical Studies, University of Sheffield

Professor John M. Hull, Professor of Religious Education, University of Birmingham

Dr Edward Kessler, Executive Director of the Centre for Jewish Christian Relations, Cambridge

Dr Larry J. Kreitzer, New Testament Tutor, Regent's Park College, University of Oxford

Dr Martin O'Kane, Lecturer in Biblical Studies, Newman College of Higher Education, Birmingham

Dr Gaye Ortiz, Lecturer in Religious and Cultural Studies, York St John College, York

Dr Wendy J. Porter, McMaster Divinity College, Hamilton, Ontario, Canada

Professor Stephen Prickett, Regius Professor Emeritus, of English Literature, University of Glasgow

Dr Joy Sisley, Centre for British and Comparative Cultural Studies, Warwick University

Dr Margarita Stocker, Freelance, Author of *Judith, Sexual Warrior*

INTRODUCTION

Martin O'Kane

Reading the Bible: Breaching Borders, Crossing Boundaries was the title of a biblical conference held at Newman College, Birmingham in April 1999. *Characters and Heroes of the Bible: challenging traditional assumptions* was the title of the conference in the subsequent year, April 2000. Both conferences grew out of the Bible and Arts Programme, Newman College and were supported by the Higher Education Funding Council and the Catholic Biblical Association. Their aim was to explore more inclusive ways of reading and understanding the Bible. This collection of essays derives directly from both conferences.

The conference themes were chosen because they relate broadly—and easily—to the way in which the Bible has been communicated and interpreted in Catholic tradition in Western Europe over the centuries. Frequently, the familiarity Catholics have with biblical stories comes not from the text itself but from interpretations of the text in art, music, apocryphal stories or dramatic re-enactments (including liturgical celebrations). The borders and boundaries of the canonical story change as the story is enhanced or appropriated by artist, musician or writer. Literal, fundamentalist readings of biblical stories have had little or no effect on Catholic readership of the Bible for the simple reason that, until recently, Catholics were not encouraged to engage in any kind of personal or detailed reading of the text. Ironically, while the Church authoritatively safeguarded its role in interpreting scripture for its flock, it also enthusiastically engaged the finest artistic and musical talents of the age to depict canonical and apocryphal stories. The result was that biblical scenes were depicted visually—and often with great flair and originality—and made a profound impact on the Catholic laity's knowledge of and familiarity with the Bible. In the Catholic consciousness, a knowledge of the Bible and a familiarity with its cultural representations are inseparable. The connection between the Catholic experience of relating to art and its symbols and the

approaches of those biblical commentators today who use cultural interpretations to elucidate the text is both natural and appealing.

The articles contained in Part I of this book, and delivered at the first
conference, *Reading the Bible: Breaching Borders, Crossing Boundaries*,
explore how moving beyond the strict borders and boundaries of the
biblical text enriches our understanding of it and continues the broad
Catholic tradition of embellishing canonical stories in order to provide
greater opportunity for the reader or viewer to identify with the theme or
characters of the story. The articles in this section are characterised by a
trend to move away from traditional interpretations of the text and offer
new readings from a variety of artistic, literary, musical or other inter-
disciplinary perspectives. Sadly, Robert Carroll who gave the opening
address, *Removing an Ancient Landmark*, died before submitting his final
draft. However, his article, though incomplete, has been included because
it offers a serious challenge as to how the Bible should be read (or viewed)
in the twenty-first century and how biblical exponents and commentators
must move quite radically beyond the strict boundaries of the canonical
text. A range of articles illustrate how biblical themes lend themselves
easily to moving beyond these boundaries. Martin O'Kane shows how the
theme of the *Flight into Egypt* has been interpreted and appropriated as a
symbol of hope for the refugee. Mary Douglas, through the eyes of an
anthropologist, offers new insights into the world of Leviticus. Edward
Kessler explores traditions associated with the Sacrifice of Isaac across the
traditions of Judaism and Christianity. Larry J. Kreitzer traces the New
Testament theme of kingship in a novel by Kipling. Wendy Porter investigates how musical composers have brought biblical texts to life creatively
and imaginatively. John Hull—as one who is blind—challenges the negative presuppositions made about blindness in the Bible and questions
whether he is able to identify with any perspective on blindness that
biblical authors offer.

The articles contained in Part II of this book, and delivered at the second
conference, *Characters and Heroes of the Bible: challenging traditional
assumptions*, explore aspects of character related to the Bible. The speakers at the conference presented different dimensions and approaches to the
topic. The emphasis on the idea of character during the conference provided an opportunity to relate the topic to contemporary biblical scholarship, to the religious background and consciousness of a largely Catholic
audience and to the challenging of traditional assumptions made about
characters within the Bible.

The notion of *character* is embedded deep in the Catholic conscious-ness. Catholics traditionally have given a central importance to the place of saints both in the Church and in their lives. Saints have been held up as models to be imitated, and their strengths and weaknesses have been reflected upon for centuries in endless hagiographies. It is especially striking—at first—how in so many works of art, European saints appear in biblical scenes defying any credible notion of geographical or historical context; for example, why should St Francis or St Barbara be depicted within a Nativity scene or why should St Dominic appear at the foot of the cross? To the viewer, their presence may be little more than a distraction from the central theme of the painting. Gradually, however, as the viewer becomes more accustomed to their presence in biblical scenes, they appear less incongruous as the boundaries between the saints and the biblical characters become blurred in the mind of the viewer. The characteristics of the saint are transferred onto the biblical character or hero so that the way we view, reflect upon and identify with both the saint and the biblical character is essentially the same. The blurring between the roles of both—and our perception of them—is reflected in the titles given to important New Testament characters; for example, John the Baptist, Peter, Joseph and frequently the Virgin Mary are given the title of "Saint" in a loose sense of the word. This has the effect of reinforcing in the Catholic con-sciousness the link between the idea and function of a saint and that of a biblical character.

The emphasis on *character* in the Catholic consciousness relates easily and naturally to contemporary literary approaches to the Bible which explore the place and role of biblical characters, not only in the plot of the canonical story but also in their cultural afterlives as expressed in art, literature, music and film. However, as Rabbi Adin Steinsalz remarks, in spite of the considerable attention given to it in contemporary scholarship, the essential idea of character and its importance in the Bible remains unacknowledged and unchallenged:

> The characters and heroes of the Bible are without doubt some of the best-known figures in history. Even people not well versed in the Scriptures and who do not read the Bible regularly, know at least the names of some of the major personalities. We encounter them again and again directly and indirectly in art, in literature, in speech or in folklore. And yet these men and women remain among the most elusive, enigmatic and least understood of any heroes. This lack of knowledge and understanding is not necessarily a function of ignorance but stems rather from the fact that the biblical personae are so familiar, so 'famous' that they have become almost

stereotyped. They have fallen victim to accepted patterns of thinking, been fitted into conventional moulds and subjected to unquestioning assumptions that have prevented any attempt at a deeper understanding. It is not uncommon for the very thing that 'everyone knows' not to receive the attention it deserves.[1]

In the first article of Part 2, Stephen Prickett explores the idea of character in literature with specific reference to Joseph the Patriarch. The character of Joseph is further explored in Susan Docherty's article on the presentation of Joseph in early post-biblical literature. Larry Kreitzer examines the detail of a well known painting, Holbein's *The Ambassadors*, and reflects upon the way its most important subject is used to relate to a key idea in Pauline literature. Margarita Stocker, in her article on the afterlives of Judith and Esther, explores how both have been appropriated in American literature. J. Cheryl Exum searches for *the* authentic representation of the character of Delilah in film. Two further articles evaluate the way in which biblical characters have been presented in film: Joy Sisley assesses how American frontier myths have been translated into biblical epics while Gaye Ortiz reviews film representations of the holy family. Finally, Anthony Axe, O.P., looks at the effectiveness of the genre of opera in portraying the biblical hero. It has not been possible to include the wealth of artistic, musical and cinematic audio-visual presentations that were used to support these papers; however, a representative sample of art work has been included.

I am most grateful to a number of people who have encouraged and assisted me during the conferences and in the preparation of this volume: first, Professor J. Cheryl Exum for her inspiration, enthusiasm and support for the project; second, the late Professor Robert Carroll for the inspiration he has left us in his writings and for his generosity in helping and advising me; and finally, Professor Philip Davies for his support—and patience—in publishing these papers from the two conferences.

Martin O'Kane
Newman College of Higher Education
Birmingham
Spring 2002

---

1. Rabbi Adin Steinsalz, *Biblical Images* (Northvale, New Jersey and London: Jason Aronson Inc, 1994), p.ix.

Part I

REMOVING AN ANCIENT LANDMARK:
READING THE BIBLE AS CULTURAL PRODUCTION

Robert P. Carroll*

We want to know what the Delphic oracle said. We want to read the Bible. It has been argued that the discipline of literary criticism 'originates in medieval efforts to interpret what is in many ways the most challenging of sacred Hebrew poetic texts, the Song of Songs'. The Bible consists of several books of stories, laments, exclamations, many of them hard to understand and therefore hard to live with or live by. We need help from commentators, rabbinic scholars, interpreters from different religious traditions, adepts of hermeneutics skilled in the ways of biblical writing. The Bible, interpreted in one spirit or another, then becomes part of the public domain: it may eventually appear in an unlikely place, as Genesis did, on television. Without those interpretations, many parts of the Bible would be darkness visible. It would still be available to the clerisy of scholars, but not to the laity. Every homily preached in a church is an attempt to add the force of spiritual or moral presence to the public domain of speech, belief, and practice.[1]

To start at the beginning: in traditional Christian and Jewish circles the Bible is read as the story of the Jewish nation or of the Church—from the creation of the world until the end of time—give or take a few centuries. It is also read as the 'story of salvation' (*Heilsgeschichte*) by many Christian reading communities. Whilst for me all discourse about *Heilsgeschichte* is just 'baggage out of Noah's ark that should have been abandoned on Mount Ararat' in terms of contemporary readings of the Bible,[2] I start with

    * Robert P. Carroll died in 2000. The following is the unfinished written draft of his lecture delivered to the Catholic Biblical Association at Newman College in 1999.
    1. Denis Donoghue, *The Practice of Reading* (New Haven and London: Yale University Press, 1998), p. 81. The citation about the Song of Songs is from Susan Noakes, 'Gracious Words: Luke's Jesus and the Reading of Sacred Poetry at the Beginning of the Christian Era', in Jonathan Boyarin (ed.), *The Ethnography of Reading* (Berkeley: University of California Press, 1993), pp. 40-55 (46).
    2. I am mindful here of Alasdair MacIntyre's emphasis on the differing (and

such a reading in order to be able to sketch the framework of this lecture or, at least, to indicate one possible starting-point over against which my lecture takes its leave. I do not really want to address here issues of traditional or conventional religious readings of the Bible.

The Great Intertext

Of course that may be a very optimistic and perhaps even a rather wildly over-exaggerated statement about how 'we read today' because there is a real 'problem of literacy' in the West today. Apart from the general problems of literacy in our contemporary audio-visual Western cultures, I doubt if many people, even biblical scholars for that matter, necessarily read the Bible as an Intertextual Book. I would, however, want to insist that such a reading strategy is probably the most viable one for the coming century and millennium. But it is a matter of perspective as well as a matter of education. It is up to our teachers, academics and writers to insist upon the intertextual nature of the Bible and to teach their students of such matters, that is, the notion and concept of the Bible as being both a book with a prehistory and a book with a reception-history.

The implications of the fact of the intertextual nature of the Bible are very many, but space does not permit an expansive treatment of them. I shall just pause over two of them because they seem to me to have some intrinsic interest for the Catholic Biblical Association conference. In the first instance I would want to say that the Bible as a collection of written documents seems to have emerged out of the Semitic—that is, Hebrew/ Palestinian/Phoenician—literary/oral reflections on the experience of the consequences of imperial forces occupying the Palestinian landmass between Babylonia and Egypt.[3] Of course the biblical literature is not just a response to the experience of the invasion and hegemony of foreign imperial powers, but it is certainly that at base. Out of that impact and influence came the images and metaphors of the imperial god signalled by the use of the tetragrammaton Y-H-W-H.

---

competing) narratives available today to which we may join ourselves in order to make sense of post-Enlightenment existence: see his *After Virtue: A Study in Moral Theory* (London: Duckworth, 2nd edn, 1985).

3.   Issues of orality and literacy are bound up together when dealing with the Bible: see William A. Graham, *Beyond the Written Word: Oral Aspects of Scripture in the History of Religion* (Cambridge: Cambridge University Press, 1987).

When the Western world accepted Christianity, Caesar conquered; and the received text of Western theology was edited by his lawyers. The code of Justinian and the theology of Justinian are two volumes expressing one movement of the human spirit. The brief Galilean vision of humility flickered throughout the ages, uncertainly. In the official formulation of the religion it has assumed the trivial form of the mere attribution to the Jews that they cherished a misconception about their Messiah. But the deeper idolatry, of the fashioning of God in the image of the Egyptian, Persian, and Roman imperial rulers, was retained. The Church gave unto God the attributes which belonged exclusively to Caesar.[4]

In the second instance, a further point about the imperial experience out of which the Hebrew Bible came ought to be made here by way of balancing the above point. Ancient or 'biblical' Israel experienced the hegemonic influence of various imperial powers—whatever its writers may have internalized in their representations of deity—as victim and object of severe imperial oppression. Out of their experiences under the armed boot of Assyria, Babylon, Persia, Greece and perhaps even Rome (especially in relation to the New Testament) one of the strongest traces left on the biblical writings of such imperial oppression is that of reactions to experience of deportation, displacement and relocation elsewhere. What I have in mind here is sometimes romantically called 'exile', but in point of fact any exile that lasts for more than twenty-five hundred years really needs to be redescribed.[5]

Englishing the Bible

What is also fundamental to understanding our *Oxford World's Classic Bible*[6] is a deep sense of the Englished Bible from the sixteenth century onwards. This point which is very important need not necessarily be

4.   A.N. Whitehead, *Process and Reality: An Essay in Cosmology* (The Gifford Lectures in Edinburgh 1927–28; New York and London: The Free Press, paperback 1979 [1929]), p. 342; see also my Presidential Address, 'Beyond Kritik and Kerygma', to the Winter Meeting of SOTS in Birmingham on 4 January 1999 which incorporates Whitehead's critique and comments on it.

5.   See James M. Scott (ed.), *Exile: Old Testament, Jewish, and Christian Conceptions* (SJSJ, 56; Leiden: E.J. Brill, 1997); on distinctions between 'ancient' and 'biblical' Israel see the writings of Philip R. Davies, especially his *In Search of 'Ancient Israel'* (JSOTSup, 148; Sheffield: Sheffield Academic Press, 1992).

6.   *The Bible: Authorized King James Version* (With an Introduction and Notes by Robert Carroll and Stephen Prickett; Oxford World's Classics; Oxford and New York: Oxford University Press, 1997), pp. xi-xlvi; 321-441 (Explanatory Notes).

confined to that very Protestant practice and cultural habit of 'Englishing the Bible'—after all, Englishing the Bible was also a 'good' Catholic practice in the sixteenth century (see Douai and Rheims Testaments)—though it is arguable that it has tended to be much more a Protestant predilection, until after Vatican Two. But 'our Bible' project had as its starting point the emergence of the Gutenberg world; it participated in the project of modernity rather than as part of the mediaeval world-view (or project). As the King James Bible or, what is commonly called 'The Authorized Version'—though 'authorized' is a misconception or misreading (misprision) of the actual history.[7]

So for me, among the absolute prerequisites for seeking to understand the English Bible as a cultural production of its time—that is as the product of the sixteenth and seventeenth centuries—would have to be some knowledge of the vexed history of those ancient religious controversies which gave rise to the wars of religion in that period. The English Bible, though not necessarily to the same extent in all its forms and versions, is, has been and ever shall be a highly political, politicized and ideological document. Whatever else may be said about it and however much it may be granted a religious identity or a role in the long history of the Christianizing of European culture and the creation of Christendom, its classical English forms are very heavily inscribed with political ideology. Just read the prefaces, addresses and 'The Translators to the Reader' section of the King James version.

Removing an Ancient Landmark

I have called this lecture 'Removing an Ancient Landmark' in conscious echo of the biblical prohibition which commands readers 'you shall not remove your neighbour's landmark' (Deut. 19.14; cf. the curse form of the prohibition in Deut. 27.17) because I want to signal clearly that this approach to handling the Bible is not necessarily a traditional, conventional nor even a religious approach. I consciously and unapologetically acknowledge that my position in this paper is that of a post-Enlightenment, modernist, even secular, reader.[8] It is offered in contradistinction to

7.   I have written a very brief statement about such matters in my contribution on 'Biblical Translations' in Adrian Hastings (ed.), *The Oxford Companion to Christian Thought* (Oxford: Oxford University Press, 2000).

8.   A self-description, if one is required, would have to include reference to such features of my history, upbringing and thinking as might be incorporated into the terms

all the very many different religious strategies for reading the Bible which have been around the place for nearly the past two millennia. My main concern here is with approaching the Bible in the full light of the past three hundred years of thinking, researching and reflecting on the Bible.

Perhaps I should explain the biblical allusion a bit further. The original biblical prohibition and curse have to do with shifting one's neighbour's landmark boundary (*gebûl*, 'boundary, border, territory, limit'). That is, the injunctions forbid any Israelite from enlarging their own property by means of extending it through the loss of their neighbour's property. However, it is only as a metaphor that I wish to take up the biblical rulings. And I want to do so because I strongly believe that it is high time both biblical scholars and cultural historians recognized the plain fact that for centuries now the Bible has been a cultural object at play within different human cultures. It is not simply or not only a collection of ancient documents with religious dimensions nor does it only constitute the sacred scriptures of various Jewish communities and Christian churches.

So it is in those senses that I wish to remove the ancient landmark of the Bible as sacred scripture and cultural generator in our contemporary culture. Outside fundamentalistic and missionary environments it has not been such a generator of culture for generations now. I want to take such a fundamental change fully into account when writing about the Bible; and as one example of how one might construct such a cultural-literary account of the Bible—divorced or separated from theological metaphysics, as it were—I would commend you to read the 'Introduction' and 'Explanatory Notes' to the Oxford World's Classics Bible. However, just in case anybody here thinks I am now indulging in 'simony' or some such ecclesiastical crime, I hasten to add that your purchase and reading of our Oxford paperback Bible will not add one penny to the wealth of myself or of my colleague, Stephen Prickett!

Some of you who may be more theologically minded than others may object to the secular use or takeover of the Bible as if religious property had been stolen, kidnapped or generally transferred to a different category. However, let me remind you of some obvious truths. There is no copyright on the Bible.[9] There is, of course, copyright on specific editions and translations of the Bible and all such copyrights tend to belong to publishers

---

'postmodern, post-Christian, humanist thinker and scholar'.

    9.   Here I would recommend to everybody Leslie Howsam's book *Cheap Bibles: Nineteenth Century Publishing and the British and Foreign Bible Society* (Cambridge: Cambridge University Press, 1993).

and committees—but never to God! Also I would have to say that the Bible has been in the cultural mainstream for centuries, so it belongs to everybody and nobody. Or if you prefer the matter expressed differently: the Bible is out of copyright. While I am always ready to acknowledge the roles played by the historical churches and synagogues in the matter of acting as temporal guardians and transmitters of various versions and editions of the Bible nevertheless the Bible must be seen as essentially a cultural product.

Shakespeare and the Bible

Let me offer you an analogy from which I may argue to make the substantive point. Consider the collected works of William Shakespeare. They too are cultural literature available and accessible to anybody and everybody who can appropriate them. In fact they are such an iconic or symbolic collection of cultural material that they are on the syllabuses of our schools, colleges and universities. They belong to the kind of cultural literature which has also become ideological literature in some cases—just like the Bible. Now I would not deny for a moment that Shakespeare was an actor and a playwright who wrote his plays to be performed. Nor would I assert for a moment that only actors and playwrights should have access to his works or that only such and such as they can or could understand the plays of Shakespeare.

I am not here to tell you that enacting the Bible is illegitimate in any sense. *Au contraire*, I recognize that as a collection of texts which have through time been given the enhancement of recognition or designation as sacred or inspired Scriptures, the Bible also can be enacted in (sacred) space just as Shakespeare may be acted on the stage. Of course enacting the Bible may take somewhat different forms than Shakespearean drama does—even allowing for straightforward dramatizations of parts of the Bible (such as biblical narratives or the stories of Job, Joseph and Jesus)— and these forms may be categorized as lectionaries, liturgies and litanies. But beyond or apart from all such liturgical enactments of sacred Scripture, the plain reading of the Bible as text or as literature remains as a legitimate cultural activity.[10]

---

10. In my book, *Wolf in the Sheepfold: The Bible as Problematic for Theology* (London: SCM Press, 1997; original edition SPCK, 1991), I tried to say something about this principle, among so many other things, relating to the Bible in the modern era.

If you want pedigree or parentage for the notion of reading the Bible as if it were a book like any other book, then all you need do is to go back to the writings of Coleridge on the Bible. It is a good post-Enlightenment view of the Bible. Now I know that there are very strong—I hesitate to say 'good', in fact I refuse to say good—opinions against reading the Bible as literature and those who have such opinions must both entertain them and shut up while I am trying to put the counter or opposite case. Whatever your opinion may be about the literary nature of the Bible, I fear it is far too late in human history for the Bible to be thought of by many people as other than human, cultural literature and the product of such human activity. The day of the magic book approach to the Bible is over for general culture, though within sacred enclaves the luxury of other points of view remain.[11]

> For the fact is that being inside a whale is a very comfortable, cosy, home-like thought. The historical Jonah, if he can be so called, was glad enough to escape, but in imagination, in day-dream, countless people have envied him. It is, of course, quite obvious why. The whale's belly is simply a womb big enough for an adult. There you are, in the dark, cushioned space that exactly fits you, with yards of blubber between yourself and reality, able to keep up an attitude of the completest indifference, no matter what happens. A storm that would sink all the battleships in the world would hardly reach you as an echo. Even the whale's own movements would probably be imperceptible to you. He might be wallowing among the surface waves or shooting down into the blackness of the middle seas (a mile deep, according to Herman Melville), but you would never notice the difference. Short of being dead, it is the final, unsurpassable stage of irresponsibility.[12]

While that final sentence may not apply to sacred enclave folk, I include it because it is part of Orwell's dismissive take on Henry Miller. Appropriating the Orwell trope for my own purposes here, without its original Orwellian attachment to Henry Miller or whoever, all I want to say is that outside the whale/sacred enclave the Bible comes across to most people today as a deeply difficult book to read and, for some, even a largely irrelevant book—however, it is to be read as a book. Escaping into the

---

11. On the dethroning of the Bible see Christopher Hill, *The English Bible and the Seventeenth-Century Revolution* (London: Allen Lane, 1993).

12. George Orwell, 'Inside the Whale', in Orwell, *Inside the Whale and Other Essays* (Harmondsworth: Penguin Books, 1962), pp. 9-50 (12).

whale (sacred enclave) may encourage the illusion of its readability, but outside the whale the real world persists in existing.

Of course I would want also to say about the principle and practice of reading the Bible as a book just like any book that it is both like any other book and it is also completely different—like every book. It is different because it is, among many other things, a library or collection of books rather than one book. It is also a collection of writings in different languages from different cultures and periods of time. From beginning to end—whether such a totality of writings is to be comprised of Genesis to Chronicles or Genesis to Revelation—it covers centuries of time and was written over centuries of time. Shall we say from 400 BCE to 100 CE? That is, more or less five hundred years. Even Shakespeare did not take as long to write all his plays (whichever you are prepared to allow to him). Hebrew and Greek, with a little Aramaic thrown in, are very different languages.

The Bible as Cultural Literature

So what do I mean by the phrase 'Reading the Bible as Cultural Literature' or 'cultural production'? I use such a phrase as 'cultural literature' or 'cultural production' because I want to make a fundamental point about the cultural-textual realities of the Bible.[13] The book—whether regarded as sacred or otherwise makes no difference to me at this stage of the argument—is a cultural production.[14] Or better yet, not so much a book as a

13. The literature is too vast here for me to provide an adequate footnote, but see S.L. Greenslade (ed.), *The Cambridge History of the Bible*. III. *The West from the Reformation to the Present Day* (Cambridge; Cambridge University Press); Klaus Scholder, *The Birth of Modern Critical Theology: Origins and Problems of Biblical Criticism in the Seventeenth Century* (London: SCM Press; Philadelphia: Trinity Press International, 1990); Henning Graf Reventlow, *The Authority of the Bible and the Rise of the Modern World* (London: SCM Press, 1984); cf. Anthony Grafton, April Shelford and Nancy Siraisi (eds.), *New Worlds, Ancient Texts: The Power of Tradition and the Shock of Discovery* (Cambridge, MA and London: The Belknap Press of Harvard University Press, 1992). I have tried to say something about this changing tradition of reading the Bible in my article 'The Reader and the Text', in A.D.H. Mayes (ed.), *Text in Context* (Oxford: Oxford University Press, 2000), pp. 3-34.

14. On culture in a general sense and in relation to the Bible, see J. Cheryl Exum and Stephen D. Moore (eds.), *Biblical Studies/Cultural Studies* (The Third Sheffield Colloquium; JSOTSup, 266; Sheffield: Sheffield Academic Press, 1998) and my own contribution to that Colloquium, 'Lower Case Bibles: Commodity Culture and the

collection of ancient books (scrolls) written in Aramaic, Greek and Hebrew, but usually read in the vernacular languages of some translated version—whether Latin or otherwise is less important. It was originally the cultural production of many anonymous writers about whom we know extremely little, if not nothing at all. That is, the original writings—however we may conceive of them—were the cultural products of very sophisticated authors.

I will conclude this lecture (paper) by making the following observations. In an age of failing literacy what are the prognostications for a reading public which will be able to read the Bible intelligently in the twenty-first century? Assuming that such a thing is a desideratum in the first place, what and how should such a public read? How widespread, deep and great will Donoghue's Miltonic trope 'darkness visible' be in the next century? What are we as biblical scholars to say to 'earnest seekers after truth' when they ask us then 'how should we read this ancient collection of documents called the Bible?' Few of us would be prepared to or feel that we ought to give the same answer to such enquiries as the Apostle Philip did to the Ethiopian official in the story in Acts 8 (vv. 26-40). Nineteen hundred years have changed everything, including how we are to read and especially how we are to understand the Bible in the new millennium.[15]

Bible', pp. 46-69. See also the writings of Pierre Bourdieu and Paul Bohannan.

15. Elsewhere I have also meditated on the nature of the Bible as literature: see Carroll, 'The Hebrew Bible as Literature—a Misprision?', *Studia Theologica* 47 (1993), pp. 77-90.

THE FLIGHT INTO EGYPT:
ICON OF REFUGE FOR THE H(A)UNTED

Martin O'Kane

Exile is not a material thing, it is a spiritual thing. All the corners of the earth are exactly the same. And anywhere one can dream is good, providing the place is obscure, and the horizon is vast (Victor Hugo).

Introduction

This article sets out to explore the significance of the Matthaean narrative of the Flight into Egypt, to review some of its artistic representations, evidence of its universal appeal, and concludes by focusing on its particular significance in the twentieth century.[1] The title of the study, 'The Flight into Egypt: Icon of Refuge for the H(a)unted', anticipates some of its conclusions, namely, that this narrative, uniquely, offers an image with which many have identified—those who have experienced exile or displacement literally (the hunted), as well as those for whom the experience of exile or diaspora has been, or continues to be,[2] an issue which they must confront in terms of their own personal or communal identity (the haunted).

'The Flight into Egypt' (Mt. 2.13-23), unique in the Gospels to Matthew, recounts the story of a family of refugees who flee the violence of their homeland, find safety in exile in a foreign land and eventually return to live and work in their homeland. Although Matthew's narrative of the episode appears brief and unsatisfactory in its detail, it has received universal fame and attention far and beyond the limited space it occupies in the Gospel. Artistic representations adorn almost every gallery in the

---

1.   I am grateful to a former student, Damien McGarrigle, who researched some of the apocryphal material used in this article.

2.   See especially Marc H. Ellis, *A Reflection on the Jewish Exile and the New Diaspora* (Liverpool: Friends of *Sabeel* UK, 1998), pp. 2-19.

world[3] and its associations with Christmas has for many, especially in the West, made it part of the cultural baggage of the Christian world and an image familiar to many from childhood.

The drama and romanticism of the legend ensures that Jesus starts off his career in true heroic style, matching any of the great movers of history; heroes and great people, it would appear, thrive in later life, if they have experienced exile or displacement in their youth. Such heroes are not restricted to the Bible, to Abraham, Joseph or Ruth[4] but are celebrated throughout history. While the New Testament heralds the start of Christianity with a story of a fugitive refugee child (φεῦγε εἰς Αἴγυπτον, Joseph is told), the *Aeneid* prepares for the glory of the Roman empire by proudly celebrating, in its opening lines, Aeneas's origins as a *profugus*, a fugitive:

> arma virumque cano, Troaie qui primus ab oris Italiam fato profugus Lavinaque venit litora
>
> I sing of arms and the hero who first came from the shores of Troy, an exile by Fate, to Italy and its Lavinian shore (*Aeneid* 1.1-4).

Romulus and Remus,[5] too, start off their lives abandoned and exiled, while Odysseus must wander through many perils in strange and hostile territories before reaching home. Although his chief characteristics in the *Odyssey* are his longing for home and his endurance of suffering in order to reach it, there is the constant danger, during his ten years' wandering, that Odysseus might succumb to the attractions of exile and abandon his determination altogether.[6] He is warned by the goddess Circe of the lure of

3.   For example, in the spring 2001 exhibition, *The Genius of Rome 1592–1623*, held at the Royal Academy of Arts, London, no less that 15 paintings of the theme were included in the catalogue from this period alone. See nn. 23 and 24 for the more significant artistic representations.

4.   For a discussion on Exile in the Bible as *plot motif* and *character type* see 'Exile' in Leland Ryken, James C. Wilhoit, Tremper Longman III (eds.), *Dictionary of Biblical Imagery* (Downers Grove, IL and Leicester, England: Intervarsity Press, 1998), pp. 250-51.

5.   'Later Gentile-Christian readers of Matthew's Gospel would have been reminded (when reading Mt. 2.12-23) of the childhood narratives of Cyrus, Cypsalus, Zoroaster and Romulus'. Ulrich Luz, *The Theology of the Gospel of Matthew* (Cambridge: Cambridge University Press, 1996), p. 25.

6.   Elazar Barkan and Marie-Denise Shelton (eds.), *Borders, Boundaries, Diasporas* (Stanford, CA: Stanford University Press, 1998), p. 1, discuss how in her novel *Le Chant des sirènes* (Port-au-Prince, Haiti: Editions du Soleil, 1979), p. 33 the Haitian

false gods and the seductions of the winds bringing him to foreign shores.[7] She describes the dangers awaiting Odyseus and his men as they sail past the Sirens' isle and face the terrors of Scylla and Charybdis:

> First you will come to the Sirens, who bewitch eveyone who comes near them. If any man draws near in his innocence and listens to their voice, he never sees home again, never again will wife and little children run to greet him with joy; but the Sirens bewitch him with their melodious song. There in the meadow they sit and all round is a great heap of bones, mouldering bodies and withering skins. Go on past that place, and do not let the men hear; you must knead a good lump of wax and plug their ears with pellets.[8]

Odysseus alone can hear the Sirens' wonderful voices, but to enjoy their song he must have his men tie his body tight to the ship's mast. Circe speaks to everyone and not just to Odysseus: the moral of the story is that, although travel may indeed broaden the mind, the ransom of the journey is loneliness, separation, shattered dreams, madness and forgotten love. The voyager who has tasted the pleasures or displeasures of exile is often unable to steer the ship back home.[9]

novelist, Marie Thérèse Colimon allegorizes the modern exodus of Haitians to foreign lands in search of freedom and self-redemption in the light of this episode from the Odyssey. Walter Brueggeman, *Cadences of Home: Preaching among Exiles* (Louisville, KY: Westminster/John Knox Press, 1997), pp. 1-3, defines the metaphor of exile as 'not primarily geographical but social, moral and cultural'.

7.   James E. Miller, *The Western Paradise: Greek and Hebrew Traditions* (San Francisco: International Scholars Publications, 1997), pp. 19-21, associates Elysium with the Garden of Eden. In the *Odyssey*, Elysium is a land without sorrow across the Ocean-stream associated specifically with the West Wind (zephyros), often considered a favourable and gentle wind.

8.   Homer, *The Odyssey* (trans. W.H.D. Rouse; New York: New American Library, 1937), p. 138.

9.   Patristic exegesis saw the voyages of Ulysses as a 'type' of the Christian's journey; the ship figures the Church or Faith and Christ the invisible pilot. The typology was prevalent during mediaeval times: 'Navigating through this world as though on the open sea, we must employ great caution lest we endanger our lives. For often we are deceived under the appearance of good'. See Franco Mormando, 'An Early Renaissance Guide for the Perplexed: Bernardino of Siena's *De inspirationibus*', in John C. Hawley (ed.), *Through a Glass Darkly: Essays in the Religious Imagination* (New York: Fordham University Press, 1996), pp. 24-49 (33). While the exilic experience of Adam's Fall was seen to bedevil all mortal sojourners, the penitent person could move beyond exile and return to 'the harbour of salvation'. In Joyce's *Ulysses*, Stephen, the modern Telemachus, on an internal voyage of self-discovery, is unable to accept the commitment of a goal outside the self. For a synopsis of the theme of

Events of the twentieth century have left behind many unresolved issues: the plight of the exile, the status of the refugee, the rights of asylum seekers, the voluntary and enforced displacements of ethnic groups and the cultural identity of diaspora communities. Images of fleeing individuals and mass departure of families, beamed across the world by the media, remind us daily of the immediacy of the issues. In 1952, Pope Pius XII suggested in his encyclical, *Exsul Familia*, that the Flight into Egypt should be seen as *the* symbol of hope to the refugee in every age:

> The emigré Holy Family, fleeing into Egypt, is the archetype of every refugee family. Jesus, Mary and Joseph, living in exile in Egypt to escape the fury of an evil king, are, for all times and places, the models and protectors of every migrant, alien and refugee of whatever kind who, whether compelled by fear or persecution or by want, is forced to leave his native land, his beloved parents and relatives, his close friends and to seek a foreign soil (*Exsul Familia* 1952)

But can the image of the Flight into Egypt be regarded as such a comprehensive and inclusive symbol? Is the term *archetype* justified?[10] After all, Jesus' status as a refugee is very temporary and he does return home safely and, in any case, isn't he simply rehearsing the Exodus/Exile experience of the Old Testament? Does the Holy Family provide a model for those who seek exile voluntarily?

Clearly, the emotional image of the innocent mother and new-born child fleeing from a dangerous and evil situation ensures that it can be appropriated easily by the refugee. The fact that even a child with divine status can be so vulnerable and find himself at the mercy of the whims of a dictator draws attention more universally to the precarious balance that exists between rootedness and displacement, justice and injustice, good and evil. But this simple and direct image is also full of symbolism: in Matthew's narrative, it must be interpreted through the twin filter of Old Testament

biblical exile in English literature, see 'Exile and Pilgrimage', in David Lyle Jeffrey (ed.), *A Dictionary of Biblical Tradition in English Literature* (Grand Rapids: Eerdmans, 1993), pp. 254-59.

10. In Ryken, Wilhoit and Longman (eds.), *Dictionary of Biblical Imagery*, p. 251, an archetype is defined as 'an image or pattern that recurs through literature and life' (p. xvii). Four pages, complete with charts, explain how archetypes are among the chief building blocks for writers of the Bible (pp. xvii-xx). It states that 'Christ was the archetype exile: a person who in this life had nowhere to lay his head' (Mt. 8.20) and who in his death 'suffered outside the gate in order to sanctify the people through his own blood' (Heb. 13.12).

Exodus and Exile and in the light of all the theological associations that accompany both these major biblical themes. Readers have identified with the narrative either literally or metaphorically; for some, the refugee status of Jesus is immediately recognisable in their own experience of displacement either individually or collectively while others accompany the Holy Family spiritually on a type of pilgrimage, reflecting on its significance for their own lives. It has been in the twentieth century, however, when the paradigm of exile, diaspora and return seems to be invariably connected with the Jewish experience, that the image has been invested with a particular significance and interpreted through the lens of that paradigm.

The Coptic Orthodox Church takes pride in associating its origins with the Flight into Egypt and, like an experienced desert guide, describes in vivid topographical detail the route taken by the family, being careful to stress the etiological significance of the Arabic place names:

> It is most probable that the holy family avoided taking the usual route at that time after escaping from Palestine to Egypt. They probably joined it after passing through the Sinai Desert, at Farma or Pelusium, which stands between Al-Arish and Port-Said. Their route took them to Basta near the city of Zagazig then to Belbies and on to Ein Shams, now called Al-Matariah, where they rested under a tree, which is still named after the Holy Virgin. Then the holy family headed southward to Babylon, of Old Cairo, where they stayed for some time in the cave which is now part of St. Sergius's church. Later the holy family continued its flight to the site, which is known now as Al-Muharak Monastery. Throughout all the places visited by the holy family, miracles have taken place and faith still shines. Tourists and local visitors throughout the year visit them. A spot of light in a world of darkness.[11]

Whereas one can easily appreciate the simple and striking image of the mother in flight and imagine the vivid, colourful route describe by the Copts, the full significance of the metaphor of exile which the Matthaean narrative contains is more difficult to unravel. It has not received the same scholarly attention as the metaphor of exile in the Old Testament where much creative and explorative work has been done, for example, by Brueggeman,[12] Carroll, Davies, Grabbe and Jeppesen[13] especially in

11. This description is found in *Cornerstone* 13 (Autumn 1998), published by *Sabeel* Ecumenical Liberation Theology Center in Jerusalem.

12. See, for example, Brueggemann, *Cadences of Home.*

13. Articles on the subject by all of these scholars appear in Lester L. Grabbe (ed.), *Leading Captivity Captive* (European Seminar in Historical Methodology, 2; JSOTSup, 278; Sheffield: Sheffield Academic Press, 1998).

reviewing how the exile has been presented historically and ideologically by the authors of the Hebrew Bible. Matthaean commentators generally regard Matthew's allusion to the Old Testament exile as referring to a definite historical event which took place in 587 BCE and restricted to only one possible theological interpretation. Old Testament scholarship, in contrast, argues that there were in fact several exiles and displacements within the Hebrew Bible and many biblical voices with divergent views willing to comment on their significance from their own particular standpoint. In other words, the effectiveness of the metaphor of exile in the Flight into Egypt pericope has not been fully appreciated because commentators have confined and restricted its significance to the traditional interpretation of the Jewish exile to Babylon in 587 BCE. Current explorative investigations into the many ways in which the metaphor of exile in the Old Testament may be read will inevitably throw new light also on the way we read Matthew's pericope.

There is a further dimension which makes the Flight into Egypt an especially rich narrative to investigate. Our reading of it will be influenced not only by whether we ourselves have actually experienced exile but also by our encounter with and response to the cultural, especially artistic, representations of the passage. J. Cheryl Exum notes:

> It is not simply a matter of the Bible influencing culture; the influence takes place in both directions. What many people know or think they know about the Bible often comes more from familiar representations of biblical texts and themes in the popular culture than from study of the ancient text itself... Not only will our knowledge of the biblical text influence the way we view, say, a painting of a biblical scene, our reading of the biblical text is also likely to be shaped by our recollection of that painting.[14]

More than any other passage in the Bible, it is virtually impossible to read this story without calling to mind a visual representation of it, either in a gallery, a church or perhaps more implicitly from a television documentary which deals with situations of war where both the visual imagery and accompanying commentary are often intended to recall the refugee Holy Family in order to increase the emotional impact. Phrases such as 'a refugee crisis of biblical proportions' or families forced to flee a tyrant 'as in biblical days' frequently trip off the tongues of news reporters and

---

14. J. Cheryl Exum, *Plotted, Shot, and Painted: Cultural Representations of Biblical Women* (JSOTSup, 215; Sheffield: Sheffield Academic Press, 1996), pp. 7-8.

resonate with the audience's subconscious familiarity with the story of the Flight into Egypt.

The Biblical Narrative

Matthew 2.13-23

The Flight into Egypt in Mt. 2.13-23 forms a compact and discrete literary unit. It is preceded by an account of the birth of Jesus and the subsequent visit of the Wise Men to Bethlehem and their adoration of the child Jesus (1.18–2.12) and followed by a description of John the Baptist, his ministry and the baptism of Jesus (3.1-17). The narrative itself forms a chiasmic structure[15] with the massacre of the children (vv. 16-18) at its core:

A (13) Now after they had left, an angel of the Lord appeared to Joseph in a dream and said 'Get up, take the child and his mother, and flee to Egypt and remain there until I tell you; for Herod is about to search for the child, to destroy him'

B (14) Then Joseph got up, took the child and his mother by night, and went to Egypt (15) and remained there until the death of Herod. This was to fulfil what had been spoken by the Lord through the prophet, 'Out of Egypt I have called my son'

C (16) When Herod saw that he had been tricked by the wise men, he was infuriated and he sent and killed all the children in and around Bethlehem who were two years old or under according to the time that he had learned from the wise men. (17) Then was fulfilled what had been spoken through the prophet Jeremiah (18) 'A voice was heard in Ramah, wailing and loud lamentation. Rachel weeping for her children; she refused to be consoled because they are no more'

A[1] (19) When Herod died, an angel of the Lord suddenly appeared in a dream to Joseph in Egypt and said (20) 'Get up, take the child and his mother, and go to the land of Israel for those who are seeking the child's life are dead'

15. Raymond E. Brown, *The Birth of the Messiah* (New York: Doubleday, 1993), p. 109, reconstructs a pre-Matthaean version which considerably shortens the material within the chiasmus. In particular, he omits vv. 22-23 which he attributes to Matthew who added these verses as his own appended composition and argues that this history of composition explains the awkwardness of several revelations involved in the return from Egypt. Luz, *Theology of the Gospel of Matthew*, p. 28, sees vv. 22-23 as an addition for similar reasons. Richard J. Erickson, 'Divine Injustice? Matthew's Narrative Strategy and the Slaughter of the Innocents (Matthew 2.13-23)', *JSNT* 64 (1996), pp. 5-27, offers (in Greek) a chiasmic structure, similar to the above, and places the Slaughter of the Innocents and its fulfilment quotation (Jer. 31.15) at the very heart of the narrative.

B¹ (21) Then Joseph got up, took the child and his mother, and went to the land of Israel. (22) But when he heard that Archelaus was ruling over Judea in place of his father Herod, he was afraid to go there. And after being warned in a dream, he went away to the district of Galilee. (23) There he made his home in a town called Nazareth so that what had been spoken through the prophets might be fulfilled 'He will be called a Nazorean'.

Elements A and B of the chiasmus describe the safe passage of Jesus by night to Egypt while in elements A1 and B1 the journey is reversed when the family returns to the land of Israel. At the heart of the narrative is element C in which the massacre takes place in Bethlehem; v. 16 interrupts the peace and calm of the midnight escape, shows that the dramatic flight was indeed justified and leaves the reader feeling relieved that the child Jesus is safe, even though it may also raise ethical questions as to why other children did not receive a similar warning.[16]

However, the brevity and intensity of the Matthaean style requires considerable unravelling to appreciate the impact of the episode. First, for whom was the narrative intended? Commentators on Matthew's Gospel agree on its Jewish orientation, one of the central aims being to present Jesus as the fulfilment and culmination of the Old Testament, and most are of the opinion that it was written for a Jewish-Christian audience towards the end of the first century, perhaps shortly after 70 CE.[17] The location of the community is still disputed but several commentators suggest Antioch in Syria as a strong probability.[18] The Flight into Egypt is characteristic of the author's attempts to make the background of the infancy of Jesus fit into its Old Testament background and to make it appealing to the reader familiar with Jewish tradition. The geographical sweep from Israel to Egypt (vv. 13-14) and back again (vv. 19-23) reminds the reader of the

16. For the ethical issues raised, see Erickson, 'Divine Injustice?', pp. 25-27, for a detailed discussion and his proposed explanation. Elizabeth Wainwright, 'The Gospel of Matthew', in Elisabeth Schüssler Fiorenza (ed.), *Searching the Scripture: A Feminist Commentary* (London: SCM Press, 1995), pp. 635-77 (644), contrasts the male and heartless despot Herod with the female and compassionate mother Rachel. She speaks of the image of 'womb compassion' and discusses v. 18 in the light of Jer. 31.20 where God describes a child whom he claims as his own and describes the deep and moving feelings of love, warmth and mercy which he has for the child.

17. See Luz, *Theology of the Gospel of Matthew*, pp. 11-21; Donald Senior, *What Are They Saying about Matthew?* (New York: Paulist Press, 1996), pp. 7-20; M.A. Powell, *The Gospels* (Philadelphia: Fortress Press, 1998), pp. 71-75.

18. See a summary of positions in Powell, *Gospels*, pp. 73-74.

patriarch Joseph's journey to and stay in Egypt (Exod. 37–50)[19] and the return of Jesus to Israel reminds the reader of Moses' return at the time of the Exodus (Exod. 14). Joseph plays the role of Joseph the patriarch and Jesus plays that of the new Moses.[20] The narrative replete with Old Testament names, places and themes[21] makes it clear that Matthew is much more interested in creating a symbolic journey through the past for the reader than simply re-telling a historical childhood tradition associated with Jesus.

But the key to interpreting the narrative and unravelling its symbolism lies in discovering the function of the three so-called *fulfilment quotations*.[22] Of the 12 fulfilment quotations in the Gospel, 5 occur in chs. 1–2 and 3 of these are found in the narrative of the Flight into Egypt (v. 15, v. 18 and v. 23). Matthaean commentators, while at odds over the precise sources of Matthew's *fulfilment quotations* and his adaptation of them, agree that Old Testament quotations are not mere embroideries on the gospel story but are an integral part of the Gospel's message, placing the story of Jesus in the broader context of Israel's history.[23] As a literary and editorial technique, the *fulfilment quotation* serves the purpose of conveying to the reader the full significance of events within the narrative; it ensures that the reader is more aware of their symbolism than the actual characters are within the story.

19. In Isa. 30.1-7 and 31.1-3, the prophet condemns those who 'seek refuge' in Egypt and not in Yahweh. The implication is that they believe the gods of Egypt are more powerful to save than Yahweh. The irony in Matthew is that Jesus himself should have to seek refuge there. See too the importance of Yahweh himself as 'refuge' in the psalms in Jerome F.D. Creach, *Yahweh as Refuge and the Editing of the Hebrew Psalter* (JSOTSup, 217. Sheffield: Sheffield Academic Press, 1996), pp. 106-21.

20. For detailed similarities with Old Testament texts dealing with the childhood of Moses, see Brown, *Birth of the Messiah*, p. 113.

21. See Brown, *Birth of the Messiah*, pp. 203-13; Robert H. Gundry, *Matthew* (Grand Rapids: Eerdmans, 1994), pp. 35-37; and Augustine Stock, *The Method and Message of Matthew* (Collegeville, MN: Liturgical Press, 1994), pp. 37-39. Erickson, 'Divine Injustice?', pp. 13-15, provides a comprehensive bibliography and detailed summaries of the main points of comparisons, as does Douglas R.A. Hare, *Matthew* (Interpretation Series; Louisville: John Knox Press, 1993), pp. 15-17.

22. For a comprehensive discussion of this peculiarly Matthean device, see Gundry, *Matthew*, pp. 24-25; Luz, *Theology of the Gospel of Matthew*, pp. 37-41; Powell, *Gospels*, pp. 69-70; Senior, *What Are They Saying about Matthew?*, pp. 51-61; Stock, *Method and Message of Matthew*, p. 30.

23. Senior, *What Are They Saying about Matthew?*, p. 61.

In the first occurrence, v. 15, Matthew quotes Hos. 11.1 which refers to the Exodus of Israel from Egypt; Jesus relives in his own life the Exodus experience of the Jewish people. In the second occurrence, v. 18, Matthew quotes Jer. 31.15 where the dead Rachel is imagined to be weeping at Ramah, the site where the Israelites were gathered for the march into the Babylonian exile, lamenting their departure. In this fulfilment quotation, Matthew links the massacre of the children in Bethlehem with the earlier tragedy of the exile to Babylon.[24] In combining Egypt, the land of the Exodus in v. 15 with Ramah, the site of the departure for the Babylonian exile in v. 18, Matthew skilfully offers a succinct history of Israel from Exodus to Exile and identifies Jesus with this history; Jesus, the refugee, relives the history of the Jewish people first in their voluntary exile in Egypt and secondly in their enforced exile in Babylon. The two fulfilment quotations in v. 15 and v. 18 draw out clearly for the reader the comparison between both events. Commentators have noted the significance of the association made between Bethlehem, Egypt and Ramah; Brown speaks of 'the summing up of the theological history of Israel in geographical miniature'[25] while Stock notes that 'the fulfilment citations give us three names (Bethlehem, Egypt and Ramah) evocative of the great moments of the Old Testament'.[26]

Although the last fulfilment quotation (v. 23) is very problematic since it does not actually appear in the Old Testament and the prophet concerned is not cited, it is clear, however, that its purpose is to make a definite association between Jesus and Nazareth.[27] Since Nazareth is in Gentile Galilee, commentators see the purpose of this verse as an attempt to show that Jesus returns from Egypt to the area of the Gentiles where he can begin his mission. By combining the reference to Israel (v. 20) with Galilee of the Gentiles (vv. 22-23), Matthew has Jesus divinely directed to the two groups that make up the Matthaean community: Jew and Gentile.[28] In

24. The theme of exile is important in the Infancy Narrative also since in the genealogy of Mt. 1, it is the only specific episode to be mentioned (1.11, 17).

25. Brown, *Birth of the Messiah*, p. 218.

26. Stock, *Method and Message of Matthew*, p. 41. Luz, *Theology of the Gospel of Matthew*, pp. 29-30, also emphasizes the importance of the geographical locations for an understanding of the passage.

27. For a comprehensive discussion on the problems which this fulfilment quotation presents, see the detailed treatment of the problem and possible solutions in Brown, *Birth of the Messiah*, pp. 207-13 and 617. Also Erickson, 'Divine Injustice?', p. 20, for an interesting perspective on the issue.

28. See Stock, *Method and Message of Matthew*, p. 41.

short, the narrative of the Flight into Egypt, the symbolism of which has been interpreted for the reader through three fulfilment quotations, is intended to speak to both Jewish and Gentile readers, presumably in Antioch towards the end of the first century CE, to further their sense of identity with the person and mission of Jesus.

The Text and the Reader

But this conclusion is inherently problematic, first with regard to the Jewish reader and secondly the Gentile. Since the Gospel was written after the destruction of Jerusalem in 70 CE, the Jewish-Christian community in Antioch has presumably either left Jerusalem or never lived there in the first place, having been part of an earlier diaspora. Does the narrative of the Flight into Egypt with its emphasis on themes of displacement, Exodus and Exile at its centre offer a credible history to the Jew living in Antioch with which he or she can identify? The return of Jesus, representing the new people of Israel, to 'the land of Israel'[29] (vv. 20-21), the only use of the phrase in the New Testament, appears re-assuring but it is a less than satisfactory closure to the narrative of Jesus' escape from Herod since his return puts his life in more, not less, danger[30] and also because he cannot return directly to his home in Bethlehem from which he fled since he is diverted away from Judaea to Nazareth in Galilee, a town with no Old Testament associations.

One could argue that, for the reader with a Jewish background, the *symbolism* of Jesus' return would have been immediately obvious.[31] One could also argue that the return of Jesus to 'the land of Israel', even though

---

29. Brown, *Birth of the Messiah*, p. 206, suggests Matthew's use of the phrase is inspired by Ezek. 20.36-38.

30. Many commentators associate Herod's search for Jesus to destroy him with Jesus' trial and death. For example, they point out that the verb in v. 13, *apollynai*, to destroy, appears in the Passion narrative in Mt. 27.20 and the verb in v. 16, *empaizein*, to ridicule, is used for the mockery of Jesus as king in 27.29, 31, 41. See Brown, *Birth of the Messiah*, p. 204. Stock, *Method and Message of Matthew*, p. 37, notes that the manner in which Herod reacts to the perceived threat posed by the infant Jesus anticipates the manner in which the religious leaders will later respond to the adult Jesus.

31. Jacob Neusner has shown how the historical-geographical experience of exile has become a paradigm for Judaism, so that Jews who did not share the actual concrete experience of exile must nonetheless appropriate its paradigmatic power in order to be fully Jewish. See Jacob Neusner, *Understanding Seeking Faith: Essays on the Case in Judaism* (Atlanta: Scholars Press, 1986), pp. 137-41.

it resulted ultimately in the death of Jesus, was the event that would bring about salvation. Yet at the same time, Matthew, in suggesting that Jesus' return reverses the Jewish exodus and exile shows that his concept of exile is a negative and punitive one. Would Matthew's diaspora readership in Antioch, prosperous Alexandria or elsewhere have agreed with his view?

An interesting perspective, of help in appreciating the impact of the geography of the passage, is Robert Carroll's discussion of the situated-ness of the reader in relation to texts dealing with Exile in the Old Testament.[32] He draws attention to the 'narratological obsession' of the Hebrew authors with Exodus and Exile which act as root metaphors in Hebrew narrative:

> Exile and exodus: these are the two sides or faces of the myth that shapes the subtext of the narratives and rhetoric of the Hebrew Bible. Between these twin topoi is framed, constructed and constituted the essential story of the Hebrew Bible they reflect a deep narratological structure and constant concern with journeys into or out of territories.[33]

He argues that although there were many instances of exile and deport-ations in the Hebrew Bible,[34] the predominant tradition that there was one major Exile has come to us through an ideological shaping of biblical history carried out in the service of a Jerusalem-centred ideology:

> From the position of modern readers of the Bible, there can really only be a sense of exile as something propounded by a Jerusalem- or Palestinian-orientated point of view. From a Babylonian Jewish community, an Egypt-ian Jewish community or even a modern reader's point of view, life in the Diaspora may not have been seen as exilic at all. It is all a question of point of view and perspective... To talk about *the* exile is to take a position following or favouring the Jerusalem-orientated point of view.[35]

It could be argued that in the narrative of the Flight into Egypt, constructed around the same twin topoi of exodus and exile, Matthew re-enforces for his Jewish Christian audience the same Old Testament

---

32. Robert P. Carroll, 'Exile! What Exile? Deportation and the Discourses of Diaspora', in Lester L. Grabbe (ed.), *Leading Captivity Captive* (European Seminar in Historical Methodology, 2; JSOTSup, 278; Sheffield: Sheffield Academic Press, 1998), pp. 62-79.

33. Carroll, *Exile! What Exile?*, p. 63.

34. Brown, *Birth of the Messiah*, p. 216 n. 8, too, admits 'how difficult it is to decide which Exile is meant by Matthew; he may have intended a conglomerate picture of exile'.

35. Carroll, 'Exile! What Exile?', p. 67.

perspective of exodus and exile; just as the Old Testament perspective is centralized in Jerusalem, so too Matthew's viewpoint of the Exodus and Exile is seen from within 'the land of Israel' (vv. 19-20). But can such a viewpoint be shared by Matthew's diaspora community, the Gentiles within his community or subsequent readers of his narrative, including the modern reader for whom there is no link either geographically or culturally? For Matthew, there is a *centre and periphery*, with Bethlehem (v. 16) or the land of Israel (vv. 19-20) at the centre and Egypt (vv. 13-15) and Nazareth (v. 23) as peripheral locations in the story. This may be Matthew's ideological view but every reading and every re-reading of the story must be situated and that situatedness of the story is dependent on the location and identity of the reader.[36]

To interpret Jesus' return to the land of Israel as a fulfilment of, and satisfactory conclusion to, the Old Testament events of Exodus and Exile is problematic. It suggests that Exile and Diaspora must always be seen as punitive, negative and temporary, a position with which not everyone would agree.[37] Matthew, in the structure of his chiasmus, determines for the reader *his* view of exile, a view that already existed in the Old Testament and which was centred on Jerusalem; the implication is that exile is a state from which people need rescuing – a view not always shared by subsequent interpreters.

Cultural Interpretations of the Flight into Egypt

Appropriation of the Text

From the early Christian centuries, re-readings of the Flight into Egypt were not focused on the *centre* of Matthew's pericope, the Massacre of the Innocents,[38] nor on its twin theme of Exodus from Egypt and return from Exile. Rather, interest was focused on the *periphery* of the pericope, on the flight of the family out of Israel and on their time of exile in Egypt.

---

36. See Philip R. Davies on the importance of identity as a major factor in this discussion. Philip R. Davies, 'Exile? What Exile? Whose Exile?', in Lester L. Grabbe (ed.), *Leading Captivity Captive* (European Seminar in Historical Methodology, 2; JSOTSup, 278; Sheffield: Sheffield Academic Press, 1998), pp. 128-38.

37. See Davies, 'Exile?', pp. 134-35.

38. Erickson, 'Divine Injustice?', p. 8, provides references where the centre of the pericope, the Slaughter of the Innocents, has been used as a platform to speak to such issues as the Holocaust, abortion and the Vietnam War.

The family, after their flight to Egypt, remains hidden in the background of the narrative during the massacre of the infants, until their re-appearance and return.[39] Their absence, the secrecy of their journey and their unknown destination have exercised the imagination of many throughout the centuries; the desire to complete the details of the terse narrative parallels similar attempts to offer closure to other unsatisfactorily short biblical narratives.[40] The brevity and lack of detail allowed interpreters, especially artists, to expand the biblical narrative and to apply it to their own situation.[41] Paolo Berdini,[42] with reference to the religious art of Jacopo Bassano, shows how a biblical painting is not just a representation of the text but the artist's *reading* of the text, influenced by his or her historical or political situation:

> What the painter visualises is not the narrative of the text but its expanded form as it emerges from the painter's reading of it. In compliance with a specific mode of reading—Christian Exegesis—the visualisation of a text is intended to have a specific effect on the beholder. I call the dynamics of visualisation 'visual exegesis' and suggest that painting visualises a *reading* and not a text.[43]

Similarly, many artists, informed and inspired by early apocryphal legends, offered *readings* of the biblical Flight into Egypt and highlighted

39. The absence of the Virgin is particularly noticeable in the panel depicting the Slaughter of the Innocents in Duccio's masterpiece, *The Maestà*, painted for the Duomo in Siena in 1317. Mary is present in all the narrative panels portraying her life except in the Slaughter of the Innocents which portrays the weeping mothers alone with their injured expressions of grief. See Enzo Carli, *Duccio's Maestà* (Florence: Istituto Fotocromo Italiano, 1998), p. 9.

40. Several writers have shown how biblical narratives have been extended and completed in art, music, literature and film. See especially, J. Cheryl Exum's treatment of the Samson and Delilah narrative in *Plotted, Shot, and Painted*, pp. 184-88; Mieke Bal, *Reading Rembrandt: Beyond the Word Image Opposition* (Cambridge: Cambridge University Press, 1991); Paolo Berdini, *The Religious Art of Jacopo Bassano: Painting as Visual Exegesis* (Cambridge: Cambridge University Press, 1997); David Curzon, *Modern Poems on the Bible: An Anthology* (Philadelphia: Jewish Publication Society, 1994); Larry J. Kreitzer, *Film and Fiction in the Old Testament: On Reversing the Hermeneutical Flow* (The Biblical Seminar, 24; Sheffield: Sheffield Academic Press, 1994); Martin O'Kane, 'The Biblical King David and his Artistic and Literary Afterlives', *Biblical Interpretation* 6 (1998), pp. 313-47.

41. For the importance of the theme in film, see Gaye Ortiz, 'Jesus, Mary and Joseph! (Holy) Family Values in Film', in this volume.

42. Berdini, *Religious Art of Jacopo Bassano*.

43. Berdini, *Religious Art of Jacopo Bassano*, p. xi.

various aspects of the journey so that what was originally either peripheral to or non-existent in the Matthaean account now becomes central, even assuming a life of its own.[44] The artists' reading of the narrative may be inspired by other biblical subject matter, for example, the exile of Adam and Eve from the garden, the Babylonian exile or the 'exile' of Christ as he is condemned to death. Ironically what Matthew omits from his text— the context and details of the family's stay in Egypt—becomes a focus for the artist to suggest, visualize and reflect upon several divergent aspects of biblical exile.

Early Apocryphal Legends
Early Christian apocryphal legends betray an insatiable interest in the characters of Jesus, Mary and Joseph and especially in the events of their journey and stay in Egypt—legends mostly clustered together in *The Gospel of Pseudo-Matthew*.[45] *Pseudo-Matthew*'s embellishments which focus on the actual escape and subsequent exile are important because such legends were instrumental in the way artists, especially in the mediaeval period and after, read the story. Elliot notes that the *Gospel of Pseudo-Matthew* was so influential in the Middle Ages, that much mediaeval art is indecipherable without reference to it.[46]

Pseudo Matthew 17-25 corresponds to Mt. 2.13-23 and documents a number of miracles performed by or because of Jesus. It locates the events two years after the birth of Jesus (*Ps. Mt.* 16) and describes the journey in colourful and fanciful language. Having found a cave in which to shelter and find rest, Mary is frightened by lions, panthers and various other kinds of wild beasts, but is pacified by Jesus' words and the submission of the animals to him. In fulfilment of Isa. 65.25 the beasts walk with them and yet not one of them was hurt (*Ps. Mt.* 19). Mary found shelter in the shade of a palm-tree and desired to eat the fruit from the branches which were

---

44. For the evolution of the Flight into Egypt iconography, see Gaston Duchet-Suchaux and Michel Pastoureau, *The Bible and the Saints* (Flammarion Iconographic Guides; Paris: Flammarion Press, 1994), pp. 149-51; and Peter Murray and Linda Murray, *The Oxford Companion to Christian Art and Architecture* (Oxford: Oxford University Press, 1996), pp. 157-59.

45. J.K. Elliot, *The Apocryphal Jesus: Legends of the Early Church* (Oxford: Oxford University Press, 1996), pp. 3-6.

46. J.K. Elliot (ed.), *The Apocryphal New Testament: A Collection of Apocryphal Christian Literature in an English Translation based on M.R. James* (Oxford: Clarendon Press, 1993), p. 84.

well out of even Joseph's reach. However, on Jesus's command, the branches of the palm-tree stooped low so that Mary could pick enough fruit with which to refresh herself, Jesus and Joseph (*Ps. Mt.* 20). Jesus commanded the tree to 'open from [its] roots a vein of water which is hidden in the earth and let the waters flow, so that [they] might quench [their] thirst' (*Ps. Mt.* 20). The tree duly complied and the family had more than enough water from the spring which emerged for themselves and for their animal companions (*Ps. Mt.* 20). The palm tree which provided the Holy Family with shelter and refreshment anticipates the palm branches used by the crowds to pave Jesus' way as he triumphantly entered Jerusalem immediately prior to his passion, death and resurrection.

The final miracle recounted by the *Gospel of Pseudo-Matthew* (22-24) is, perhaps, the most dramatic. On reaching Sotinen in Egypt and not knowing anyone there, the family went to the temple. In fulfilment of Isa. 19.1, when they entered the temple the 365 idols fell off their plinths and shattered into tiny fragments 'and thus they plainly showed that they were nothing' (*Ps. Mt.* 23). This single event, the gospel declares, 'led to the conversion of the whole city because the governor proclaimed that unless this were the God of our gods, our gods would not have fallen on their faces before him, nor would they be lying prostrate in his presence: therefore they silently confess that he is their Lord. Unless we do what we have seen our gods doing, we may run the risk of his anger and all come to destruction' (*Ps. Mt.* 24).

A further legend[47] which developed around the biblical story was that of the sower: being pursued by Herod's soldiers, Mary and Joseph asked a sower, whom they passed by, to tell the soldiers that he had seen them go by at the time of sowing. Immediately, a field of corn grew up, giving the impression that sowing had occurred many months previously. When the soldiers arrived and saw that it was nearly time for the harvest they gave up their search thinking that they were much too late and thereby allowed the family to continue their escape without fear of being caught.

Artistic Representations
Even at an early stage in the narrative's interpretation, the emphasis on divine protection in perilous circumstances obviously appealed to the reader and the potential of the subject could easily be appropriated by

---

47. Cited in Maryan W. Ainsworth and Keith Christiansen (eds.), *From Van Eyck to Bruegel* (New York: Metropolitan Museum of Art, 1998), p. 266.

artists to encourage the viewer to identify with the scene.[48] In some cases, the artist simply depicts the embellishments made to the biblical text by the apocryphal stories. For example, *The Flight into Egypt* (National Gallery, London, c. 1515) (Fig. 1), a panel from a wooden altarpiece by the Master of 1518, is typical of the way the subject was treated in the fourteenth and fifteenth centuries.[49]

Figure 1. *The Flight into Egypt*, The Master of 1518
(c. 1515, The National Gallery, London).

48. Although there is no recent bibliography specifically on this topic, two biblical commentators from the end of the last century explore the theme in some depth— H. Van Dyke in *Harper's New Monthly* (December 1889) and Frederic W. Farrar, 'The Massacre of the Innocents and the Flight into Egypt', in *The Life of Christ as Represented in Art* (London: A. & C. Black, 1894), pp. 263-70.

49. There is a detailed description of this painting in Anabel Thomas, *Illustrated Dictionary of Narrative Painting* (London: National Gallery Publications, 1994), pp. 38-39.

Here, the artist depicts, on the right, the plinth from which a pagan idol is falling and, on the left, the miracle of the wheatfield. Painted as an altar-piece, the work was intended to act as a devotional aide and is representative of many similar paintings. Joseph is leading the donkey which carries Mary as she suckles the infant Jesus; his gaze towards Mary directs the attention of the viewer to her and especially to the suckling child.

A second and more interesting interpretation is found in stained glass from the early twelfth century above the Royal Portal in Chartres Cathedral in the Incarnation Window which depict in five narrative panels the Flight into Egypt.[50] That so much space in the window was given over to the theme testifies to its importance. Of particular significance is the way in which the family is welcomed at Sotinen in Egypt; the city is represented in great detail with ramparts, streets, turrets and towers, houses with windows and hinged, nail-studded doors and a high red city gate, before which Aphrodisius the governor and a great retinue stand to welcome the Christ Child. The detail and sophistication of the depiction of Sotinen, the city of the Gentiles, create the effect of stability and security while the warmth of Aphrodisius's welcome contrasts with the harsh cruelty of King Herod in Bethlehem. But especially noteworthy is the way in which the place of exile, in Sotinen, becomes for the viewer the centre and focus of the Matthaean narrative.

Mediaeval Books of Hours and Vespers Art
Of the very many depictions of the Flight into Egypt, those associated with the liturgical hours of Vespers offer some of the richest interpretations. They are found especially in the Books of Hours[51] and most notably in a painting by Carravaggio, *Rest on the Fight into Egypt*.

50. Malcolm Miller, *Chartres Cathedral* (Andover, Hampshire: Pitkin, 1996), pp. 32-36.

51. See Christopher de Hamal, *A History of Illuminated Manuscripts* (London: Guild Publishing, 1986), and his second edition, *A History of Illuminated Manuscripts* (London: Phaidon, 1994), in which many sections have been modified and updated with many new illustrations. However, while the Flight into Egypt is included in the first edition (p. 174), it is omitted in the second. John Harthan, *Books of Hours and their Owners* (London: Thames & Hudson, 1978), includes three colour plates of the Flight into Egypt (pp. 71, 122, 126). See also his *The History of the Illustrated Book* (London: Thames & Hudson, 1997), especially 'Section 1: Manuscripts to the Sixteenth Century', pp. 11-58. Robert G. Calkins, *Illuminated Books of the Middle Ages* (London: Thames & Hudson, 1983) includes an illustration and brief discussion of the Flight into Egypt from the *London Hours* in the British Library from the first decade of

The mediaeval Books of Hours, 'the late medieval best-sellers'[52] with their devotional decorations and illustrations based on biblical scenes indicated those portions of the day which were to be set aside for religious or business purposes. The contents of the Books were divided into three elements: essential, secondary and accessory texts.[53] One of the essential texts is the *Little Office* or *Hours of the Virgin* in which each Hour was usually illustrated by a full or half page miniature of the following scenes.[54]

Matins	The Annunciation
Lauds	The Visitation
Prime	The Nativity
Tierce	The Angel's Announcement of Christ's Nativity to the Shepherds
Sext	The Adoration of the Magi
None	The Presentation in the Temple
Vespers	The Flight into Egypt
Compline	The Coronation of the Virgin

In the *Little Office*, the Hours are seen principally as episodes in the life of the Virgin, for example, at Lauds Mary visits Elizabeth and at Vespers she flees with the Christ child to Egypt. No doubt the reason for the association of the Flight with Vespers was Matthew's report that the journey took place at night. (For this reason, the chronological order of events is disrupted; one would expect the Flight to come before the Presentation and not after it.) A typical artistic representation of the Flight into Egypt which served to introduce the texts of Vespers in the Books of Hours is found in *The Hours of Marguerite de Foix, Duchess of Brittany* (Fig. 2).

the fifteenth century (pp. 261 and 266). Janet Backhouse, *The Illuminated Page: Ten Centuries of Manuscript Painting in the British Library* (London: The British Library, 1997), includes three early representation of the Flight into Egypt: first, a surviving leaf from a late-twelfth-century Psalter showing 12 scenes from the Christmas story including the Flight into Egypt (p. 47); second, several scenes from apocryphal incidents from the Holkham Bible Picture Book, early fourteenth century (p. 237); and third, a very finely decorated miniature of the Flight introducing Vespers in a Book of Hours, which was started in 1520 and completed more than a century later in 1643 for Louis XIV when luxury devotional manuscripts made an unexpected return to fashion in France during the reign of the 'Sun King'. Nancy Grubb, *The Life of Christ in Art* (New York: Abbeville, 1996), p. 53, has a depiction from the thirteenth-century *Miniatures of the Life of Christ*, p. 50.

52. Harthan, *Books of Hours and their Owners*, p. 9.
53. Harthan, *Books of Hours and their Owners*, p. 14.
54. Harthan, *Books of Hours and their Owners*, p. 28.

Figure 2. *The Flight into Egypt* (c. 1470–80, from The Hours of Marguerite
de Foix, Duchess of Brittany, Victoria and Albert Museum, London).

In the depiction of the Flight into Egypt from the *Hours of Marguerite de
Foix, Duchess of Brittany*, distant mountains, towers and a river landscape
lead the eye down to the walled city of Bethlehem from where the family
is fleeing.[55] Immediately behind the mule, an angel stands as if protecting
the little group from the soldiers sent in pursuit by King Herod. The

---

55. The figure of Joseph is differentiated from that of Mary and Jesus because he
does not have a halo; he is denied the sanctity given to them. This might possibly be
explained by a particular devotion that Marguerite de Foix may have had for the Virgin
Mary, the 'immaculate daughter of Anne', which is suggested by a prayer at the end of
the book. See Harthan, *Books of Hours and their Owners*, p. 124.

peasant cutting corn illustrates the apocryphal Miracle of the Sower in which Mary asked the sower to tell the soldiers that he had seen a family go past at sowing time. The soldiers then abandon the pursuit in the belief that the refugees must now be too far away to be apprehended. Below the text, the Massacre of the Infants takes place in Bethlehem. Herod stands on the right pointing with his sceptre as the soldiers go about their work. The artist presents the viewer with images of great immediacy. As well as incorporating faithfully the Matthaean narrative of the Massacre of the Infants at Bethlehem, he includes an apocryphal legend of *Pseudo-Matthew*. The written text, opening Vespers, imploring God to come to the reader's help, serves to associate the dangers conveyed in the miniature with the vicissitudes of his/her own life and, by implication, commends the reader to pray for divine assistance.

No doubt, the reason for the choice of the Flight into Egypt to illustrate the texts of Vespers was that it offered yet another incident—and a nocturnal one—in the life of the Virgin. But there is a further explanation. Vespers, which included five psalms and the Magnificat,[56] was a favourite and an important devotion. Paolo Berdini, in a detailed study of the religious art of Jacopo Bassano, notes its importance in the Middle Ages:

> Regarding the ordinary Christian, the liturgy of the hours provided the structure within which the continuity and interplay between the two Testaments could be recognised. In particular, Vespers were conceived and perfected as evening prayers with the intention of positing clearly the link between creation and salvation, between the story of the sinful Adam and the redemptive sacrifice of Christ.[57]

Berdini relates the underlying exegetical exercise present in the reading of biblical texts at Vespers, to the interpretation of Bassano's *The Journey of Jacob* (1578)[58] and suggests that an understanding of the structure of Vespers offers a rich 'reading' or 'visual exegesis' of that painting. He argues that the overriding impression of night and darkness in *The Journey of Jacob* reveals 'an exegetical character that can be related to the structure of Vespers'.[59] He notes that the biblical passages which Vespers contained (from the Psalms and Genesis) were selected for the purpose of

56. Harthan, *Books of Hours and their Owners*, pp. 16-17.

57. Berdini, *Religious Art of Jacopo Bassano*, p. 84.

58. Unfortunately, it is not possible to include this painting here. It is included in Berdini, *Religious Art of Jacopo Bassano*, and also on the website of the Museo del Palazzo Ducale, Venice.

59. Berdini, *Religious Art of Jacopo Bassano*, p. 85.

relating the events of creation to the events of Christian revelation. Light as a divine manifestation was considered the unifying force of the Old and New Testaments. In the Old Testament, light signals the beginning of creation; it is the first sign of life given to Adam but, in the New Testament, the light of Christ indicates the path of salvation itself. Vespers, at the last light of day, provided an opportunity to reflect on light and darkness, labour and rest. Central to all scriptural selections forming Vespers since early Christianity, Psalm 104 initiated Christian thanksgiving and introduced night as the time for praying. Psalm 104.20-24 describes a nocturnal landscape where night is broken by the daylight of labour which lasts until evening. Darkness disrupts labour and brings rest:

> You make darkness and it is night, when all the animals of the forest come creeping out. The young lions roar for their prey, seeking their food from God. When the sun rises, they withdraw and lie down in their dens. People go out to their work and to their labour until evening (Ps. 104.20-23).

Berdini's method of 'visual exegesis', of applying the same interpretive process to a biblical painting as applied to biblical texts at Vespers, illumines artistic representations of the Flight into Egypt. A work which cannot be fully appreciated unless interpreted as Vespers Art is Caravaggio's *Rest on the Flight into Egypt* (Fig. 3).

Figure 3. *Rest on the Flight into Egypt* (c. 1603 by Michelangelo Merisi da Caravaggio [1571–1610], Galleria Doria Pamphilj, Rome/Bridgeman Art Library).

Caravaggio based his work on Tintoretto's painting of *The Flight into Egypt* (1583–87), in the Scuola di San Rocco, Venice, which dramatically presents the Holy Family as they furtively and hesitatingly leave Bethlehem. While the theme of the Flight into Egypt was common in Italy,[60] Rest on the Flight into Egypt, in contrast, was a northern subject[61] and in Venice there was no major example depicting the family resting on the way. In depictions of the theme in Italy, landscape normally took second place to the central image of the Virgin, to which Joseph and the donkey

60. See, for example, paintings of the theme by di Buoninsegna (c. 1280, Cathedral Museum, Siena); Giotto (c. 1305, Scrovegni Chapel Padua [see Grubb, *Life of Christ in Art*, p. 50]); Corregio (c. 1515, Galleria degli Uffizi Florence); Barocci (c. 1528, Pinacoteca Vaticana, Rome); da Fabriano (c. 1400, Galleria d'Arte Antica e Moderna, Florence). The theme in Duccio's *Maestà* can be seen in Carli, *Duccio's Maestà*, p. 27; Giotto's version in the Church of St Francis, Assisi, can be seen in Eric Santoni, *La Vie de Jésus* (Paris: Editions Hermé, 1990), p. 35, and Carracci's version (1603) in the Doria Gallery, Rome, can be seen in Susan Wright, *The Bible in Art* (New York: Smithmark, 1996), p. 85; di Paolo's version (c. 1450) in the Pinacoteca Nazionale di Siena can be seen in Marco Torito, *Pinacoteca Nazionale di Siena* (Genova: Sagep Editrice, 1993 edn), p. 49. The Flight into Egypt forms part of Simone Martini's famous frescoes of the Church of San Gimignano, Tuscany: see J.V. Imberciadori, *The Collegiate Church of San Gimignano* (Poggibonsi, Tuscany: Nencini, 1998), pp. 20-21. For a discussion of the painting *Holy Family with a Donatrix as Saint Catherine of Alexandria* and the psychological intensity of the grouping of the figures, see Carolyn C. Wilson, *Italian Paintings XIV—XVI Centuries in the Museum of Fine Arts, Houston* (The Museum of Fine Arts, Houston, in association with Rice University Press; London: Merrell Holberton, 1996), pp. 350-56.

61. See, for example, de Cock (c. 1520), National Gallery, Dublin; Patener (c. 1520, National Gallery, London); Lastman (1620, National Gallery, London); Poussin (1657, Hermitage, St. Petersburg); van der Werff (1706, National Gallery, London); Boucher (c. 1750, Hermitage, St. Petersburg). For Lucas Cranach, see Alexander Stepanov, *Lucas Cranach the Elder* (Bournemouth: Parkstone, 1997), p. 27. For Bruegel, see Rose-Marie Hagen and Rainer Hagen, *Pieter Bruegel* (Cologne: Taschen, 1994), p. 93. For Elsheimer (c. 1600), see Jacques Duquesne, *La Bible et ses Peintures* (Paris: Fixot, 1989), p. 149. For Patel (c. 1650), see Frances Lincoln, *The First Christmas* (London: The National Gallery, 1992), p. 25. For Doré, see Gustave Doré, *La Bible* (Paris: Ars Mundi edition, 1998), p. 326. For Rossetti, see Farrar, *Life of Christ in Art*, pp. 266-77. For Edward Burne-Jones, see Joseph Rhymer, *The Illustrated Life of Jesus Christ* (London: Bloomsbury, 1994), pp. 32-33. Depictions of the theme exist in Islamic art from Isfahan, Iran, in the eighteenth century when Western influence was at its greatest. In one of these, Mary and Joseph pass through the desert with Jesus in Bedouin dress with a Bedouin tent in the background. See Na'ama Brosh and Rachel Milstein (eds.), *Biblical Stories in Islamic Painting* (Jerusalem: Israel Museum, 1991), pp. 125-26.

were generally loosely connected at a distance. Caravaggio subdued the dramatic impact of the family's departure in Tintoretto's painting by showing the family at rest and by making the figures impressively present.[62] He distinguished the landscape according to the adult figures, with the angel positioned as a hinge between the two. A strong geometrical layout divides the oblong space into the barren half occupied by Joseph. Almost incidentally, behind the angel's wings, mother and child appear. Old age on the left hand of the picture is contrasted with youth as the quintessence of eternal life; on the right, the eye is drawn from the stony earth on the left across the world to the distant perspectives of eternity.

The composition fans out from an angel who is playing music and who has his back to the viewer. He divides the picture centrally with the outline of his right side and his left wing, which projects vertically towards the viewer in the foreground picture area. Nothing grows on the stony ground to the left. Joseph now an old man sits there beside a travelling bottle and bundle. He wears clothes of earth-colour and is holding a book of music from which an angel is playing a violin solo.

In setting out violin music for the angel to play, Caravaggio offers a key to the painting's meaning. By painting a meticulous copy of a music book which contains a motet which begins with the letter Q, we can identify a passage from Song of Songs 7.6-7, as the text appropriate to the music; the score shows the cantus part of a motet by the Flemish composer, Noel Baulduin, first published in 1519. The quotation forms part of the Vespers of the Virgin Mary and runs:

> Quam pulchra es et quam decora carissima in deliciis. Statura tua assimilata est palmae et uba tua botris.

> How beautiful are you, my beloved, you creature of bliss! As you stand there, you are like the palm tree and your breasts are like the grapes.

Caravaggio takes the relationship of the Flight into Egypt to Vespers so literally that instead of depicting the fleeing Holy Family, usual in Italy, he chooses to show them resting as befits the hour of sunset and makes the music a lullaby. König points out that the sleep of Mary and Jesus anticipate the death of Jesus—sleep and death being often intimately linked in art. The painting is a Vespers picture, in which Caravaggio evokes the

---

62. See Eberhard König, 'On Deciphering the Pictures of the *Rest during the Flight into Egypt*—a Pastoral or Caravaggio's First Great Work?', in König, *Caravaggio* (Cologne: Konemann, 1997), pp. 88-92. My discussion of the painting relies on his description and analysis.

hours that the Virgin Mary spends with her child, the pastoral character of the angelic music and the nearness of sleep and death. The motet from the Song of Songs, applied to the Virgin Mary at Vespers, suggests that the focus of the painting is on Mary's role not only now but also at the death of Jesus.

The key to appreciating the painting is an understanding of the process of Vespers, the liturgical separation of work and rest, light and darkness, consciousness and sleep; the angel's wings act as a hinge to highlight the separation. On the left half of the painting, Joseph, the angel and the donkey (with its huge eye) stay awake to celebrate Vespers and watch over Mary and the child on the right as they sleep. The viewer identifies with the left side of the picture with the group who are awake and conscious and not with Mary and Jesus who are unaware of what is happening. The viewer is further attracted to the group on the left because the music score is positioned at such an angle that only the angel and the viewer can read it. As the angel plays the Vespers motet which Joseph holds and as the viewer reads it, s/he becomes part of the Vespers picture and joins in the devotion to Mary suggested by the text of the Song of Songs.[63]

The Flight into Egypt as Metaphor for the Journey of Life
Lew Andrews[64] and David Freedberg[65] discuss the importance of internal visual representation from the thirteenth century onwards as an aid to prayer and meditation. Andrews[66] draws attention to the anonymous text, *Giardino di Orationi* (Garden of Prayer), written in 1454 and widely available during the fifteenth and sixteenth centuries, which instructed the faithful how best to meditate upon and remember the story of the Passion. It advised them to make a 'memory place' of their own familiar surround-

63. Helen Langdon, in her interpretation of this painting in *Caravaggio: A Life* (London: Chatto and Windus, 1998), pp. 123-26, ignores completely the aspect of Vespers, preferring instead to emphasize the 'passionate eroticism' of the Song of Songs in the motet which she applies to the 'sweetly erotic' angel. However, she does state that 'In the Christian centuries the eroticism of the Song of Songs had become virginal, and its most ardent words the words of the soul…Mary becoming the symbolic Bride of Christ' (p. 125).

64. Lew Andrews, *Story and Space in Renaissance Art: The Rebirth of Continuous Narrative* (Cambridge: Cambridge University Press, 1995).

65. David Freedberg, *The Power of Images: Studies in the History and Theory of Response* (Chicago: University of Chicago Press, 1989).

66. Andrews, *Story and Space in Renaissance Art*, pp. 29-33.

ings in order to visualize the successive events of the Passion to be remembered in various locations within that space:

> The better to impress the story of the Passion on your mind and to memorise each action of it more easily, it is helpful and necessary to fix the places and people in your mind: a city for example will be the city of Jerusalem— taking for this purpose a city that is well known to you...and then too you must shape in your mind some people, well known to you, to represent for you the people involved in the passion...[67]

Andrews notes that this spiritual exercise was readily translated into paint, the best example being Memling's depiction in Turin of the Passion, which is an illustration of the advice of the handbook. The episodes within the picture act as aides memoire to the viewer's recall as well as to dazzle the eye:

> Their illusionistic brilliance spurs both the imagination and memory, permitting the viewer to enter the painting's fictive world, to move through the picture's space as though traversing the imaginary room or houses of the ancient treatises or the familiar environments of the devotional handbook. Viewing or looking is presumed to be an active process, a kind of devotion.[68]

Freedberg, too, discusses how the painter was 'a professional visualiser of the holy stories' and how his pious public were practised in spiritual exercises that demanded a high level of visualization of the central episodes in the life of Jesus.[69] As an example, he cites the detailed instruction of the Flight into Egypt in the *Meditations of the Life of Christ* from the mid-thirteenth century by Pseudo-Bonaventure:

> Jesus was carried to Egypt by the very young and tender mother, and by the aged saintly Saint Joseph, along wild roads, obscure rocky and difficult, through woods and uninhabited places—a very long journey. They are said to have gone by the way of the desert which the children traversed and in which they stayed for 40 years. Where did they rest and spend the night? Have pity on them. Accompany them and help to carry the child Jesus and serve them in every way you can. Here there comes a compassionate meditation. Make careful note of the following things do they live or did they beg? You must contemplate all these things. Enlarge on them as you please.

67. Cited in Andrews, *Story and Space in Renaissance Art*, p. 29.
68. Andrews, *Story and Space in Renaissance Art*, p. 33.
69. One might also note here how the popular thirteenth-century Franciscan tract, the *Meditations on the Life of Christ*, stressed the defencelessness of the Holy Family, alone in a strange land. See I. Ragusa and R.B. Green (eds.), *Meditations on the Life of Christ* (trans. I. Ragusa; Princeton, NJ: Princeton University Press, 1961), p. 67.

Be a child with the child Jesus! Do not disdain humble things for they yield devotion, increase love, excite fervour and raise hope.[70]

Freedberg demonstrates, with illustrations from the Passion of Christ, how the imaginative intensity of such tracts was greatly increased by painters 'to arouse the empathetic responses necessary for successful meditation'.[71] Two paintings of the Flight into Egypt also illustrate Freedberg's point.

Figure 4. *The Rest on the Flight into Egypt*, Gerard David, (1510, The Metropolitan Museum of Art, New York, The Jules Bache Collection, 1949).

70. See Ragusa and Green (eds.), *Meditations on the Life of Christ*, p. 67.

71. The spirituality of van Gogh too, stemmed from the mediaeval traditions of an inward piety which taught that the spiritual journey is interior and intensely personal. It is expressed in Thomas à Kempis's *The Imitation of Christ* which had a profound

In *The Rest on the Flight into Egypt* (Fig. 4),[72] Gerard David was inspired by two late mediaeval works of literature: the *Life of Christ* of Ludolph of Saxony and the *Meditations on the Life of Christ* by Pseudo-Bonaventure. Popular expanded versions of the latter, contemporary with David's painting, present the Flight in terms of a pilgrimage on which the reader should accompany the Holy Family. They describe the arduous journey of the aged Joseph and Mary carrying the child Jesus 'through dark and uninhabited forests, and by very long routes past rough and deserted places to Egypt'.

A tiny scene in the right middle ground shows the family emerging from the woods to the broad open plain where Mary nurses the child. In the centre image as in the forest scene, David has recalled the description of Ludolph of Saxony: 'the eye of devotion observes the little Jesus who sweetly drinks at the breast of the glorious…what could be more pleasant or delightful to see?' At the left a spring has opened near Mary's feet to quench their thirst since they were refused water along the way by the inhabitants of Materca. Just as the Virgin provides the child with her milk, so in turn Christ nourishes the faithful with his own body and blood. This is indicated by the posture of Jesus who turns towards the viewer, as if extending an invitation. It is shown in details directly below the child: the glimpse of the Virgin's underdress which is red (the colour of Christ's passion) and the broad leaf plantain, popularly known for its medicinal value as a stancher of blood. The ivy on the left is a symbol of salvation and the bough with the apples to the right of the Virgin is a reminder of the sin and subsequent exile of Adam.

David draws the viewer into the painting in a number of ways: for example, the way in which the Virgin and child tower, in a pyramid-like shape, over the viewer with whom the child establishes eye contact and through the many symbols which anticipate the death of Jesus, interpreted as a saving activity. But, most importantly, the journey of the family becomes the individual's own journey through life. Drawn into the

---

effect on van Gogh in the early years. See Kathleen Powers Erickson, *At Eternity's Gate: The Spiritual Vision of Vincent van Gogh* (Grand Rapids, MI: Eerdmans, 1998), pp. 42-49.

72. David painted two versions of the subject. The second is in the Washington Art Gallery. Both paintings inspired numerous replicas and versions, e.g. a copy of the Metropolitan *Flight* is in the Prado. For detailed descriptions of both, see Ainsworth and Christiansen, *From Van Eyck to Bruegel*, p. 308, on whom I rely in my description of the above two paintings.

painting, we now accompany the refugee family—their journey becomes our journey.

A painting by the so-called Master of the Female Half-Lengths (Fig. 5) provides a second example, showing how the viewer is invited to become part of the episode.

Figure 5. *The Rest on the Flight into Egypt*, The Master of the Female Half-Lengths (c. 1515, The Metropolitan Museum of Art, New York. H.O. Havemeyer Collection, Bequest of Mrs H.O. Havemeyer, 1929).

The details of this painting[73] have been inspired by *Pseudo-Matthew* and include many of the episodes mentioned there. The subject of the Flight into Egypt, which at first glance seems to be merely the pretext for the creation of a charming landscape,[74] is in fact discreetly referred to in

73. The artist was inspired by a contemporary of Gerard David, Joachim Patiner whose two surviving depictions of the themes are in the Prado and the Gemäldegalerie, Berlin. See Ainsworth and Christiansen, *From Van Eyck to Bruegel*, p. 266. I rely on their description of this painting.

74. The landscape in depictions of the Flight is never without significance. It may perhaps at first glance suggest the idealized and artificial world of *Arcadia*, the perfect pastoral world free from concern and danger as symbolized by the Forest of Arden in

motifs and scenes scattered in the foreground and background. The painting was conceived of as a type of *Andachtsbild* in which a worshipper might follow the story from scene to scene during private devotion, travelling the various paths of the landscape. The journey was understood by contemporary viewers as a metaphor for pilgrimage, in particular the pilgrimage of every human life, confronting at each step along the way the choice between the easy path of a sinful existence and the more difficult one of virtue.[75]

Mary is seated on the ground surrounded by flowering plantain, a lowly plant that symbolizes the well-worn path of the faithful who seek Christ. The fountain to the left suggests the refreshment provided by a miraculous spring of water. The broken figure suggests the idols that were toppled off their pedestals. In the foreground are a traveller's basket and saddlebags wrapped around a pilgrim's staff. The wheatfield behind conveys the story of the wheat which in *Pseudo-Matthew*, sprang up miraculously. The most prominent feature of the middle distance is the architectural fantasy that is surrounded by water and approached over a footbridge by an elegant woman in a long pink robe. No doubt the viewer is intended to journey along from image to image reflecting on the significance of each episode. The elegant lady in pink corresponds to the image of the Virgin. It has been suggested that the castle in the middle distance is common in paintings of this period and intended to address the increasingly secularized middle class.[76] The viewer is invited to contrast the lady with the Virgin, the wealthy lady entering her castle with Mary, the homeless and refugee mother.

The landscape situates the episode for the viewer: it is not the landscape of Egypt but a familiar one, situated within their own experience. The viewer enters into the painting and is invited to join in the journey. The pilgrim's staff and clothing at the forefront of the painting may suggest that we take on this journey with some urgency.

As You Like It. However, it can also suggest the Garden of Eden from which humankind experienced their first exile and banishment and act as a reminder that Christ is the new Adam restoring this lost world. In discussing the landscape in Bassano's *Journey of Jacob*, Berdini (*Religious Art of Jacopo Bassano*, p. 86), states that 'man and the created world are still a multitude of survivors in need of leadership and salvation'. This is reflected in *The Journey of Jacob* through a disordered and discordant landscape.

75. See Ainsworth and Christiansen, *From Van Eyck to Bruegel*, p. 266.

76. Ainsworth and Christiansen, *From Van Eyck to Bruegel*, p. 266.

The theme of the Flight into Egypt also offered the viewer an opportunity to reflect on the passion of Christ. Gentileschi's version[77] (Fig. 6) (unlike many depictions of the scene which are characterized by a sense of serene romanticism) captures the harsh realism suggested by the story; stripping away the idealism of other depictions, he leaves the viewer with 'a family exhausted in their human ordinariness from their nocturnal journey'.[78]

Figure 6. *Rest on the Flight into Egypt* ([oil on canvas] by Orazio Gentileschi [1565–1647], Birmingham Museums and Art Gallery/Bridgeman Art Library).

He situates the episode in a setting which highlights the bleakness, isolation and poverty of the refugee family; there is no natural landscape, no source of food or water; instead a large decaying wall covers almost a third of the canvass. Their worldly possessions are contained in one small sack. The menacingly tempestuous sky is symbolic of the violent drama

77. The theme was a favourite of Gentileschi. Other versions are found in the Louvre (see Santoni, *La Vie de Jésus*, p. 36) and in the Paul Getty Museum in Malibu. In the Louvre version, the donkey is omitted. Some think that this makes the image more universally applicable to any refugee family since the inclusion of the donkey links the image unmistakably to the holy family.

78. Wendy Beckett, *The Gaze of Love: Meditations on Art* (London: Marshall Pickering), p. 98.

which is unfolding in Bethlehem and from which the family has escaped. From just above the lower part of the wall, on the left of the painting, a glimmer of light emerges, heralding a new dawn.

The painting anticipates the death of Jesus in a number of ways.[79] First, the donkey, whose head seems extraordinarily large and prominent in the centre of the painting,[80] reminds the viewer of the journey to Jerusalem at the beginning of Christ's passion in Mt. 21.1-11. Beckett[81] suggests that the donkey symbolizes the divine protection which appears to be absent on first viewing in Gentileschi's painting, but which is much more immediately obvious in the paintings of Giotto and Caravaggio in the form of choirs of angelic hosts. Second, as Joseph collapses with fatigue, his lifeless body[82] is reminiscent of artistic portrayals of the body of Jesus taken from the cross, the Deposition, a common theme in Renaissance art. Third, the Christ child, feeding at the breast of Mary, may anticipate the giving of his body as food in the Eucharist.

Gentileschi invites the viewer to enter the scene, beckoned by the gesture of Jesus' right arm and his eye contact. The wall clearly protects the family (and the viewer who stands on the same side) from everything that happens in the world beyond it, symbolized by the tempestuous sky. From this vantage point, the viewer is invited to reflect on where safety, rest and security lie in a storm-filled world and is invited to reflect on the passion and death of Jesus.

Exile as a Positive and Spiritual Experience

A review of artistic representations of the Flight into Egypt indicates that artists were attracted by both the literal and metaphorical aspects of the story. The stark image of the fleeing family obviously provided the artist with opportunities in terms of characterization, landscape and colour. With regard to the metaphorical aspect, artists almost invariably depict exile as

---

79. For a description of the development of the traditions which associated the infancy of Christ with his passion and death, see Anne Derbes, *Picturing the Passion in Late Medieval Italy: Narrative Painting, Franciscan Ideologies and the Levant* (Cambridge: Cambridge University Press, 1998), pp. 1-11.

80. The point is discussed by Richard Harris in *A Gallery of Reflections: The Nativity of Christ* (Oxford: Lion Publishing, 1995), p. 80.

81. Beckett, *Gaze of Love*, p. 98.

82. Note his *red* tunic—symbol of the Passion in other paintings.

a potentially positive experience. In some cases, the journey takes on the connotations of pilgrimage, inviting the viewer to travel with the family on a journey of personal and spiritual enrichment; the dangers of the journey are seen as providing an opportunity to strengthen one's faith. For other artists, the rest on the Flight was invested with the same liturgical significance as Vespers. What many cultural representations of the Flight into Egypt have in common is that they encourage the viewer to reflect on the experience of exile, be it physical or metaphorical, and on its causes and effects. They take on the role of Brueggemann's 'primal speaker', a phrase he uses to describe Old Testament prophets as they comment on the causes and effects of exile in the Old Testament.

> It is clear that exiles must pay careful and sustained attention to speech, because it requires inordinately disciplined and imaginative speech to move through the shattering to newly voiced meaning.[83]

Mintz[84] suggests that in exile the primal speakers attempt:

> first to represent the catastrophe and then to reconstruct, replace, or redraw the threatened paradigm of meaning, and thereby make creative survival possible.

When artists take on the role of 'primal speaker', they acknowledge the catastrophe by including an image of the Massacre of the Infants or of King Herod; but they also replace the danger of Bethlehem with the security of Egypt; they reconstruct by including in depictions of the flight symbols which anticipate the passion and death of Jesus which ultimately offer salvation: the donkey which takes the family to Egypt anticipates the entry of Jesus to Jerusalem at the beginning of his passion; the apple which Jesus holds indicates that he is the new Adam reversing the Fall; the red of the garments anticipate his death; the posture of Joseph as he sleeps may anticipate the deposition of Jesus from the cross. In short, artists, in their depictions of the story, suggest that through danger and death, there comes resurrection and new life. The artist is not interested in portraying the safe return of the family to Bethlehem as a logical solution which reverses their current dilemma; he is more interested in suggesting to the viewer that new meaning must be given to a situation of catastrophe and

---

83. Brueggemann, *Cadences of Home*, p. 15.
84. Ian Mintz, *Hurban: Responses to Catastrophe in Hebrew Literature* (New York: Columbia University Press, 1984), p. 2.

invites the viewer to reconstruct, in Mintz's words, 'a new paradigm of meaning'. The situation of exile becomes an opportunity to rebuild and reconstruct.

The Twentieth Century[85] and Chagall

Pablo Picasso

Picasso's *Poverty* (1903) (Fig. 7), painted during his so-called 'Blue Period' which was characterized by his preoccupation with the poor and destitute of society anticipates the importance given to the theme throughout the entire twentieth century.[86] In *Poverty*, painted with palettes of blue, the frail and destitute family bear a strong resemblance to the Holy Family on the Flight to Egypt.[87] The sense of despair in much of his work at this time has been associated with the grief Picasso felt at the suicide of his friend Casegames in 1901. Mortality is communicated by the skull-like appearance of the heads of both mother and baby.

The simplicity of the image with its slow death-like movements of the family suggests that exile can be internal as well as external, in the words of Brueggemann 'Exile is not primarily geographical but it is social, moral and cultural'.[88] (This statement is especially true for the nineteenth century where many British and French artists, painting scenes of destitution to arouse the national social conscience, used the motif of the Flight into Egypt to depict the poor or evicted rural and urban family.)[89]

---

85. In the twentieth century, photography became a popular means of capturing the plight of the refugee. See Josef Koudelka, *Exiles* (London: Thames & Hudson, 1997). Described in *The Times* as 'the most potent and powerful photographer alive today', Koudelka's book of photographs taken since leaving the Czech Republic and in his many years of wandering in Europe and the US 'sum up in his images the alienation and disconnection of the 20th century'. For a recent twentieth-century painting, see *The Flight into Egypt*, by He Chi, from China in *Christ and Art in Asia* (76) September 1998, p. 5. The painting symbolizes the alienation of the Chinese Christian at the end of the millennium.

86. *Art Treasures of England: The Regional Collections* (Catalogue of 1998 exhibition; London: Royal Academy of Arts, 1998), p. 317.

87. For other twentieth-century depictions of the Flight into Egypt, see Nicholas Usherwood, *The Bible in 20th Century Art*, pp. 6, 49, 99.

88. Brueggemann, *Cadences of Home*, p. 2.

89. For example, Hubert von Herkomer, *Hard Times* (1885, Manchester City Art Galleries) and William-Adolphe Bouguereau, *Charity* (1865, Birmingham Museum and Art Galleries).

Figure 7. *Poverty*, Pablo Picasso (1903, The Whitworth Art Gallery,
The University of Manchester. ©Succession Picasso/DACS 2001).

Marc Chagall

Images depicting fleeing mothers and children, alongside other biblical
images, were commonly used before, during and after World War Two by
Jewish artists, to depict the horror and intensity of the suffering of the
Jews.[90] The defencelessness of the mother and child is conveyed by the

90. For a survey of Jewish artists' depiction of Holocaust themes, see Ziva
Amishai-Maisel, *Depiction and Interpretation: The Influence of the Holocaust on the
Visual Arts* (Oxford: Pergamon Press, 1993). My section on Chagall relies substantially
on her work.

conspicuous absence of the father in many of the Holocaust works and their innocence and purity by their implied Christian overtones of the Madonna and Child and the Flight into Egypt, associations which Chagall exploited openly.

Chagall used three basic symbols to depict the Jew fleeing into exile or to depict the refugee. The first was that of the Wandering Jew, the second the Jew carrying the Torah and the third the Mother and Child; but frequently all three themes were combined.[91] With regard to the latter, he sometimes used the *static* Madonna and Child image especially in his early career (1920s and 1930s), while from 1941 he concentrated on the *fleeing* mother and child. Chagall emphasized the similarity of this theme to the Flight into Egypt, a comparison not pursued by most of the other artists.

After his flight from Europe in 1941, while seeking a self image as a refugee, he found in the Flight into Egypt an autobiographical precedent for his present state and an image which clearly suggested the fact that he had been *saved* while others had not. It is this creation of an intensely personal iconography of the refugee mother and child that really differentiates him from other contemporary Jewish artists who used the theme.[92]

Very specifically and consciously, Chagall stressed the Christian innuendoes of the theme to arouse the sympathy of his Christian audience in a more direct way than could be achieved by either of his specifically Jewish refugee types; he was attempting to call attention to the plight of the Jews in Europe by addressing Christians in their own language of images.[93] The Flight into Egypt with its long history in Christian iconography, its associations with the Christian liturgy and its cultural and sentimental links with Christmas was an ideal means to express to Christian Europe the plight and suffering of the Jewish people.

---

91. For Chagall's life-long inspiration from the Bible, see his introduction to the newly opened Musée National Message Biblique Marc Chagall in Nice in 1973 in *Marc Chagall 1887–1985* (Nice: Musée National Message Biblique Marc Chagall, 1998), p. 7, and *Marc Chagall: Die großen Gemälde der Biblischen Botschaft* (Stuttgart: Belser Verlag, 1992), p. 5.

92. Chagall was especially inspired by icons of the Madonna and he had a personal interest in the process of birth and motherhood which came to the fore especially in connection with the birth of his daughter, Ida (see Amishai-Maisel, *Depiction and Interpretation*, p. 23).

93. Amishai-Maisel, *Depiction and Interpretation*, p. 24.

Figure 8. *The Harlequin Family*, or *The Flight into Egypt*, Marc Chagall
(1942–44, Indianapolis Museum of Art, Gift of Mrs. James W. Fesler.
©ADAGP, Paris and DACS, London, 2001).

In *The Harlequin Family* (1942–44) (Fig. 8), also called *The Flight into Egypt*, the mother and child ride out of the deserted snow-covered village on the traditional donkey with Joseph the Harlequin perched precariously behind them. The image is very similar to the traditional iconography of the flight into Egypt; to the Christian viewer, the painting is reminiscent of a Christmas card scene with its background of snow. In *The Yellow Crucifixion* (1943),[94] the same motif appears in the foreground where the Wandering Jew replaces the Harlequin in the role of Joseph. In preparation for this painting, Chagall drew a sketch forming a rich tapestry of biblical imagery which he adapted and applied to the situation of the Jews in Central Europe. In the original sketch, the sacrifice of Isaac and the Massacre of the Innocents played an important part alongside Christ, the Crucified Jew. During the war, the figure of Jesus, for Chagall, was

94. The title may well be an ironic homage to the more tranquil and religiously conventional *Yellow Christ* painted by Gauguin in 1889 (see Bohm-Duchen, *Chagall*, p. 245).

predominantly a symbol of Jewish martyrdom,[95] an image which he constantly combined with his other Holocaust motifs: the Mother and Child and the Wandering Jew. Later, Jesus came to symbolize the artist himself. The message he had originally intended to convey through these desperate images was that everyone is finally sacrificed, Abraham, Isaac, the ram and all the other innocent victims. However, in the painting itself, he simplified the imagery and preferred to use the Crucifixion as the most comprehensible image of a sacrifice which had taken place. To underline Jesus' Jewish identity, Chagall juxtaposed a Torah scroll to the Crucifixion and placed a phylactery on the head of Christ.[96]

The Yellow Crucifixion relates to the sinking of the ship, the *Struma*, in 1942. In it, both Jewish and Christian elements are strongly emphasized. Jesus wears phylacteries as well as his prayer shawl/loincloth and an open Torah scroll covers his right arm to form a single image. The scroll, in which the original sketch had depicted slaughtered children and the Sacrifice of Isaac is now empty and is illuminated by a candle held by an angel who blows a ram's horn, the symbol of salvation. But redemption is still far away; the cross is planted in the burning shtetl from which Jews try to escape while the fleeing mother and child below connect these refugees to the Flight into Egypt. But at present there is no escape: the refugees move left to join those on the sinking *Struma*. His personal identification with the theme can be seen in his sketch for *The Yellow Crucifixion* in which he wrote his name and that of Vitebsk on the open Torah in Hebrew.[97]

Two images in this painting refer to Christ: the Crucified Christ and the Christ child fleeing into Egypt. Chagall's style, in organizing his pictures by balancing the two 'semi-autonomous episodic fragments within a shallow visual setting',[98] may imply further desperation: just as the Christ

95. 'For me, Christ has always symbolised the true type of Jewish martyr. That is how I understood him in 1908 when I used this figure for the first time...it was under the influence of the pogroms. Then I painted and drew him in pictures about ghettos, surrounded by Jewish troubles, by Jewish mothers, running terrified with little children in their arms' (Chagall in 1977), cited in Amishai-Maisel, *Depiction and Interpretation*, pp. 184-85.

96. This description is taken from Amishai-Maisel, *Depiction and Interpretation*, p. 168

97. Amishai-Maisel, *Depiction and Interpretation*, p. 168.

98. The phrase is adapted from Stephanie Barron, *Exiles and Emigrés: The Flight of European Artists from Hitler*, p. 115, where she sums up Chagall's artistic style: 'Chagall dispensed with conventional rules of spatial and narrative unity and instead

child, even though he escaped Herod, will ultimately die as an innocent victim, so too although the Jewish refugee may escape the present calamity, his or her future remains similarly threatened. Will the place of exile be significantly better than the destruction from which the refugee flees?

In *Christmas 1943*, a sketch done for *Vogue Magazine*'s Christmas issue of 1943[99]—the drawing appeared opposite an appeal to donate to various charities over Christmas—Chagall depicted a terrified woman carrying a worried child, fleeing under the direction of an angel instead of the happy Madonna and Child, one might expect. The drawing reflects his preoccupation with the theme during his American years and his desire to keep the image before the Christian West, especially at Christmas.

Chagall's personal identification with the image of the Flight into Egypt emerges in *Obsession* in 1943 (Fig. 9). Here the mother and child are in a wagon hitched to a blue horse and escape from a building burning in Russia, which he symbolized by the green-domed church and the men bearing a red flag at the upper right. This image is based on two illustrations from Chagall's autobiography: visually it derives from the drawing of a cart driving away from a house; thematically, it was inspired by the story of Chagall's mother being removed on her bed from the house which burned down at the moment the artist was born. *Obsession* symbolizes the darkest days of the war and parallels the crushing of the Warsaw Ghetto revolt.[100] Here the whole world goes up in flames and a green Jesus lies helpless in the streets of the burning ghetto, mourned by the matriarch Rachel in the blazing sky above. Beside him, a bearded Jew holds aloft the candelabrum usually used to illuminate the cross but now one of its branches, the green one which parallels the green Christ, totters, its flames darkened, symbolizing a life that has been extinguished. On the right, Chagall sets his symbols of hope, the mother and child fleeing from the burning house. But their grinning satanic mule refuses to move so that their escape is blocked and the child—Chagall himself—realizing this, covers his face with his hands. Above them the Red Army come to the rescue but these few staggering soldiers are unarmed and they too seem consumed by the flames.

organised his pictures by balancing semiautonomous episodic fragments within a shallow visual setting'.

99. Amishai-Maisel, *Depiction and Interpretation*, p. 24.
100. Amishai-Maisel, *Depiction and Interpretation*, p. 184.

Figure 9. *Obsession* (1943 [oil on canvas] by Marc Chagall [1887–1985].
Private Collection/Peter Willi/Bridgeman Art Library
©ADAGP, Paris and DACS, London, 2001).

In *Obsession*, Chagall powerfully and dramatically subverts traditional Christian iconography of the Flight into Egypt by means of his character-istic style of using semi-autonomous episodic fragments, drawn from biblical or Christian imagery. In the traditional iconography of the Flight into Egypt (for example, *The Master of 1518*, see Fig. 1), Joseph is usually depicted leading the donkey and protecting Mary and the Child; on their journey, in many paintings of the theme, pagan idols fall from their pedestals as the Christ child approaches. Often too the background reflects a unified composition of a peaceful and serene landscape which invites the viewer to reflect and meditate on the order and stability of the world, particularly in Vespers pictures. Frequently, the family is guided by angels and so are divinely protected.

In *Obsession*, however, such imagery is subverted: the absence of Joseph is particularly noticeable, leaving the mother and child especially vulnerable; it is not the pagan gods which tumble in front of the mule, blocking its way. The Crucified Christ, the Christian symbol of the saving power of God, falls down helplessly—the colours of the lifeless body implying that he is well and truly dead, beyond revival and so powerless to defend. The background, far from suggesting a unified landscape of peace and calm, is literally on fire, the flames about to envelop the mother and child. Rachel, not included in Christian iconography, floats above the scene and mourns as she does in Matthew's account of the episode. By using familiar Christian symbols and re-inforcing them with Rachel from the biblical narrative,[101] Chagall speaks to Christian viewers of the plight of the Jews in imagery easily appreciated. Jesus is both the martyred innocent Jew but also represents the powerlessness of the Christian God; not only is he a fallen, ineffective idol but also his lifeless body even blocks the escape for the Jewish family. Chagall's inferred comment appears to be that the Christian West, like their god, is either powerless or lacks the will to save the Jews in their plight.

The autobiographical connection of the fleeing mother with his birth and hence with his own fate as a refugee also explains his russification[102] of the theme at this time by a sleigh instead of a cart. In the large painting *War* (1943), the mother and child flee in a sleigh from a snow-covered village alight with flames and inhabited only by a corpse. They abandon both the Wandering Jew who escapes in a different direction and the horse and wagon which seems to have been bogged down in blood.[103] The theme was repeated in a later version, *War* (1964–66, Fig. 10). The mother and child also flee on *The Flying Sleigh* (1945), accompanied by a Russian. The sleigh is now drawn by a creature which is half horse and half rooster and thus will have no difficulty in escaping.[104]

Chagall and the Text of Matthew

More closely than any other artist, Chagall mirrors the detail of the Matthaean story of the Flight into Egypt and reflects the purpose for which Matthew wrote his Gospel; and so a number of similarities may be drawn between the situation of Matthew, the first-century narrator of the story of the Flight into Egypt and that of Chagall, its twentieth-century artistic interpreter. First, Matthew created the story to speak to his first-century

---

101. The only time that the New Testament reader meets Rachel is Mt. 2.18. Only in Matthew too is the child Jesus born in a *house*, which Chagall paints as on fire.

102. For Chagall's early Russian themes, see Ruth Apter-Gabriel (ed.), *Chagall: Dreams and Drama* (Jerusalem: Israel Museum, 1993), pp. 13-18.

103. The sketch for *War* (1943), now in the Musée national d'art modern, Paris, depicts an even more horrific image of a desperate mother and child in flight. See Jacob Baal-Teshuva, *Marc Chagall* (Cologne: Taschen, 1998), pp. 160-61.

104. Amishai-Maisel, *Depiction and Interpretation*, p. 24.

Jewish/Christian audience in a language and with symbols that they would understand. In his narrative, he defines the future role of Jesus in terms of Exodus and Exile and interprets his narrative through three Old Testament fulfilment quotations; Old Testament history has been fulfilled in the person of Jesus (the Jew *par excellence),* a fulfilment centred on his return from exile in Egypt. From its Jewish roots and heritage, Matthew's community develops into a Christian Church.

Figure 10. *War* (1964–66 [oil on canvas] by Marc Chagall [1887–1985]. Kunsthaus, Zurich/Bridgeman Art Library ©ADAGP, Paris and DACS, London, 2001).

Chagall, too, speaks to both Jews and Christians in the twentieth century and uses symbols from both traditions. Early in his career, realizing that using purely Jewish themes was too parochial, he gradually developed his use of Christian symbols, the best example being the Crucified Jew, which to many Jews proved controversial.[105] But Chagall especially wanted to confront and accuse Christians/Gentiles using their own language and symbolism with regard to the plight of his fellow-Jews. Just as Matthew, in the Flight into Egypt, used Jewish Old Testament imagery to speak to Jews in the first century about Christ and his identity, so Chagall used Christian New Testament imagery to speak to Christians in the twentieth century about Jews and their identity. The immediacy and poignancy of the episode in Matthew, which in the mediaeval period had lost something

---

105. Baal-Teshuva, *Marc Chagall,* p. 161.

of its sharpness and focus due to a reliance on florid apocryphal embellishments, are picked up again by Chagall in the very real, life-death situation of World War Two. This was helped by the strong autobiographical factor in Chagall's paintings. More than any other artist who depicted the theme, Chagall was very keen to include himself in his paintings and to identify personally with the subject, which he was to use as his self-image of exile. This, coupled with his personal identification with Christ, whom he saw as the perfect martyred Jew, ensured that he shared much of Matthew's own perspective.

It is Chagall's explicit self-identity as an exile and his reading of the Flight into Egypt *from the point of view of an exile* which makes us return to the issue of the *situatedness* of the reader of the Matthaean account, discussed in the first section of this article. There, Matthew centred his story in Bethlehem and structured his literary account from the point of view of 'the land of Israel'; the episode is resolved and closed by Jesus returning there. But, subsequent readings in the apocryphal traditions, in paintings and in the Books of Hours emphasize the exile, the stay in Egypt and not the return. Chagall's depictions of the theme raises the question of 'centredness' again; born in Russia, working in Paris and exiled in the Unites States, Chagall highlights his *un-situatedness*—he is the person floating around in his paintings or the baby being rushed away by a terrified mother. For Chagall and for the Jews of Eastern Europe for whom he speaks, exile is a continuous experience because there is nowhere to return to:

> The man in the air in my paintings…is me… It used to be partially me. Now it is entirely me. I'm not fixed *anyplace. I have no place of my own*… I have to live *someplace*.[106]

Even in the post-war years and with the establishment of the State of Israel, Chagall does not depict the return of the Holy Family to the land of Israel.[107]

Conclusion

The Flight into Egypt, which Matthew portrays as temporary and negative and in which he focused on the return, has, ironically, been most often

106. Amishai-Maisel, *Depiction and Interpretation*, p. 22.
107. For Chagall's paintings and political views in the post-1948 period, see Amishai-Maisel, *Depiction and Interpretation*, pp. 324-26.

interpreted as potentially a rewarding, even spiritual, experience. In the apocryphal legends, the episode provided the opportunity to emphasize the miraculous powers of Jesus so that the Gentiles of Egypt acknowledge him. In the stained glass of Chartres, the details of his sojourn in Egypt are more important than those of his return. The Holy Family is frequently depicted as resting in a lavish landscape which provides the viewer with an opportunity to reflect and meditate. In fifteenth- and sixteenth-century paintings, many characteristics of the passion and death of Jesus are subtly brought together; the Flight into Egypt allows the viewer to anticipate the various elements of the passion. Chagall emphasises the flight and depar- ture of the family, without any reference to their return.

Ironically, in the context of yet another exile in the latter half of the twentieth century, Marc Ellis, in his essay on reconstructing a meaning and identity for diaspora life, compares and contrasts the Jewish experi- ence to the post-1948 displacement and subsequent diaspora of the Palest- inians. His view that 'a condition of exile becomes an opportunity and its pain an affirmation'[108] echoes many interpretations of the theme of the Flight into Egypt in art. Naim Ateek, Palestinian Christian and Director of *Sabeel* Ecumenical Liberation Theology Centre, in his Autumn 1998 newsletter, places Jesus the Palestinian refugee at the centre of his theo- logy; the return of Jesus to 'the land' justifies the hope of return for all Palestinians in exile. There is a notable irony in the fact that a story, originally written by Matthew to encourage and value the Jewish heritage of his community, could have been used in the mid-twentieth century by Chagall to accuse Christians in Europe of the persecution of his fellow- Jews and subsequently by a Palestinian Christian in Jerusalem to accuse Jews who have returned to the land of making *his* fellow-Palestinians into refugees and exiles.[109] Ateek's theology mirrors the details of Matthew's narrative; unlike the artistic representations discussed above, which view the story from the standpoint of exile, Ateek reads the story from the same geographical centre (Jerusalem) as Matthew and, just as in the text the story is resolved in the return of Jesus to the land, Ateek also sees the plight of the Palestinian exiles resolved in their right of return:

108. Ellis, *A Reflection on the Jewish Exile*, p. 5.
109. Another 'political' interpretation is evident in a Spanish colonial folk artist's interpretation of the theme where the Holy Family is given a local guide to lead them in their exile; the implication is that the family, fleeing form the motherland, are wel- comed and sustained by those living in the colonies. See *Story of Jesus*, p. 64.

It is paradoxical that in Jesus' day, there were more open borders than at the end of the 20th century. The holy family was able to return from Egypt to Palestine. The repatriation of refugees is a right and not a courtesy.[110]

At the end of this century, in Ateek's theology, the centre of the narrative has returned to Jerusalem.

After some 2,000 years, the Flight into Egypt continues to be appropriated in the Arts. In a recent play, *La Fuite en Égypte*,[111] first performed in January 1999, the modern Parisian playwright, Bruno Bayen, dramatizes part of the life of Io from Greek mythology. Zeus fell in love with Io, the daughter of Inachus, king of Argos, and turned her into a heifer to conceal her from the jealousy of Hera. But Hera sent a gadfly to persecute Io and forced her to undergo long wanderings in the course of which she came to Egypt. Here Zeus came to her and changed her back into a woman and by touching her body with his hand begot his son Epaphus. Epaphus ruled Egypt and Africa and was eventaully worshipped as a god; Io was worshipped thereafter by the Egyptians as Isis.[112]

In the play, set in Egypt after her arrival there, Io is presented as the 'same age as the Virgin Mary at the birth of her son'.[113] She reflects with her young daughter and another character about her fate, driven as she is by the mercy of the gods, her continual wanderings and the prophecies of the gods.[114] The fate of Io and that of the Virgin Mary are implicitly

110. Ateek, *Living in the Hope of Return*, p. 2.

111. Bruno Bayen, *La Fuite en Égypte* (Paris: L'Arche, 1999).

112. Paul Harvey, *The Oxford Companion to Classical Literature* (Oxford: Oxford University Press, 1986 edition), pp. 222-23. Michael Grant and John Hazel *Who's Who in Classical Mythology* (London: Routledge, 1996), pp. 186-87.

113. Bayen, *La Fuite en Égypte*, p. 9.

114. Farrar, *Life of Christ in Art*, mentions two paintings which closely associate Mary with Io (Isis). The first is *In the Shadow of Isis*, by Luc Olivier Meeson, from the end of the nineteenth century. In it, 'the Virgin, with her sleeping Child in her arms, is seated at the angle of a ruined temple of Isis…they are seated on the shattered colossal head of some fallen Egyptian idol. On the wall of the temple we see the sculptured bas-relief of the Divine Egyptian Mother, Isis, with the half-moon on her head; she is giving suck to Thoth. The lotus of life and another deity bend low before Isis. The Virgin is gazing up at the sculpture with a look of intense curiosity and awe' (p. 266). In the second, *Anno Domini*, by Edwin Long, there is an elaborate rendering of the actual arrival in Egypt where there is a huge procession led by the High priest of Isis. The multitudes adore the image of Isis as it is carried past them. A slave offers for sale a tray of Egyptian gods, Isis, Osiris and Thoth. With these idols some girls are trying to cure a sick child. In an opposite direction comes the Holy Family. The Virgin refuses

compared: both have sons fathered by Zeus and God and their two sons are gods also. In his introduction, Bayen notes that the story of Io and her metamorphosis has been told differently by Aeschylus, Ovid and Herodotus, and the accounts of her journeys and the number of her children are never agreed upon. Furthermore, her story has been culturally assimilated and interpolated so many times by Western authors and painters that one is led to ask whether she has *a* story at all or whether her life is simply a 'geography and constellation of Mediterrenean legends?'[115] There is no *one* way of looking at her life.

Perhaps the same observation applies to the narrative of the Flight into Egypt. It has been depicted in so many ways by so many interpreters from different ages and backgrounds that the original significance of the story has become unimportant; but the fact that it has inspired so many artists in every age is a testimony to its power to inspire the artistic imagination in every century, offering consolation to those who have been displaced forcibly (the hunted) as well as to the exile and émigré who have left voluntarily, yet remain haunted by the memories and love of their homeland.

to buy the statue of the gods…instead her eyes gaze at the despairing mother and dying child for whom the idols are of no avail' (p. 268).

115. Bayen, *La Fuite en Égypte*, p. 7.

The Compassionate God of Leviticus and his Animal Creation

Mary Douglas

Introduction

This study concerns an interesting set of animals described in Leviticus and Deuteronomy as creeping, crawling, teeming or swarming. These creatures are abominated and not to be eaten. Much has been written about why they should be abominated, but I have elsewhere[1] proposed that there is nothing abominable about the swarming animals at all. On the contrary, according to this reading God loves them as the rest of his animal creation. What is abominable is to do anything to hurt them. This is unorthodox, but I believe it makes more sense than traditional interpretations. Based on this argument, I will call for a new idea about the identity of the swarming animals.

Why does Leviticus teach that God created animals which are abominable and unclean? Was it not arbitrary and capricious to make creatures he did not like? Such a teaching conflicts with the Book of Wisdom's saying:

> For you love all things that exist, and detest none of the things that you have made, for you would not have made anything if you had hated it...
> (Wis. 11.24).

It also conflicts with many other biblical sayings about God's compassion and mercy. So why did he tell his people to abhor these harmless animals? There are two answers, one to do with uncleanness and one to do with abominability.

This brand-new reading starts with Jacob Milgrom's observation that impurity and abomination in Leviticus are not equivalent terms.[2] This is a

---

1. *Leviticus as Literature* (Oxford: Oxford University Press, 1999). Special acknowledgements are due to Professors Jacob Milgrom and John Sawyer for their unstinted help.

2. J. Milgrom ('Two Biblical Hebrew Priestly Terms: *Sheqetz* and *Tame'*, *MAARAV* 6 [1992], pp. 107-16) states that these two concepts are different. Since he

significant correction to the traditional view. The two words describe acts which trigger different sequences of action. *Uncleanness* or impurity is a contagious condition of a person, place or thing, incompatible with the service of the cult; after touching an *unclean* corpse the person has to wash and be unclean until evening. Contrary to most traditional readings of the texts, he shows that contact with the corpse of a water swarmer or air swarmer is not unclean, it is an *abomination*. And no cleansing action at all is required.

This puts a very different complexion on all previous commentaries that have tried to combine Deuteronomy 14 and Leviticus 11. The two books, with nearly the same list of animals, are traditionally taken to be giving the same law. The Deuteronomic text makes uncleanness (or impurity) a synonym for abomination. Rabbinic usage tried to conflate the two books whenever possible, while favouring the Deuteronomic usage in case of conflict. Deuteronomy organizes all the dietary rules under the uncleanness rubric, and Leviticus organizes them under two distinct rubrics: uncleanness and unholiness, which are not the same thing. The difference was not noticed before.

It could be important that Leviticus makes a difference between impure and abominable animals, while in Deuteronomy there is no difference. Furthermore, Leviticus keeps impurity (uncleanness) for land animals and abominability for air and water animals. For Leviticus, nothing is abominable that goes on land (except land swarmers which are impure as well as abominable) and nothing is impure (unclean) that flies in the air or swims in the water. The attempt to bring all the dietary rules under the one rubric of impurity makes havoc with the purity idea. All these are major issues in interpreting Leviticus which is the main source on biblical purity. It seems fair to ask that impurity be studied according to Leviticus, and not according to Deuteronomy which is, after all, not a book especially concerned with ritual. The obscurity cast over Leviticus by trying to make it accord with Deuteronomy needs to be lifted.

Forbidden Animals in Other Religions

There are serious problems with the present interpretations of the Mosaic dietary laws, which should not be left unsolved. The main one is that the

does not consider the book to be one composition he can attribute divergences to the first or second author. But here, partly for lack of competence in distinguishing the two writers, and largely because of the belief that the composition is a unity, I make reference throughout to 'the Leviticus writer'.

current traditions make nonsense of God's compassion toward his creation. In other religions, gods often impose dietary rules upon their worshippers. The thing to notice is that if an animal is forbidden as food, it is
usually not because there is anything wrong with the animal, or anything
abhorrent or disgusting about it. Rather the other way, the animal often
turns out to have featured in the mythology as a strong and kindly being
which has rendered a service to the god, or in some prehistoric exchange a
human ancestor incurred a debt of great magnitude towards the ancestor of
an animal species. They formed a pact of everlasting friendship, in consequence of which the human descendant of the first beneficiary is forbidden to eat the animal descendants of the ancestor's benefactor. It would
be an act of gross ingratitude and impiety—one might say it would be
abominable. Comparisons teach us to search the text for explanations
somewhere other than in harmful or unattractive features of the animal
itself. The writer of Leviticus finds the world divided into two kinds of
humans, those under the covenant and the rest, and two kinds of land
animals, those under the covenant and the rest. But the rest are not evil, the
picture is not painted in black and white. It was the work of the later
commentators to read good and bad into the divisions between pure and
impure.

Clean Land Animals

In Leviticus, clean and unclean are terms that only apply to the land
animals. Either they are part of the domestic flocks and herds of the
people, or not. The domestic cattle, sheep and goats are cultically clean,
which means that they have to be consecrated and sacrificed at the altar
before they can be eaten; elaborate rules provide for how they are to be
treated. These are the clean land animals. Clean simply means available
for the cult and for human diet. All the other land animals are unclean,
which simply means not available for cult or food. Uncleanness is contagious. The carcasses of the unclean animals cannot be touched without
incurring uncleanness. In effect the law rules out using any part of the
animal's body for any purpose: if you cannot touch its carcass at all, you
cannot eat it. The paradoxical result is that both kinds of land animal come
under God's protection, the clean species are destined for highly regulated
consecration, sacrifice, and human use; the other land species cannot be
used at all after death. The dietary rules for land animals concern the cult
and for those land animals unconnected with the cult the uncleanness rules
are a protection. In other words, the so-called dietary rules are misnamed.

They do much more than regulate culinary and alimentary matters; their function is nothing less than to regulate the relations between humans and the animal creation.

Since the rules for the cult were given to Moses as part of the covenant at Sinai, it may be safe to assume that the clean animals which are offered in sacrifice come under the covenant in appropriate ways. And there is textual support for this: Exod. 20.8 requires that the work animals observe the sabbath, and that the male first born of the flocks and herds be consecrated to God at the altar (Exod. 22.30, Deut. 15.19). The fact that they are all land animals suggests something more. The idea of covenant has territorial implications and principles of ownership and control which do not apply to the populations of the water and the sky.

The effect of the rules in Lev. 11.1-8 is to identify the land animals which can be consecrated, and to mark all the other land animals as off-limits for human food and to prevent their corpses from being used in any way at all. The neatness of this rule is that it does not prevent humans making use of unclean animals while they are alive, so there is nothing against dogs herding or hunting with their masters, nor against people riding horses or asses; vermin and predators can be chased off or killed. After they are dead, their skins and bones and teeth cannot be put to use. Only the clean animals, after they have died a consecrated death, can provide leather goods, sandals, bags, garments, horns for trumpets and so on. In their lives and their deaths they belong to their owners as the latter belong to their God, by virtue of the covenant of Sinai.

Swarming and Creeping

For the denizens of air and water a different principle is involved. Leviticus never applies the term *unclean* to water or air animals. These are either *abominable* or not. The non-abominable creatures can be eaten, the abominable ones cannot be eaten and their carcasses cannot be touched. Here we can start to cast doubt on whether the translation of 'abominable' makes sense. In Leviticus and Deuteronomy it is applied to swarming or creeping live things. But nothing derogatory is ever said about swarming or creeping and the words do not have a negative sense in other parts of the Pentateuch. In Genesis, God quite obviously took a benign view of all his creatures and saw the creeping swarmers as good:

> God said: 'Let the waters *bring forth swarms* of living creatures...' God
> created the great sea monsters and every living creature that moves with

which the waters *swarm,* and all the winged creatures of every kind. And God saw that this was good (1.20-21).

God made wild beasts of every kind and cattle of every kind, and all kinds of *creeping things of the earth.* And God saw that this was good (1.25).

God made wild beasts of every kind and cattle of every kind, and all kinds of *creeping things of the earth.* And God saw that this was good (1.25).

In the story of Noah, God instructed Noah to bring into the ark three classes:

of every living thing of all flesh…of the birds according to their kinds, and of the animals according to their kinds, of *every creeping thing of the ground* according to its kind… (Gen. 6.19-20).

of clean animals, and of animals that are not clean, and of birds, and of everything that *creeps on the ground,* two and two, male and female, went into the ark with Noah… (Gen. 7.8-9).

they and every beast according to its kind, and all the cattle according to their kinds, and *every creeping thing that creeps on the earth* according to its kind, and every bird according to its kind, every bird of every sort. They went into the ark with Noah, two and two of all flesh in which there was the breath of life… (Gen. 7.14-16).

After Noah's sacrifice had appeased his anger, God made a covenant with the people—and note especially that he made it with the animals too.

Behold I establish my covenant with you and your descendants after you, and with every living creature that is with you, the birds, the cattle, and every best of the earth with you, as many as came out of the ark (Gen. 9.8-10).

There is nothing about abominability in any of this.

However, I am going to suggest a different interpretation by drawing a parallel between the unclean land animals and the air/water creatures that must not be eaten or touched when dead. Just as the rule against corpse contact with unclean animals on land acts to protect them from human predation by making it impossible to profit from their corpses, so the rule against corpse contact for the air and water animals protects the swarmers.

As I mentioned above, Deuteronomy simply states that the creatures in the waters without scales and fins are unclean (or impure). Leviticus, at greater length, does not mention uncleanness, but says that these species are to be an abomination to the people of Israel. At this point, it will be useful to be reminded of what the two books say.

Figure 11. *In the Waters*

Deuteronomy 14.9-10	Leviticus 11.9-23
9 Of all that are in the waters you may eat these: whatever has fins and scales you may eat.	9 These you may eat, of all that are in the waters. Everything in the waters that has fins and scales, whether in the seas or in the rivers, you may eat.
10 And whatever does not have fins and scales you shall not eat, it is unclean for you.	10 But anything in the seas or in the rivers that has not fins and scales, of the swarming creatures in the waters and of the living creatures that are in the waters, is an abomination to you.
	11 They shall remain an abomination to you; of their flesh you shall not eat, and their carcasses you shall have in abomination.
	12 Everything in the waters that has not fins and scales is an abomination to you.

The category of water creatures not to be eaten is residuary: they are only those that remain after the scaly-finned ones have been set aside. As to the creatures of the air, Deuteronomy and Leviticus give almost the same list of winged life that is not to be eaten, but, again, Deuteronomy uses the word unclean while Leviticus simply states that the forbidden birds are an abomination, and again, nothing about impurity.

Figure 12. *In the Air*

Deuteronomy 14.11-20	Leviticus 11.13-19
12 You may eat all clean birds. But these are the ones you shall not eat: the eagle, the vulture, the osprey,	13 And these you shall have in abomination among the birds, they shall not be eaten, they are an abomination; the eagle, the vulture, the osprey.
13 the buzzard, the kite, after their kinds;	14 the kite, the falcon according to its kind,
14 every raven, after its kind;	15 every raven according to its kind,
15 the ostrich, the nighthawk, the sea gull, the hawk, after their kinds;	16 the ostrich, the night hawk, the sea gull, the hawk according to its kind,
16 the little owl and the great owl, the water hen,	17 the owl, the cormorant, the ibis,
17 and the pelican, the carrion vulture and the cormorant,	18 the water hen, the pelican, the carrion vulture,
18 the stork, the heron, after their kinds; the hoopoe and the bat.	19 the stork, the heron according to its kind, the hoopoe, and the bat.

These lists of birds are less interesting than they sound, because no one knows what the ornithological nomenclature would be, and so the birds are not identified. The names given here have always been recognized to be very speculative.

For completeness sake, let us add two columns for insect life.

Figure 13. *Insect Life*

Deuteronomy 14.19-20		Leviticus 11.20-23	
19	And all winged insects are unclean for you; they shall not be eaten.	20	All winged insects that go on all fours are an abomination to you.
		21	Yet among the winged insects that go on all fours you may eat those which have legs above their feet, with which to leap upon the earth.
20	All clean winged things you may eat.	22	Of them you may eat; the locust according to its kind, the bald locust according to its kind, the cricket according to its kind, and the grasshopper according to its kind,
		23	But all other winged insects which have four feet are an abomination to you.

The edible and corpse-touchable air animals have wings and two legs, and the edible water creatures have fins and scales, all the rest are abominable. (Four feet without four legs is abominable.)

The hypothesis here is that all the species of abominable birds and abominable water animals are in a single residuary class. It is the same logical structure as for clean land animals, which are specified, and all the rest are grouped together. The named birds are not offered as an exhaustive list of forbidden flying species. We do not have to try to find out what it is about the hoopoe as a species, or the little owl, the heron, or the pelican, that makes them abominable. Their original names have only been given to *exemplify* a class, and this is clearly defined in the text. We have to suppose that the readers of this book also know their Genesis and know what swarming means:

> Every swarming thing that swarms upon the earth is an abomination, it shall not be eaten. Whatever goes on its belly, and whatever goes on all fours, or whatever has many feet, all the swarming things that swarm upon the earth, you shall not eat; for they are an abomination (Lev. 11.41-42).

Unfortunately, the lists of forbidden creatures in the air and water have not been read in this sense since earliest times, and we have to conclude that there was a break in the continuity of reading Leviticus. Since we are supposed to know what swarming means, to have names of some of the kinds of birds that qualify is just an extra help, or it would be if we knew which birds they are. But the commentators have assumed that they are birds of prey, an assumption which throws an unwarranted moral meaning over the idea of abominability.

Likewise in the water the finless, scaleless water creatures are a parallel residual class. They swarm, like shoals of shrimps, or creep like crabs and lobsters, or glide on their bellies like eels. They are not named, but if the congregation merely reads the texts carefully without adding what is not there, they can see the swarming going on before their eyes. If they do not have fins and scales they go on their bellies, they have many feet, they crawl or creep, and, above all, they swarm (Lev. 11.41-43). We have read Genesis so we are supposed to know that this is a burgeoning, prolific form of life blessed at the Creation.

The case of land swarmers is consistent, but more complicated. Being land animals they come under the rules for land animals, so they have to be counted as unclean from the point of view of the cult, and also as abominable from the point of view of their being swarmers. Eight land swarmers are named, 'the weasel, the mouse, the great lizard, the gecko, the land crocodile, the lizard, the sand lizard, and the chameleon' (Lev. 11.29-30). The list is not exhaustive; again, it merely exemplifies by pointing to particular cases. It does not even include all the kinds of land swarmers mentioned (we can easily think of more, with many feet, such as woodlouse or centipede). To all of them, and to the whole class to which they belong, the law applies:

> These are unclean to you, among the swarming things that swarm upon the earth (Lev. 11.29).

Like other land animals that are not defined as fit for sacrifice, the land swarmers are unclean; and, as are the other swarmers in Leviticus, they are an abomination. I conclude that the swarmers are the one residual class that covers all three environments, land, air and water, and includes all the animals not listed as edible.

Translating Swarming

The word *sheretz* which is commonly translated as 'swarming' is closely associated in Hebrew with breeding, bringing forth, and fertility in general.[3] But in translations of Leviticus 11 its relation to fertility is ignored. The connection between breeding and swarming must have seemed to Maimonides difficult to interpret literally. He presented a far-fetched theory that the swarming creatures in Lev. 11.42 breed within seeds or fruits,[4] the label pointing not to their own fertility but to the fruitfulness of their breeding ground. Levine acknowledges a connection with germinating when he says that it means 'to come to life, crawl, swarm'.[5] But the connection with fecundity, abundance and proliferation in a good sense, which is so prominent for 'swarming' in Genesis, has been dropped in interpreting Leviticus.

Genesis clearly connects the word with fecundity. The swarmers are specialized for 'bringing forth'. It is the verb for God's command to the waters to bring forth. After the flood, when he made his covenant with Noah, he said again,

Be fruitful and multiply, *bring forth abundantly* on the earth and multiply in it (Gen. 9.7).

When '*bring forth*' is used in Genesis fecundity is positive, in the good sense of blessing, as in God's blessing to Abraham. Somehow in reading Leviticus the meaning of the word has been shifted to a negative sense. In Leviticus the class of the abominable contains not only swarming but also creeping and this too has been given a negative sense that it does not normally carry.

The Leviticus writer has a literary trick of using a closely matched pair of words in spiralled apposition. He writes about creatures which are 'brought forth' in 'swarms' as if they are assimilated to the living things that 'creep' on the earth. In Hebrew the meaning of the two terms, *creeping* and *swarming,* are distinct, but in English they have come together, very likely as a result of the great influence of the Bible on the English language.

In English 'teeming' would translate the aspect of fertility: to bring forth, produce, give birth to, bear (offspring), to be prolific, or fertile; to abound, teem, swarm (*Oxford English Dictionary*). It hardly does much for the second, sinister meaning of 'festering' and 'rot'. There is an

---

3.   M. Jastrow, *Dictionary of the Targumim, the Talmud Babli and Jerusalmi, and the Midrashic Literature* (New York: The Judaica Press, 1982), pp. 16, 33.

4.   P. Cohen, *Ramban on the Torah* (Massachusetts: Rubin, 1985), p. 91.

5.   P. Levine, *Leviticus* (The JPS Torah Guide; New York: Schocken Books, 1989), p. 67.

English word that exactly catches both these meanings: the word is *pullulate*. It is an intransitive meaning to 'sprout out', 'spring forth', 'spread', 'grow', 'increase'

> a) of a growing part, shoot or bud,
> b) of a seed, to sprout, to germinate, to breed, to multiply,
> c) to put forth morbid growths.

It also means 'to teem, to swarm, to spring up abundantly' (*Oxford English Dictionary*).

There is no reason to suppose that in ch. 11, Leviticus uses 'swarm' in any negative sense, but rather keeps its own commands with reference to swarming creatures in harmony with the commands to them in Genesis to bring forth abundantly. Typically, commentators on Leviticus 11 have tended to adopt a darker meaning which depends entirely on a dubious translation of 'to creep' (*remes*).

Translating Creeping

Creeping does not necessarily have a negative sense, though it often suggests furtive, hidden movement. Snaith conflated creeping and swarming when he suggested:

> This collective noun includes all small creatures that go about in shoals and swarms, insects that fly in clouds, such as gnats and flies generally (compare Ethiopic, germinate), and small creatures such as weasels, mice and lizards that are low on the ground (compare Aramaic, crawl).[6]

The Genesis commentary says that 'creep' is:

> A general term for creatures whose bodies appear to move close to the ground. Here it seems to encompass reptiles, creeping insects and very small animals.[7]

The translation has lost the main idea of the Hebrew word, the idea of motion and life which opens its meaning to include the signs of life as in Genesis where it refers to any breathing thing.

> And to every beast of the earth, and to every bird of the air, and to every thing that creeps on the earth, everything that has the breath of life (Gen. 1.30).

6. N.E. Snaith (ed.), *Leviticus and Numbers* (London: Nelson, 1967), p. 82.
7. N.M. Sarna, *Genesis* (The JPS Torah Guide; New York: Schocken Books, 1989), p. 11.

This is true of land animals, and can apply to air or water swarmers when they come on to the ground. In Genesis where 'moving' is taken to be the sign of life, the sensitive translator has used 'moved' or 'stirred' instead of 'crept' (Gen. 7.21-22).

The two words, 'swarming' and 'creeping', come so close together in modern English that 'teem' is found in the dictionaries for both. By referring to the generative principle that belongs to 'swarming' and to the life principle that belongs to 'moving', the word 'teem' bridges the two meanings. It would help the reinterpretation if instead of 'swarming' we could use 'teem', and for 'creeping', to come closer to the Hebrew, we could simply say 'moving'. Then the questions about why the carcasses of teeming, living things should be avoided can be posed afresh.

Translating Abomination

The Leviticus text is translated as saying that eating a creeping swarmer is an *abomination* in the eyes of the Lord. We have sought to establish that *swarmer* means an abundantly fertile creature. No reason is given for the swarmer being abominable. Leviticus does not use any of the vivid Hebrew pejorative forms, or any pejorative at all, for the animals in this chapter. The word that Leviticus uses and which we translate into English as 'abomination' is very rare outside Leviticus.[8] It seems to have been specially chosen by the Leviticus writer, or even specially coined, to avoid the pejorative association. The Leviticus term for 'abomination' is a word from the same stem as a more common word for 'abomination', but here it is used idiosyncratically in a form which does not have detestable and idolatrous associations.[9] There is therefore a case for seeking to establish a new translation instead of 'abomination' in the dictionary sense of 'detestable', or 'abhorrent', as of idolatrous practices. Here it would seem to be used in a 'technical' sense, as a specialized levitical concept. 'Detest' and 'abhor' are emotional terms, but a legal injunction would need a more directive and precise term, less emotional than 'revulsion' or 'detestable'. A more kinetic and spatial translation might be: 'You shall completely

---

8.   J. Milgrom, *Leviticus* (New York: Doubleday, 1991), p. 655. Only Ezek. 8.10 and Isa. 66.17 are both clearly exceptional.

9.   Leviticus evidently uses the form *sheqetz* in preference to the heavily pejorative term *shiqqutz*. The noun *shiqqutz* has a form which clearly associates it with nouns like *piggul* (Lev. 7.18) and *gillul* (Lev. 26.30). See J. Sawyer, 'Root Meanings in Hebrew', *JSS* 12/1 (1967), pp. 37-50 (42) n. 2. Deuteronomy uses *to'eba*.

shun', or 'You shall utterly reject', rather than 'You shall abominate'. The test line would then read, 'You shall shun everything that swarms, etc.'

This shift would resolve our initial problem as to why God ever made abominable things. On this reading they are not abominable in the Deuteronomic sense of abomination. If the Leviticus word, wrongly translated as 'abominate', when stripped of its subjective quality means 'to avoid' or 'shun', then God would simply be telling his people to avoid certain things, keep out of their way, not harm, still less eat, them. Deuteronomy uses the other word, also translated as 'abomination', to indicate that an action is wrong. For example:

> You shall not do so to the Lord your God; for every abominable thing which the Lord hates they have done for their gods (Deut. 12.31).

Likewise Lev. 11.43 points the same way when it condemns 'making yourself abominable with them'. The translation in the *JPS Torah Guide* suits the present argument even better: 'You shall not draw down abomination upon yourselves'. In other words, what is held to be abominable in that text is the doing. In English we can say that cannibalism is abominable or even that human flesh is abominable, and it does not mean that the victim is abominable or to be detested. There would be no theological problem about an arbitrary God if what is abominable is the action of eating or mutilating the carcasses. Everything becomes consistent, the animals in question are a part of God's beautiful creation, saved from the flood by his express command, and the people of Israel are forbidden to attack them.

> Anything in the seas or the rivers that has not fins and scales, of the teeming creatures in the waters and of the living creatures that are in the waters, is *an abomination* to you (to be shunned by you) (Lev. 11.10-12).

> And those you shall have *in abomination* (avoid) among the birds, they shall not be eaten, they are *an abomination* (to be shunned) (11.13-19).

> All winged insects that go on all fours are *an abomination to you* (to be shunned by you) (11.20-23).

> Every teeming thing that teems upon the earth is *an abomination* (to be shunned). It shall not be eaten. Whatever goes upon its belly, and whatever goes on all fours, or whatever has many feet, all the teeming things that teem upon the earth, you shall not eat: *they are an abomination* (to be shunned). You shall not make yourselves *abominable* (to be shunned) with any teeming thing that teems, and you shall not defile yourselves with them, lest you become unclean... (11.41-43).

If this usage can be accepted it means that, though contact with these creatures is not against purity of the cult, harming them is against a more general commitment to holiness. Surely it is not puzzling that these abounding creatures which proliferate freely and glide lightly in the water or over the land should not be harmed? They are symbols of fruitfulness in animal creation. Eating the teeming creatures offends God's avowed concern for fertility. The ancient association of the temple with fertility supports the idea that harming the teeming creatures is wrong. The fertility principle is central enough and important enough to be balanced against the principle of cultic purity throughout ch. 11. Divinely blessed natural proliferation on the one hand, the life-restoring cult on the other, the two principles of creation and covenant make a double-stranded twist through the chapter.

Conclusion

When the dietary laws of Leviticus are re-examined in this perspective, the revised translations help to see that ch. 11 was much simpler than had been supposed. An overall survey of land animals has classed all except the flocks and herds of the people as unclean, not to be eaten or offered for sacrifice...that is all. And the animals classified as unclean turn out to be not abominable at all, just unclean. An overall survey of the other animals separates fishes and birds from swarming things, and requires the bodies of teeming things to be respected...that is all.

Leviticus makes sense of animal creation when it is read as a sermon on God's pattern of the universe. In this reading, covenant and fertility are two contrasted principles. Covenant gives the paradigm of the laws at Sinai and the tabernacle, hedged by purity rules expressing God's over-lordship and his justice. His compassion towards teeming things belongs to the other dispensation that has to do with Genesis and his blessing on abundant fruitfulness. The protective laws that tell humans to avoid teeming creatures demonstrate God's compassion. The balance between the divine attributes of justice and mercy gives a more intelligible reading than does God's horror of impurity and his unexplained dislike of swarmers.

THE SACRIFICE OF ISAAC (THE *AKEDAH*) IN CHRISTIAN AND JEWISH TRADITION: ARTISTIC REPRESENTATIONS

Edward Kessler

Introduction

The story of the Sacrifice of Isaac in Genesis 22 (known in Jewish tradition as the *Akedah*, 'the Binding of Isaac') has been, and continues to be,
the subject of much discussion in Christian and Jewish literature. It is a
story which intersects the two religions, linking them together. It is
generally examined from a literary perspective but the focus of this article
is to consider the story from the perspective of the artist. We should, of
course, consider first whether the artist has been allowed to play a role at
all in interpreting the story. In the past, scholars turned to the following
biblical verses:

> You shall not make for yourself a graven image, or any likeness of anything
> that is in the heaven above, or that is in the earth beneath, or that is in the
> water under the earth; you shall not bow down to them or serve them; for I
> the Lord your God am a jealous God (Exod. 20.4-5)

This command has been interpreted to mean that Jews and Christians
would automatically have opposed every form of figurative visual
representation.

In support, scholars referred to Josephus, who was clearly hostile to
images,[1] as well as to Tacitus, Pliny and others, who remarked about the
absence of statues and images in Jewish cities and synagogues. Yet their
writings were not necessarily typical. Even Josephus reported that there
existed groups, such as the Hasmonaean family in the first century BCE,
who produced human representations.

As far as the rabbis were concerned, there were, as so often, differing
views. For instance, there is the well-known story about R. Gamaliel II,
head of Yavneh, who was criticized for going to a bath house which

---

1.   Josephus, *War* 2.195; *Ant.* 17.151.

boasted a statue of Aphrodite.[2] Many rabbinic passages make reference to the widespread existence of Jewish figurative art but opposing views existed.[3] The Targum mentions that figurative art in synagogues was approved as long as it was used not for idolatrous purposes but only for decoration:

> You shall not set up a figured stone in your land, to bow down to it, but a mosaic pavement of designs and forms you may set in the floor of your places of worship, so long as you do not do obeisance to it.[4]

Figurative art was also a significant part of everyday life in the early Church. Like the rabbis, the Church Fathers were concerned about the idolatrous nature of art in places of worship. For example, at the Council of Elvira in approximately 300 CE, the thirty-sixth canon stated that there should be no pictures in a church in case the object of worship was depicted on the walls (*picturas in ecclesia non debere, ne quod colitur et adoratur in parietibus depingatur*). Nevertheless, the Early Church was not as hostile to art as has been almost universally assumed. Tertullian, like R. Gamaliel II, states that figurative representation was not forbidden because it was not idolatrous.[5] Murray shows how later commentators misrepresented the Church Fathers by either ignoring or minimizing comments about the acceptability of figurative art.[6]

The first extant examples of Christian imagery appear as early as the beginning of the third century CE in funereal art such as the catacomb frescoes. The Dura-Europos chapel makes it clear that other forms of art, such as Christian iconographic paintings, appear from the mid-third century. Thus already a century before the Edict of Tolerance, art was an important element of Christian life and consequently artistic interpret-

---

2.   Mishnah, *'Abod. Zar.* 3.4: '"Why does thou bathe in the Bath of Aphrodite?" He answered, "One may not make an answer in the bath". And when he came out he said, "I came not within her limits: she came within mine!" They do not say, "Let us make a bath for Aphrodite", but, "Let us make an Aphrodite as an adornment for the bath". Moreover, if they would give thee much money thou wouldest not enter in before thy goddess naked or after suffering pollution, nor wouldest thou make water before her! Yet this goddess stands at the mouth of the gutter and all the people make water before her. It is written, *their gods*, only; thus what is treated as a god is forbidden, but what is not treated as a god is permitted.'

3.   Rabbinic acceptance of figurative art is found Jerusalem Talmud, *'Abod. Zar.* 3.3, 42d and Jerusalem Talmud, *'Abod. Zar.* 3.2. Rejection is illustrated by the *Mek. SbY., Ki Tisei* 31.

4.   Targum, *Ps.-Jon.* (to Lev. 26.11).

5.   Tertullian, *Against Marcion* 2.22.

6.   C. Murray, 'Art and the Early Church', *JTS* 28 (1977), pp. 313-45.

ations of the Bible became a significant feature of Christian exegesis. We can be certain, therefore, that figurative art plays an important role in the study of both Judaism and Christianity in late antiquity and evidence exists to show that it fulfilled an important function in everyday life.

The Sacrifice of Isaac was one of a small number of popular biblical images. These included Noah, Daniel in the Lion's Den, the Twelve Tribes of Israel and King David. Each character suggested the promise of deliverance. Images have also been found on glass, jewellery, amulets, seals and even ivory. However, this article will focus on representations depicted on mosaics and frescoes, in synagogues and churches, in chapels and catacombs.

The Sacrifice of Isaac in Christian Art

The Sacrifice of Isaac in Christian tradition
The Sacrifice of Isaac was a very popular subject for early Christian art and is found among a small number of selected biblical images. These include Noah, Daniel, and Jonah as well as the Raising of Lazarus and the Good Shepherd. It appears in many forms, including frescoes, sarcophagi and mosaics. In the classical writings of the Church Fathers there are a number of references to its portrayal. Gregory of Nyssa, for instance, wrote:

> I have seen many times the likeness of this suffering in painting and not without tears have I come upon this sight, when art clearly led the story before the sight.[7]

Augustine also discussed this subject:

> The deed is so famous that it recurs to the mind of itself without any study or reflection, and is in fact repeated by so many tongues, and portrayed in so many places, that no-one can pretend to shut his eyes or his ears from it.[8]

For many years, scholars of early Christian art, like those of Jewish art, have been excessively influenced by trends in the *written* tradition. As a result, images were understood primarily in terms of the Crucifixion of Christ. Scholarly debates centred on whether the artistic representations should be understood in terms of typology or in terms of deliverance. Some scholars suggested that because patristic writings do not offer a detailed typological understanding of the relationship between the figures

---

7. Gregory of Nyssa, *On the Son of God and the Holy Spirit* (PG 46.573).
8. Augustine, *Reply to Faustus the Manichaen* 22.73.

of Isaac and Jesus until after the conversion of Constantine (312 CE), typological representations could not appear in art before then. They, therefore,
placed an emphasis on deliverance[9] and pointed out, for example, that
Isaac was never portrayed as bound on the altar until the mid-fourth
century. More recently Jensen, who has offered a critique of the existing
scholarship, has questioned the validity of arguments based on a few existing pre-Constantinian images and challenged the accuracy of their dating.
Jensen also suggested typology could be discovered in early Christian
literature (cf. Melito, Tetullian, Origin).[10]

The weakness with all these arguments is that they are based upon the
literary tradition. They do not begin from the image but from the word.
The image supports the word rather than the word supporting the image.
None of the works I have read examines artistic interpretation in its own
right, as illustrated by Jensen who suggests that, 'homilies and liturgies
were the most important sources from which early Christian imagery
derives meaning for its audience'.[11] While I agree that it is important to
evaluate the context of the image, I would suggest that this is already the
third stage. The first stage is to examine the image on its own; the second
is with reference to the biblical story; the third is with reference to the
context. After these three stages are completed we are then in a position to
offer a full and thorough examination of the artistic interpretation.

Before discussing Christian artistic representations of the Sacrifice of
Isaac, it is worthwhile to summarize the views expressed in the writings of
the Church Fathers. This will enable us to see the similarities as well as the
differences between artistic and literary interpretation. There are a number
of important developments in the interpretation of the Sacrifice of Isaac in
early Christian literature. First, it is worth noting that there are only a few
explicit references to the story in the New Testament, suggesting that it
does not play an important role. Abraham's faith is seen in terms of

---

9. I. van Woerden, followed by other scholars, argued that 'since the greater part
of the early monuments has to do with death and burial the emphasis seems to lie on
'deliverance in need... From 313 onwards it appears transformed'. I. van Woerden,
'The Iconography of the Sacrifice of Abraham', *VC* 15 (1961), pp. 214-55.

10. R. Jensen states that the altar was a place not where the victim was killed but
where the offerings were laid, i.e., after the killing. 'By the late fourth century the
illustrators may simply have forgotten the earlier practices or sensed no need to make
the scene look familiar or correct to their audience.' R. Jensen, 'The Offering of Isaac
in Jewish and Christian Tradition', *Biblical Interpretation* 2 (1994), pp. 99-120 (105).

11. Jensen, 'Offering', p. 106.

obedience and trust in response to suffering; the significance of the Sacrifice of Isaac lies in supporting the authors' exhortations to remain faithful to the Christian gospel. From the end of the first century onward, we find the development of a typology. Beginning with *Barnabas*, developed in detail by Melito (Bishop of Sardis 160–70 CE) and Origen (185–251 CE), the story of Isaac was compared to the story of Jesus. Typology was used by Christians to support a number of assertions such as the view that biblical events foretold the coming of Christ. Similarities between Isaac and Jesus were highlighted: both carry wood to the place of slaughter; both assent to the will of God; both are led to the sacrifice by their father. In sum: Isaac was a model of the Christ who was going to suffer.

Typology did not solely link Isaac to Christ, but also Christ to the ram. According to Melito, there was a parallel between the sacrifice of the ram in substitution for Isaac and the sacrifice of Christ as a ransom for mankind. The deliverance of Isaac by the slaughter of the ram foreshadowed the deliverance of mankind by the death of Christ.[12] Origen developed this further and, in a discussion on the verse, 'a ram was caught by its horns' (Gen. 22.13), suggested that the ram represented the flesh which suffered while Isaac represented the Word, that is the Spirit which remained incorruptible.[13] This verse lent itself to christological interpretation. Typical are the words of Basil of Seleucia (bishop of Seleucia 440–68 CE), 'the ram caught in the plant was like Christ on the Cross'.[14] Other fathers such as Tertullian (200 CE) interpreted the bush to represent the crown of thorns.[15]

In Christian literary tradition, there is an emphasis on the fact that Jesus actually died while Isaac did not. The Sacrifice of Isaac was itself a model of the sacrifice to come, a pale shadow of the future event. Jesus died; Isaac was saved. This type of exegesis emphasized the efficacy of the Christian gospel and, at the same time, responded to Jews who emphasized the Sacrifice of Isaac as atoning in its own right. In addition, the Sacrifice of Isaac became bound up with early Christian liturgy. It was (and still is) used in the Eucharist ceremony, in the Easter liturgy and in the prayer for the dying. Finally, there exists a modest literary tradition, which portrays Sarah playing a more significant role. This tradition is found primarily in Syriac writings where she is described by Ephrem, for example, as willing

---

12. Melito, 'Fragment 10', in S. Hall (ed.), *Melito* (Oxford: Clarendon Press, 1979), p. 76.

13. Origen, *Homilies on Genesis* 8 (*PG* 12.208-209).

14. Basil of Seleucia, *Oration* 7 (*PG* 85.110).

15. Tertullian, *Against the Jews* 13.

to give up her son. Ephrem compares Sarah to Mary and points to a number of parallels including both questioning God, both having miraculous births and both giving up their son.[16]

The Sacrifice of Isaac in Funereal Art

Funereal art does not simply consist of imagery associated with the fears and sorrows surrounding death. The images illustrate examples of divine intervention and express the desire that God may show the same favour to the deceased. Funereal art is divided into two sections—sarcophagi and catacomb paintings. Both proclaim the same hope—that the deceased may find happiness beyond the grave.

The earliest catacomb frescoes illustrate the theme of deliverance. For instance, the Callixtus catacomb in Rome (Fig. 14) is dated from the first half of the third century CE. Abraham and the child Isaac are offering thanks for their deliverance. In the foreground, to their right stands the ram, erect and proud. Quite clearly, the three main characters are Abraham, Isaac and the ram. Behind the ram are an olive tree and the wood for the sacrifice.

Figure 14. *Detail from the Callixtus catacomb in Rome.*

16. See S. Brock, 'Sarah and the Aqedah', *Le Muséon* 87 (1974), pp. 67-77.

Figure 15. *Detail from the Priscilla catacomb in Rome.*

Another (late) third-century fresco located in the Catacomb of Priscilla, Rome (Fig. 15) illustrates the same theme. It shows the boy Isaac carrying wood and Abraham, according to Van Woerden,[17] pointing to the fire on an altar. I would suggest, however, that Abraham is pointing to a tree. Nearby (presumably) stands the ram. Abraham is looking up to the heavens, perhaps hearing the word of God.

Two other fourth-century frescoes have very similar images. Although the similarity between them has not been noticed, I would suggest that there is a clear link. In the late third- or early fourth-century fresco in the Catacomb of Peter and Marcellinus (Fig. 16) Abraham holds a knife in his raised right hand and at his feet is the child Isaac—naked, kneeling and bound for the sacrifice. The ram appears on the far side of the altar, which is alight, and the image is above a scene of the paralytic carrying his bed. Cubiculum C in the Via Latina (Fig. 17), from the late fourth century, reproduces this image almost exactly. The altar has wood burning upon it; to the left is the ram, which appears to be looking for Abraham who has a sword in his hand. Abraham is looking at something (an angel? the voice of God?) while Isaac is kneeling with his hands behind his back. Below is a representation of a servant with a donkey, possibly at the foot of the mountain.

17. Van Woerden, 'Iconography of the Sacrifice of Abraham', p. 222.

Figure 16. *Detail from the Peter and Marcellinus catacomb in Rome.*

All the examples of catacomb art emphasize the aspect of deliverance and do not indicate typology. This artistic interpretation either parallels, or perhaps even precedes, the early Christian prayer for the dead, which contained a cycle of deliverance. The earliest reference to this prayer is from the seventh century although it is believed to have originated much earlier.

In addition to frescoes, we commonly find images of the Sacrifice of Isaac in early Christian sarcophagi. The Mas d'Aire Sarcophagus from the third century is the earliest. It shows the child Isaac, bound and kneeling. Abraham grasps his hair from behind and raises the knife to strike. Abraham's eyes are not on Isaac but the ram, which is standing at his side (almost nuzzling him). The ram appears eager to be sacrificed. Sarcophagi provide a variety of altars—sometimes Isaac is bound upon an altar or next to the altar, and sometimes, as at Mas d'Aire, there is no altar. Sarcophagi also fail to portray the ram caught by its horns or caught in a bush. Thus, the evidence suggests that the christologically interpreted ram was not of importance to the artists. None of the sarcophagi shows Isaac carrying wood as a model of Christ carrying the cross. The concern of the artist is significantly different to that of the literary exegete as there is little interest in typology.

Figure 17. *Detail from Cubiculum C in the Via Latina.*

Many of the sarcophagi, which are dated in the fourth and fifth centuries provide evidence of post-biblical interpretation which cannot be found in contemporary Christian literature. For instance, several depict two or three assistants or onlookers which implies that the Sacrifice of Isaac did not take place in secret. This may also indicate that artistic interpretations contain traditions, which would otherwise have been lost. For example, in a Luc-de-Bearn sixth-century sarcophagus, a man and woman are watching the sacrifice. The woman, who has her hand to her mouth—to indicate dismay—may be Sarah. The appearance of Sarah at the sacrifice is mentioned in the poems of St Ephrem of Syria and other Syriac writings but rarely in the Greek or Latin Fathers. She is also portrayed in the chapels of the El Bagawat (Egypt) necropolis, which are dated from the fourth century CE.

In El Bagawat the story is depicted several times. It is found in the chapel of Exodus where Abraham stands next to an altar, which is already alight. On the other side of the altar stands Isaac with his arms crossed while his mother Sarah stands at his side under a tree and lifts her arms to the sky in an act of prayer. The ram stands under a tree and the hand of God is seen to the right of the name Abraham. In the fifth-century Chapel of Peace (also known as Byzantine Museum) we find the Sacrifice as one in a number of images (Fig. 18); these include the symbols of peace, justice and prayer, alongside Adam and Eve, the ark with Noah and his family, Jacob, Daniel and the lions, the annunciation and Paul and Thecla (described in the apocryphal *Acts of Paul* as a convert and companion of Paul).

Figure 18. *Detail from the Chapel of Peace.*

In the image of the Sacrifice of Isaac a hand (of an angel?) is throwing two knives in the air and another is held by Abraham. Isaac, a child, is unbound and his arms are outstretched, perhaps in supplication. Archaeologists have suggested that mother and son are holding incense.[18] Sarah has a halo around her head and Abraham, Isaac and Sarah are all identified. A tree/plant with flowers is drawn on the right hand side, probably to balance the tree on the left. As a result of the inclusion of Sarah in the representation of the Sacrifice of Isaac the artists of El Bagawat expand the biblical story and portrays its significance for the whole family. They do not follow the biblical account, which depicts the story in terms of a father-son relationship but offer their own interpretation.

The Sacrifice of Isaac in Church Mosaics

There are two famous Byzantine mosaics in sixth-century Ravenna—San Vitale and San Apollinare in Classe. Both associate the Sacrifice of Isaac with the offerings of Abel and Melchizedek, which are linked to the liturgy of the Eucharist. For example, in San Vitale we find a portrayal (Fig. 19) of the mosaics of Cain and Melchizedek sharing a church altar near which are placed the bread and wine. Nearby appear the three angels announcing the promise of a son while Abraham offers them a calf and Sarah stands in the doorway of a tent. To the right is a representation of the Sacrifice of Isaac.

Figure 19. *Detail from San Vitale in Ravenna.*

18. A. Fakhry, *The Necroplis of El Bagawat in Kharga Oasis* (Paris: Services des Antiquités de l'Egypte, 1951), p. 73.

Isaac is kneeling on the altar and Abraham's sword is raised but the hand of God appears to prevent the sacrifice. At Abraham's feet is the ram looking at Abraham, striking a typical christological pose. These mosaics flank the real church altar where the Eucharist was celebrated. The biblical figures are linked by the following prayer:

> Be pleased to look upon these offerings with a gracious and favourable countenance, accept them even as you were pleased to accept the offerings of your just servant Abel, the sacrifice of Abraham, our patriarch and that of Melchizedek, your high priest—a holy sacrifice, a spotless victim.

This prayer and its reference to the Sacrifice of Isaac came into use by the fourth century CE and it is clear that artistic interpretation paralleled the liturgical development. In early Christian liturgy, the Sacrifice of Isaac is mentioned during the offertory prayers, associated with epiclesis (a petition for the descent of the Holy Spirit upon the bread and wine), alongside Abel, Noah, Moses and Aaron, and Samuel. The reading of Genesis 22 was an important element of the lectionary cycle and was mentioned by Egeria during her visit to Jerusalem in the late fourth century CE. The Easter cycle was the major feature of the liturgical year and Genesis 22 was commonly read on the Thursday before Easter and, considering that readings were often quite different from church to church, this consensus is quite remarkable. We should also note that the homilies of Melito, as well as the interpretations of Gregory of Nyssa (*In Sanctum Pascha*) and Athanasius (*Epistle* 6), each of which discuss the Sacrifice of Isaac, were all composed at Easter.

Thus in early Christian art, the Sacrifice of Isaac focused on deliverance and the Eucharist as represented by images of the communion and divine deliverance. Images are found in funereal art because the story was understood in relation to death and resurrection. The ram is significant in artistic interpretation, not because of any christological significance, but because of its allusion to deliverance. The Isaac-Christ typology is rarely found in artistic interpretation during this period, and when it is found it is associated with liturgy, not literature.

The Akedah *in Jewish Art*

The Akedah *in Jewish tradition*
In classical rabbinic thought there are a number of significant developments in the interpretation of the *Akedah*. First, Isaac becomes a central character and is no longer a passive victim. For the rabbis he is a grown

man and joins Abraham and God as a principal actor. Isaac allows himself to be offered upon the altar and such is his stature that he is able to 'view the perfection of the heavens'. He becomes the paradigm of martyrdom as he voluntarily offers himself to be sacrificed.

Secondly, in Jewish thought the *Akedah* was linked to Passover as well as Rosh ha-Shana. *Jubilees*, the targums and the *Mekilta* link the Passover lamb with Isaac's sacrifice. Isaac is placed on the same theological level as the Passover lamb. 'By a lamb Isaac was redeemed; by a lamb Israel was redeemed.' In a comment on Exod. 12.13, 'And when I see the blood (of the Passover lamb), I will pass over you', we are asked, 'What does God see?' We are told, 'The blood of Isaac's *Akedah*'.[19] The association with Rosh ha-Shana eventually triumphed and the *Akedah* became part of the new-year liturgy. In the *Mishnah*, it is closely associated with the concept of human atonement and divine forgiveness.[20] Indeed, in the targums (and elsewhere) we are told that whenever the children of Israel ask for forgiveness God will remember the *Akedah*.

Thirdly, even though Isaac was not sacrificed, the *Akedah* is regarded by the rabbis as a true sacrifice and wholly acceptable to God. The reason why the sacrifice was not completed was because the son was exchanged for the ram—in the words of the rabbis, 'although the deed was not carried out, He accepted it as though it had been completed'.[21] For the Church Fathers, the son was exchanged because Isaac was not acceptable and it was not yet time to complete the test. In the words of Melito, 'Christ suffered, whereas Isaac did not suffer for he was the model of the Christ who was going to suffer'.[22] Fourthly, Mount Moriah is linked to the Temple. Following 2 Chron. 3.1, Josephus and the rabbis associate the site of the *Akedah* with the site of the Temple.[23]

The Akedah *at Dura-Europos*
When the Dura-Europos synagogue was uncovered in 1932 a new era in the history of Jewish art began because the synagogue contained the earliest known cycle of biblical images (244–45 CE). Externally, Dura-Europos

---

19. *Mek.*, *Pisha* 7. Cf. Targum to the Song of Songs, 1.13.
20. *Meg. Ta'an.* 2.4, 'He who answered Abraham on the mountain of Moriah, may He answer you and hearken this day to the voice of your pleading.'
21. *Gen. R.* 55.5.
22. Melito 'Fragment 9', in Hall (ed.), *Melito*, p. 74.
23. Josephus, *Ant.* 1.226; 7.333; *Gen. R.* 55.7.

was modest in the extreme, being located in a private house and could not compare architecturally with Sardis. However, its uniqueness lay in its interior for its wall decorations were second to none (Fig. 20). The city itself was founded by Seleucus I in approximately 300 BCE and remained a Seleucid outpost until mid-second century BCE when it was captured by the Parthians. For the next three centuries it flourished as a centre for east-west trade. In the second century CE it was captured by the Romans until it was destroyed by the Persians in 256 CE and never resettled.

Figure 20. *Detail from the synagogue at Dura-Europos.*

Dura-Europos contained 16 temples catering to the needs of an eclectic pantheon of Roman, Greek and Persian gods. It also contained a modest Christian chapel. In the synagogue there are more than 30 scenes covering the four walls of a 40-foot room. Several images surround the Torah shrine (on the base level):

- Esther
- Elijah restoring life to the son of the widow of Zarephath (1 Kgs 17)
- Samuel anointing David (1 Sam. 16)
- Moses as a baby floating in the Nile and rescued by the daughter of Pharaoh (Exod. 2)

To illustrate the elaborateness of the paintings I have selected part of the Ezekiel Cycle (Fig. 21). The painting is based on Ezekiel 37 and the description of the resurrection of the dead. God is symbolized by the hand and Ezekiel is depicted three times as he receives the divine commission. At the prophet's feet lie numerous body parts instead of the bones mentioned in the biblical text and beside him the mountain has split in two with an olive tree on each peak. To the right is a fallen house, illustrating an earthquake during which the resurrection would occur, and to the right of one mountain stands Ezekiel whose right hand is raised to the hand of God stretched out to him. His left hand points to the three lifeless bodies besides which stands a female figure who probably represents the *pneuma* providing the *ruah* to revive the dead. Further right stands Ezekiel again pointing to the three *psychai* who renew the lifeless bodies.

Figure 21. *Detail from the Ezekiel Cycle from Dura-Europos.*

In addition to the richness of the painting, I would emphasize two features which are depicted elsewhere—the hand of God and the gesture of Ezekiel's right hand. In this gesture, the palm is turned outward and the second and third fingers are held extended while the thumb, the fourth and fifth fingers are doubled back against the palm. The most familiar analogy is the Christian gesture of benediction, found commonly in Byzantine art. The archaeologist, Kraeling, associates this gesture with general pagan practice[24] and Goodenough links it with the Sabazius cult, suggesting that it was a cultic gesture—just as Sabazius brought immortality to his

24. Kraeling refers to two Roman senators who made the gesture when they addressed magistrates before a tribunal. C.H. Kraeling *The Synagogue: The Excavations of Dura-Europos Final Report VIII, Part 1* (New Haven: Yale University Press, 1956), p. 194.

followers, so Ezekiel worked a comparable miracle by bringing life to the corpses.[25]

The image of the *Akedah* (Fig. 22) is found over the opening for the ark, the Torah shrine. This was the most prominent feature of the synagogue and was always built on the Jerusalem orientated wall. The ark of the scrolls (*aron*), which housed the Torah, stood inside the shrine and several images and inscriptions refer to it. This feature became so well known that John Chrysostom accused the Jews of exaggerated veneration for their 'Holy Ark'. In Dura-Europos the Torah shrine belonged to a phase of synagogue decoration that was distinct from and earlier to the other paintings and must therefore be examined separately. Unlike the other images, which were replaced during repainting, it was retained and not touched.

Figure 22. *Detail from the* Akedah *at Dura-Europos.*

Our eye moves from left to right focusing first on the menorah, the palm branch (*lulav*) and citron (*etrog*). At the centre we see the Temple and to the right the *Akedah*. The symbols of *Sukkot* and the Temple suggest a vision of a future feast of Tabernacles to be celebrated in Jerusalem by all nations as described in Zechariah 14. The Temple could be viewed as much in terms of the future as well as the past and might represent a new Temple to be built on the site of the destroyed Temple. The synagogue

25. E. Goodenough appears to have been the first to make this suggestion. See *Jewish Symbols in the Greco-Roman Period* 10 (Princeton: Princeton University Press, 1953–68), p. 184.

building had been dedicated 170 years after the destruction of the Second Temple and restoration was a realistic dream as Julian the Apostate would make clear 120 years later.

Let us examine the characters in more detail. A primitively drawn Abraham, knife in hand, stands resolutely with his back to the onlooker, as does the little bundle of Isaac lying on the altar. This is emphasized by the shock of black hair that we see on both figures rather than facial features. Isaac is clearly a child and appears unbound. In the distance a tiny figure, also with a shock of black hair, stands before a tent, with an opening on the top. This figure has been variously interpreted as Abraham's servant,[26] Ishmael,[27] Abraham himself in his house[28] and Sarah.[29] However, arguments are readily available to render each proposal unlikely. For instance, the figure appears to be wearing a man's clothing and is therefore unlikely to be Sarah; he is not wearing the same clothes as Abraham (and therefore unlikely to be Abraham); the traditions concerning hostility between Isaac and Ishmael were influenced by the rise of Islam (seventh century) which rules out Ishmael. My own opinion is that the character is Isaac. The tent is touching the altar and is thus linked to Isaac. The figure is the same size as Isaac and both have black hair. We should also remember that Sarah died after the *Akedah* and that the first time Isaac was comforted was when Rebecca was brought to him and taken into his mother's tent (Gen. 24.67). The open hand of God appears beside the tent. This representation of the hand is the earliest surviving image. The hand symbolizing the *bat kol* is found in many literary works including both rabbinic and non-rabbinic writings.[30]

Although I have pointed out a number of developments and changes to the biblical story (such as Isaac being unbound, the third character and the presence of the hand of God) the representation of the *Akedah* at Dura-Europos is closer to the biblical text than many other representations. For instance, the ram is behind Abraham and Isaac is lying on the altar. In the lower foreground the rather large ram waits patiently, tethered to a tree.

26. Kraeling, *The Synagogue*, p. 343.
27. P. Prigent, *Le Judaisme et l'Image* (Tübingen: Mohr, 1991), p. 116.
28. Mesnil du Buisson, *Les Peintures de la Synagogue de Doura-Europos* (Rome: Analecta Biblica, 1939), pp. 24-27.
29. Goodenough, *Jewish Symbols*, p. 189.
30. E.g., Josephus, *Ant.* 1.13; 4.233; Philo, *Abr.* 32, 176; *Tan. Va-Yera* 23; *PRE* ch. 31.

The Hebrew text is probably the source for this illustration for, unlike the LXX, it describes the ram as 'behind' Abraham. It is centrally located which emphasizes its importance to the artist. Although the rabbis suggested that the ram had been created on the sixth day of creation and was waiting since for its moment of destiny,[31] they did not give a great deal of attention to it nor did they describe it being tethered to a tree. There appears no Jewish literary source for this artistic interpretation. However, the fourth-century Coptic Bible, mentions a 'ram tied to a tree'[32] which may indicate the existence of a Jewish artistic interpretation retaining a tradition no longer found in Jewish literature. This suggestion is supported by artistic evidence elsewhere, both Jewish and Christian, which depict the ram tied to a tree.[33]

The Akedah at Beit Alpha

In 1929 an excavation in the eastern Jezreel valley, just south of Galilee, unearthed a mosaic floor of a sixth-century synagogue. A sequence of three scenes, bordered like a carpet, make their way to the Torah located in a wall orientated towards Jerusalem (Fig. 23). These scenes are:

- the Akedah
- the zodiac with Helios and his four horses
- the ark

At the entrance, a mosaic lion and a bull flank bilingual inscriptions, which in Greek acknowledge the artists and in Aramaic thank the donors. These inscriptions date the synagogue to the reign of Justin (518–27).

The narrative plane (Fig. 24) moves from left to right, from the donkey to the ram to Isaac, from the accompanying youths to Abraham. The Hebrew, naturally, moves from right to left identifying Isaac, the ram and the command issuing from the hand of God. Abraham throws Isaac into the fire on the altar while the hand of God, as at Dura-Europos, prevents the sacrifice. A large ram is tied to a tree and is standing erect. The ram, following the biblical story, is caught by one horn and tied to a tree.

---

31. *Targ. Ps.-Jon.*, Mishnah, *Pirkei Ab.* 5.6; *PRE* ch. 31.
32. A. Ciasca (ed.), *Sacrorum Bibliorum: Fragmenta Copto-Sahidica*, I (Rome: Musei Borgiani, 1885), p. 22.
33. See discussion below on Beit Alpha and Sepphoris.

Figure 23. *Depiction of the* Akedah *at Beit Alpha.*

The ram is significant for it is even bigger than the tree, emphasizing the importance of the ram to the artist—in contrast to Jewish literary tradition. The fact that early literary tradition, except in a few instances, does not refer to the role of ram, is especially noteworthy when we see that later rabbinic writings such as *Pirke de Rabbi Eliezer* of the eighth century discuss the ram in detail. This development might be viewed as having been influenced by artistic interpretations such as depictions of the ram looking for Abraham (see below). Since this literary development occurred much later than the artistic representations we could justly argue that the literary interpretation is based upon the artistic.

Figure 24. *Detail from the* Akedah *at Beit Alpha.*

In the mosaic, two servants, one of whom has a whip in his hand, hold the ass which has a bell around its neck. Above, the hand of God presents some interesting features for it extends from a dark area, which looks like the end of a sleeve and is described by archaeologists as a 'cloud'.[34] Perhaps the most remarkable figure is the child Isaac, floating beyond Abraham's fingertips. Does Abraham hold him close, or at arm's length, in preparation for the loss? Isaac is suspended and his arms are crossed but not bound, swinging precariously between the flames of the sacrifice and his obedient father. The trial is still Abraham's—but not unequivocally for we focus on the helpless, dangling figure of the son.

The ambiguity of the mosaic raises the question of Isaac's willingness. As mentioned earlier, the literary tradition emphasizes Isaac's voluntary obedience by describing his maturity and giving his age as 37 years.[35] The artistic portrayal of Isaac as a child suggests that he has little active role in the sacrifice. It is even possible to view him as a reluctant participant. Once again, we can see that artistic interpretation possesses its own emphasis, significantly different from the literary interpretation.

34. E. Sukenik, *The Ancient Synagogue of Beith Alpha* (Jerusalem: Hebrew University, 1932), p. 40.

35. *Gen. R.* 56.8.

The Akedah *at Sepphoris*

In 1993, a well-preserved early fifth-century synagogue was discovered in the city of Sepphoris, capital of the Galilee. Judah ha Nasi lived in Sepphoris in the early part of third century bringing with him institutions of Jewish leadership, and the city enjoyed a renaissance. Sepphoris had 18 synagogues at the time of Judah ha Nasi and remained the capital of the Galilee until the end of the third century CE when the Sanhedrin and Patriarchate moved to Tiberias. A general overview shows that it was a Jewish city similar to the pagan cities of the region—there were no clear separate neighbourhoods on the basis of religious, social or economic criteria.

The mosaic floor is the most important part of the synagogue that has survived, covering the building's entire floor and consisting of 14 panels. The central band depicts the zodiac. Each of the 12 signs, which surround the sun, is identified with the name of the month in Hebrew. Most have images of young men, the majority clothed but some naked; the four seasons are depicted in the corners accompanied by agricultural objects characteristic of each season.

The *Akedah* is depicted in two panels and the first (Fig. 25) has a Greek inscription, 'be remembered for good, Boethos (son) of Aemilius with his children. He made this panel. A blessing upon them. Amen.' The word 'amen', written in Hebrew, ends the benediction. Archaeologists, Weiss and Netzer, suggest that the panel shows the two servants who remain at the bottom of the mountain with the ass. One holds a spear while his other hand is raised slightly in a gesture we have already seen made by Ezekiel in Dura Europos. The other servant sits under a tree, at the foot of the mountain holding the ass.[36]

There is no other instance of a servant making the special sign and I would suggest an alternative explanation is required. Rather than a servant, I propose that the figure is Abraham instructing the servant to remain behind. The shoes of Abraham appear to be exactly the same as those portrayed in the right-hand panel (Fig. 26). This panel is badly damaged and depicts the head of an animal tethered to the tree by its left horn; below are two upturned pairs of shoes—a small pair for Isaac and a

---

36. Z. Weiss and E. Netzer, *Promise and Redemption: A Synagogue Mosaic from Sephhoris* (Jerusalem: The Israel Museum, 1996), pp. 30-31.

large pair for Abraham. In another small section of the panel Weiss and Netzer suggest there exists the blade of a vertically held knife with traces of a robe to its right.

Figure 25. *Depiction of the* Akedah *at Sepphoris.*

The small pair of shoes again emphasizes that, for the Jewish artistic exegetes, Isaac was not the youth of the biblical story nor the adult of rabbinic literary interpretation. His shoes indicate that he was a boy. The idea of removing shoes is probably derived from other biblical passages such as Moses at the burning bush (Exod. 3.5) and Joshua in the presence of the Lord's Host (Josh. 5.15). The artist has clearly decided that when Abraham and Isaac reached the sacred spot they would have removed their shoes out of respect for the sanctity of the site.

Figure 26. *Detail from the* Akedah *at Sepphoris.*

Once again we notice a conflict with the literary interpretation. In *Genesis Rabbah*, Abraham is compared favourably to Moses. One of the reasons why he was superior to Moses was because he was not asked by God to remove his shoes at Mount Moriah.[37] The artistic interpreter provides evidence for an alternative tradition, perhaps in a debate about the significance of the removal or non-removal of shoes.

37. *Gen. R.* 55.6.

In conclusion, the first point to make is that the *Akedah* was part of an extensive tradition of synagogue decoration. It is highly unlikely that the existence of the *Akedah* in three synagogues was mere chance. Secondly, in artistic interpretation, far more than in literary interpretation, the *Akedah* is linked to the Torah and the Temple. Artistic interpretation associated the *Akedah* with the Jewish people's redemption and reminded God of his promise to Abraham and his children. Thirdly, Isaac is always portrayed as a child. Artistic interpretation does not follow literary interpretation but remains consistent with the biblical story; it emphasizes the helplessness of the child and not the voluntary self-offering found in literary exegesis. Fourthly, artistic interpretation expands the role of the ram. Whereas in the biblical story the ram appears to have been on Mount Moriah by chance, the artistic representation emphasizes the significance of the ram through its size and prominent position. Artistic interpretation offers its own insight into the development of the *Akedah* in Jewish thought. An examination of the literary interpretation on its own, although illustrative of the diversity of literary tradition, does not tell the whole story.

Conclusion

The diversity of Jewish and Christian representations of the Sacrifice of Isaac is striking. For many, the biblical story has been viewed solely from a literary perspective but I have shown that artistic representations are extremely important and should not be ignored. Indeed, artists who created images based on the biblical story should be viewed as exegetes in their own right for they have offered their own interpretations, some of which conflict with the better-known interpretations found in the writings of the Church Fathers or the rabbis.

An investigation of the biblical story from the perspective of the artist shows a number of significant similarities between the representations of Jewish and Christian artists. Indeed, a number of these show variations from the biblical text such as the ram being tied to a tree (rather than caught by its horns in a bush). We should not be surprised to discover that Christian artistic interpretation sometimes follows the same pattern as Jewish (or vice versa). They simply indicate a positive interaction between Jew and Christian and, as such, provide a good example of Jews and Christians working together in ancient times.

It is worth emphasizing the rich diversity of Jewish and Christian artistic interpretations of the *Akedah*. Some scholars and religious leaders have criticized these artistic representations, seeing in their diversity the possibility of danger and error. Jean D'Espagne, a seventeenth-century French Protestant theologian was annoyed that in the contemporary Bible, 'Isaac is here painted on his knees before an altar and Abraham behind him holding a knife in his hand, which is lifted up to give the blow. But this picture is false and doth bely the holy History.'[38] Martin Luther also complained that 'the picture commonly painted about Abraham about to kill his son is incorrect'.[39] In fact, from the very beginning the portrayal of the *Akedah* exhibits not *errors* but *interpretations* of the biblical text. Sometimes these interpretations mirror liturgical or literary developments. On other occasions, they are not found elsewhere.

Artistic interpretation is bound to the biblical text but has developed its own rules of interpretation. Artistic interpretation must be examined as a form of biblical exegesis and is critical to any study of biblical interpretation. In the words of the Church Father, Gregory of Nyssa, and valid for Jewish as well as Christian art, there are occasions when 'art clearly led the story'.[40] For this, students of biblical interpretation should be truly grateful.

38. J. D'Espagne, *Shibboleth: or the Reformation of severall places in the Translation of the French and English Bible* (London, 1655), pp. 148-49.

39. Jaroslav Pelikan (ed.), *Luther's Works: Lectures on Genesis* (St Louis, MO: Concordia Publishing House, 1964), p. 110.

40. Gregory of Nyssa, *On the Son of God and the Holy Spirit* (PG 46.573).

'THE SON OF GOD GOES FORTH TO WAR':
BIBLICAL IMAGERY IN RUDYARD KIPLING'S
'THE MAN WHO WOULD BE KING'

Larry J. Kreitzer

For years Rudyard Kipling has been relegated to one of the lower divisions of the literary league table. Despite having won the Nobel Prize for Literature in 1907, Kipling's literary star had begun to wane long before his death in 1936. His reputation in the literary establishment declined markedly after World War One, and his academic reputation hit rock-bottom in the 30s and 40s. Though it was considered unwise to show much admiration for him at high-table in the 1950s, the revival of his fortunes is usually dated to an essay by Edmund Wilson (included in *The Wound and the Bow* [1941]), another by George Orwell from (1942), and—perhaps more important than either—T.S. Eliot's magisterial introduction to his *A Choice of Kipling's Verse* (1941). That was the highbrow poetic establishment speaking in the loudest voice it could manage at the time. The general reader, of course, had gone on buying the books, most of which had remained in print: perhaps the surest guide to the durability of a literary reputation. Kipling got noticed in the universities after the publication of J.M.S. Tompkins's *The Art of Rudyard Kipling* (1959). The later stories, with their often impenetrable ambiguities and quasi-modernist credentials benefited especially. Andrew Rutherford's two volumes of *Selected Short Stories* (1966) were enormously influential, and fanned interest in Kipling for a new generation. The 60s, 70s and 80s saw major new studies of Kipling, usually critical-biographical in nature. This resurgence of interest has continued apace as the new biography by Harry Ricketts entitled *The Unforgiving Minute* (1999) testifies. It is once again becoming fashionable to read Kipling.

The short story 'The Man Who Would Be King' first appeared in Kipling's *The Phantom Rickshaw and Other Eerie Tales* (1888),[1] the fifth

---

1. It was later re-issued in his *Wee Willie Winkie and Other Stories* (1888). A

volume of the so-called Railway Series of paperbacks which were designed for a popular market in India and sold for one rupee each.[2] Kipling was only 22 years old when he wrote it while staying with Professor S.A. Hill and his wife Edmonia at their bungalow in Allahabad.[3] It was to be one of the last substantial works he produced while living in India, the country of his birth. It is an imaginative tale of two ne'er-do-wells, Peachey Carnehan and Daniel Dravot, former sergeants in the British Army serving in India, who conceive of a plan whereby they will disguise themselves, slip into the wilds of neighbouring Afghanistan through the Khyber Pass with a load of smuggled rifles, train a local army, and establish themselves as Kings of Kafiristan, a remote province in the northeastern area of the country. 'The Man Who Would Be King' remains one of Kipling's best-known stories, and its popularity has been enhanced by the 1975 film adaptation of it by director John Huston. Indeed, it is probably true to say that more people know of the story through the film adaptation than have read the story; the fact that it starred Sean Connery and Michael Caine no doubt has something to do with its abiding appeal among film enthusiasts. Pan Books in London even sought to cash in on the resurgence of interest in Kipling associated with the release of the film by publishing a new edition of the story in 1975, complete with a bright red cover and colour photographs of the two principal stars on the front.

Within this study I would like to examine 'The Man Who Would Be King' (both Kipling's short story and Huston's film adaptation), with a particular view to exploring some of the biblical and theological ideas which it contains. First, some preliminary remarks of the work as a piece of literature are in order.

facsimile of the original volume was published in Frome, Somerset, by The R.S. Surtees Society in 1988. The pagination used throughout this study is that of this facsimile edition.

2.   See F.A. Underwood, 'The Indian Railway Library', *The Kipling Journal* 46 (March 1979), pp. 6-15, and *The Kipling Journal* 46 (June 1979), pp. 10-17.

3.   Kipling lodged with the Hills for much of his last year in India (1887–88). A letter of Mrs Hill dated July 1888 describes the writing of the story, including some recollections about how Kipling came to name the central characters Peachey Talliafero Carnehan and Daniel Dravot. See Edmonia Hill, 'The Young Kipling', in Harold Orel (ed.), *Kipling: Interviews & Recollections*, I (London: Macmillan, 1983), p. 99, for details.

'The Man Who Would Be King': *An Allegory of Empire*[4]

Kipling's story has been variously assessed by critics over the years. Kingsley Amis judged it to be a 'grossly overrated long tale', noting that it has an unusually elaborate narrative frame which is frequently mistaken for complexity.[5] Arthur Conan Doyle, in contrast, included the story in his list of the best short stories of all time,[6] while J.M. Barrie declared it a masterpiece, 'the most audacious thing in fiction',[7] and H.G. Wells once described it as 'one of the best stories in the world'.[8]

While 'The Man Who Would Be King' has been widely praised as a short story, critical discussion of the work has not been great. Full-length discussions of it have been rather few on the ground, although I am not entirely sure why this is the case. Two possible explanations come to mind, however.

The first reason may be the fact that 'The Man Who Would Be King' is so intimately associated with the heyday of British imperialism and the patronizing and racist attitudes towards other peoples and faiths contained within the story makes it unattractive as an object of study for many.[9] In

---

4.   Mark Paffard, *Kipling's Indian Fiction* (London: Macmillan, 1989), p. 32, describes the work as 'an allegory of Empire in which the epic, the tragic and the farcical are finely balanced'.

5.   K. Amis, *Rudyard Kipling* (London: Thames & Hudson, 1975), pp. 62-63. Philip Mason, *Kipling: The Glass, the Shadow and the Fire* (London: Jonathan Cape, 1975), pp. 82-83, agrees. In contrast, Charles Carrington, *Rudyard Kipling: His Life and Work* (London: Macmillan, 1955), p. 99, remarks, 'The method of picture-and-frame is nowhere more effectively developed'. The story 'On Greenhow Hill' is another excellent example of a complex frame device.

6.   Cited in Roger Lancelyn Green (ed.), *Kipling: The Critical Heritage* (London: Routledge & Kegan Paul, 1971), p. 302. Also see Morton Cohen, *Rudyard Kipling to Rider Haggard: The Record of a Friendship* (Rutherford: Farleigh Dickinson University Press, 1965), p. 71.

7.   Cited in Green (ed.), *Kipling*, p. 81.

8.   Cited in Green (ed.), *Kipling*, p. 305.

9.   In this regard, Kipling is often compared to Joseph Conrad, another writer for whom the intricacies and perplexities of a collapsing colonialism provide the impetus for much of his writing. See Edmund A. Bojarski, 'A Conversation with Kipling on Conrad', *The Kipling Journal* 34 (1934), pp. 12-15; John A. McClure, *Kipling and Conrad: The Colonial Fiction* (Cambridge, MA: Harvard University Press, 1981); James Harrison, *Rudyard Kipling* (Twayne's English Author Series 339; Boston: Twayne Publishers, 1982), pp. 149-58; John Lyon, 'Half-Written Tales: Kipling and

the words of C.S. Lewis: 'Most of us begin by regarding Kipling as the panegyrist of the whole imperial system'.[10] Thus, most critics note the strongly imperialist streak that runs through the story, the tendency within Kipling's work to proclaim the virtues of King and Country. Little wonder, then, that Kipling has been described as an Apostle of the British Empire[11] and 'The Man Who Would Be King' as an allegory of imperialism,[12] which stands as something of a parody of the British acquisition of India.[13] Indeed, the American critic Edmund Wilson describes the story as 'a parable of what might happen to the English if they should forfeit their moral authority' in such imperial matters.[14]

Certainly there are many allusions to decisive moments of British imperial history scattered throughout the story. It seems clear that the attempt by British forces under the command of General Frederick Roberts (1832–1914) to invade Afghanistan provides a historical backdrop for the story as a whole. This campaign, which lasted from 1878–80, was a brilliant, but ultimately pointless exercise and would have been much discussed at the time, perhaps capturing the imagination of an impressionable young teenager like Kipling. At one point in the story, as Peachey and Daniel are

Conrad', in Phillip Mallett (ed.), *Kipling Considered* (London: Macmillan, 1989), pp. 115-34.

10. C.S. Lewis, *Selected Literary Essays* (Cambridge: Cambridge University Press, 1969), p. 240. Oliver B. Pollak, 'The Man Who Would Be King', *The Kipling Journal* 46 (September 1979), pp. 10-13, is also worth consulting.

11. Although George Orwell, 'Rudyard Kipling', in Andrew Rutherford (ed.), *Kipling's Mind and Art* (London: Oliver & Boyd, 1964), pp. 70-84 (72), rejects the suggestion that Kipling was a 'prophet of British imperialism in its expansionist phase'. For more on the relationship between Orwell and Kipling, two men who might at first glance represent opposite ends of the political spectrum, see Richard Cook, 'Rudyard Kipling and George Orwell', *Modern Fiction Studies* 7 (1961–62), pp. 125-35.

12. On this point see Louis L. Cornell, *Kipling in India* (London: Macmillan, 1966), pp. 161-65. Bonamy Dobrée, *Rudyard Kipling: Realist and Fabulist* (Oxford: Oxford University Press, 1967), p. 156, is not so sure that this assessment is correct.

13. See Harrison, *Rudyard Kipling*, pp. 40-41.

14. Edmund Wilson, 'The Kipling That Nobody Read', in Andrew Rutherford (ed.), *Kipling's Mind and Art* (London: Oliver & Boyd, 1964), pp. 17-69 (55). He goes on to suggest that Kipling's high sense of moral responsibility is to be seen in and through the story. Wilson remarks: 'The Wesleyan preacher in Kipling knows that the valiant dust of man can build only on dust if it build not in the name of God; and he is prepared to pound the pulpit and call down the Almighty's anger when parliamentarians or ministers or generals debauch their office or hold it light'.

examining maps and planning their campaign into Kafiristan, Daniel notes a position on a map and says, 'Up to Jagdallak, Peachey and me know the road. We was there with Roberts' Army' (p. 76).[15] Other allusions to British imperialism are also to be found in the short story. For example, again when Peachey and Daniel appear in the narrator's office and first lay out their audacious scheme to become kings of Kafiristan, an image from an earlier episode of British rule in the Far East is invoked. Daniel explains to the narrator the extent to which he and Peachey have considered their plan, 'We have slept over the notion half a year, and require to see Books and Atlases, and we have decided that there is only one place now in the world that two strong men can Sar-a-*whack*. They call it Kafiristan' (p. 75).

The mention of Sarawak (whose spelling is deliberately altered and the final syllable italicized in the story to intimate the kind of forceful subjugation which is involved in becoming Kings of Kafiristan) is telling. It refers to the exploits of James Brooke (1803–68), who put down a rebellion in Sarawak (Borneo) and was subsequently installed as Rajah in 1842. For his efforts, Brooke was later made a Knight Commander of the Order of the Bath in 1848. He is even referred to by name later on in the story after Peachey and Daniel have established themselves as kings. Daniel begins to get delusions of grandeur, dreaming that he can forge a Kafiristani Empire which he will hand over to Queen Victoria herself, thereby bringing two million additional people into the British realm (he even describes them as 'English' subjects). Referring back to the situation in Sarawak, he says excitedly, as he further spins out his fantasy to Peachey, 'Rajah Brooke will be a suckling to us' (p. 93). Similarly, following the disastrous attempt to wed one of the native women, when Peachey and Daniel realize that their game is up and that the peoples of Kafiristan no longer believe them to be gods and are moving against them, Peachey says to Daniel, 'This business is our Fifty-Seven' (p. 100). Clearly this is an allusion to the so-called Indian Mutiny of 1857 in which there was an attempt by native peoples to throw off the yoke of British rule.

In other words, despite the fact that 'The Man Who Would Be King' has the intelligence, precision and vivacity of myth, the atmosphere of an oppressive British imperialism seems to hang cloyingly over the tale, choking off any interest further on the part of many modern, marginally curious readers.

---

15. In Huston's film, the ex-Gurkha interpreter Billy Fish describes himself as the sole survivor of Roberts's fated incursion into Afghanistan.

A second possible reason why the story has not received the attention of critics that one might have expected is its prevalent use of Masonic imagery. For most people Freemasonry remains a strange and foreign world, a closed society which is shrouded in mystery and marked by its practice of bizarre and incomprehensible rituals. By its very nature Freemasonry is elitist and, consequently, it is viewed by many as socially divisive, if not downright offensive. Kipling himself became a Freemason in April of 1886, having been admitted to the Lodge 'Hope and Perseverance, No. 782 E.C.' in Lahore when he was just 20 (the usual minimum age was 21). He used Masonic imagery and allusions frequently in his writings,[16] but nowhere more effectively than in 'The Man Who Would Be King', where all of the major characters are Masons. This is both a strength and a weakness as far as the story itself is concerned. The fact remains that although Masonic imagery is clearly an essential feature of the form of 'The Man Who Would Be King' it also constitutes something of a barrier for contemporary readings of, and interest in, the story. Insofar as Freemasonry is viewed as a relic of a bygone era, so too is Kipling's 'The Man Who Would be King'.

Nevertheless, there are some good critical explorations of the story which open it up in a manner helpful for our consideration. The brief discussion of it by Cleanth Brooks, Jr, and Robert Penn Warren in their *Understanding Fiction* (1943) is often cited. They see it as a story primarily concerned with exploring the paradoxical nature of kingship and suggest it involves 'a contrast between kinds of kingship, between kinds of power, external and internal, power over others and power over oneself'[17]. Probably the most penetrating study thus far is that offered over 40 years ago by Paul Fussell, Jr.[18] Fussell does an admirable job in laying out the supreme sense of irony which pervades Kipling's story, the way in which

16. See H.S. Williamson, 'Masonic References in the Works of Rudyard Kipling', *The Kipling Journal* 31 (1934), pp. 76-92; Basil M. Bazley, 'Freemasonry in Kipling's Works', *The Kipling Journal* 16 (1949), pp. 13-14, and *The Kipling Journal* 17 (1950), pp. 7-11; Carrington, *Rudyard Kipling*, p. 69; Bazley, 'Freemasonry in Kipling', *The Kipling Journal* 28 (1961), pp. 7-13; Norman Page, *A Kipling Companion* (London: Macmillan, 1984), pp. 185-86. It may be that Kipling took his inspiration for incorporating Masonic ideas within his fiction from Edgar Allen Poe, who parodied it to great effect in his *The Cask of Amontillado* (1846).

17. Cleanth Brooks Jr and Robert Penn Warren, *Understanding Fiction* (New York: Appleton-Century-Crofts, 1943), p. 63.

18. Paul Fussell Jr, 'Irony, Freemasonry, and Humane Ethics in Kipling's "The Man Who Would Be King"', *English Literary History* 25 (1958), pp. 216-33.

he playfully juxtaposes alleged 'true' kingship of monarchs in the real world and the 'make-believe' kingship of monarchs such as Peachey Carnehan and Daniel Dravot who reign in the mythical world of Kafiristan. More importantly, for our considerations, is the way in which Fussell suggests that Peachey Carnehan and Daniel Dravot are, in their experiences as kings of Kafiristan, acting out a parody of biblical history. As Fussell states:

> From their initial appearance as 'gods' and law-givers to the wicked tribes, to Dravot's 'redemption' and Peachey's crucifixion, their actions are played before an ironic background constructed of kingly acts, both temporal and spiritual, legalistic and symbolistic, Hebraic and Christian, of the Bible.[19]

Fussell contends that the way in which Carnehan and Dravot rule over the various tribes of Kafiristan is intended to convey to the reader a sense of the biblical account of creation and the establishment of the leadership of the early Hebraic kings, as well as the settling of the factious disputes among the early tribes of Israel. He also suggests that Kipling intends a deliberate association between Mosaic Law and Masonic Law insofar as Peachey Carnehan and Daniel Dravot attempt to impose their ethical standards upon the lives of the subjugated people of Kafiristan. At one point, Fussell notes, Dravot goes so far as to equate the reformed people of Kafiristan with the Lost Tribes of Israel, and contemplates the appointment of 12 hand-picked Englishmen to rule over them. The Old Testament idea of a covenant between God and his people which is sanctified by means of the sacrificial spilling of blood is even alluded to within the story. Here Peachey Carnehan describes how one village is allowed to move to a more fertile area, but not without the cost of sacrificial blood. Peachey explains, 'They were a poor lot, and we blooded 'em with a kid before letting 'em into the new Kingdom' (p. 87).

Even the ill-fated attempt by Dravot to take a wife from among the local people is presented as if it is a violation of biblical principles that make a distinction between the divine realm and the human realm (as in Gen. 6.1-4 where the 'sons of God' marry the 'daughters of men'). Carnehan objects strenuously, saying, 'The Bible says that Kings ain't to waste their strength on women, specially when they've got a new raw Kingdom to work over' (p. 96).

Building upon this insight, some critics of the story have suggested that the real moral of 'The Man who Would Be King' is not that we should

---

19. Fussell, 'Irony', p. 221.

observe the proper boundary between the mortal man and immortal God, but that there is a price to be paid for the improper treatment of women by men. Thus, Nora Crook, who offers what is in effect a deconstructionist reading of the text and attempts to subject it to a feminist critique says,

> Dravot's fall comes about because of his ignorance of poetry, history and legend, which could have told him that he was behaving dangerously in taking a wife from a community which sacrifices women to sate the lust of gods, for the woman has nothing to lose, and something to gain, by testing his divinity. Peachey was right to warn him off dealings with women, not because women are intrinsically evil and clogs on the realisation of men's dreams, but because they have a long score to settle.[20]

Or again, in a related interpretative approach, Phillip Mallett assesses the story from the standpoint of it being an illustration of the typically Kiplingian narrative device in which characters plot deceits and arrange elaborate hoaxes as part of a larger plan. Innumerable Kipling stories (including some of his very worst) are about hoaxes and jokes—some of his best, too, such as 'The Village That Voted the Earth Was Flat' (1917) and the brilliant 'Dayspring Mishandled' (1928). In 'The Man Who Would Be King' the central deceit, or hoax, is that Peachey and Daniel are gods, the descendants of Alexander the Great. According to Mallett, Kipling is here giving voice to what amounts to racist assumptions about the superiority of whites. He says:

> That white men who find themselves among non-whites will naturally rise to a position of authority is more or less a reflex response among white writers, from Defoe's *Robinson Crusoe* to John Boorman's film *The Emerald Forest*, and the idea of the white incomer being taken for a god is at least as old as Shakespeare's *The Tempest*. Typically, Kipling draws the reader's attention to these assumptions, but then having flaunted them, declines to register any anxiety about them.[21]

---

20. Nora Crook, *Kipling's Myths of Love & Death* (London: Macmillan, 1989), p. 59. It is worth remembering that Kipling was the author of the line 'The female of the species is more deadly than the male'. One of the central means whereby the fear of women is expressed within the story is the prohibition against liquor and women within Article Two of the 'Contrack' drawn up between Peachey and Daniel: 'That you and me will not, while this matter is being settled, look at any Liquor, nor any Woman black, white, or brown, so as to get mixed up with one or the other harmful'. It may well be that T.S. Eliot has this declaration in mind within his famous poem 'The Journey of the Magi'. See Kenneth Muir, 'Kipling and Eliot', *Notes & Queries* 1 (1954), pp. 400-401 for more on this point.

21. Phillip Mallett, 'Kipling and the Hoax', in Phillip Mallett (ed.), *Kipling*

Taken together, these observations serve to illustrate how 'The Man Who Would Be King' has captured the imaginations of a few critics who have produced a range of different critical readings of it as a piece of literature. Let us move now to consider the theological content of the story more closely.

Kipling's Story: A Parable on the Cost of Kingship

Clearly, Kipling was very familiar with biblical stories, alluding to them frequently within his various writings.[22] Although he was by no means an active churchgoer, he did come from a family with strong Methodist connections (both of his grandfathers were Methodist ministers).[23] Above all, Kipling appreciated the importance that religion had within human societies, without getting caught up in debates about whether the morality and customs associated with religious belief were right or wrong. For Kipling, such things were a fact of human existence and that was all that mattered.

There are three specific ways in which the biblical material and, in particular, Christian imagery associated with the life and ministry of Jesus Christ come through in the story. We now turn to discuss this imagery.

The Passion Predictions of the Would-Be Kings

The ominous fate of the adventurous pair is hinted at several times in the beginning of the story. Some of these hints are more subtle than others; occasionally they are so craftily done that they are almost invisible. For example, should we make something out of Daniel Dravot's words, spoken to the narrator early on in the story? Dravot says, 'It isn't so easy being a King as it looks' (p. 77). Similarly, a sharp-eyed reader *might* detect a deliberate allusion to the fate of Carnehan and Dravot in the unusual hyphenation that Kipling adopts in the following sentence, put on

Considered (London: Macmillan, 1989), p. 103.

22. For more on this see Sandra Kemp, *Kipling's Hidden Narratives* (Oxford: Basil Blackwell, 1988), pp. 82-100. Also note G.F. MacMunn, 'Kipling's Use of the Old Testament', *The Kipling Journal* 32 (1934), pp. 110-19. Kipling alludes to several other literary sources in the story, including Tennyson's 'Gareth and Lynette' when he mentions in passing when comparing the blank page of a newspaper's report to the blank shield of Modred. For more on this particular point see S.A. Courtauld, 'Kipling's Literary Allusions', *The Kipling Journal* 25 (1933), pp. 7-20.

23. Angus Wilson, *The Strange Ride of Rudyard Kipling: His Life and Works* (Harmondsworth: Penguin Books, 1979), pp. 7-10, discusses Kipling's religious heritage.

the lips of Dravot as he explains to the narrator the audicious plan to become kings of Kafiristan:

> We shall go to those parts and say to any King we find—'D'you want to vanquish your foes?' and we will show him how to drill men; for we know that better than anything else. Then we will subvert that King and seize his Throne and establish a Dy-nasty (p. 75).

Does Kipling intend us to understand this final word as 'Dynasty' or 'Die-Nasty'? One cannot help but wonder if he deliberately inserted the double entendre, given the otherwise inexplicable insertion of the hyphen into the word.[24]

However, it is in the scene where the narrator meets Peachey and Daniel at the Kumharsen Serai, the great trading bazaar, that we see most clearly hints of the passion which is to come. It is at the Serai that arrangements are made for the would-be kings to travel from Peshawar into Afghanistan with their smuggled cargo of 20 Martini rifles and ammunition, hidden under a load of mud toys and loaded onto 2 camels. The men are disguised, with Daniel posing as a mad priest and Peachey pretending to be his servant. Three references to the fate which awaits them are made, functioning in much the same way that the three predictions of Jesus Christ made on the road to Caesarea Philippi serve to set up the Passion Narratives within the Synoptic Gospels (see Mt. 16.21/Mk 8.31/Lk. 9.22; Mt. 17.22-23/Mk 9.31/Lk. 9.44; and Mt. 20.18-19/Mk 10.33/Lk. 18.31-33). The first of these is made by a horse-dealer, who remarks to the narrator about the pair:

> The *mullah* is mad... He is going up to Kabul to sell toys to the Amir. He will either be raised to honour or have his head cut off. He came in here this morning and has been behaving madly ever since (p. 78).

The second passion prediction is made by Dravot himself a little later as he and Peachey have moved a little further down the road with their camels and its load of rifles. Dravot makes a reference to becoming a king of Kafiristan and this allows the narrator to see through his priestly disguise. Out of earshot of the people in the bazaar, the narrator and Dravot exchange words:

---

24. I once heard Germaine Greer make a similar comment about the American television soap-opera *Dynasty*. She remarked that she and her mother referred to it as 'Die Nasty'.

'Have you got everything you want?' I asked, overcome with astonishment. 'Not yet, but we shall soon. Give me a memento of your kindness, Brother. You did me a service yesterday, and that time in Marwar. Half my kingdom shall you have, as the saying is.' I slipped a small charm from my watch-chain and handed it up to the *mullah* (p. 80).

This is a carefully veiled allusion to the fate that awaits Dravot, one that is not always immediately recognized by the reader of the story. The reference to having 'half my kingdom' is drawn from the story of the beheading of John the Baptist (Mt. 14.3-12/Mk 6.17-29). In particular, it refers to the foolish promise that King Herod makes to Salome (the daughter of his wife Herodias) after she has danced publicly at the King's birthday party. Thus Mk 6.22-23 records:

> For when Herodias' daughter came in and danced, she pleased Herod and his guests; and the king said to the girl, 'Ask me for whatever you wish, and I will grant it.' And he vowed to her, 'Whatever you ask me, I will give you, even half of my kingdom.'

The result is, of course, that John the Baptist is beheaded in order to fulfill Salome's whim. Herod's importunate promise to Salome has its parallel in Dravot's brash declaration to the narrator; Dravot's words become a self-directed prophecy in that he, like John the Baptist, will eventually suffer beheading. Thus, Kipling cleverly injects an allusion to such a fate at this point within the story. This is done subtly, and with not a little touch of irony, but the effect is all the more powerful as a consequence.

The third allusion to the awful fate that awaits Carnehan and Dravot is made two paragraphs later, as the narrator is made to speculate as to the future of the intrepid adventurers. The narrator remarks:

> Then the camels passed along the dusty road, and I was left alone to wonder. My eye could detect no failure in the disguises. The scene in the Serai proved that they were complete to the native mind. There was just the chance, therefore, that Carnehan and Dravot would be able to wander through Afghanistan without detection. But beyond, they would find death—certain and awful death (p. 80).

How the narrator *knows* that a certain and awful death awaits them is not disclosed, but this matters little. On this particular point within the story the narrator is omniscient, and the identity of narrator and author (Kipling) is deftly asserted.[25] In short, within the Serai episode, Kipling com-

---

25. For more on the complex way in which Kipling uses ambivalent narrative

municates to his readers a trio of hints, passion predictions if you will, of what is to come in the story.

One further passage is also worth mentioning in this regard, although it comes a little further on within the story. This occurs after Peachey and Daniel have established a Masonic lodge in one of the villages and used Masonic rites and ceremonies as a means of unifying the people under their authority. Dravot is bubbling over with enthusiasm about the way things are going. We read of Dravot: 'You are my people, and by God,' says he, running off into English at the end—'I'll make a damned fine Nation of you, or I'll die in the making!' (p. 92).

The Crucifixion of Peachey Carnehan

The close relationship between the two adventurers is a central motif throughout the short story, especially as they have to pay the price of their kingship. This comes in the form of a mutual suffering and passion, wherein the promises of their commitment to one another are tested to the limit. There are several points at which the mystical identification of Peachey Carnehan with Daniel Dravot in death is stressed along these lines, notably within passages where Peachey reveals to the narrator what happened to them once they had entered Kafiristan and had been proclaimed as kings. What is remarkable about these passages is the way in which Peachey is made so to identify with Daniel, that the death of the latter is described as if it incorporates the death of the former. In short, from Peachey's perspective, when Daniel dies, so too does Peachey himself. In this sense, the article within the 'Contrack' that the two will stand by each other, come thick or thin, is made complete.

As illustrations of this virtual absorption of Peachey into Daniel as dual kings of Kafiristan, particularly as the latter dies at the hands of the people of the province, we note the following three passages. First, Peachey, in a semi-delirious state, responds to the narrator's question:

> 'What did you and Daniel Dravot do when the camels could go no farther because of the rough roads that led into Kafiristan?' 'What did which do? There was a party called Peachey Taliaferro Carnehan that was with Dravot. Shall I tell you about him? He died out there in the cold. Slap from the bridge fell old Peachey, turning and twisting in the air like a penny whirligig that you can sell to the Amir—No; they was two or three-ha'

voices within his fiction, see Kemp, *Kipling's Hidden Narratives*. Although she does not discuss 'The Man Who Would Be King' directly, there is much that is of relevance to our understanding of the story within Kemp's provocative study.

pence, those whirligigs, or I am much mistaken and woeful sore... And then these camels were no use, and Peachey said to Dravot—"For the Lord's sake let's get out of this before our heads are chopped off"' (pp. 83-84).

What is intriguing about this paragraph is the way in which Peachey describes *himself* as falling from the bridge. In point of fact, we learn later on in the story that it is Daniel Dravot (and not Peachey) who is executed in this way. The point here seems to be that Peachey so identifies with his companion Daniel that when his friend is killed on the rope bridge he somehow interprets this as his own execution.[26] And yet, ironically, the whole episode is set within a mournful appeal by Daniel that he and Peachey extract themselves from this dangerous situation before 'our heads are chopped off'. The significance of the word 'our' is not to be missed here.

A similar passage is found a little later on within the story, as Peachey continues his account of Dravot's martyrdom. He describes how they came to their first village and Daniel made motions for something to eat.

Then he opened his mouth and points down it, and when the first man brings him food he says—'No', but when one of the old priests and the boss of the village brings him food, he says—'Yes,' very haughty, and eats it slow. That was how we came to our first village, without any trouble, just as though we had tumbled from the skies. But we tumbled from one of those damned rope-bridges you see, and—you couldn't expect a man to laugh much after that? (p. 85).

Here again it is the *'we* tumbled' that is striking about Peachey's recounting of the episode, as if he falls from the bridge with his companion Daniel.

The description of Dravot falling from the rope bridge is brought up a third time by Peachey as he relates their story to the narrator. Once again, he is in something of a confused state, mixing up the images of beheading and falling from the rope bridge, Dravot's death and his own identification with it. As their guide and translator Billy Fish is executed, and Peachey

---

26. J.M.S. Tompkins, *The Art of Rudyard Kipling* (London: Methuen & Co., 1959), p. 112, notes, 'Carnehan's confused identification of his own fate with the death of the man he loved and admired'. On this point, also note the perceptive comments of J.I.M. Stewart, *Rudyard Kipling* (New York: Dodd, Mead & Company, 1966), p. 62, 'Was it Dravot who was prodded to his death on the rope bridge, or was it Carnehan? He is not quite sure. But the mental darkness which thus from time to time obscures the story merely serves to throw the total picture into brilliant relief'.

and Daniel are surrounded by angry villagers, we hear Peachey continue the tale:

> There was a man called Billy Fish, a good friend of us all, and they cut his throat, Sir, then and there, like a pig; and the King kicks up the bloody snow and says: 'We've had a dashed fine run for our money. What's coming next?' But Peachey, Peachey Taliaferro, I tell you, Sir, in confidence as betwixt two friends, he lost his head, Sir. No, he didn't neither. The King lost his head, so he did, along o' one of those cunning rope-bridges ... It tilted this way. They marched him a mile across the snow to a rope-bridge over a ravine with a river at the bottom. You may have seen such. They prodded him behind like an ox. 'Damn your eyes!' says the King. 'D'you suppose I can't die like a gentleman?' He turns to Peachey—Peachey that was crying like a child. 'I've brought you to this, Peachey,' says he. 'Brought you out of your happy life to be killed in Kafiristan, where you was late Commander-in-Chief of the Emperor's forces. Say you forgive me, Peachey.'—'I do,' says Peachey. 'Fully and freely do I forgive you, Dan.'—'Shake hands, Peachey,' says he. 'I'm going now.' Out he goes, looking neither right nor left, and when he was plumb in the middle of those dizzy dancing ropes—'Cut, you beggars,' he shouts; and they cut, and old Dan fell, turning round and round and round, twenty thousand miles, for he took half an hour to fall till he struck the water, and I could see his body caught on a rock with the gold crown close beside (p. 102).

In the very next paragraph of the story Peachey Carnehan explains his own fate following the death of Daniel Dravot in terms which are quite moving and filled with pathos. He explains to the narrator what happened to him at the hands of the people of Kafiristan following the death of Daniel Dravot:

> 'But do you know what they did to Peachey between two pine trees? They crucified him, Sir, as Peachey's hands will show. They used wooden pegs for his hands and feet; and he didn't die. He hung there and screamed, and they took him down next day, and said it was a miracle that he wasn't dead. They took him down—poor old Peachey that hadn't done them any harm— that hadn't done them any...' He rocked to and fro and wept bitterly, wiping his eyes with the back of his scarred hands and moaning like a child for some ten minutes (pp. 102-103).

Two other brief allusions to the physical dimensions of Peachey's crucifixion are also worth noting. Both occur quite early on in the story as part of the account of Peachey's relation of his experiences to the narrator. First, we note the following statement in which the narrator describes his own actions in listening to Peachey's tale:

> I leaned forward and looked into his face as steadily as I could. He dropped one hand upon the table and I grasped it by the wrist. It was twisted like a bird's claw, and upon the back was a ragged red diamond-shaped scar (p. 82).

Clearly, the scars made by nails during a crucifixion are meant here. Similarly, we also have a tantalizing allusion made to such crucifixion nails a little further on in Peachey's recollections. The narrator asks Peachey for more information and gets a startling reply:

> He paused for a moment, while I asked him if he could remember the nature of the country through which he had journeyed. 'I am telling you as straight as I can, but my head isn't as good as it might be. They drove nails through it to make me hear better how Dravot died' (p. 84).

Much has been made of the meaning of Peachey's crucifixion, whether or not Kipling intended it to be viewed against the backdrop of Christianity and its concentration on the Crucifixion of Jesus of Nazareth as the focus of faith. Occasionally, critics of Kipling's work have suggested Masonic imagery as an alternative background, given the fact that Freemasonry perpetuated the cult of the Dying and Rising God and the associated fertility cults.[27] It is difficult to know how much weight can be given to this idea, however. At the very least, it seems clear that Kipling alludes to the biblical accounts of the Passion and Crucifixion of Jesus Christ at several points within 'The Man Who Would Be King'. The fact that he does so is illustrative of the theological undergarment of the story as a whole, and suggests that there is a great deal going on theologically within Kipling's work here. There is one further facet of the story which also points in this direction and needs to be considered, namely, the singing of a Christian hymn by Peachey at the conclusion of the tale.

The Reworked 'Son of God' Hymn by Reginald Heber

The hymn 'The Son of God goes forth to war' was written by Reginald Heber D.D. (1783–1826); it remains one of his best-known hymns, perhaps superceded only by 'Holy, Holy, Holy, Lord God Almighty' or 'Brightest and best are the sons of the morning'. 'The Son of God goes forth to war' was written for St Stephen's Day, with vv. 3 and 4 referring specifically to Stephen as the first martyr of the faith (see Acts 7.55-60).

---

27. See Fussell, 'Irony, Freemasonry, and Humane Ethics in Kipling's "The Man Who Would Be King"', p. 228, for more on this point.

Heber was educated at Brasenose College, Oxford, and pursued a brilliant academic career as a cleric, delivering the Bampton Lectures in 1815. Interestingly (from the standpoint of our study of the Anglo-Indian Kipling) Heber became the Bishop of Calcutta in 1823 (after having twice declined the post), with his diocese covering the whole of India. The pressures of his duties and the constant traveling they involved, together with the difficult climate, eventually broke his health and he died of a stroke after three short years of service in the Indian sub-continent. In any event, the fact that he had such an intimate relationship with British concerns in India makes Kipling's choice to include one of his hymns within the story an understandable one. The hymn concerned runs:

1. The Son of God goes forth to war,
   A kingly crown to gain;
   His blood-red banner streams afar!
   Who follows in His train?

2. Who best can drink his cup of woe,
   Triumphant over pain,
   Who patient bears his cross below,
   He follows in his train!

3. The martyr first, whose eagle eye
   Could pierce beyond the grave;
   Who saw his Master in the sky,
   And call'd on Him to save.

4. Like Him, with pardon on his tongue,
   In midst of mortal pain,
   He pray'd for them that did the wrong!
   Who follows in his train?

5. A glorious band, the chosen few
   On whom the spirit came,
   Twelve valiant saints, their hope they knew,
   And mock'd the cross and flame.

6. They met the tyrant's brandished steel,
   The lion's gory mane;
   They bow'd their necks the death to feel!
   Who follows in their train?

7. A noble army—men and boys,
   The matron and the maid,
   Around the Saviour's throne rejoice,
   In robes of light array'd:

8. They climb'd the steep ascent of Heaven,
   Through peril, toil, and pain!
   O God! to us may grace be given
   To follow in their train.

The opening stanza of the hymn is cited by Kipling at the end of the story. It is sung by the broken and defeated Peachey Carnehan as he begs in the streets of Lahore. The former king of Kafiristan is delirious, suffering from sunstroke, singing to an unknown audience through his nose and looking neither to the right nor to the left,

The Son of Man goes forth to war,
A golden crown to gain;
His blood-red banner streams afar—
Who follows in his train? (p. 104)

What is intriguing is the fact that the messianic title in the opening line is shifted in the story from 'Son of God' to 'Son of Man'. What is the significance of this? Is it perhaps because of the greater militaristic associations the latter term was thought to have held? There is certainly something in this, in that many New Testament interpreters detect a subtle change of nuance between messianic declarations of Jesus as 'Son of God' and him as 'Son of Man'. But this is a rather modern distinction, one that cannot be legitimately applied to Kipling and the late nineteenth century. It is more likely that this is a deliberate alteration of Heber's hymn on Kipling's part, one that cleverly *shifts the focus of the hymn as a declaration of deity to it as a proclamation of humanity.* In other words, the alteration emphasizes the *humanity* of Carnehan and Dravot, at the expense of any false claims to *divinity*, claims which, as the story relates, result ultimately in death and crucifixion.

This represents what might at first glance appear to be an insignificant change of wording within the hymn, but it seems to me that the alteration of a single word here summarizes quite succinctly the essential point of the story as a whole. Peachey Carnehan, as the solitary, legitimate follower of his friend and regal colleague Daniel Dravot, dares to proclaim the message of the Son of *Man*, to the Christian missionaries in Lahore. These Christian missionaries have hitherto failed to recognize the full significance of the declaration regarding a 'Son of Man', and ultimately are brought face to face with an unexpected truth about the nature of kingship and the genuine discipleship that flows from it. The only mention of Christian missionaries in the short story up to this point has appeared earlier in the story in an (apparently) unrelated context. Within the opening paragraphs of the story, Kipling offers a satirization of mission-aries as people wholly concerned with keeping grudges and pursuing vendettas against one another in the narrator's newspaper:

> A newspaper office seems to attract every conceivable sort of person, to the prejudice of discipline... Missionaries wish to know why they have not been permitted to escape from their regular vehicles of abuse and swear at a brother-missionary under special patronage of the editorial We (p. 71).

Yet here at the conclusion of his story, in a remarkable inversion of roles, Kipling has the missionaries confronted with the proclamation that the kingly 'Son of Man goes forth to war'. Even more, it is the faithful follower Peachey, the crucified, who brings this message to them from the heathen. It is surely not without significance that Daniel Dravot was the king of Kafiristan, the king of the Land of the Infidels, an area untouched by either Islamic civilization or British imperialism (*kafir* in Arabic means 'unbeliever' or 'infidel'—a fact which Kipling was almost certainly exploiting throughout the story).[28] In other words, far from taking the gospel *to* the heathen, the missionaries receive a prophetic declaration *from* them. This is a good illustration of Kipling's use of irony, and is in keeping with what we know of his general antipathy to Christian mission-ary activity in India.

We turn now to consider the film adaptation of Kipling's 'The Man Who Would Be King', keeping in mind the various theological themes which we have identified as integral to the story.

Huston's Film: The Parable is Re-Cast

The celebrated actor-director John Huston admitted a life-long fascination for Kipling, even to the point of having committed much of his verse to memory as a child. Huston toyed with the idea of making a screen adaptation of 'The Man Who Would Be King' as early as 1952. In the end, Huston himself wrote the screenplay along with Gladys Hill (an earlier version by Peter Viertel was eventually abandoned),[29] and filming began in late 1975. Over the long period during which the film germinated in Huston's mind, various actors were considered for the central characters of

28. On this point, see Paffard, *Kipling's Indian Fiction*, p. 77.
29. See Peter Viertel, *Dangerous Friends* (Middlesex: Penguin Books, 1992), pp. 180-83, 200-10; Laurence Grobel, *The Hustons* (London: Bloomsbury, 1990), pp. 680-88, for more details about the production of the screenplay.

Peachey Carnehan and Daniel Dravot, including Humphrey Bogart and Clark Gable, Peter O'Toole and Richard Burton, Burt Lancaster and Kirk Douglas, and Paul Newman and Robert Redford. Ultimately, it was Paul Newman who suggested to Huston that the roles needed to be taken by British actors, such as Michael Caine and Sean Connery. Huston, wisely, saw the logic of this proposal and cast the two in the parts.[30] Other international cast members were brought into the project, with the Canadian actor Christopher Plummer taking the role of Rudyard Kipling, while the role of Roxanne was played by the Guyanian actress Shakirah Caine (Michael Caine's wife), the role of Billy Fish by the Indian actor Saeed Jaffrey, and the role of Ootah by the Moroccan actor Doghmi Larbi. Huston's film was generally well-received by critics[31] and was acknowledged as a significant effort by the various film-industry awarding bodies. Thus, Maurice Jarre, who composed the music for *The Man Who Would Be King*, received a Golden Globe nomination for producing the Best Original Score for a Motion Picture at the 1976 Golden Globe awards. In addition, the film was nominated for two British Academy of Film and Theatre Awards (BAFTA): one for Edith Head for Best Costume Design and one for Oswald Morris for Best Cinematography. It also received four Oscar nominations by the Hollywood Academy of Motion Picture Arts and Sciences: one for Russell Lloyd for Best Film Editing, one for Edith Head for Best Costume Design, one for Tony Inglis, Alexandre Trauner and Peter James III for Best Art Direction-Set Direction, and one for John Huston and Gladys Hill for Best Writing of a Screenplay Adapted from Other Material. Unfortunately, it won none of these nominations. It did, however, receive a Royal Premiere at the Odeon, Leicester Square, in London in December of 1975. A new print of the film was released in 1997 and Michael Caine and Sean Connery presented it at the Edinburgh Festival for that year.

30. John Huston, *An Open Book* (London: Columbus Books, 1988), pp. 341-60, discusses the film. Also see Axel Madsen, *John Huston* (London: Robson Books, 1979), pp. 244-49; Michael Caine, *Acting in Film* (New York: Applause Theatre Book Publishers, 1990), pp. 101-103, 128; Anne Billson, *My Name Is Michael Caine: A Life in Film* (London: Muller, 1991), pp. 104-108; Andrew Yule, *Sean Connery: Neither Shaken Nor Stirred* (London: Little, Brown and Company, 1993), pp. 179-86; John Parker, *Sean Connery* (London: Victor Gollancz, 1993), pp. 185-92.

31. Including Pauline Kael, *When the Lights Go Down* (London: Boyars, 1980), pp. 107-12.

Scenes from the film were shot on location in a variety of locations, including Glen Canyon, Utah, the Grande Montée, Chamonix, France, and the city of Marrakesh in Morocco (which served as a suitable site for the market and street scenes). An elaborate set for the city of Sikandergul was made, costing in excess of $500,000. Much of the outdoor scenery was shot in the Atlas Mountains of Morocco, including the scenes depicting the notorious Khyber Pass, the entrance-way from India to the wilds of Pakistan and the mysterious lands beyond (the picturesque Gorges du Todra at Tinghi served as the setting in this respect). The film even contains a brief exchange between Peachey and Daniel as they consider the last time that they travelled through the pass, under heavy gunfire. One cannot help but recall an incident in Kipling's own life when he was on a walk through the Khyber Pass and was shot at by an Afghan freedom-fighter. In this sense, the film promotes a nice link between Kipling's story and his own life.[32] Local villagers were also brought in as extras, most notably a 103-year-old man named Karroom Ben Bouih whom Huston cast as the High Priest Kafu-Selim.[33] The fact that much of the dialogue among the Kafiristani people is conducted in an exotic-sounding dialect, adds considerable realism to the film as a whole.[34]

Several interesting additions to the basic storyline of the Kipling tale are added within the film's screenplay. Huston interjects a substantial amount of humour into the film, as the scenes where Peachey and Danny attempt to drill the people of Kafiristan in military tactics illustrates. Also, within the film the unnamed journalistic narrator of the story is explicitly identified with Rudyard Kipling himself—a natural and helpful clarification of the short story. Meanwhile, the Masonic links between Peachey Carnehan and Kipling are made much of, initially in the scenes detailing Peachey's theft of Kipling's pocket-watch, complete with its Masonic charm-emblem, at the train station in Lahore, thus setting the tale in motion.

---

32. Kipling claimed to have been shot at in May of 1885. See Thomas Pinney (ed.), *Something of Myself and Other Biographical Writings* (Cambridge: Cambridge University Press, 1990), p. 28.

33. Huston, *Open Book*, p. 360, relates how excited the man was when he was shown the daily rushes of himself on screen. It was the first time he had ever seen movie film and he said (through an interpreter), 'We will never die!'

34. Saeed Jaffrey, *Saeed: An Actor's Journey* (London: Constable, 1998), pp. 194-200, discusses this. He explains how he concocted an Eastern-sounding language which was a mixture of Hindi and Arabic to make the film feel more authentic to the region. Thus, his character Billy Fish introduces himself as Macchendra Bahadur Gurung ('the brave fish from the Gurung clan').

Ultimately this becomes the means whereby Kipling agrees to assist his Lodge brother Carnehan and pass a message on to Dravot at Marwar Junction.[35] In addition, the very first scenes in the film effectively add yet another layer to the complex framing technique of the short story in that they have Peachey Carnehan approach the newspaperman Kipling in his offices at *The Northern Star* and announce that he has returned from the adventures in Kafiristan. After asking for and receiving a drink, Carnehan reminds Kipling of their first meeting on the train from Lahore some three years ago. In contrast, in the short story the narrative opens with the encounter between Carnehan and Kipling on the train from Lahore, while the return of Carnehan from Kafiristan to Kipling's office takes place much later in the storyline.

Another crucial addition to the storyline concerns the historical framing of it against the backdrop of the history of the region. Much is made in the film of the conquering of Kafiristan by Alexander the Great in 328 BCE, which effectively allows Danny, in particular, to be portrayed as the reincarnation of this revered ruler of the past. Not only is Danny addressed as Sikander the Second (*Sikander* being a local corruption of *Alexander*), but the central city where the chief priest lives and from which Danny rules is known as Sikandergul—city of Sikander (as Billy Fish at one point patiently explains). Most importantly, the historical backdrop of Alexander the Great allows Huston to name the woman whom Danny attempts to marry, thereby bringing about his own downfall (in Kipling's story the would-be wife of the would-be king is never named). In the film the woman is given the name Roxanne, the name of the daughter of the Bactrian ruler Oxyartes, who married Alexander in 327 BCE. A further link between Alexander the Great and Daniel Dravot/Sikander the Second is thus forged.

Finally, we note one further crucial addition to the storyline within the film. This concerns Daniel Dravot's ability to survive after having been shot in the chest with an arrow during the first military skirmish with the native peoples of Kafiristan. The arrow strikes the ammunition belt that Dravot wears under his tunic and he miraculously plucks the arrow from his chest, an action which results in the native people falling down and worshipping him as a god. This 'sacred arrow' then becomes a symbol of

---

35. This somewhat bizarre episode in the book was based on a true incident in Kipling's life involving fellow-Masons. He relates it in a letter to Margaret Burne-Jones dated 27 January 1888. See Thomas Pinney (ed.), *The Letters of Rudyard Kipling, Volume 1: 1872–1889* (London: Macmillan, 1990), pp. 152-53, for details.

Dravot's imperial power and he carries it through much of the film as a conquering British military officer might carry a swaggering stick. The significance of this arrow incident is hard to overestimate within the overall storyline of the film. It provides a tangible reason for the Kafiristani people to begin to worship Daniel Dravot as a god, something which the short story never quite manages to convey clearly. Indeed, there is even a deliberate shot of the arrow being trampled underfoot by the angry crowd of people from Sikandergul after they realize that they have been duped by Peachey and Dravot.

We turn now to consider how the theological themes identified above as integral to the storyline of Kipling's work are handled within Huston's film.

Intimations of Passion for the Would-Be Kings

What about the three-fold passion predictions of the Kumharsen Serai, so suggestive within Kipling's short story? How are these portrayed in the film? Somewhat surprisingly (given the closeness of the screenplay to the short story), none of these intimations as to the fate that awaits the would-be Kings of Kafiristan is depicted within Huston's film. The closest thing that we get to them is a suggestive little warning uttered by Kipling to the pair of intrepid adventurers as they prepare their camels laden with the concealed Martini rifles and ammunition. He says, 'Don't do it! The odds are too great'. However, the film does have its own special way of hinting at the passion that Dravot and Carnehan will eventually endure, one which owes its genius to Huston himself and his passion for Kipling's poetry. The film opens with scenes of Kipling working late into the night at his desk. He is a journalist for *The Northern Star* (an alteration to the short story which gives the name of the paper as *The Backwoodsman*), and he is writing some verses to be included within the paper. The sharp-eyed critics of Kipling will note the significance of the verses that he is shown to be composing: they are the opening lines from 'The Ballad of Boh Da Thone', a poem written in 1888 about an incident during the Burma War (1883–85) involving the rebel leader mentioned in the title. Kipling writes:

> Boh Da Thone was a warrior bold:
> His sword and his rifle were bossed with gold,
> And the Peacock Banner his henchmen bore
> Was stiffened with bullion, but stiffer with gore.

This is the first clue as to what will be the eventual fate of Daniel Dravot: Bo Da Thone was also killed for his rebellion against the imperial forces, the powers that be, and his head was sent to the military officer, Captain O'Neil, who had pursued him for so long. In short, anyone familiar with 'The Ballad of Boh Da Thone' would know that it is a tale which ends in a gruesome beheading. The stage is thus set to see how Daniel Dravot and Peachey Carnehan will fare in comparison.

The Crucifixion of Peachey Carnehan

Huston's film does not dwell upon the crucifixion of Peachey Carnehan as such. It does not depict the crucifixion itself, although it might well have done so. However, the episode in the story where Peachey reveals to the narrator (Kipling) that he was crucified by the angry Kafiristani people is quite faithfully portrayed within the film. In fact, we have two scenes in which Peachey is shown talking to Kipling after his arduous return across the Himalayas.

The first occurs at the very beginning of the film where Peachy first approaches Kipling and announces that he has returned and then proceeds to tell his story (which is then narrated through most of the rest of the film). The second is at the very end of the film when Peachey concludes his story, reveals his own passion, and leaves the head of his beloved companion Daniel Dravot on the desk. Michael Caine's rather gruesome make-up certainly adds to the overall effect of these scenes, as does the horrified expression on the face of Christopher Plummer (in his role as Kipling) when he beholds the spectacle of the shrivelled head. The fate of Dravot, together with the crucifixion of Peachey himself, is thus portrayed in this fashion:

Peachey: And old Danny fell, round and round and round and round, like a penny whirligig, twenty thousand miles. But it took him half an hour to fall before he struck the rocks. And do you know what they did to Peachey? They crucified him, Sir, between two pine trees. As Peachey's hands will show. (*He lifts his mangled hands to illustrate.*) And poor Peachey, who never did them any harm, he just hung there and he screamed. But he didn't die. And the next day they come, and they took him down, and they said it was a miracle he wasn't dead. And they let him go. And Peachey come home in about a year. And the mountains tried to fall on old Peachey. But he was quite safe because Daniel walked before him And Daniel *never* let go of Peachey's hand; and Peachey never let go of Daniel's head.

Kipling: His *head*?

Peachey: (*nodding*) You knew Danny, Sir?

Kipling: Oh, yes!

Peachey: You knew, most worshipful Brother, Daniel Dravot, Esquire. (*Peachey removes a leather bag from under his cloak and places it on the desk.*) Well, he became the King of Kafiristan, with a crown on his head. And that's all there is to tell. I'll be on my way now, Sir. I've got urgent business in the south. I have to meet a man at Marwar Junction. (*He shuffles, painfully, out of the room. Kipling moves forward to unwrap the leather bag and finds it contains the dessicated head of Daniel Dravot, complete with golden crown. The reporter falls back, astonished, as the camera focuses in upon the head, blurs its focus, and the theme music and final credits begin to run.*)

The Re-worked 'Son of God' Hymn by Reginald Heber

In Huston's film version of Kipling's story Daniel Dravot is made to sing the fifth and sixth verses of the hymn immediately prior to his execution. He sings the fifth verse, including the opening line 'The Son of *God* goes forth to war', as the crowd of angry villagers surrounds him. The sixth verse is sung as he stands on one of the rope bridges which connect Sikandergul with the outside world. The guy-lines to the bridge are cut by one of the priests of Sikandergul under the orders of Kefu-Selim and Daniel plunges headlong to his death in the valley below, leaving the final line of the sixth stanza to be sung by a weeping and choking Peachey Carnehan. Interestingly, he alters the line slightly, changing the plural 'their' to a singular 'his', as if to emphasize the significance of Daniel as a martyr whose example is worthy of emulation.

The hymn is sung to a rousing tune that serves as a leitmotif throughout the film. Maurice Jarre's tune is heard over the opening credits, in addition to several other key scenes in the film. A variation of it is heard in a scene depicting a military parade by the people of the Bashkai as they march onto a neighbouring city in the area. In this instance, native instruments such as yak horns, kettle drums and cymbals are used, but the tune is clearly recognizable amid the cacophony. The same variation is heard during the closing credits. Most importantly, vv. 1 and 5 of the hymn are sung by Danny as he and Peachey cross over the Himalayan mountains into Afghanistan. Peachey warnes him against the danger of causing an avalanche due to his raucous singing, and Dravot utters a line in reply which is taken straight from the short story, 'If a king can't sing, it ain't worth being a king!' Finally, the music of the hymn is also heard during the closing scenes as Peachey Carnehan leaves the head of Daniel Dravot, wrapped in a cloth and sporting his golden crown, with Kipling at his office at *The Northern Star*. At one level, the deliberate alteration that Kipling makes to Heber's hymn (the change of 'Son of God' to 'Son of Man') is lost within the film adaptation. This happens in two ways. First, Danny's singing of v. 1 in the Himalayan mountains keeps Heber's original opening line intact, with 'The Son of God goes forth to war' clearly heard in the form of Sean Connery's rich baritone voice. In short, here it is not 'the Son of *Man*' who goes forth, but the 'Son of *God*'. Second, the film ends not with Peachey's death and the mysterious disappearance of the crowned head of Daniel Dravot (as does the short story), but with Peachey shuffling slowly out of Kipling's office, having deposited his precious cargo on the desk. Peachey thus leaves the newspaper reporter, and the viewer, to contemplate the significance of the shrunken and crowned head of Daniel Dravot. In other words, there is no depiction of the final episode of the short story where Peachey sings the 'Son of Man' hymn. Nor is there any depiction of Peachey's death a few days later among the missionaries at the asylum. In the short story the narrator attempts to discover what has happened to the severed head of the executed king of Kafiristan, but to no avail—it has vanished, like the earthly body of the resurrected Christ, and is no longer available to confirm the extraordinary events which had taken place. Unfortunately, we see nothing of this open-endedness with regard to Dravot's remains within the film. All of which is to say that the ending is perhaps the most unsatisfactory feature of Huston's film, for it provides no proper closure for the character Peachey Carnehan. As viewers we are left wondering what happens to him. We are given no hint as to where he goes and how he discharges his responsibility as a 'son of man' who follows in the train of his friend and fellow-king, Daniel Dravot, whose blood-red banner (his reddish, blood-stained beard?) has gone before him. However, despite the fact that there is no altered 'The Son of Man goes forth to war' hymn within the film, there is one explicit reference to 'Son of Man' in it. This is in a scene which has no parallel within the short story, but does nevertheless serve as a point of connection to the citation of the first stanza of Heber's hymn at the end of the story as mentioned above. It occurs after Danny has made his fateful decision to take the beautiful, but deadly, Roxanne as his wife. Billy Fish comes to Peachey and expresses his worry about this decision and the impact that it will have among the priests of Sikandergul, and through them upon the people of Kafiristan. In particular, he is concerned about the natural signs of the displeasure of the chief god Imbra (animals miscarrying, failure of crops, etc.). The following exchange takes place between the two men:

Peachey: Well, Billy, what's going on?
Billy Fish: Times very bad, Peachey! Priests open up birds. All green inside, and stinking most horrid! Imbra very angry!

Peachey: They probably cut the spleen. The green's only bile. Don't worry, Billy. The girl won't go up in smoke. I'll promise you that.

Billy Fish: Girl don't matter! Many girls here. No difference. Two girls more or less. But cows, now. They dry up! And goats throw babies too soon. And corn do not ripen. Everybody go hungry!

Peachey: Now Billy, you know as well as I do that Dravot's no god. He himself told you about the arrow.

Billy Fish: Then priests must be mistaken about Imbra. He not angry because god marrying mortal. But because Son of Man pretend to be a god.

Indeed, the interplay between 'Son of Man' and 'Son of God' implied within this dialogue is remarkably reminiscent of one of the most theologically significant lines within Kipling's story. As we have already noted, the film portrays Peachey telling Kipling (the narrator) about his crucifixion. However, Peachey's speech (as it appears in the story) is cut short within the film and he is not allowed to go on to describe what the villagers did to him after they took him down from the pine trees of his crucifixion. Kipling's short-story goes on to have Peachey say, 'They were cruel enough to feed him up in the temple, because they said he was more of a God than old Daniel that was a man' (p. 103). Humanity and divinity are thus carefully juxtaposed and the reader is left to contemplate how one relates to the other. Is Peachey 'more of a God' simply because he survives the crucifixion? Or is it that he somehow manages to convey the true nature of kingship in his dealings with the Kafiristani people over the past three years? Or could it be that the false divinity of Daniel Dravot is cast aside in favour of his true humanity, particularly as he takes full responsibility for the situation and willingly gives up his life for the sake of his friend Peachey? In this sense, Dravot might be said to discover his true kingship at the very moment that he lays aside his false kingship. In other words, he enters into his divinity precisely as he acknowledges his humanity.

In the end, Kipling doesn't offer a definitive answer as to the meaning of this theological conundrum. He is content to pose the question and leave us as readers to contemplate its enormity. It seems that by means of the alteration of a single word within the short story (the change of the first line of Heber's hymn from 'Son of *God*' to 'Son of *Man*'), Kipling points suggestively to the wonder and mystery of the incarnation itself. In short, this is the unfathomable secret of 'The Man Who Would Be King'.

Conclusion

I have sought within this study to explore something of the Christian imagery which underlies Kipling's beloved short story 'The Man Who Would Be King', as well as John Huston's imaginative adaptation of the work to film. We might even be tempted to think that insofar as Peachey Carnehan has managed to survive the terrible crucifixion between two pine trees, and make a subsequent appearance before the astonished narrator/ newspaper reporter (Kipling), he stands as something of a Christ-figure who has undergone terrible suffering.[36] Such a 'second-coming' on the part of Peachey is certainly unexpected, if not miraculous, and one is left wondering if this was part of Kipling's original intentions in writing the story, or even of Huston's intentions in adapting it. Whatever we might think about the implications of such a suggestion for assessing both Kipling's and Huston's primary intentions and aims within their work, it seems certain that 'The Man Who Would Be King' will remain one of the most imaginative, and memorable, of fictional stories exploring the nature of kingship and imperial rule.

36. Harry Ricketts, *The Unforgiving Minute: A Life of Rudyard Kipling* (London: Chatto & Windus, 1998), p. 331, suggests that the death of Kipling's only son John during the First World War altered the way in which he used biblical allusions in his writing. Prior to his son's death the Old Testament predominated, but after his death allusions and images from the New Testament became much more prevalent, as if the idea of sacrificial death of the Son/son becomes a fixation.

THE COMPOSER OF SACRED MUSIC AS AN
INTERPRETER OF THE BIBLE

Wendy J. Porter

Introduction

The role of the composer of sacred music as an interpreter of the Bible is one yet to be fully explored. The musical settings of biblical texts can provide not only insights into the composer's interpretation of the passage itself but also a window into the history of interpretation as it is represented at the time of the composition. Approaches that a composer may have taken include altering a biblical passage, juxtaposing several biblical passages together, using a non-biblical text to provide commentary on a biblical one, or specifically setting individual words or phrases in a way that highlights them.

I would like to comment briefly on five specific works that span the two millennia of Christianity. Each one contributes uniquely to the corpus of sacred music, in that the composer has interpreted some aspect of the Bible. The first two are not works that can easily be performed—the first, because there is no musical notation, and the second, because both the text and the music are fragmentary and the musical notation itself can only be read with some difficulty. The first of these two is in Greek, is found in the New Testament and has sometimes been referred to as 'the earliest Christian hymn';[1] the second is also in Greek, but is written on a scrap of papyrus (P.Oxy. 1786) and is the earliest known example of a Christian hymn with musical notation. The final three examples are readily available in recorded form: the first of these is a Latin work by an English composer of the Reformation period in Britain, John Sheppard; the second is a German motet by Johann Sebastian Bach; and the final work is a Latin

---

1. G.S. Barrett, *The Earliest Christian Hymn* (London: James Clarke, 1897), p. 6. Of course, other passages in the New Testament might also have this claim made about them, such as Phil. 2.6-11.

motet by the twentieth-century French composer, Francis Poulenc.

What do these five disparate works—separated by centuries or even millennia—have in common that could possibly draw them into the same discussion? In some respects, very little; yet each one has a specific relationship to the New Testament and to the Christian Church. This is the common thread that I would like to follow throughout this grouping, by presenting the text, introducing the composer, identifying some features about the work and, finally, discussing one or more aspects about the composer's role in interpreting the biblical passage found within the work. In each case, the composer has contributed some form of interpretation of the biblical passage.

1 Timothy 3.16: An Early Christian Hymn
(First Century)

The Text

καὶ ὁμολογουμένως μέγα ἐστίν τὸ τῆς εὐσεβείας μυστήριον·
  ὃς ἐφανερώθη ἐν σαρκί,
     ἐδικαιώθη ἐν πνεύματι,
     ὤφθη ἀγγέλοις,
     ἐκηρύχθη ἐν ἔθνεσιν,
     ἐπιστεύθη ἐν κόσμῳ,
     ἀνελήμφθη ἐν δόξῃ.

And beyond all question, the mystery of godliness is great:
  who was manifested in a body,
     was vindicated by the Spirit,
     was seen by angels,
     was preached among the nations,
     was believed on in the world,
     was taken up in glory.

The Composer

Traditionally, Paul the Apostle has been thought to be the author of 1 Timothy, which would date the letter to about 62–63 CE. However, many scholars now think that the letter is pseudepigraphal and was written later than the time of Paul, with proposals ranging from the end of the first century to as late as mid-second century.[2] There is still significant

2. For a brief overview of the various positions on dating, see D. Guthrie, *New Testament Introduction* (Downers Grove, IL: Inter-Varsity Press, rev. edn, 1970),

evidence for Pauline authorship of 1 Timothy, which I tend to accept, but it will be seen that the present discussion is not necessarily dependent on this view.

There is a similar lack of consensus regarding who wrote the specific passage found in 1 Tim. 3.16. Since the beginning of the twentieth century, the view that has found increasing acceptance is that the writer of 1 Timothy, whether Paul or a later writer, quoted an early Christian hymn or credal statement.[3] Nonetheless, assuming that Paul did write the letter, it remains entirely possible that he also wrote the passage in 3.16. First, it is early in the history of the Christian Church for there to have existed such a theologically developed Christian hymn to quote if Paul did not write it himself. Secondly, we know of no other writer besides Paul who could have written this hymnic passage so early in the period. If there was someone else, we would surely have heard the name of this person or at least of his fame, and would have some indication of his writing.[4] Thirdly, the shift in the style of writing of the verse is frequently cited as evidence for a quotation of another writer, but this shift can be accounted for in the fact that this is a different genre of writing than the surrounding letter.[5] Whether or not Paul had written the section earlier than the time of writing the letter, so that he is quoting himself, is not particularly relevant here. It seems to me that Paul is the reasonable choice for the author of the passage in v. 16.

pp. 623-24. For discussion of the implications of authorship, see, S.E. Porter, 'Pauline Authorship and the Pastoral Epistles: Implications for Canon', *BBR* 5 (1995), pp. 105-23; cf. D. Guthrie, *The Pastoral Epistles: An Introduction and Commentary* (TNTC; Leicester: Inter-Varsity Press; Grand Rapids: Eerdmans, rev. edn, 1990), pp. 224-40.

3.　E. Norden, *Agnostos Theos: Untersuchungen zur Formengeschichte religiöser Rede* (Stuttgart: Teubner, 1913; repr. Darmstadt: Wissenschaftliche Buchgesellschaft, 1956), pp. 250-63. See the recent analysis and critique of this subject in S.E. Fowl, *The Story of Christ in the Ethics of Paul: An Analysis of the Function of the Hymnic Material in the Pauline Corpus* (JSNTSup, 36; Sheffield: JSOT Press, 1990), pp. 37-45.

4.　This would also make Paul the likely candidate as author of v. 16 even if he did not write the letter.

5.　The argument that the first word, ὅς, is an indication that the 'quotation' is drawn from a larger text could also be evidence for Paul's role as an interpreter in his use of language. Paul may refer back to the neuter word 'mystery' in the opening statement by using the masculine relative pronoun ὅς, since a similar shift from neuter to masculine is found in Col. 2.2: 'in order that they may know the mystery of God, namely Christ', where the author 'personifies' the mystery as the person of Christ.

The Passage and Features of its Interpretation

Here we encounter the question of whether this passage is a hymn or a credal statement. In Ralph Martin's outlining of characteristics of a creed compared with those that would define a hymn,[6] it is apparent that the categories are not exclusive. In fact, in Martin's article, 1 Tim. 3.16 fits with some of the criteria of a creed, but, in even more cases, with those of a hymn. Some of the features that are known to be characteristics of ancient hymns are worth noting. For instance, the Greek word ὕμνος was used for many centuries in Greek classical culture before Christianity's inception. For instance, at least since the time of Homer, a hymn was a song of adoration to a god. This can be seen in the Homeric hymns,[7] but also in a later example, such as Cleanthes' *Hymn to Zeus*.[8] Performance of a hymn addressed to a god was even the focus of competitions in the ancient world.[9] In Stephen Fowl's investigation of New Testament hymns, he discusses perspectives that early Christians may have had of hymns. Although the word they used was the same, there are differences in usage that must be taken into account. When the hymn was introduced into New Testament literature, the sense was radically altered from its previous usage. For instance, although the Greek meaning of hymn was a song of adoration *to a god*, the passage in 1 Timothy is not addressed *to God*, but is written in such a way that it is specifically *about Christ*. From the perspective of a Greek-speaking Jew, a hymn might represent what is found in the headings of some of the Psalms that are not songs of praise, but are nonetheless addressed *to God*. Here again the same distinction must be made, and that is that the 1 Timothy passage is not addressed *to God*, but is *about Christ*.[10] Using these Greek and Jewish definitions,

6.   R.P. Martin, 'Aspects of Worship in the New Testament Church', *Vox Evangelica* 2 (1963), pp. 6-32 (14-17). For a much more recent treatment, see Fowl, *Story of Christ*, pp. 31-45.

7.   T.W. Allen and E.E. Sikes, *The Homeric Hymns* (London: Macmillan, 1904).

8.   *SVF* I, no. 537.

9.   See I. Henderson, 'Ancient Greek Music', in E. Wellesz (ed.), *The New Oxford History of Music*. I. *Ancient and Oriental Music* (London: Oxford University Press, 1957), pp. 336-403 (363): ' "The First Delphic Hymn" or paean to Apollo...was composed almost certainly in the later second century B.C., and written in the "vocal" notation on stone at Delphi, where it must have won a prize in the Pythian festival'. For a recent treatment of this subject, see M.L. West, *Ancient Greek Music* (Oxford: Clarendon Press, 1992), pp. 14-21.

10.   Fowl, *Story of Christ*, pp. 31-34.

1 Tim. 3.16 would not strictly be considered a hymn. However, Fowl comments that the term hymn can still be used for what we find in 3.16, for the definition is 'the construction of a later, critical community, and not a straightforward translation of ὕμνος in either its specific or generic sense'.[11] As a result, the passage in 3.16 might still be called a hymn, but a hymn in a new sense. This hymn is perhaps one of the early templates for Christian hymns, a pattern that can be seen in hymns of the Christian faith throughout the centuries to follow.[12]

The structure and language of this hymn are also indicators of the interpretive role in which the writer is engaged. 1 Tim. 3.16 uses a different style of writing that sets it apart from the rest of the letter.[13] The writing is extremely compact, using a total of eighteen words in six lines. Some commentators divide these lines into three groups of two lines each, and some divide it into two groups of three lines each, but in either case, the writing is distinctly poetical.[14] However, the content of these six lines is expansive, summarizing six events in which Christ is central. The use of the six verbs in the passive voice are a means by which Christ is understood as the grammatical subject of each phrase. This may be a new way of writing a hymn, that is, using language to poignantly highlight important events that are focused on Christ but are not written as though addressed to him. Paul may have reinvented the procedure of hymn writing as he interpreted the story of Christ in these six brief and memorable lines.

Finally, the context of 1 Timothy in which this hymn is placed has implications for the role of Paul as an interpreter. The simple fact that this hymn was placed within the letter provides not only an insight into the author's view of the story of Christ, but also how he saw it functioning within the larger context of the letter.[15] For the sake of brevity, I will mention just one point. Throughout 1 Timothy, a recurring subject is that of negative forms of speech, such as 'meaningless talk' (1.6), 'malicious talkers' (3.11), 'godless myths and old wives' tales' (4.7), 'gossips and

---

11. Fowl, *Story of Christ*, p. 33.

12. See also W.J. Porter, 'Sacred Music at the Turn of the Millennia', in S.E. Porter *et al.* (eds.), *Faith in the Millennium* (Roehampton Institute London Papers, 7; JSNTSup; Sheffield: Sheffield Academic Press [in preparation]).

13. See Norden, *Agnostos Theos*, pp. 250-63.

14. See Martin, 'Aspects of Worship', pp. 22-26.

15. Fowl, *Story of Christ*, pp. 175-94.

busybodies' (5.13), 'unhealthy interest in controversies and quarrels about words...malicious talk' (6.4-5), and 'godless chatter' (6.20). The emphasis here seems to prompt Paul to invoke not only several 'trustworthy sayings', which may stem from earlier sources,[16] but also the hymn in 3.16, which may well be his own. The hymn can be seen as a means to oppose the then current hold that asceticism had on the Church, as well as the generally destructive effects of negative speech among its members.[17] The succinct and poetical nature of the words of the hymn, particularly apparent in its Greek form with its six passive verbs, makes it a hymn that is highly memorable and easy to say (or sing), even though the content of the hymn still engages scholars 2000 years later.

P.Oxy. 1786: A Christian Hymn with Musical Notation (Third Century)

The Text

]ομου πασαι τε θεου λογιμοι α[   ]αρ
]υτανηω σιγατω μηδ' αστρα φαεσφορα λ[αμπ]ε
[σ]θων [απ]ολειπ [οντων] ρ[ιπαι πνοιων πηγαι] ποταμων ροθιων
πασαι υμνουντων δ' ημων
[π]ατερα χυιον χ' αγιον πνευμα πασαι δυναμεις επιφωνουντων αμην
αμην κρατος αινος
[αει και δοξα θεωι] δ[ωτ]η[ρι] μονωι παντων αγαθων αμην αμην[18]

16. See the discussion in G.W. Knight, III, *The Faithful Sayings in the Pastoral Letters* (Kampen: Kok, 1968), pp. 148-52.

17. See Guthrie, *Pastoral Epistles*, pp. 39-43 (42-43).

18. This reading of the text is largely that of M.L. West, 'Analecta Musica', *ZPE* 92 (1992), pp. 1-54 (47), following E. Pöhlmann, with reconstructions included in square brackets. It is presented here in a way that visually represents the lines as they are seen on the papyrus fragment.

E. Pöhlmann's edition (*Denkmäler altgriechischer Musik: Sammlung, Übertragung und Erläuterung aller Fragmente und Fälschungen* [Nürnberg: Verlag Hans Carl, 1970], pp. 106-109) includes a reconstruction of the possible beginning part of the text, with translation, as follows:

[Σὲ πάτερ κόσμων, πάτερ αἰώνων, μέλπωμεν] ὁμοῦ πᾶσαί τε θεοῦ λόγιμοι δο[ῦλα]ι. [ὅσ]α κ[όσμος]
[ἔχει πρὸς ἐπουρανίων ἁγίῳ σελάων πρ]υτανήῳ, σιγάτω, μηδ' ἄστρα φαεσφόρα λ[αμπ]έ⁻
[σ]θων, [ἀπ]ολειπ[όντων] ῥ[ιπαὶ πνοιῶν, πηγαὶ] ποταμῶν ῥοθίων πᾶσαι.
ὑμνούντων δ' ἡμῶν

M.L. West's translation: '…Let it be silent, let the luminous stars not shine, let the winds(?) and all the noisy rivers die down; and as we hymn the Father, the Son, and the Holy Spirit, let all the powers add "Amen, amen". Empire, praise always, and glory to God, the sole giver of all good things. Amen, amen.'[19]

E. Werner's translation: '…all splendid creations of God…must not keep silent, nor shall the light-bearing stars remain behind… All waves of thundering streams shall praise our Father and Son, and Holy Ghost, all powers shall join in: Amen, Amen! Rule and Praise (and Glory) to the sole Giver of all Good. Amen, Amen'.[20]

The Composer

It is unknown who originally wrote this hymn or who wrote it down with its musical notation, but it is dated to the latter part of the third century.[21] The fact that the hymn was written down may suggest that it had been known previously, for the passing on of music was largely by means of oral tradition and this would have been the means to preserve the hymn. In that case, it may represent beliefs and musical practices of the Church from some time earlier than the late third century There is also some reason to believe, however, that the hymn was a new composition.[22] In either case, the hymn is representative of at least some aspects of the music of the Christian Church in the latter part of the third century.

The Work

This musical fragment was found written on the back of a papyrus that had earlier been used to record an account for corn. The fragment was

[π]ατέρα χυἱὸν χἅγιον πνεῦμα πᾶσαι δυνάμεις ἐπιφωνούντων ἀμὴν ἀμὴν. κράτος ἆινος
[ἀεὶ καὶ δόξα θεῶ] δ[ωτ]ῆ[ρι] μọνῳ πάντων ἀγαθῶν. ἀμὴν ἀμήν.

…[Father of the world, Father eternal, celebrate with song and dance as one all creatures of God, notable slaves. As far as the world has toward the holy heaven shine to the president(?), be not silent stars shine…]

19. West, *Ancient Greek Music*, p. 325.

20. E. Werner, 'Music', in G.A. Buttrick (ed.), *The Interpreter's Dictionary of the Bible* (4 vols.; Nashville, TN: Abingdon Press, 1962), III, pp. 457-69 (467-68).

21. See the original edition of this papyrus by B.P. Grenfell and A.S. Hunt, '1786. Christian Hymn with Musical Notation', in *The Oxyrhynchus Papyri*, XV (Egyptian Exploration Society Graeco-Roman Memoirs; London: Egypt Exploration Society, 1922), pp. 21-25 (21).

22. West ('Analecta Musica', p. 50) suggests this by his reference to the composer having studied the works of the composer Mesomedes.

analyzed and first published in 1922 by two of the great early papyrologists, B.P. Grenfell and A.S. Hunt. They called it a 'Christian Hymn with Musical Notation' in that first publication and, to this day, this particular fragment, known as P.Oxy. 1786,[23] remains the earliest known Christian hymn with musical notation (although some recently edited documents may have some bearing on this particular claim).[24]

There is much discussion about the foundations of the hymn itself. Scholars such as Grenfell and Hunt came from a classical background and commented on the Greek influence that they saw in the text and in the notation of the hymn. They provided some clues as to its environment (found as it was in Oxyrhynchus, Egypt), its function, and even its possible sound. The papyrus with its musical notation was thought to give insight into hymns and hymn writing of the third-century Christian Church, and possibly earlier. However, a question that must be raised is how the text of the hymn fits with statements by some scholars that nonbiblical texts were not used in the Christian Church at this time. Was this, perhaps, considered a 'biblical' text at the time?[25]

Towards the middle of the twentieth century, scholars such as Eric Werner began to argue for an almost exclusively Jewish background to, and influence on, the hymn. Werner posited that the formulaic 'Amen, Amen' found near the end and again at the very end of the musical fragment had been taken over almost directly from Jewish chant. He based his statement on the melismatic characteristics of the music on the words 'Amen, Amen' and on the corresponding melismatic nature of Jewish

23. Grenfell and Hunt, 'Christian Hymn with Musical Notation', pp. 21-25.

24. There is now the possibility that the newly edited fragments of P.Oxy. 4462, which are dated to the second century, could fit in this category. See M.L. West, 'Texts with Musical Notation', in M.W. Haslam *et al.* (eds.), *Oxyrhynchus Papyri*, LXV (Egypt Exploration Society Graeco-Roman Memoirs, 85; London: Egypt Exploration Society, 1998), pp. 81-102 (88), where West writes: 'It looks as if these verses may have been of a philosophical or religious cast', and remarks on similarities to Gregory of Nazianzen, *Carm.* 2.2.4.55.

25. M.H. Shepherd (*IDB*, II, p. 668) writes about 'the reaction in orthodox circles, about the turn of the third century, against the use in the liturgy of all nonbiblical psalms and hymns. It was not until the middle of the fourth century that Christian hymnody once more blossomed in the church's worship'. This does raise some questions as to what status this particular hymn had in the context of the Christian Church: was it acceptable in the Church liturgy or was it perhaps only used in a private context?

chant.[26] However, in M.L. West's recently published editions of new fragments of texts with musical notation, he writes that two of the new texts 'reveal that the evolution of the melisma had gone further by the third century than we were aware'.[27] In other words, the use of more than one note for a syllable, found on the 'amen, amen' of P.Oxy. 1786, is now thought to have been used much earlier in Greek music than was previously thought. This calls into question the positions of both Werner, who, based on the use of melismatic formulas or several notes per syllable in Jewish music, posited that this was a specifically Jewish feature,[28] and Egon Wellesz, who argued that the hymn must be specifically Syrian in background, also because of the melismatic nature of Syrian music.[29]

The system of notation used in this hymn is generally agreed to be Greek. The notes are roughly equivalent to a modern tenor part, ranging an octave from F below middle C to F above middle C. The symbols used for vocal notation, at least in this range of the voice, are taken basically from the Greek alphabet, with increasing adaptation of the letters as one moves further away from the middle range, either higher or lower.[30] The symbols used in P.Oxy. 1786 are written above the words and are recognizable letters, such as: R ϕ c o ξ ι ζ ε. The rough equivalent of these notes to modern ones are R = F; ϕ = G; c = A; o = B; ξ = C; ι = D; ζ = E; ε = F. Other signs that are found indicate rests, lengthening of notes and legato. Because of the lacunae, scholars have offered various reconstructions and readings of both the text and the musical notation.[31]

26. Werner, 'Music', p. 467. Melisma refers to the use of multiple notes per syllable of text, as compared with the restrictive use of one note to each syllable.

27. West, 'Texts with Musical Notation', p. 81.

28. Various other studies have also called into question the notion of a predominantly Jewish influence, e.g., J.A. Smith, 'The Ancient Synagogue, the Early Church and Singing', *Music & Letters* 65.1 (1984), pp. 1-16; J. McKinnon, 'On the Question of Psalmody in the Ancient Synagogue', in I. Fenlon (ed.), *Early Music History: Studies in Medieval and Early Modern Music*, VI (ed. I. Fenlon; Cambridge: Cambridge University Press, 1986), pp. 159-91; and J. McKinnon (ed.), *Music in Early Christian Literature* (Cambridge Studies in the Literature of Music; Cambridge: Cambridge University Press, 1987); see also West, 'Analecta Musica', pp. 47-54.

29. E. Wellesz, *A History of Byzantine Music and Hymnography* (Oxford: Clarendon Press, 1961, 2nd rev. edn, 1961, repr. 1998), pp. 152-56 (155-56).

30. West, 'Analecta Musica', pp. 36-42.

31. See, e.g., T. Reinach, *La musique greque* (Editions d'aujourd'hui; Paris: Payot, 1926), pp. 207-208; J.F. Mountford, 'Greek Music in the Papyri and Inscriptions', in J.U. Powell and E.A. Barber (eds.), *New Chapters in the History of Greek Literature*

Questions of Interpretation

Grenfell and Hunt summarized the contents of the hymn as: 'Creation at large is called upon to join in a chorus of praise to Father, Son, and Holy Spirit, and the concluding passage is the usual ascription of power and glory to the "only giver of all good gifts" '.[32] A doxology, such as this 'usual ascription' might be termed, was already well established in the Christian Church by this time. M.A. Bischel writes that the lesser doxologies, such as the Latin *Gloria Patri* ('Glory be to the Father, and to the Son, and to the Holy Spirit: as it was in the beginning is now, and ever shall be, world without end. Amen'), were already in use in Rome at the time of Clement (c. 91), and that in later centuries a doxology was used after each psalm.[33] It is possible that this is how the doxology at the end of the hymn fragment is being used—formulaically—but it also suggests that the writer was integrating the Old Testament-like sections (see below) with the doxology, clearly placing the hymn within the Christian tradition by referring to 'the Father, the Son, and the Holy Spirit'.

Eric Werner states that the 'scriptural influence upon this composition is undeniable',[34] and mentions three psalms whose influence can be seen, Ps. 93.3-4, Ps. 148.4 and Ps. 19.1-2.[35]

Ps. 93.3-4	LXX (92.3-4)
The seas have lifted up, O Lord	ἐπῆραν οἱ ποταμοί, κύριε,
The seas have lifted up their voice;	ἐπῆραν οἱ ποταμοὶ φωνὰς αὐτῶν
The seas have lifted up their pounding waves	ἀπὸ φωνῶν ὑδάτων πολλῶν
Mightier than the thunder of the great waters	θαυμαστοὶ οἱ μετεωρισμοί; τῆς θαυλάσσης,
Mightier than the breakers of the sea—the Lord on high is mighty.	θαυμαστὸς ἐν ὑπηλοῖς ὁ κύριος,

(Second Series; Oxford: Clarendon Press, 1929), pp. 146-83 (177); Pöhlmann, *Denkmäler altgriechischer Musik*, pp. 106-109; and for discussion of the origin or adaptation of the musical notation, see West, 'Analecta Musica', pp. 36-46.

32. Grenfell and Hunt, 'Christian Hymn', p. 22.

33. M.A. Bischel, 'Hymns, Early Christian', *ABD* 3 (1992), p. 351.

34. Werner, 'Music', p. 467.

35. But here it must be remembered that this perceived influence is particularly dependent upon his translation, as opposed to West's, and that West is a classicist and a specialist in ancient Greek documents. West's translation, which negates the participation of all the elements, has quite a different focus than that found in these psalms.

Ps. 148.4	LXX (148.4)
Praise him, you highest heavens	αἰνεῖτε αὐτόν, οἱ οὐρανοὶ τῶν οὐρανῶν
And you waters above the skies.	καὶ τὸ ὕδωρ τὸ ὑπεράνω τῶν οὐρανῶν

Ps. 19.1-2	LXX (18.2-3)
The heavens declare the glory of God;	οἱ οὐρανοὶ διηγοῦνται δόξαν θεοῦ,
the skies proclaim the work of his hands.	ποίησιν δὲ χειρῶν οὑτοῦ ἀναγγέλλει τὸ στερέωμα
Day after day they pour forth speech; night after night they display knowledge.	ἡμέρα τῇ ἡμέρᾳ ἐρεύγεται ῥῆμα, καὶ νὺξ νυκτὶ ἀναγγέλλει γνῶσιν.

Several influences that Werner does not mention, however, are, for instance, Rev. 5.13, which includes part of the doxology:

> Then I heard every creature in heaven and on earth and under the earth and on the sea, and all that is in them, singing: 'To him who sits on the throne and to the Lamb be praise and honor and glory and <u>power, for ever</u> and ever!'.

> καὶ πᾶν κτίσμα ὃ ἐν τῷ οὐρανῷ καὶ ἐπὶ τῆς γῆς καὶ ὑποκάτω τῆς γῆς καὶ ἐπὶ τῆς θαλάσσης καὶ τὰ ἐν αὐτοῖς πάντα ἤκουσα λέγοντας τῷ καθημένῳ ἐπὶ τῷ θρόνῳ καὶ τῷ ἀρνίῳ ἡ εὐλογία καὶ ἡ τιμὴ καὶ ἡ δόξα καὶ τὸ κράτος εἰς τοὺς αἰῶνας τῶν αἰώνων.

and Rev. 7.11b-12:

> They fell down on their faces before the throne and worshiped God, <u>saying</u>: 'Amen! Praise and <u>glory</u> and wisdom and thanks and honor and <u>power</u> and strength be <u>to our God</u> for ever and ever. <u>Amen!</u>'

> καὶ ἔπεσαν ἐνώπιον τοῦ θρόνου ἐπὶ τὰ πρόσωπα αὐτῶν καὶ προσεκύνησαν τῷ θεῷ λέγοντες ἀμήν, ἡ εὐλογία καὶ ἡ δόξα καὶ ἡ σοφία καὶ ἡ εὐχαριστία καὶ ἡ τιμὴ καὶ ἡ δύναμις καὶ ἡ ἰσχὺς τῷ θεῷ ἡμῶν εἰς τοὺς αἰῶνας τῶν αἰώνων ἀμήν.

There are also some echoes of 1 Tim. 1.17:

> Now to the King <u>eternal</u>, immortal, invisible, <u>the only God</u>, be honor and <u>glory for ever</u> and ever. <u>Amen.</u>

> τῷ δὲ βασιλεῖ τῶν αἰώνων, ἀφθάρτῳ ἀοράτῳ <u>μόνῳ</u> θεῷ, τιμὴ καὶ δόξα εἰς τοὺς αἰῶνας τῶν αἰώνων, ἀμήν.

While there are only six examples of the use of some lexical form of the word ὑμνέω in the Greek New Testament (Mt. 26.30; Mk 14.26; Acts 16.25; Eph. 5.19; Col. 3.16; Heb. 2.12), there are many examples of it in the Septuagint. However, it is unclear whether there is significant influence from the Septuagint on this hymn, or whether it reflects the later writings of the New Testament and perhaps other writings of the period. Certainly there is some similarity with other hymn-like writing that precedes or is roughly contemporary with P.Oxy. 1786, such as where Clement of Alexandria writes of Terpander's hymn to Zeus: 'Zeus, beginning of all, ruler of all, Zeus, to you I send this beginning of hymns'.[36]

That textual criticism is a significant factor in determining even the basic reading of this text is seen in the different glosses of West and Werner. In West's version, the created elements are commanded to cease their normal activity while the created beings 'hymn' God, a common use of the term in Greek hymns.[37] In contrast, in Werner's version, the created elements are commanded to marshal their forces in the acclamation of praise to God. If West's translation of the fragmentary text is more accurate, then the Old Testament influence is less obvious at this point, since there are very few prayers in the Old Testament that command silence (see Hab. 2.20: 'But the Lord is in his holy temple; let all the earth be silent before him'). However, in Cleanthes' *Hymn to Zeus*, the statement in lines 38-39, 'For neither men nor gods have any greater privilege than this: to sing for ever in righteousness of the universal law',[38] by inference suggests that *only* men and gods have this privilege of hymning God.[39] Conversely, the reading of Werner, or of Grenfell and Hunt's original summary of 'Creation at large' being 'called upon to join in a chorus of praise to Father, Son, and Holy Spirit', brings the Old Testament influence more to the forefront; for instance, Ps. 148.5 calls upon all creation to 'praise the name of the Lord', with all manner of created beings and heavenly bodies and elements called upon to praise the name of the Lord.

In either case, this hymn seems to have some roots in the words of a psalm, some in verses such as are found in Revelation, and some in the

---

36. McKinnon (ed.), *Music in Early Christian Literature*, p. 35 no. 59, citing Clement of Alexandria, *Stromata* 6.11.88.

37. For phrasing similar to 'hymn God', see Cleanthes, *Hymn to Zeus*, line 6 (*SVF* I, no. 537): 'Therefore I shall hymn you and sing forever of your might', translation taken from A.A. Long and D.N. Sedley, *The Hellenistic Philosophers* (2 vols.; Cambridge: Cambridge University Press, 1977), II, p. 54.

38. *SVF*, I, no. 537, trans. in Long and Sedley, *Hellenistic Philosophers*, p. 54.

39. In contrast, the powers in P.Oxy. 1786 are commanded only to add 'Amen, Amen'.

language of Greek hymn writers. There are three distinct elements that distinguish the final form of this hymn. First, the composer in his interpretation of his sources, has changed reference from 'the Lord', which is found in the psalms of the Hebrew Bible or Old Testament, to 'the Father, Son and Holy Spirit', which incorporates a Christian element into this hymn. Secondly, he has integrated the Old and New Testaments rather than simply citing the Old Testament. Thirdly, he has incorporated language that is characteristic of sources such as Cleanthes' *Hymn to Zeus*. The result is that the composer of this hymn seems to have synthesized and reinterpreted earlier documents in an unprecedented way.

John Sheppard: Verbum caro factus est / 'The Word Was Made Flesh' (Sixteenth Century)

The Text

> *Verbum caro factum est et habitavit in nobis;*
> *cuius gloriam vidimus quasi unigeniti a patre,*
> *plenum gratiae et veritatis* (Jn 1.14).

> *In principio erat verbum et verbum erat apud Deum, et Deus erat verbum* (Jn 1.1).

> *Gloria Patri et Filio et Spiritui Sancto* (Doxology).[40]

> The word was made flesh and dwelt among us:
> and we beheld his glory as of the only Son of the Father,
> full of grace and truth (Jn 1.14).

> In the beginning was the Word, and the Word was with God, and the Word was God (Jn 1.1).

> Glory be to the Father and to the Son and to the Holy Spirit (Doxology).

---

40. A similar but not identical form of this text can be found in the *Liber Usualis Missae et Officii* (Typis Societatis S. Joannis Evang.; Paris, Tornaci and Rome: Desclée & Sons, 1929), *In Nativitate Domini*, Resp. 8, p. 357. The text reads as follows (with repetitions not indicated here): *Verbum caro factus est, et habitavit in nobis: et vidimus gloriam ejus, gloriam quasi Unigeniti a Patre, plenum gratiae et veritatis. Omnia per ipsum facta sunt, et sine ipso factum est nihil. Gloria Patri, et Filio, et Spiritui Sancto.* The Jn 1.1 text of the second part of Sheppard's setting is found in the first verse of Lesson IX, which follows the respond.

The Composer

John Sheppard (born as early as 1512[41] or as late as 1520,[42] died c. 1559/60) composed his music during the shift from Latin to the English vernacular in the Reformation in Britain. There is little documented about his life, but he is known to have been Master of the Choristers at Magdalen College, Oxford, in 1542.[43] As far as his musical output, however, le Huray says that 'In terms of sheer quantity Shepherd has no mid sixteenth-century rival'.[44] Because much of his music has only been systematically published in more recent years, little has been known about it.[45] Today, Sheppard's music is increasingly being included in the standard repertoire of cathedral, church and college choirs.

The Work

Sheppard's settings of responsories are a significant part of his oeuvre. Hugh Benham writes that the responds of Sheppard 'contain some of his most impressive writing',[46] part of the significance being in the fact that of the 16 choral responds, 12 of them are settings of texts that had not previously been set.[47] In the setting of *Verbum caro factum est*, we have one of those early settings.[48] The manuscript that includes this Latin respond-motet is housed at Christ Church, Oxford,[49] and the work is set for six

41. D. Chadd (trans. and ed.), *John Sheppard*: I: *Responsorial Music* (Early English Church Music, 17; London: Stainer & Bell, 1977), pp. ix-xi (ix).

42. H. Benham, *Latin Church Music in England 1460–1575* (London: Barrie & Jenkins, 1977), p. 195.

43. P. le Huray, *Music and the Reformation in England 1549–1660* (Cambridge Studies in Music; Cambridge: Cambridge University Press, repr. with corrections 1978 [London: Herbert Jenkins, 1967]), p. 208.

44. Le Huray, *Music and the Reformation*, p. 208.

45. This is largely due to the fact that entire parts of his music are missing, a common problem in music of this period, partly because of the practice of writing separate parts in separate books and, it is thought, partly because of the destruction that took place in the sixteenth century in English churches and cathedrals.

46. Benham, *Latin Church Music*, p. 197.

47. Benham, *Latin Church Music*, p. 197; see also, F.L. Harrison, *Music in Medieval Britain* (Buren, The Netherlands: Fritz Knuf, 1980), pp. 366-81 (370-72).

48. See M. Hofman and J. Morehen (eds.), *Latin Music in British Sources c1485–c1610* (EECM Sup. vol. II; London: Stainer & Bell, 1987), p. 174, who list only two settings of this Latin text known in British sources at this time, citing Sheppard's as the earliest setting, followed by only one other, that of (Edward?) Blancks (c. 1550–1633).

49. Mus. MS 979.

voice-parts: treble, mean, alto 1, alto 2, tenor and bass.[50] The setting is for Christmas Day, the ninth respond at Matins[51] (or the third respond of the third nocturn) and the processional respond at Mass.

There is a long history of responsorial psalmody, of which the responsory is a later development and variation. St Augustine, for instance, describes a psalm that is sung by a soloist, and mentions that the congregation responds with a short interjection, although the exact nature of this interjection is not known. It is thought that, at this time, an entire psalm was sung. Later, the psalm became abbreviated, until eventually a single verse of a psalm was used. Dom Gregory Murray writes that 'the regular form of a responsorial chant is that after the whole has been sung, the first section is repeated as far as the beginning of the verse'.[52] However, he also observes that 'the Roman method was to repeat the whole of the first part of a responsory, while the Gallican method (which now prevails in the Divine Office) was to repeat only the last clause of the R[esponse] after the V[erse]'.[53] Later, texts other than the Psalms were treated in a similar way. Benham defines a respond during the fifteenth and sixteenth centuries as

> a chant which followed a lesson, often commenting on it in some way... Every respond consisted of two main parts, the 'response' (begun by a soloist or small group of soloists, and continued by the choir) and the verse or verses (solo throughout). At its simplest the pattern was response, verse, latter part of response repeated... The third, sixth and ninth responds at Matins, and those at Vespers normally had the first part of the Gloria Patri as a second verse sung to the same melody as the first, after the repeat of the response; this was followed by a second, often shorter repeat...[54]

---

50. The tenor part of this setting is lost, but Harrison (*Music in Medieval Britain*, p. 370) writes that 'thanks to the monorhythmic method of writing the plainsong...it is possible to reconstruct with certainty those responds in which the cantus firmus was in the tenor', and, in note 4 (pp. 370-71), lists *Verbum caro factum est* as being one of those responds that has been reconstructed in this way.

51. But note that in the *Liber Usualis* (1929), p. 357, it is indicated as Resp. 8.

52. Dom Gregory Murray, *The Choral Chants of the Mass* (The Society of St Gregory, 7; Bristol: Burleigh Press, 1947), p. 16.

53. Murray, *Choral Chants*, p. 16.

54. Benham, *Latin Church Music*, pp. 17-18. See also A. Hughes, *Medieval Manuscripts for Mass and Office: A Guide to their Organization and Terminology* (Toronto: University of Toronto Press, 1982), pp. 26-33; W. Apel, *Gregorian Chant* (Bloomington, IN: Indiana University Press, 1958), pp. 95-96 and 182. See also Harrison, *Music in Medieval England*, p. 61, where he writes the following description:

This corresponds to the pattern that we see in Sheppard's setting. However, he sets the text in such a way that the reading of it is significant. This is in contrast to some settings where the common use of the style of the responsory or respond in Psalm texts progressively abbreviated the response of the choir until the text was unintelligible as a whole.[55]

The Interpretation

The text of Sheppard's responsory is short and comes from two verses in the New Testament as well as part of a traditional doxology of the Christian Church, known as the Lesser Doxology, which is included here in its traditional manner for the third respond of a nocturn (see note 52). The verses are quoted from the Latin *Vulgate*, the first being Jn 1.14, and the second Jn 1.1. The third is the doxology, which is not unlike the text of the baptismal command in Mt. 28.19. As mentioned above, one of Sheppard's significant contributions is that of setting to polyphonic music texts that had not otherwise been set in this manner. This particular setting represents one of those contributions, and the very nature of its setting contributes to a new way of reading the text, for even though it follows a familiar pattern, the pattern would have existed in the form of chant and not in a combination of polyphony and chant. The setting of Jn 1.14 and Jn 1.1 alternates between a single chant line, sung by three soloists in unison, and the polyphonic setting of all six voices, with the plainchant as *cantus firmus*. The use of this alternating pattern of chant and polyphony can also be seen, for instance, in the works of Sheppard's contemporary, Thomas Tallis. Benham's description of a responsory above corresponds basically with Sheppard's setting of this passage, but Benham continues:

'Though the antiphon and the respond both had their origin in the early forms of psalmody, they had, in general, distinct forms and ritual functions in the Middle Ages. While the antiphons were choral chants sung with a psalm the responds were more elaborate chants sung after lessons. Hence Matins with nine lessons had also nine responds. In its normal form a respond was begun by one or a few singers and continued by the choir; then the verse was sung by the soloist or soloists and the respond was repeated from mid-point by the chorus. The third, sixth and ninth responds at Matins, i.e., the third respond of each nocturn, were distinguished by the singing of the first half of the Gloria patri (to the same music as the verse) after the repeat, followed by the same or a still shorter repeat'.

55. See Hughes, *Medieval Manuscripts*, p. 27, who mentions that this practice of abbreviation occurred already in the ninth century.

> The earliest settings of responds, as of Alleluias, had polyphony for the solo sections. Choral treatment began much later than in the case of Alleluias, in Taverner's day...
>
> It is almost certain that Taverner's *Dum transisset* I and II are the first choral responds; but Tallis and Sheppard made the major contributions to the type, treating some sixteen new texts between them.[56]

Paul Doe writes that, before the first half of the sixteenth century, 'Earlier Responsory settings had been limited to a very small number of texts, mostly for Compline or certain ceremonies, in which only the solo parts of the plainsong were set in polyphony. These new festal Responsories, however, are fundamentally different in that they set the choral part of the chant', referring specifically to the 'transfer of polyphony from solo to choral chant, and the clear presentation of the plainsong as an equal-note *cantus firmus*'.[57] Sheppard's use of this new distribution of polyphony and plainchant between the parts, and his setting of the John passage, are the means by which he takes traditional elements and very subtly reworks them into a new interpretive work.

Within the individual lines of the polyphonic section of this work, Sheppard makes use of the highest note of each voice range to set up a formal and symmetrical pattern of emphasis. This use of the highest note in the upper four voices is clearly symmetrical between the three sections of the Jn 1.14 text: the highest note in the treble is used four times in section I, once in section II, and four times in section III; the highest note in the mean is used three times in section I, five times in section II, and three times in section III; in the first alto part, the usage of the highest note is three times in section I, four times in section II and three times in section III; and in the second alto part, the usage is evenly divided between the three sections, being used three times in each. The specific plan in evidence here is further supplemented in that each of these four upper voices uses the upper note of its range the same number of times: thirteen in each. In the lowest two voices, tenor and bass, the use of the highest note is heard only three times, and in this case, the division is spread between the two voices: the bass uses it in section I, the tenor in section II and the bass again in section III. It is difficult to determine the exact meaning of this structure, but it certainly suggests that Sheppard worked out his presentation of music and this text with great care and attention to

56. Benham, *Latin Church Music*, p. 18.

57. P. Doe, 'Latin Polyphony under Henry VIII', *Proceedings of the (Royal) Musical Association* 95 (1968–69), pp. 81-95 (93-94).

detail. The combination of the use of the highest notes of the individual six lines with the corresponding syllables of the words (where at least in three instances the highest note is used) gives a reading of the text that is emphasized or highlighted as follows:

I   *Ver*bum caro factum est et habi*ta*vit in *no*bis;
     (The *word* was made flesh and *dwelt* among *us*)

II   *cui*us *glori*am vidimus *qua*si unigeniti a *pat*re,
     (and *we* his *glory* beheld *as of* the only Son of the *Father*)

III plenum *grat*iae et veri*tat*is.
     (full of *grace* and *truth*)

A fairly natural reading of the text can be seen to be held in high esteem, although at this late stage in the development of Latin polyphony one might expect to see more focus simply on musical elaboration and perhaps even a disregard for the text.

There are also several elements of Sheppard's setting that make use of the unique features of responsories in order to reshape these particular texts. John 1.14 is the verse that is treated polyphonically, while the other two verses are sung in chant by the three designated soloists.[58] The pattern of repetition in the text is as follows:

> The word was made flesh and dwelt among us
> and dwelt among us
> and dwelt among us
> We beheld his glory as of the only Son
> as of the only Son
> as of the only Son of the Father
> of the Father
> Full of grace and truth
> and truth and truth and truth
> and truth and truth.

In the beginning was the word and the word was with God and the word was God.

> We beheld his glory as of the only Son
> as of the only Son
> as of the only Son of the Father
> of the Father

---

58. As mentioned above, this is in contrast to the standard practice of setting the soloists' parts in polyphony and the response part in plainchant.

> Full of grace and truth
>> and truth and truth and truth
>> and truth and truth.

> *Glory be to the Father and to the Son and to the Holy Spirit.*

>> Full of grace and truth
>>> and truth and truth and truth
>>> and truth and truth.

Sheppard, using the techniques of a responsory, gives increasing prominence to the second and third parts of Jn 1.14. By giving this text a polyphonic setting and inverting the traditional choral pattern, Sheppard has given increasing prominence to the penultimate phrase that is sung by the choir in full polyphony—'full of grace'—and even more prominence to the final phrase, 'of truth', by its many repetitions. In Jn 1.14, the words 'we beheld his glory as of the only Son of the Father' follow directly after the preceding phrase 'the word was made flesh and dwelt among us', but in the second setting, a new context is set up that reads: 'In the beginning was the word and the word was with God and the word was God / 'we beheld his glory as of the only Son of the Father'. This is then taken one further step in the last section, where 'and we beheld his glory as of the only Son of the Father / full of grace and truth' now reads 'Glory be to the Father and to the Son and to the Holy Spirit / full of grace and truth'. Similarly, this drawing of attention back to the text of Jn 1.14 is a means of giving full focus to this verse as fundamental to the reading of the other two texts. Sheppard has taken a liturgical practice and applied it to a text that had not been set polyphonically in this way. In doing so, he has provided a new perspective on this New Testament text.

J.S. Bach: Der Geist hilft unser Schwachheit auf /'The Spirit helps us in our weakness' BWV 226 (Eighteenth Century)

The Text

Der Geist hilft unser Schwachheit auf	The Spirit helps us in our weakness.
denn wir wissen nicht, was wir beten sollen, wie sichs gebühret;	We do not know what we ought to pray
sondern der Geist selbst vertritt uns aufs beste	but the Spirit himself intercedes for us
mit unaussprechlichem Seufzen (Rom. 8.26).	with groans that words cannot express (Rom. 8.26).

Der aber die Herzen forschet,	And he who searches our hearts
der weiß, was des Geistes Sinn sei;	knows the mind of the Spirit,
denn er vertritt die Heiligen nach dem,	because the Spirit intercedes for the saints
das Gott gefället (Rom. 8.27).	in accordance with God's will (Rom. 8.27).
Du heilige Brunst, süßer Trost,	Look down, Holy Dove, Spirit bow;
nun hilf uns, fröhlich und getrost	Descend from heav'n and help us now:
in deinem Dienst beständig bleiben,	Inspire our hearts while humbly kneeling,
die Trübsal uns nicht abtreiben.	To pray with zeal and contrite feeling!
O Herr, durch dein Kraft uns bereit	Prepare us, through Thy cleansing pow'r
und stärk des Fleisches Blödigkeit	For death, at life's expiring hour:
daß wir hie ritterlich ringen,	That we may find the grave a portal
durch Tod und Leben zu dir dringen	To Thee in heav'n, and life immortal!
Halleluja, halleluja (Martin Luther).	Hallelujah! Hallelujah! (Martin Luther).

The Composer

The name Johann Sebastian Bach seems to be universally known. In fact, it would be surprising to meet someone who had not heard of Johann Sebastian Bach and did not know something about him, and yet this composer's work still merits further study and exploration. This man, who lived from 1685–1750 and was only considered the third choice, and a poor third choice at that, for the position of choirmaster at the Thomas-schule in Leipzig, is today revered simply as one of, if not the greatest, of composers. As incomprehensible as it seems today, after his death, much of his music was forgotten. Among others, Felix Bartholdy-Mendelssohn can be given credit for re-introducing Bach's *St Matthew Passion*[59] and thus sparking a revived interest in Bach's choral works. Bach's settings of both the St Matthew and the St John Passions, as well as his *Mass in B Minor*, are substantial works that, appropriately, are now often performed.

---

59. The performance took place on 11 March 1829, in the Berlin Singakademie; see A. Schweitzer, *J.S. Bach* (2 vols.; trans. E. Newman; Leipzig: Breitkopf & Härtel, 1911), I, pp. 241-43 (242); for a very interesting account of the events leading up to the performance and the evening itself, as recounted by Eduard Devrient, who handled the business negotiations and also sang the part of Christ in the performance, see H.T. David and A. Mendel (eds.), *The Bach Reader: A Life of Johann Sebastian Bach in Letters and Documents* (New York: W.W. Norton, 1945), pp. 376-86.

His works for organ are part of the standard repertoire of the great organists. His cantatas, although perhaps infrequently used in liturgical settings outside the Lutheran context, nonetheless are included in many choral repertoires and performed as part of sacred or secular musical concerts. Pianists like Edwin Fischer in the early part of the twentieth century reintroduced the concertos for keyboard by performing them in several concerts (and recording them) in 1933–38, in Berlin,[60] and Claudio Arrau, in a series of 12 recitals in 1935–36, also in Berlin, performed all of Bach's keyboard works, introducing some if not most of them for the first time to the general public of the twentieth century. Glenn Gould, arguably one of the most remarkable and intellectual pianists of the twentieth century, can be heard using a concert venue as the platform from which to present a pianistic treatise on the fundamental supremacy of Bach's 'Goldberg Variations', with works by Sweelinck, Schoenberg and Mozart as foils.[61] But simultaneously, there is continued and revived interest in the levels of interpretation that Bach brought to the texts of his music, whether they be passions, masses, cantatas, or, as in this case, motets. Study has been done on the notations that Bach wrote alongside Bible passages,[62] and certainly, in his music, there seems always to be either musical commentary on the texts of the works that he presents, or an indirect commentary based on the compilation of the texts themselves.

The Work
Bach's contribution to the history of interpreting the New Testament by means of his musical-textual settings includes his motet, *Der Geist hilft unser Schwachheit auf.* This is one of Bach's six known motets.[63] In contrast with the several hundred cantatas of Bach, six of anything, especially works this short, seems unexpected. However, they were not settings that had a regular place in the Lutheran service of Leipzig in the eighteenth century, apart from being specially commissioned works for specific occasions. This motet is the only one that has an autograph registering its

60. E. Fischer, *J.S. Bach, EMI* 1989, CDH7630392.
61. G. Gould, 25 August 1959, Salzburg Concert, Sony 1994, SMK53474.
62. See H.H. Cox (ed.), *The Calov Bible of J.S. Bach* (Ann Arbor, MI: UMI Research Press, 1985); and R.A. Leaver, *J.S. Bach and Scripture: Glosses from the Calov Bible Commentary* (St Louis: Concordia, 1985).
63. There is some discussion about this number: in the past there were several other motets attributed to J.S. Bach, which are no longer considered authentic, and there are at present some possibilities of others being attributed to him that until now have not been.

intended purpose. It was written 'for the burial of the late professor and rector Ernesti',[64] which dates it to October 1729. Johann Heinrich Ernesti was rector of St Thomas School as well as professor of poetry in the University.[65] The main part of the text comes from Rom. 8.26-27:

> In the same way, the Spirit helps us in our weakness. We do not know what we ought to pray, but the Spirit himself intercedes for us with groans that words cannot express. And he who searches our hearts knows the mind of the Spirit, because the Spirit intercedes for the saints in accordance with God's will.

The remainder of the text is from the third stanza of Martin Luther's hymn, 'Komm, Heiliger Geist, Herre Gott', from 1524; the choral arrangement that forms the third part of this motet is based on the melody of this same hymn.[66]

There are three main sections in this work, which in its entirety lasts approximately eight minutes in performance. The first section uses the first of the two verses from Romans 8. This section is entirely set for double choir of soprano, alto, tenor and bass. The second section uses the second verse of the Romans text, v. 27, which is marked 'Alla breve' in the score. Here the two choirs are merged into one four-part choir. The third and final section is again for the combined voices of the two choirs and is in the style of the chorale that would normally be found at the end of a cantata.

The Interpretation

In this work, the word 'Geist' or 'Spirit' is frequently set to a long fluctuating or undulating line; in Bach's language of setting text to music, this seems to symbolize the nature of the word 'ghost' or 'spirit' by its movement of the line. Later in the first section, the word that is given a long melismatic line is the final word of the phrase *mit unaussprechlichem Seufzen* or 'with inexpressible *groanings*'. Here Bach uses more chromatic notes and angular intervals than in the rest of the work, a means of expressing the anguish of the text; for instance, in the highest voice of the

---

64. 'Bey Beerdigung des seel. Hn. Prof. und Rectoris Ernesti', as cited by K. Hofmann in his preface in K. Ameln (ed.), *Johann Sebastian Bach Motetten Motets BWV 225–230* (Kassel: Bärenreiter-Verlag, 1995), pp. 2, 4.

65. C.S. Terry, 'Johann Sebastian Bach', in E. Blom (ed.), *Grove's Dictionary of Music and Muscians* (10 vols.; New York: St. Martin's Press, 1954, 5th edn), I, pp. 293-321 (306).

66. This hymn comes from the fourth edition of the *Gesangbuch Eisleben* (1598).

first choir (measure 130) at the word *Seufzen*, the soprano sings an ascending diminished fifth or tritone, and finishes the word on the same interval, but descending this time. This interval is notoriously difficult to sing and, at least in the seventeenth and eighteenth centuries, was generally avoided in good voice-leading. Here, however, Bach seems to use it specifically because of these properties. Similarly, he uses minor seconds and the outline of a diminished seventh chord to emphasize the text and its accompanying expression.

Another example is in the alto voice in Choir I (measures 132-33), which begins the word *Seufzen* on the notes A, Ab-G, Ab-G. These intervals of minor seconds are sometimes used by Bach to signify sorrow or pain, and here the repetition of Ab-G seems to accentuate this factor. Many such examples of this use of chromatic notes and difficult intervals in the individual voices can be found in this section. From the extended passages of this particular word-setting, it seems clear that Bach intended the music and the text to fully reflect each other, and in fact, for the music to elucidate the text at this point.

This first section of the motet is the longest of the three sections and presents the part of the text that speaks of suffering in its most extended passages (although this is not readily captured by the choirs that perform it). In the second section, where the biblical text shifts its emphasis more from the personal dimension to that of the 'mind of the Spirit' and 'God's will', the music becomes more straightforward and less densely written. Removing the antiphonal aspect of two choirs by merging them into one and changing the style of the section to 'alla breve' results in a more spacious sense, which seems to underline the more pragmatic and cerebral aspect of this second verse, a characteristic underlined also by its fugal setting.

The third section is the most brief and straightforward and brings the listener, at least presumably the traditional church-person of Bach's day and location, back to the familiarity of Luther's hymn. The writing is in the familiar chorale style, and the verse, selected specifically for its appropriateness to the situation, speaks of help from the Holy Spirit—in keeping with the earlier Romans text—of preparation for death, finding the grave a door or portal to God in heaven, and to life immortal. The concluding 'Hallelluja, halleluja' at this point seems oddly fitting and provides a victorious if brief conclusion to the work. By means of Bach's setting of two verses in Romans and their juxtaposition with Luther's hymn, one journeys through a text illustrating suffering and pain to one that moves to the mind of God and ultimately to the hymn that speaks of life immortal. Certainly Bach's interpretation of Rom. 8.26 and 27 in this context gives an insight into the spirit of the passage.

Francis Poulenc: Tenebrae factae sunt /
'It became dark' (Twentieth Century)

The Text

Tenebrae factae sunt	It became dark
dum crucifixissent Jesum Judaei,	when the Jews had crucified Jesus,
et circa horam nonam	and around the ninth hour
exclamavit Jesus voce magna.	Jesus exclaimed in a loud voice:
Deus meus, ut quid me dereliquisti?	'My God, why have you forsaken me?'
Et inclinato capite,	and with inclined head
emisit spiritum.	He gave up the spirit.
Exclamans Jesus magna ait.	Crying out, Jesus with a loud voice said:
Pater, in manus tuas	'Father, into your hands
commendo spiritum meum.	I commend my spirit'.
Et inclinato capite,	and with inclined head
emisit spiritum.[67]	He gave up the spirit.

The Composer

Francis Poulenc (1899–1962), known as one of the French *Les Six* or 'The Six', was not a likely candidate for that of a serious composer of sacred music, but around 1936 he did turn seriously to the art of composing sacred choral music.[68] Poulenc himself said that he hoped that when his sacred works were better known that the public would see he was not just a 'frivolous author'.[69] H. Hell's statement that the 'predominantly sober aspect of Poulenc's choral works is one of the most interesting features of his art'[70] suggests that Poulenc's desire was fulfilled. Certainly his sacred choral works have become a solid part of the choral repertory of the twentieth century.

67. This text can be found in *Liber Usualis, Feria* VI in *Parasceve, Nocturn* II, *Lectio* V, pp. 597-98.

68. K.W. Daniel, *Francis Poulenc: His Artistic Development and Musical Style* (Studies in Musicology, 52; Ann Arbor, MI: UMI Research Press, 1980, 1982), p. 199.

69. F. Poulenc, *Entretiens avec Claude Rostand* (Paris: R. Julliard, 1954), taken from the publication of radio interviews between Poulenc and Rostand.

70. H. Hell, *Francis Poulenc* (trans. E. Lockspeiser; London: John Calder, 1959 [French original: Paris: Librairie Plon, 1958]), p. 44.

The Work

Although Wilfred Mellers characterizes Poulenc as 'all sentimentality and nostalgia',[71] this one of *Quatre motets pour le temps de pénitence* / 'Four Motets for a Time of Penitence' is not about sentiment and nostalgia. Undoubtedly the motets are 'personally expressive', as Mellers later writes in his biography of the composer.[72] Poulenc's own comment about setting texts to music in songs is: 'I find myself able to compose music only to poetry with which I feel total contact—a contact transcending mere admiration'.[73] While this motet is not in the category of 'song', one's impression is that Poulenc experiences that same sense of connectedness or contact with the text of this work, and places himself within the environment of the event that it depicts. Daniel writes that 'Controlled, sustained dramatic effect is the key aspect of these motets...and examining the means Poulenc uses to achieve this...reveals their true beauty',[74] while Hell writes that this work for *a cappella* choir 'is a work of the standing of the *Mass* with the difference that the choral writing is less subtle and the religious message rather more dramatically conveyed'.[75] Mellers describes the motets as 'powerfully subjective, even "expressionist", pieces while being also devotional music that may function as an act of worship in church'.[76] All three authors concur that this is a highly significant work.

The text is the key to this powerful motet, which was written with the other three motets in 1938–39. The text that forms the basis of Poulenc's third of 'Four Motets for a Time of Penitence', *Tenebrae facta sunt*, is a standard text for Holy Week[77] (but it is by no means a standard musical interpretation of it, for which brief discussion, see below). This composite of the four Gospel accounts of the Crucifixion of Christ is as follows. The

71. W. Mellers, *Man and his Music: The Story of Musical Experience in the West: Romanticism and the Twentieth Century*, IV (London: Barrie & Jenkins, repr. 1977 [London: Barrie & Rockliff, 1962]), p. 227.

72. W. Mellers, *Francis Poulenc* (Oxford: Oxford University Press, 1993), p. 152.

73. Cited in J. Machlis, *Introduction to Contemporary Music* (New York: W.W. Norton, 2nd edn, 1979 [1961]), pp. 207-208.

74. Daniel, *Francis Poulenc*, p. 227. He also writes that he thinks *Tenebrae facta sunt* 'is the most striking of the pieces' (p. 227).

75. Hell, *Francis Poulenc*, p. 59, where he also further comments on the 'tragic note in the sombre *Tenebrae facta sunt*, remarkable for its violent climaxes and its skilful use of the varied registers of the voices'.

76. Mellers, *Francis Poulenc*, p. 79.

77. It is used in the second Nocturn of Matins on Good Friday.

first phrase of the text, 'It became dark when the Jews had crucified Jesus', is paraphrased from the three Synoptic Gospel accounts of Matthew, Mark and Luke.[78] These opening words are the least similar to the biblical text, for the Gospel accounts do not state that 'it became dark *when the Jews had crucified Jesus*', only that it became dark. The second portion of the text, 'and around the ninth hour Jesus exclaimed in a loud voice: "My God, why have you forsaken me?"', follows closely the passages from Matthew and Mark.[79] The next section, 'and with inclined head, he gave up his spirit', although it seems to follow on directly from the preceding line, is not as closely connected in the New Testament texts. This can be seen in John's Gospel: 'When he had received the drink, Jesus said, "It is finished." *With that, he bowed his head and gave up his spirit*',[80] and in Matthew's Gospel: 'And when Jesus had cried out again in a loud voice, *he gave up his spirit*'.[81] The lines, 'Crying out, Jesus with a loud voice said: "Father, into your hands I commend my spirit"', are found only in Luke.[82]

The Interpretation
Poulenc himself stated that he 'wrote four motets for Holy Week which are as realistic and as tragic as a Mantegna painting',[83] and that 'Mantegna...correspond[s] very closely, in fact, to my religious ideal', that of 'mystical realism'.[84] E.H. Gombrich writes that Andrea Mantegna (1431–1506) tried 'to imagine quite clearly what the scene must have looked like in reality', including both the inner meaning of the story, as evidenced in earlier painters, but also its outward circumstances.[85] The text of *Tenebrae facta sunt*, with its inclusion of two of Jesus' statements, one according to

---

78. Mt. 27.45; Mk 15.33; Lk. 23.44.
79. Mt. 27.46; Mk 15.34.
80. Jn 19.30.
81. Mt. 27.50. There is only a slight similarity to the Markan passage (Mk 15.37).
82. Lk. 23.46: '*Jesus called out with a loud voice, "Father, into your hands I commit my spirit"*. When he had said this, he breathed his last'.
83. Cited by Daniel, *Francis Poulenc*, p. 225, from Poulenc's *Entretiens*.
84. F. Poulenc, *My Friends and Myself* (conversations assembled by S. Audel; trans. J. Harding; London: Dennis Dobson, 1978; French original: Geneva and Paris: La Palatine, 1963), p. 58.
85. E.H. Gombrich, *The Story of Art* (London: Phaidon Press, 16th edn, 1995 [1950]), pp. 256-60 (259). Gombrich refers to Mantegna's paintings as being much like scenes in a play (p. 260).

Matthew and Mark, and one according to Luke, provides the kind of detail, even drama, that Poulenc wished for this depiction of the grief and sorrow of the final moments of Jesus' life before he died.

Poulenc mixes features of old with new in his writing of this work, and, in so doing, brings about a metamorphosis of the text and the scene that it depicts. Mellers, for instance, writes that 'Poulenc's techniques are... orthodox in musical terms, for the vocal lines start from the rhythms of the words, and grow from, if they do not always adhere to, vocal modality'.[86] Later, he writes that the vocal lines in the motet do not 'deny Renaissance principles', but involve 'a progressive degree of "humanization" from medieval spirituality to Renaissance physicality: which becomes overt at the fluctuating harmonies on the "ninth hour" and at Christ's frenzied chromatics and dotted rhythms in his appeal, "voce magna", to his Father'.[87] Here we can see the evidence of the change that is wrought by Poulenc.

The first muted notes of the motet give an impression of darkness and foreboding, setting the scene of the Crucifixion. One distinctive feature that I wish to draw attention to is the point in the text where Jesus exclaims in a loud voice *Deus meus, ut quid me dereliquisti?* / 'My God, my God, why have you forsaken me?' It is poignant that only the first two words are sung in 'a loud voice'. These words are then echoed very quietly, with the following words of the statement also sung quietly. Certainly in a dramatic reading of this passage, one might expect to hear the entire line spoken loudly, even increasing in volume: 'My God, my God, WHY HAVE YOU FORSAKEN ME?' However, Poulenc's depiction of this cry, in which only the first two words are a loud cry and all the following words are quiet, vividly depict Jesus having used all the breath he could muster to speak out the first two words. The echo of these words is very much like the sound of a desperate, dying and forsaken man: 'MY GOD...my God...why have you forsaken me...?' Poulenc's choice of the upper voices and upper notes to sing *Deus meus* 'My God' further suggests a strained sound, a sound that cannot be sustained and drops off to a lower range as well as dynamics. This portrayal of physical fatigue and an accompanying dryness in the heat corresponds to the image of the Crucifixion that is depicted in the Gospel accounts, as well as other historical accounts of those who have been crucified. The physical reality

86. Mellers, *Francis Poulenc*, p. 80.
87. Mellers, *Francis Poulenc*, p. 82.

of a crucifixion[88] bears out Poulenc's interpretation of the scene of Jesus on the cross.

Conclusion

While this paper has merely touched on these five works, nonetheless I think that it is evident that each one unveils and interprets at least one unique facet of the biblical text by means of its musical setting. There are features in each work that reveal the composer in his role as an interpreter of the Bible. Although the composition of sacred music often has been seen as a less creative role than that of writing music for its own sake, it seems to me that, in fact, the composer, in writing sacred music, has the unique opportunity of engaging intellectually with the text at a theological level by composing a musical work that recreates the text in a new form. In this new form, the composer has set out for performance and for evaluation a personal interpretation of the biblical text.

88. For extensive discussion of crucifixion, see M. Hengel, *The Cross of the Son of God: containing The Son of God, Crucifixion, The Atonement* (trans. J. Bowden; London: SCM Press, 1986), in particular 'Crucifixion', pp. 93-185, which was originally *Crucifixion* (trans. J. Bowden; London: SCM Press, 1977), from the German original: '*Mors turpissima crucis*: Die Kreuzigung in der antiken Welt und die "Torheit" des "Wortes vom Kreuz"', in J. Friedrich, W. Pöhlmann and P. Stuhlmacher (eds.), *Rechtfertigung: Festschrift für Ernst Käsemann zum 70 Geburtstag* (Tübingen: Mohr–Siebeck; Göttingen: Vandenhoeck & Ruprecht, 1976), with substantial later additions by the author.

Open Letter from a Blind Disciple to a Sighted Saviour[*]

John M. Hull

Introduction

When I wrote about the miracles of Jesus more than 25 years ago, I approached the problem from a historical critical point of view.[1] I was primarily interested in the world out of which the text came. I tried to set my work within the context of similar critical scholarship and that is why there were lots of footnotes. It did not occur to me to ask how blind or deaf people might react to my discussion of the healing miracles. In that respect, things have not changed much. While writing my *Open Letter to Jesus* (Section 2), I studied about a dozen articles written in the tradition of critical-historical exegesis.[2] I noticed as a blind person what I had not seen when I was sighted, that the people, presumably mostly sighted, who write articles about the symbolism of blindness in the Gospels never seem to reflect upon the implications of this for blind people.

In my *Open Letter to Jesus,* I deliberately adopted a different approach. I concentrated not upon the world out of which the texts came, but the world which the texts tended to create, the horizon towards which they seemed to point.[3] I tried to bracket out my previous familiarity with the Bible, to forget the meaning which many of those passages had had for me in my former sighted life, and to allow the biblical speech (I did it all on tape) to fall into my consciousness like rain upon the dry ground.[4]

* I am grateful to the St Peter's (Saltley) Trust whose generous grant enabled the production of this article.

1. John M. Hull, *Hellenistic Magic and the Synoptic Tradition* (London: SCM Press, 1974).

2. E.g. E.S. Johnson, 'Mark 10.46-52: Blind Bartimaeus', *CBQ* 40 (1978), pp. 191-204.

3. Paul Ricoeur, *Interpretation Theory: Discourse and the Surplus of Meaning* (Forth Worth: Texas Christian University, 1976), p. 36.

4. The result is a hermeneutic similar to that which Kwok Pui-Lan describes as

It did not seem to make any difference to my response to the text, as I heard it, whether the words of Jesus about the Pharisees being 'blind fools' are due to Matthew's editorial construction rather than being close to something Jesus may actually have said. For the same reason, I did not always study the Gospel parallels and variants, in cases where a saying or story appears more than once. I simply responded to what my tape-recorder was reading to me. However, in describing how a *particular* blind person reacts to the Bible, I believe that I have shown something about the Bible *in general* and not only something about myself.

My method of interpretation is typical of post-modern responses to the meaning of the Bible.[5] Now that we have learned from Asian, African and South American models of biblical interpretation, to say nothing of feminist and black readings, we realize that the tradition of European biblical scholarship has European characteristics.[6] Just as we have theology which represents the interests of the people with whom we stand in solidarity, so we have the Bible which sustains that solidarity. All knowledge is within the circle of human interest, and there is no unmotivated truth.[7] Nevertheless, when we understand that the knowledge and the truth about the Bible is driven by the socio-historical position of the commentators, and that 'the meaning of the Bible' is necessarily a cultural artefact, we are invited to put that meaning against the meanings of the Bible from other socio-cultural positions. The sighted truth about the Bible may be true and yet not all the truth. In so far as it is not the complete truth, we are misled if we absolutize it.

This, then, is an attempt to relativize or pluralize the Bible. Without denying the truth that the Bible is mainly a book for sighted people, I want to relativise that truth by making it obvious, and by stating the obvious to relativize it.[8] The truth that the Bible is a book for sighted people is related to the truth that the Bible is also a book for blind people. If the Bible is

'the Bible as a talking book'. Kwok Pui-Lan, *Discovering the Bible in the Non-Biblical World* (Maryknoll: Orbis, 1995), pp. 40-43.

5.   Walter Brueggemann, *The Bible and Post-Modern Imagination: Texts under Negotiation* (London: SCM Press, 1993).

6.   R.S. Sugirtharajah, *Voices from the Margin: Interpreting the Bible in the Third World* (London: SPCK, 1995).

7.   Jürgen Habermas, *Knowledge and Human Interests* (London: Heinemann Educational, 1978).

8.   Michel Pêcheux, *Language, Semantics and Ideology: Stating the Obvious* (London: Macmillan, 1982).

relatively a book for sighted people, then the Bible is also relatively a book for people, and for hearing people, and for white people, and for wealthy people and so on. Is there no end to this process of relativization? Is there, after all, no absolute truth in the Bible?

If there is an absolute truth, it is not to be found through a process of artificial and often unconscious absolutizing, but through a proliferation of many meanings until everyone's meanings are gathered in. This is the way that the Bible becomes truly ecumenical, truly catholic. We do not know how many more perspectives there might be. We do not know how many new groups and new cultures will hold up the diamond of God's word and give it a new twist, so that new patterns and colours flash forth from it, but if the Bible is to be a book for all people, this process cannot be arrested. It is necessary that all those who are spoken to by the Bible should have an opportunity to reply, and thus the conversation which is within the Bible can enter into conversation with us today, and through offering a voice and a hearing to everyone we can create a community of genuine free speech.[9]

In what sense can we say any longer that the Bible is the word of God? When I hear Jesus saying that the blind cannot lead the blind because they will both fall into a ditch, is that the word of God to me? When the Bible as a whole and the Gospels in particular, every one of them, tell me that as a blind person I represent disobedience, unbelief, ignorance and sin, am I to take that as God's word to me? This is not a word of acceptance, of forgiveness and of liberation, but a word of rejection, of oppression. In order to translate this into the word of God, we need to take out the disparaging metaphors. The truth to which faith witnesses is that our ignorance, sin and disobedience prevent us from responding to the love of God made known in Jesus Christ. It is not necessary that this witness of faith should be cast into the form of the metaphor of blindness. This is surely a case where the metaphor kills but the spirit gives life.

There are Christians who say that they believe the Bible to be literally true. Such Christians may find it difficult to recognize the metaphor of blindness and may be obliged by the nature of their faith in the authority of the Bible to adopt a condemnatory attitude toward blind people. This is the stark choice facing the biblical literalist: if you accept the Bible literally you will be more likely to accept uncritically the negative image of blindness in our culture.

---

9.   Jürgen Habermas, *The Theory of Communicative Action* (2 vols.; Boston: Beacon Press, 1984, 1987).

We may make a similar comment about the speech of Jesus himself. When Jesus is reported to have said that the blind cannot lead the blind because they will both fall into a ditch, he means that people without understanding cannot become teachers of others without understanding because in that case neither will finish up with any understanding. It is not necessary to the truth spoken by Jesus that the metaphor of blindness should be used. When Jesus warned that the salt would be no good if it lost its saltiness, he was not speaking only about salt but also about the presence of the teaching of the Kingdom of God in human lives. Nevertheless, we have to face the fact that to Jesus is attributed the use of a disparaging metaphor, a belittling and demeaning description which has oppressed and marginalized blind people down the centuries, because most Christians even when they saw the truth beneath the metaphor did not explicitly reject the metaphor, and therefore the text continued to collaborate in the building up of the cultural artefact in which blindness is belittled. As a free person in Christ and as a Christian blind person I lay this solemn charge against the Bible and against its sighted Christian interpreters.

Jesus used the metaphor, or the New Testament tradition attributed the use of the metaphor to Jesus, because the metaphor not only illustrated the truth but also was believed to contain the truth. It was believed that blind people tended to be foolish, ignorant and inconsistent. If Jesus had said, 'The blind cannot lead the blind because they will both fall into a ditch but they don't really, I'm only trying to make a point', the whole impact of the saying would have been lost. It would be like saying that the salt would be no good if it lost its saltiness—but it would be really.

The traditional authority of the Bible is now challenged on ethical as well as scientific grounds. The authority of the Bible must be evaluated in different ways. The Bible is a conversation into which we, who hear it, are drawn. It is a conversation in which we hear many voices—the rich and powerful, the poor and the oppressed. The Bible is the word of God because in it the voices of the poor and the oppressed have never been silenced.[10] We hear the voices of sighted people and, now and again, in a softer tone, the voices of blind people. The Bible is the word of God because when we understand it in terms of its own variety and not through the perspective of our own enclosed biological and social conditions, it

10. George Thompson, *The First Philosophers* (London: Lawrence and Wishart, 1955), p. 333. Ernst Bloch, *Atheism in Christianity: The Religion of the Exodus and the Kingdom* (New York: Heider, 1972).

speaks to us not only as sighted people and blind people but also as people. The biblical question is what we do with our sight, and what we do with our blindness.

I have chosen the genre of the *Open Letter* because it is an effective medium through which I can illustrate clearly and in an autobiographical way how I, as a blind person, react to the theme of blindness in the Bible and, in so doing, ensure that the Bible reveals its riches to everyone and not just to the sighted.

Open Letter to Jesus

Dear Jesus,

According to the Gospel of Matthew, you used the expression 'blind' as a term of abuse. When you were attacking certain groups of people you described them as 'blind guides' (Mt. 23.16), 'blind fools' (v. 17), and 'you blind Pharisee' (v. 26). You have given your authority to those down the ages who have disparaged others through references to visual loss. Whenever a Member of Parliament criticizes a government minister by saying that he or she shows a blind disregard for the welfare of the people of this country, whenever a sports journalist describes a cricketer as having struck out blindly with the bat, or an academic recommends blind marking, the impression is reinforced that blind people are stubborn, callous, lacking in self-control or just plain ignorant. It would have been so easy for you to have called them 'careless guides', 'stupid fools', or 'stubborn Pharisees'. If you had spoken in that way, then the disparaging image of blindness, which has caused blind people so much pain, would not have received your permission and encouragement.

When I discuss these sayings with your sighted priests and other well-meaning friends, they defend you by pointing out that your use of the expression 'blind' is only metaphorical, but I cannot understand how this is supposed to help. In general, the gospels show you as being sensitive and attentive to blind people (Mk 8.22-26; 10.46-52), so I cannot imagine that if the guides, lawyers and Pharisees were literally blind, you would have been so tactless as to refer to their blindness when criticizing them. Indeed, the problem is created precisely by the metaphorical use of blindness to suggest ignorance, stupidity and insensitivity.

Another point which your sighted friends make is that the disparaging use of blindness is confined to Matthew. The comparable passages in Mark and Luke do not use the expression 'blind' (Mk 12.38-40; Lk. 20.45-47). We can conclude, the argument goes, that these references are to be attributed to Matthew himself or to the tradition upon which he was drawing, and not to you personally.

Well, perhaps that helps a little, but on the other hand I am not at all sure that there are many sayings in any of the Gospels which represent your actual words, and in any case the offending words are part of Scripture, part of the picture which the first evangelist offers of you. When we hear these words read in church, we respond by saying, 'praise to Christ Our Lord'. So whether you actually used the words or not, or said something like them in Aramaic, if not in Greek, you are nevertheless implicated in these texts.

The problem goes deeper than the mere disparaging use of the word 'blind'. When you referred to the blind guides, you illustrated the point by saying that they strained out a gnat and swallowed a camel (Mt. 23.24). In other words, the guides are fussy about details but overlook important things. This illustration becomes more significant in the context of the eating habits of blind people. If you sat with me at a table, Jesus, would you notice that although I managed to eat the last pea on the plate, I completely ignored my glass of wine because no one had told me it was there? Would you notice how I bit into the little pat of butter wrapped up in paper, which had been placed on top of my bread roll, and failed to notice the bowl of sauce into which I was supposed to dip my carrot sticks? You will remember, Lord, how in the early days of my blindness when I was desperately trying to appear to be independent, I went along the buffet table indiscriminately, finishing up with sherry trifle on my roast vegetables.

The same sighted person's observation of blind people's behaviour is evident in the remark about first cleaning the inside of the cup and then the outside. The blind Pharisee is accused of washing the outside of the cups but ignoring the inside (Mt. 23.25). If you came to my office and shared a coffee with me, Jesus, would you be watching nervously to see whether the coffee cups were nice and clean? After all, the only way a blind person can know this is by feeling the inside of the cup, but most people do not like to drink from a cup the inside of which has been felt by someone else's sticky fingers. A blind person has to wash the cup every time to make sure it is clean, or keep the clean cups in a different place, or turn them upside down when they are washed. These techniques illustrate the difficulty of cleaning the inside as well as the outside. The fact that these observations are coupled with the accusation of blindness indicates that the word 'blind' is not used casually or accidentally, but arises from detailed observation of the behaviour of blind people.

The truth is that, in the days of your earthly ministry, Lord, you were a sighted person. You naturally grew into the view of blind people which your sighted society conveyed to you. For example, Matthew says that you said of the Pharisees, 'Let them alone; they are blind guides of the blind. And if one blind person guides another, both will fall into a pit' (Mt. 15.14). I wonder that you should have said this, Lord, because your own experience of blind people leading each other suggested otherwise. In his ninth chapter, your evangelist Matthew describes how two blind men followed you and caught up with you when you entered into a house (Mt. 9.27-31). They must have followed the noisy crowd as it passed by, and managed to catch up with you when you finally went into a house. They did not fall into a pit or a ditch. Moreover, it is more difficult to attribute this saying to Matthew than to you yourself, since Luke also reports it. 'Can a blind person lead a blind person? Will they not both fall into a pit?' (Lk. 6.39). Luke introduces this comment as being a parable, but the parable would have derived its force from the fact that it was a genuine belief held among sighted people about the behaviour of blind people. You, Lord, are described as participating in this general belief, but this says more about the assumptions and the prejudices of sighted people than about the actual behaviour of those who are blind. Blind people depend upon familiarity. A blind person who was familiar with a certain route would offer to lead a blind stranger along that way. I have myself led blind people many times, and have in turn been led. We have never fallen into ditches, been run over on the road, or fallen down stairs, although I admit to an occasional confrontation with a rose bush. It is when I am being led by a sighted person that I sometimes have bad experiences. As I am walking through a department store the floor suddenly slides away from me and I almost lose my balance. 'Sorry', my sighted friend says. 'I forgot to tell you that we are going down on the escalator'.

When I studied the New Testament as a sighted person, it did not occur to me that you, Jesus, were yourself sighted. We were in the same world, but it did not occur to me that being sighted was a world. I thought that things were just like that. When I became blind, then I realized that blindness is a world, and that the sighted condition also generates a distinctive experience and can be called a world. Now I find, Jesus, that I am in one world and you are in another.

This knowledge came to me for the first time when I read the Gospel of John as a blind person, but even then my understanding was limited. I encountered you in the Gospel of John with a sense of estrangement, because I realized as I read the Gospel in braille—the first book in braille which I read after my loss of sight—that it was not intended for people like me. I realized that sight and light were the symbols of truth and that darkness and blindness were symbols of sin and disbelief, and I realized the meaning of this symbolism in my heart, not just in my head. When, as a sighted theological student, I had written essays about the symbolism of the Fourth Gospel I knew these things only from my scholarship, such as it was. Now I knew them from my humanity, my blind humanity, but it had not occurred to me that the Bible as a whole was written by sighted people for sighted people. I felt confused and alienated by John's Gospel, but I had not realized the reason for my reaction, because I did not know that sight and blindness generate different worlds of human experience.

When I return to your Fourth Gospel today, it is very clear to me that more than any other Gospel it is a product of a sighted society. In your presence, Lord, I read the first chapter. Verse 4 tells me that you are life, and that your life was the light of all people. Your light shines on in the darkness, and the darkness has not overcome it (v. 5). The true light (v. 9) which enlightens everyone was coming into the world. No one has ever seen God (v. 18) and we (indicating your sighted followers) beheld your glory. It is by sight that John the Baptist recognized you (vv. 33, 34). John was told that the one upon whom he saw the dove descending (v. 32) would be the chosen one, and then he adds, 'I myself have seen and have testified that this is the Son of God' (v. 34). In v. 42, we read that you looked at Peter and said, 'so you are Simon son of John', and so on. Now I notice the repeated invitation to 'come and see' (vv. 43, 46). This is what you said to your disciples when they asked where you lived, and Phillip said to Nathaniel, 'come and see'. When he saw you, John said to his own disciples, 'behold the Lamb of God!' (v. 29), and, when you saw Nathaniel coming to you, you said, 'behold an Israelite indeed' (v. 47). You said to Nathaniel, 'I saw you under the fig tree' (v. 48). In John, ch. 8, you say that you are the light of the world and that the one who follows you will not walk in darkness but will have the light of life (Jn 8.12) but, Lord, I walk in darkness every day and have done so for 20 years. Yes, I know that you only meant it metaphorically, but it is not very nice to be regarded as a metaphor of sin and unbelief. Sometimes the metaphor is so graphic that I can't help feeling a twinge of pain. 'Are there not twelve hours of daylight? Those who walk during the day do not stumble, because they see the light of this world. But those who walk at night stumble, because the light is not in them' (Jn 11.9). The assumption of this passage is that work is only possible during the daylight hours but for me the daylight hours are irrelevant. It makes no difference to me whether I work by day or by night and my computers and tape recorders, like myself, know nothing of light or darkness.

There is another question which I want to ask you, Lord. Do you believe that there is a connection between disability and sin? Or, if not you yourself, then did your early followers believe this? When you had healed the lame man who lay on the steps besides the pool of Bethesda, you said to him, 'Do not sin any more, so that nothing worse happens to you' (Jn 5.14). To my mind, that clearly indicates that you thought there was a connection between his lameness and some sin or other, and when I read in Jn 5.3 that in the portico lay a multitude of invalids, blind, lame, paralysed, I cannot imagine that this comment applied only to the particular man or to lame people in general, but would also have been said if the healed person had been blind. Similarly, when you healed the lame man lowered through the roof (Mk 2.1-12) you first said to him, 'your sins are forgiven'. It was only when the implications of this comment were challenged by those who heard it that you continued with the physical healing of the lame man. It is difficult to resist the view that it was necessary first to get the sin out of the way before the disability could be healed.

When we read about the blind man in John 9 the situation is different, but presents its own problems. Your disciples anticipated a connection between disability and sin with the question, 'who did sin, this man or his parents, that he was born blind?' You rejected this suggestion, adding, 'that

God's works might be revealed in him' (v. 3). In other words, the man had been blind from birth not because of some parental sin but in order to create a sort of photo opportunity for you, Lord. When you spoke of God's works being revealed in the blind man, you were not referring to his blindness, but to the restoration of his sight. The implication is that God's works cannot be seen in a blind person but only in a blind person becoming sighted.

Towards the end of the chapter we read that you said, 'I came into this world for judgement so that those who do not see may see, and those who do see may become blind' (v. 39). Some of the Pharisees near you heard this and said to you, 'surely we are not blind are we?' You replied, 'if you were blind, you would not have sin. But now that you say, "we see", your sin remains' (Jn 9.40). When you said, 'if you were blind you would not have sin', this seems to mean 'if you were really and literally blind, you would have no sin, but now that you say, "we see", your sin remains'. The sin lies not in the literal blindness but in the self-deception of those who believe that they have insight but do not.

Now, Lord, an important problem: why was there not a blind person among your followers? I know that women and black people have been asking you similar questions about themselves, but even if there were none in your group of 12, women can find models of faith in people like Mary and Martha, and there is always your mother. As for black people, they can look to representatives such as Simon from Africa, who carried your cross and the Ethiopian traveller in the Acts of the Apostles. What models of faith do we blind people have? There is the man born blind in John, ch. 9, and there is Bartimaeus together with several unnamed people, but the trouble is that they did not become your followers until they had left their blindness behind them. This is why there was not a blind person among your disciples and why there could not have been one: you would have restored their sight and then they would no longer be blind. Given your assumptions about blindness, which you shared with the rest of the society of your day, it could not possibly have been different. After all, if a blind person was invited to follow you and did so while remaining blind, everyone would have been shocked, and I dare say that even you would have been embarrassed. People would have said of you what they said of the Lazarus business: 'Could not this man who opened the eyes of the blind man have kept this man from dying?' (Jn 11.37). Could not this man (that's you) who opened the eyes of other blind people, have restored the sight of your chosen follower? In terms of the assumptions of your day, it would have been difficult to find an answer to this question.

Furthermore, if a blind person could not have been your disciple in the days of your earthly ministry, what is the situation of your blind followers today? In spite of everything the theologians say about symbolism, most Christians tend to take the stories about you at face value, and a blind Christian is often made aware of the question, which hangs in the air unspoken: if your faith was genuine, would not Jesus have restored your sight? I have been a member of various churches in which healing services have been held from time to time. Although they have always emphasized that healing is intended in the general sense of a blessing, not necessarily or even at all a physical restoration or regeneration, I have never felt free to attend such services, because I think that my attendance would be read in an ambiguous way. Some people might think that I was coming in expectation of the restoration of my sight. Indeed, I have known Christians who belonged to more conservative congregations who have been harassed by an expectation of miraculous healing. I have known Christians who, having become blind, have had to move to a new congregation.

You remember, Lord, the disabled people's church in South Korea, which I was invited to attend. When I asked the people why they found it necessary to have their own church, they replied, 'because the people in the ordinary churches tell us that we make them feel uncomfortable'. You and I both know of similar stories from Britain, told by blind people seeking ordination to the Christian ministry. Although many are accepted and welcomed, others are met with the objection that they would not be able to care for other people since they themselves require care. Every time one of the stories about how you restored the sight of blind people is read out in church, blind Christians will imagine the thoughts of the congregation directed towards them with the question: if it happened to Bartimaeus, why not to you? Of course, the modern miracle-working evangelists often tell stories of how you have restored the sight of blind people in their meetings. You know that because of certain experiences of my own I am slightly sceptical about these stories, but perhaps it happens. Am I not like Naaman the Syrian general who had leprosy, refusing to wash in the river Jordan because it seemed too easy? All I have to do is walk down the aisle and be humble enough to accept the ministry of healing. Perhaps, the voice of the tempter continues, it would not work for me, but I will not be any worse off than I am now.

This is the dilemma which a literal interpretation of your healing miracles has created for me, and you know that I go for comfort and strength not to the stories of your miracles, which I find alienating and distressing, but to the experience of your apostle Paul. He was given some kind of physical handicap which he called a thorn in the flesh, and there are some indications that it could have been a visual problem (1 Cor. 13.12; Gal. 4.13-15; 6.11). Anyway, he prayed three times to you, asking that it should be taken away, and you said to him, 'my grace is sufficient for you; my strength is made perfect in weakness' (2 Cor. 12.8-9). Like Paul, Lord, I have no dramatic stories to tell, no accounts of wonderful happenings to amaze people with. All I have to boast of is my infirmity, my weakness.

Figure 27. *The Blind of Jericho*, or *Christ Healing the Blind* (1650 by Nicholas Poussin [1594–1665], Louvre, Paris/Giraudon/Bridgeman Art Library).

In contrast, you know and I know that the stories about your miraculous healing, whatever may lie behind them, have been interpreted symbolically in the Gospel traditions (see Fig. 27). For example, in Mark ch. 8, there is a story about your healing of a blind man in two stages. At first he saw imperfectly that people looked like walking trees. After the second intervention, the man saw perfectly. This story may contain elements of folk medicine but, in the theological imagination of the evangelist, it seems very likely that it represents the limited understanding which your disciples had in the days of your earthly ministry. It was only after the Spirit came, and the Church was formed, that a deep and true understanding of your nature and mission was achieved.[11] There are many indications in the Gospels that unbelief is spoken of as if it were a failure to see. When your disciples did not understand you, you said to them, 'Do you have eyes—and fail to see?' (Mk 8.18) and the two disciples who walked with you on the Emmaus road after your resurrection were unable to recognize you because of their unbelief, but when you had broken the bread in their presence 'their eyes were opened' (Lk. 24.31).

The negative symbolism attached to blindness runs right through the Bible. Samson, Zedekiah and Tobias were all blinded in circumstances associated with sin, folly or unbelief and the blindness of the wicked men of

11. E.S. Johnson, 'Mark 7.22-26: The Blind Man from Bethsaida', *NTS* 25 (1978), pp. 370-83.

Sodom (Wis. 2.21) and of Elymas the magician who obstructed the work of Paul in Cyprus (Acts 13.4-12) are specifically attributed to divine punishment. The wicked meet with darkness in the daytime, and grope at noonday as in the night (Job 5.14), the children of treacherous friends will be afflicted with blindness (Job 17.5), the light of the wicked is darkened so that they cannot see (Job 22.11); the Psalmist complains that since God has punished him, the light of his eyes has gone from him (Ps. 38.10), and he hopes that his enemies will be cursed with blindness (Ps. 69.23); those who have been forsaken by God complain that they grope 'like those that have no eyes' (Isa. 59.10); and when the day of the Lord comes, God will bring blindness upon people, 'that they shall walk like the blind' (Zeph. 1.17).

It is this legacy of blindness regarded as a punishment from God or as a metaphor of sin and disbelief which the New Testament inherits. The most influential passage occurs after the story of the vision of Isaiah in the temple:

> Go and say to this people 'keep listening but do not comprehend. Keep looking, but do not understand.' Make the mind of this people dull, and stop their ears, and shut their eyes, so that they may not look with their eyes, and listen with their ears, and comprehend with their minds, and turn and be healed (Isa. 6.9-10).

It is significant that this passage does not refer to blindness, but to the shutting of the eyes. This is a more acceptable way of describing unbelief and disobedience, because sighted people may close their eyes deliberately to avoid seeing, whereas the metaphor of blindness is not only negative towards people who really are blind but suggests that the people concerned could not help their disobedience and their unbelief. Isa. 6.9-10 is referred to or quoted in all four Gospels and is used to support the notion that the people have deliberately shut their eyes so as not to realize the truth of the teaching of Jesus. The text of Isaiah is retained in Mt. 13.14-15 (compare Mk 4.12 and Lk. 8.10) but in John's Gospel, the metaphor of shutting the eyes is abandoned and instead the metaphor of blindness is used:

> And so they could not believe, because Isaiah also said 'he has blinded their eyes and hardened their heart, so that they might not look with their eyes, and understand with their heart and turn—and I would heal them' (Jn 12.39-40).[12]

This is consistent with the emphasis in John's Gospel upon darkness and blindness as metaphors for disbelief (Jn 9). If any of the four evangelists had described one of your followers as being blind, it would have been a contradiction of the meaning of the symbolic universe of the ancient world as expressed in the Bible.

---

12. J.M. Lieu, 'Blindness in the Johannine Tradition', *NTS* 34 (1988), pp. 83-95.

This negative symbolism of blindness was, of course, all too natural in a world where blind people suffered from an immense disadvantage, a world without guide dogs, white canes, braille and computers. Nevertheless, I remain puzzled at the failure of the biblical authors to have any real insight into the lives of blind people. There is no reference to the cleverness and ingenuity of blind people, who must find different ways of doing things; there is no reference to the sensitivity of blind people to sounds and smells. Nothing is said in admiration of the intelligent hands of the blind weaver or the blind potter. True, there are references here and there to the alleged charisma and intuitive knowledge of blind people, but this is a mere illusion of sighted people who cannot resist the thought that blindness is either to be associated with outrageous sin or with wonderful wisdom.

One of the few indications of any close observation of the lives of blind people is in connection with the way that blind people walk. 'They meet with darkness in the daytime, and grope at noonday as in the night' (Job 5.14). Naturally, day and night are indistinguishable visually to totally blind people but the reference to groping is a typical sighted person's point of view. Blind people necessarily use their hands to find things out and to protect themselves. This is not a stupid, senseless groping but an intelligent way to respond to the blind situation. A detail is added in Isa. 59.10 where 'we grope like the blind along a wall, groping like those who have no eyes'. Yes, we blind people do make contact with the fabric, we like to keep a hand on the rail, and if we are cane-users we need something to act as a tapping board. However, this is no more than our way of glancing around, something sighted people do with their eyes, that we do with our hands, canes or with our entire body.

The impact of these observations upon sighted people is summed up in Zeph. 1.17: 'I will bring such distress on people that they shall walk like the blind'. Blind people generally worked and lived within their families. Blind craftspeople might perhaps be seen in the marketplace, but it was not until they got up to go that their peculiarities became obvious to the sighted passers-by. Blind people do have a very visible kind of walk. You, Lord, were aware of this fascination with the way that blind people walk when you made your comment about falling into ditches.

In spite of all this, Jesus, you were not unaware of the typical sins of sighted people. If I read your Sermon on the Mount, remembering that you were a sighted person, I can appreciate it as an attack on the sighted culture to which you belonged:

> You are the light of the world. A city built on a hill cannot be hid. No one after lighting a lamp puts it under the bushel basket but on the lampstand and it gives light to all in the house. In the same way, let your light shine before others, so that they may see your good works and give glory to your Father in heaven (Mt. 5.14-16).

These sayings are obviously addressed to a sighted audience, and the visual theme is continued in v. 28: 'everyone who looks at a woman with lust has already committed adultery with her in his heart' and this is immediately followed by the warning 'if your right eye causes you to sin, tear it out and throw it away; it is better for you to lose one of your members than for your whole body to be thrown into hell'. The eye is the instrument of adultery, so the tearing out of the eye, which makes this kind of adultery impossible, is equivalent to castration. Do not blind heterosexual men desire women? Yes, of course, but their desire is aroused through the erotic qualities of the female voice, which is inextricably bound up with the personality. The sighted heterosexual man, on the other hand, may be aroused by the sight of the female body, which in picturesque form can be disassociated from the personality. Thus the voice is erotic but the depersonalized body may be pornographic.

In Matthew ch. 6, the attack upon the sighted culture grows stronger still. It is because of appearances, the love of being seen, that sighted people fall into hypocrisy and falsehood, but you, Lord, suggest the limits of sight when you speak paradoxically of your Heavenly Father who sees in secret (Mt. 6.5-6). That means your Father knows in a way that surpasses sight.

I particularly like the prayer you taught your disciples, because there is nothing in it that cannot be said by a blind person. The reference to being led is particularly appropriate for blind people, and the prayer seems to suggest the superficiality and limited nature of the sighted culture (Mt. 6.9-15). In Mt. 6.22-23, you state:

> The eye is the lamp of the body. So, if your eye is healthy, your whole body will be full of light; but if your eye is unhealthy, your whole body will be full of darkness. If then the light in you is darkness, how great is the darkness!

Not only is this a comment from a sighted prophet addressing a sighted world, but suggests the horror and revulsion which a sighted person may feel towards blindness. Yes, indeed, the sighted world is full of show and vain glory, as you describe it when you speak of Solomon in all his glory (Mt. 6.29). People should not be bothered about their appearance or their clothing. The sighted world is preoccupied with these external things. The saying about seeing the speck which is in your brother's eye but not noticing the log in your own eye continues the theme in visual terms, speaking of the self-deception which a sighted culture encourages (Mt. 7.3-5).

Although you were a sighted person, you were not immersed uncritically in the values and attitudes of the world of sight. You were sharply aware of the temptations of vision. I also notice the restraint which you showed in your dealings with blind people. You were not at all like the modern healing evangelists, who invite disabled people to come to their meetings, and make a great show of healing them in public. I do not read that you ever encouraged blind people to approach you; rather, it was they who sought you out. A beautiful example of the tact and respect which you showed to blind people may be found in the story of the blind beggar, Bartimaeus. When he came to you, you did not assume that he wanted his sight restored but you asked him, 'what do you want me to do for you?' (Mk 10.51). Now, a modern blind person would have replied, 'Get me on a good training course where I can search the internet with voice synthesizers', but although Bartimaeus was not in a position to make this reply, it was at least nice to be asked.

When I turn to some of your other sayings, I get a better idea of your attitude towards blindness. 'When you give a feast, invite the poor, the crippled, the lame, and the blind. And you will be blessed, because they cannot repay you, for you will be repaid at the resurrection of the righteous' (Lk. 14.13-14). This is part of your teaching about the reversal of status between the rich and the poor. You are to extend hospitality to the powerless. So far, I agree with you. But your message is a mixed one. You seem to take the low economic condition of blind people for granted. We are among the marginalized. We are invited to the banquet precisely because we have nothing to offer. Would my hunger overcome my fear of being patronized in this way? Are there no blind people who could be invited for their amusing conversation, or because they can play the piano while the coffee is being served? Blind people are invited because they can do nothing, offer nothing. What we have to offer is our weakness. When we are weak, the host is strong, whereas the attitude of Paul was that when he was weak, he was strong. His strength lay in his own weakness not in the weakness of others. When you told the parable of the great feast, the idea is slightly different. The invited guests have refused to come to the banquet because they are too busy. So the host says to his staff, 'go out at once into the streets and lanes of the city and bring in the poor, the crippled, the blind and the lame' (Lk. 14.21-25). When this was done, there was still room, and the staff were told to go out 'into the roads and lanes and compel people to come in, so that my house may be filled' (v. 23). In this story the disabled are invited not because they have nothing to offer but in order to fill the tables. They are to be included not because they are disabled but because there is room.

I have found several relevant aspects of your life and teaching. As a sighted person you seem to share the negative attitudes of your society towards blind people. At the same time, you are highly critical of the values of the sighted culture in which you live. On an individual basis you are sensitive and tactful towards blind people and, while acknowledging their condition of economic deprivation, you insist upon their inclusion. Nevertheless, you did not include a blind person in your closest circle. In your presence blind people felt the hope and discovered the reality of the restoration of sight but you did not offer to blind people courage and acceptance in their blindness. You would have led me by the hand out of blindness but you would not have been my companion during my blindness.

This is a cause of confusion and pain to me and many blind people, and those who have other disabilities. You accepted the fishermen. Even when they left their boats and nets on the shore, they would continue, in a sense, to be fishing. You accepted the children, embraced them, and said that they were to be models of the Kingdom. You accepted the ministry and friendship of women, even those who had a shady past, but blind people had to become sighted before they could follow you.

I am confused, Lord. I am not only hurt and puzzled; I am offended. John the Baptist in prison sent messages to you asking if indeed you were the Messiah, or whether he should look for someone else. At that time, you cured many sick people, you cast out evil spirits, and on many who were blind you bestowed sight (Lk. 7.21). Then you said to the messengers,

> Go and tell John what you have seen and heard: the blind receive their sight, the lame walk, the lepers are cleansed, the deaf hear, the dead are raised, the poor have good news brought to them. And blessed is anyone who takes no offence at me (Lk. 7.22).

This answer is intended to reassure John the Baptist, and we must presume that John would have been offended if you had not been restoring sight to the blind. My position is just the opposite of his. I am offended because you did restore sight to the blind, although I am very happy for the individuals who were thus restored. What I want is inner healing, the healing that comes from acceptance, from inclusion, from the breaking down of barriers through mutual understanding, for an acceptance of different worlds, of different kinds of human life. You seem to present a convergent model of normality but I want a divergent model. This is why I am offended.

Nevertheless, your word comes home to me as it did to John in prison. I am also to be blessed if I am not offended by you, but how can I help being offended?

Your evangelist Matthew applies to you the prophecy of Isaiah. You were healing many disabled people and Matthew says that this was in fulfilment of the prophecy 'He took our infirmities and bore our diseases' (Isa. 53.4 and Mt. 8.17). But to perform miracles upon disabled people is not to take their infirmities and to bear their diseases; it is to remove them. There is a difference between taking something away and taking something upon yourself.

As I read your Gospels, thinking about these problems, I come upon a passage which I have known all my life, but it has never struck me before how relevant it is to my present life as a blind person. After they had tried and sentenced you to be condemned to death, the servants of the High Priest began to spit on you, blindfold you and strike you, saying, 'Prophesy! Who hit you?' (Mk 14.65) (Fig. 28). Luke describes the incident as follows:

> Now the men who were holding Jesus began to mock him and beat him; they also blindfolded him and kept asking him, 'Prophesy! Who is it that struck you?' They kept heaping many other insults on him (Lk. 22.63-65).

Figure 28. *The Mocking of Christ with the Virgin and St Dominic*
(1442 [fresco] by Fra Angelico [Guido di Pietro] [c. 1387–1455],
San Marco, Florence/Bridgeman Art Library).

To be blindfolded is not to be blind. To be a sighted person who cannot
see is not the same as to be a blind person. Nevertheless, it begins to come
close to it. In these moments of de facto blindness, did you begin to know
blindness from the inside? Did those words come back to you—'blind
fools'? Now you yourself are treated like a blind fool. Strangely, my indignation begins to die away. My questions are silenced. You have become a
partner in my world, one who shares my condition, my blind brother.

Later in the same day, they crucified you. From about mid-day, there was
darkness over all the land. It was then that you cried out, 'My God, why
have you forsaken me?' (Mk 15.34). In your agony and confusion, did you
realize that there was an eclipse of the sun? Or did you think that once
again they had blindfolded you? Or that perhaps you had indeed lost the
power of sight? Was that perhaps why you felt forsaken by God, the God of
light, the sighted people's God? I cannot help wondering whether, after

these experiences, your attitude to blindness is somehow different. On the road to Emmaus, the eyes of your two disciples were constrained, so that they were not able to recognize you (Lk. 24.16). You walked the road with two disciples who were in effect blind. Only when you broke the bread were their eyes opened so that they could recognize you, and then you vanished from their sight (Lk. 24.31). Again, they became blind as far as you were concerned, but now it is the blindness of recognition, no longer the blindness of a failure to recognize. Sight has become more paradoxical.

The Gospel of John foresees the end of the sighted culture. 'I am going to the Father and you will see me no longer', and later in the same chapter 'a little while and you will no longer see me; and again a little while, and you will see me' (Jn 16.10, 16). This awareness of the limits of sight is vividly expressed in the story of Thomas, who doubted your resurrection. You said to Thomas, 'Have you believed because you have seen me? Blessed are those who have not seen and yet have come to believe' (Jn 20.29). Most people think you were speaking to second- and third-generation Christians, or those living far away from Israel, who never saw your earthly ministry. However, these words can be regarded as a particular blessing upon your blind disciples.

When I began to write to you, my mind was full of questions. Then my confusion turned into indignation and then I wrote with tears when I realized that you not only died for me but you became blind for me. And what can I say to you now about the passages which offended and hurt me so much? Well, Lord, if I may say so without presumption, I forgive you. But is it not your role to forgive me? Yes, but perhaps our relationship is becoming more mutual. Blind people, after all, do lead other blind people. You have been this way before, so you are familiar with it. Take my hand, blind master, and lead me.

Yours sincerely,

John

Implications for the Education of Both Blind and Sighted People

The attitudes of people in our culture towards blindness are shaped by the classical literature of Western society, reinforced by repetition in many novels and films.[13] This cultural construct is further reinforced by the metaphorical use of blindness in everyday speech.[14]

13. Eleftheria A. Bernidaki-Aldous, *Blindness in a Culture of Light* (Frankfurt: Peter Lang, 1990); William R. Paulson, *Enlightenment, Romanticism and the Blind in France* (Princeton: Princeton University Press, 1987); D. Kent, 'Shackled Imagination—Literary Illusions about Blindness', *Journal of Visual Impairment & Blindness*, 83, 3 (1989), pp. 145-50.

14. The COBUILD Bank of English held in the University of Birmingham con-

This inherited set of attitudes and beliefs is ambivalent towards blindness. On the one hand, blind people are thought of as helpless, pathetic, useless, ignorant or even stupid, insensitive and incompetent. On the other hand, blind people are sometimes regarded as being strangely gifted. They have amazing memories and may have a weird kind of foresight. Blind people are regarded with a mixture of admiration, compassion and horror. A sighted person, sharing these attitudes towards blindness, who loses his or her sight transfers inwardly all of the previous images and presuppositions about blindness.[15] The blinded person now has feelings of horror and compassion towards the self. All the helplessness and ignorance which were imputed to other blind people now recoil upon the self. Thus blindness is a shattering blow to one's self-esteem. This is reinforced by the attitudes of compassion and horror with which the blind person is now greeted by relatives, friends and, above all, employers. The blinded person comes quickly to agree that he or she might get hurt, will have to retire and is no good at anything anymore.

Of course, the shock of blindness is very great, since it is necessary for the personality to reconstruct itself around a different balance of the senses, and the reluctance to exchange one world for another is as profound as the reluctance to lose sight in the first place.[16] Nevertheless, these elements of change in the inner and outer worlds of blindness are certainly accentuated and complicated by social attitudes towards blindness, built up over the centuries.

---

tained more than 750 examples of the word 'blind' from the pages of the *Guardian* newspaper on 23 October 1998. Of these, only 45 per cent are literal. In all but one or two cases, the remaining metaphorical uses are negative towards blindness. 13 per cent emphasize blindness as ignorance, 12 per cent as deliberate indifference, 28 per cent as culpable ignorance (often severe and violent), and 0.02 per cent refer to callous indifference. The remaining 15 per cent are miscellaneous negative expressions. We read of 'blind and insensitive planning', 'blind blithering arrogance' and 'sheer blind obsessiveness'. What use does the word blind serve in these expressions? None, except for providing the satisfaction of using as an expletive a human condition the name of which happens to begin with the letter b. These comments are not a criticism of the *Guardian*. On the contrary, if a socially aware newspaper such as this expresses the negative image so vigorously, we may assume it to be used with less sensitivity elsewhere.

15. A. Wagner-Lam and G.W. Oliver, 'Folklore of Blindness', *Journal of Visual Impairment and Blindness* 88, 3 (1994), pp. 367-76.

16. Maurice Merleau-Ponty, *The Phenomenology of Perception* (London: Routledge, 1962), p. 81.

Since the Bible has been the principal source of cultural definition in Europe, it is not surprising that it is also the principal source of the cultural construct of blindness.

The attitude of Jesus towards blindness has been the inspiration for the medical and social care of blind people in Europe and beyond.[17] The fact that blind people were the objects of the healing ministry of Jesus and that the recovery of sight was one of the main features of the coming of the Kingdom of God has undoubtedly led to improved conditions for blind people.[18] At the same time, however, the negative images of the Bible have also been significant. While the miraculous healing of blind people is obvious, external and memorable, the negative images of blindness in the Bible are subtle, often metaphorical, and almost unnoticeable. The fact that the reader of the Bible is immersed within the cultural construct of blindness largely created by the Bible means that the attitudes towards blindness in the Bible are hardly noticed even as they are read. There is no contrast between the construct of blindness in the Bible and that which is prevalent in our society. As one reads the Bible, the attitudes in the Bible towards blindness are, so to speak, camouflaged by the lack of contrast between them and what we think about blindness anyway. Thus what takes place is an unconscious process of reinforcement. We read the Bible in the light of our cultural construct of blindness, which is at the same time replicated and reinforced by what we read.

One might suppose that the moment one goes blind the truth of this collaboration in prejudice would become apparent. One might imagine that a blind person reading the Bible would quickly detect the disparaging identification of blindness with ignorance, unbelief and sin, but recognition and identification seldom take place with such immediacy and such simplicity. The blind person does not recognize the images any more than the sighted person does, and rather than pointing to the Bible as the source of the oppression, the blind reader points to himself or herself as the person described in the Bible. The blind person reads that Jesus called sighted people blind fools. The blind person, especially the blind religious

---

17. It is significant that prophets and evangelists have often sought to establish their credentials by healing or attempting to heal blind people. An example is the attempt of the millenarian prophet Richard Brothers to heal the blind in 1788. See J.F.C. Harrison, *The Second Coming: Popular Millenarianism, 1780–1850* (London: Routledge Kegan Paul, 1979).

18. Gabriel Farrell, *The Story of Blindness* (London: Oxford University Press, 1956), p. 150; Paulson, *Enlightenment, Romanticism and the Blind in France*, p. 8.

person, does not usually think that Jesus should not have used such language because blind people are not necessarily fools. On the contrary, the blind Christian simply accepts what Jesus said.

The educational implications of this situation for both blind and sighted people are far-reaching. It is essential to develop a critical metaphorical awareness of the biblical text, which is contrary to the literalness too often preferred by the devotional reader of the Bible. This attitude toward blindness has been constructed not only by the Bible but also by the self-enclosure of sighted people. It can be deconstructed by helping sighted people not to be enclosed within their sighted world. This can be attempted through helping both blind and sighted people to realize their own unconscious constructs. The techniques of personal construct psychology such as the pyramid grid are useful ways of doing this.[19] Next, these constructs, having been brought to the surface, can be placed against the images and presuppositions of the Bible. This involves a deconstruction of the cultural artefact through which we read the Bible, and also at a deeper level a reconstruction of the cultural artefact of the sighted world out of which the Bible came in the first place.

The Christian education of blind and sighted people in particular, and of so-called able-bodied and disabled people in more general terms is very much in need of such a liberating pedagogy. As a result of such a process, blind people, whether religious or not, will be able to live with more self-respect and self-understanding. If sighted people can learn to adapt to the needs of blind people without patronizing them, and if blind people can learn to accept sighted people without manipulating them, the new relationship of mutual acceptance between blind and sighted will have become a utopian whisper of a new world.

Implications for a Theology of Blindness

At a conference where I had spoken about a biblical theology of blindness I was the object of a very funny satire which was presented to the members of the conference during a concert on the final evening. My good-natured critic, much to the amusement of everyone, proposed a theology of baldness, which would be inspired by my approach. He presented several passages from the Bible which suggested a prejudice against bald people. The bald Samson was a weak Samson; the boys ridiculed Elisha by

19. Alvin Landfield and Franz R. Epting, *Personal Construct Psychology, Clinical and Personality Assessment* (London: Human Sciences Press, 1986).

shouting out, 'Get out, you bald head!' and, in general, hair is regarded as an ornament and crowning beauty, hence to be without hair was to be dehumanized and ugly. This clever parody made me re-examine my view of blindness. By identifying in detail the particular characteristics of one condition or another, we begin to grasp the fact that some human conditions are so radically different that they create different worlds.[20] A *state* of human life is a condition sufficiently distinct from others, and sufficiently radical to create its own world. Being a child is such a state, and male and female are also such states. A theology of blindness, or of any other major disability, may then be thought of as a theology of the states of life. Its theological antecedent may be found in the French school of mysticism in the seventeenth century associated with Pierre Bérulle.[21] The human states are not so foreign to each other that mutual understanding is impossible, but alternatively they are sufficiently distinct to create real challenges to self-enclosure. Such states are generated through a combination of physical and social characteristics, and the balance between the physical and the social may well vary. Skin colour can produce such states, and in societies which are acutely conscious of pigmentation there can be more than a dozen distinct social groups, each identified by a different skin colour.[22] However radical the different experience of life is for black and white people, this difference is the product of imperialism and has no secure ground in physiology as such. Speaking purely psychologically, black and white people may experience life in very much the same sort of way. That is not true of childhood since, although childhood

20. An outstanding medical psychologist, whose detailed observations have helped us to realize the character of these human states is Oliver Sacks. See especially his *Awakenings* (London: Duckworth, 1973), *A Leg to Stand On* (London: Duckworth, 1984) and *Seeing Voices: A Journey into the World of the Deaf* (London: Picador, 1991).

21. A state is a feature of the life or being of Jesus which is 'concrete, permanent and independent of powers and actions, imprinted in the depths of the created being and in the condition of its state'. Henri Brémond, *A Literary History of Religious Thought in France*, III, *The Triumph of Mysticism* (London: SPCK, 1936), p. 56. States are 'modes of being'. See Eugene A. Walsh, *The Priesthood in the Writings of the French School* (Washington, DC: Catholic University of America Press, 1949), p. 7.

22. In Haiti pigmentations may be significant by a ratio of 127.1 parts white to black. In other words, if a person has one black ancestor seven generations earlier he or she can be categorized accordingly. Thomas H. Eriksen, *Ethnicity & Nationalism: Anthropological Perspectives* (London: Pluto, 1993), pp. 63.

is very largely a cultural artefact,[23] there are necessary biological and developmental factors which would constitute childhood as a distinct state no matter what the character of the cultural construct.

The difference between a state and a non-state will be a matter of criteria which will be arranged along a continuum. Blindness is undoubtedly a state of human life, since blind people live in a world of experience which is radically different from that in which sighted people live.[24] The same may be said, perhaps even more emphatically, of the world of the profoundly deaf person. Adults who do not grow taller than three foot six have an experience of adult life which is so radically different that this condition may be said to be world-creating, but to be a bit on the short side is not the same. It is a sliding scale. In a society of equal opportunities between men and women, the degree to which gender is a world-generating state will be somewhat minimized, although never entirely absent, but in societies where there is rigid gender stereotyping, the world of women may be very different from that of men.[25]

Baldness is not a world-creating condition in our society. It is an attribute of a world but not a world. It may be regarded as a loss, perhaps an embarrassment, and if it is the result of a loss of hair following chemotherapy baldness could be a cause of acute distress. Nevertheless, it remains a distressing feature of the sufferer's ordinary world, and does not throw him or her into the sort of reconstruction of reality which is necessitated by becoming paralysed from the neck down, for example.

A theology of blindness is an example of what might be called a theology of states or conditions. It is similar to and yet different from feminist and black theologies. Like them, it will have both negative and positive aspects; it will both denounce and announce.[26] A theology of blindness will try to expose and denounce the negative imagery which flows from the sighted world,[27] and it will at the same time try to relativize the taken-

23. Philippe Ariès, *Centuries of Childhood* (London: Cape, 1962).

24. I have explored this theme in some detail in *On Sight and Insight: A Journey into the World of Blindness* (Oxford: One World, 1998).

25. John Gledhill, *Power and Its Disguises: Anthropological Perspectives on Politics* (London: Pluto, 1994), pp. 34-38.

26. Paulo Freire, *The Pedagogy of the Oppressed* (London: Sheed & Ward, 1972), p. 76, and *The Politics of Education* (London: Macmillan, 1985), p. 57.

27. Many examples could be provided to illustrate the negative image which blindness has in the Christian theological tradition. The sermon 'Christ the Light of the World', by Jonathan Edwards (1703–58), is full of negative images of blindness.

for-granted assumption of the sighted world that the sighted reality is absolute. Being sighted is also a state.

Next, a theology of blindness will be constructive. It will propose that blind people reflect the image of God in their very blindness. It will show that the metaphor of blindness suggests in a positive way the essential characteristics of the life of faith. From a theology of blindness we can derive practical suggestions about social and political life. These might include the techniques of taking one step at a time, and concentrating on the concrete particularities of an otherwise overwhelmingly abstract problem. A theology of blindness like any theology of disability will challenge prevailing concepts about what is normal. The traditional view is that when the Kingdom of God comes, the eyes of the blind will be opened, the ears of the deaf will be unstopped, and the lame person will jump like a deer. A theology of blindness will show that instead of contemplating utopia in terms of a convergence upon a single image of normality, what we must converge upon is a wider acceptance of varieties as being normal.[28] Normality must become inclusive. This will lead us into a critique of other forms of exclusion, including the most powerful of all, the exclusion of the poor by the rich. In some such way, a theology of blindness will offer a utopian promise of universal liberation.[29]

Wilson Kimnack (ed.) *Jonathan Edwards: Sermons and Discourses 1720–23* (Yale University Press, 1992), p. 535.

28. Jane Wallman, *Disability as Hermeneutic: Towards a Theology of Community* (unpublished PhD thesis, University of Birmingham, School of Education, 2000); for other recent writings on theology and disability, see Judith Z. Abrams, *Judaism and Disability* (Washington DC: Gallandet University Press, 1998), David A. Pailin, *A Gentle Touch: From a Theology of Handicap to a Theology of Human Being* (London: SPCK, 1992), and, for a recent philosophical treatment, Bryan Magee, *On Blindness: Letters between Bryan Magee and Martin Milligan* (Oxford: Oxford University Press, 1995).

29. I have tried to suggest the utopian symbolism of blindness in the postscripts of *On Sight and Insight*, p. 233.

Part II

The Idea of Character in the Bible: Joseph the Dreamer

Stephen Prickett

A title such as this declares its provenance. Only since the eighteenth century could such a romantic or post-romantic theme as 'biblical characterization' be a conceivable, let alone a legitimate, field of study. Moreover, such an *awareness* of changing patterns of biblical interpretation, with the associated notion of different (and changing) historical 'periods', belongs to the same romantic matrix.

With significant exceptions, until about 300 years ago biblical interpretation was essentially typological and figural. The richly varied protagonists of the Hebrew Bible, Abraham and Isaac, Jacob and Esau, Joseph and his brothers, or David and Solomon, had been assimilated into that specifically Christian construct, the Old Testament, by relating them not to their context but to their perceived counterparts in the Christian gospel, the New Testament. By the late Middle Ages, the general claim that Christianity was the key to understanding the Hebrew Scriptures—the message of Philip to the Ethiopian in Acts 8—was supported by an increasingly elaborate system of figurative and allegorical interpretation. Even pagan classical texts were included by some authorities who were prepared to see Virgil's *Aeneid*, for instance, as a parable of the Christian soul's journey through life. Interpreters such as Origen and Augustine were to lay the foundations of a system of exegesis so complex and polysemous that almost every event of the history of the Old Testament could simultaneously be read as world history and as the key to contemporary events.

Such interpretation, moreover, was endlessly elastic. The Bible was too important a narrative to be confined to only one (past) meaning. Different schools of thought differed as to the precise number of figural interpretations possible to a given passage of Scripture. Some Alexandrian authorities detected as many as twelve, but four was by far the most widely accepted number.[1] Even this number could itself be arrived at by typological reasoning. Irenaeus, for example, argued for the canonical primacy of the four Gospels from the fact that God's world was supplied in fours: as there were 'four zones', and 'four winds', so there were four Gospels. From this, four levels of interpretation followed easily. According to St John Cassian in the fourth century these were a literal, or historical sense, an allegorical, a tropological (or moral) and an anagogical. Tropological related to the Word, or doctrine conveyed by it, and therefore carried a moral sense; the anagogical concerns eternal things. Cassian takes as his example the figure of Jerusalem. Historically it may be seen as the earthly city; allegorically, it stands for the Church; tropologically it represents the souls of all faithful Christians; anagogically, it is the heavenly city of God.[2] As a later Latin rhyme has it:

> Littera gesta docet, quid credes allegoria,
> Moralis quid agas, quo tendas anagogia.
>
> [The letter teaches what happened, the allegorical what to believe,
> The moral what to do, the anagogical toward what to aspire.][3]

This Christian sense of 'allegory' (from the Greek *allegoria*) came to carry a quite different sense from the original classical one of a fiction fable or personification with another meaning—of the sort used by Aesop. Nor was this mode of interpretation contingent or accidental. Erich Auerbach argues convincingly that far from being merely a hermeneutic fashion, this new Christian interpretative theory was an essential ingredient in its becoming a world religion:

> Figural interpretation changed the Old Testament from a book of laws and a history of the people of Israel into a series of figures of Christ and the Redemption—so Celtic and Germanic peoples, for example, could accept the Old Testament as part of the universal religion of salvation and a necessary component of the equally magnificent and universal vision of history conveyed to them along with this religion... Its integral, firmly teleological, view of history and the providential order of the world gave it the power to

1. See John Wilkinson, *Interpretation and Community* (London: Macmillan, 1963), esp. pp. 119-57.
2. Marjorie Reeves, 'The Bible and Literary Authorship in the Middle Ages', in Stephen Prickett (ed.), *Reading the Text: Biblical Criticism and Literary Theory* (Oxford: Blackwell, 1991), p. 16.
3. A.J. Minnis, *Mediaeval Theory of Authorship* (London: Scolar, 1984), p. 34.

capture the imagination…of the convert nations. Figural interpretation was
a fresh beginning and a rebirth of man's creative powers.[4]

It was, in effect, the prime tool of the Christian appropriation of the
Hebrew Scriptures—by far the most successful piece of literary appropriation ever carried out. As Auerbach also significantly observes, the
appropriation was accompanied by a new surge of creative energies—even
if some figural interpretations strike the modern reader as little short of
grotesque. A sermon among the *spuria* of Chrysostom interprets the
Massacre of the Innocents by noting that the fact that children of two years
old and under were murdered while those of three presumably were spared
is meant to teach us that those who hold the Trinitarian faith will be saved
whereas Binitarians and Unitarians will undoubtedly perish.[5] By the
Middle Ages the literal meaning of even such writings as Paul's letters
took second place to figurative meanings. The fact that such meanings
were frequently anti-semitic illustrates with some force the extraordinary
double-focus that some Christian uses of the Bible had acquired by that
time.

It is important to realise, however, that such an interpretative system
was not *at the expense* of what we would now see as 'character' and
'historical context'. Both our modern literary and psychological idea of
character and our idea of history are themselves essentially romantic ideas.
Though we can read a later sense of character into works of the past—
in the Old and New Testaments, as in, for instance, Shakespeare or
Chaucer—that does not mean people of the past had the same sense of
individual identity as we (commonly) do. Augustine's *Confessions* give us
a glimpse into what we may feel is a modern consciousness, and in some
senses he represents just that, but, as Charles Taylor shows in his magisterial book, *Sources of the Self: The Making of the Modern Identity*, he is
a rare exception.[6] Moreover, the fact that it was Augustine who also was
responsible for so much of the traditional figural interpretation of the Bible
should alert us to the fact that for him such allegorical interpretations of
character were not a step away from 'real' characterization, but a part of it.
For him, and for the Church for another thousand years, the historical

---

4.   Erich Auerbach, *Scenes from the Drama of European Literature* (trans. R.
Mannheim; New York, 1959), p. 28.
5.   See 'The Reasonableness of Typology' , in G.W.H. Lampe and K.G.
Woollcombe (eds.), *Essays on Typology* (London: SCM Press, 1957), p. 31.
6.   Charles Taylor, *Sources of the Self: The Making of the Modern Identity*
(Cambridge: Cambridge University Press, 1989), esp. pp. 127-41.

actuality of a person was primarily a guarantee of the inner spiritual meaning of their existence.[7] The last gasp of such an attitude can be seen as late as *The Vanity of Human Wishes* (1749), where Johnson comments on the fate of Charles XII of Sweden:

> He left the name at which the world grew pale,
> To point a moral, or adorn a tale (11.221-22).

At such a transitional point, however, it is difficult to be sure of the degree of irony involved. For an earlier generation, such a fate would have hardly been 'vanity'; for a later one the vanity would have lain not in the failure of Charles's ambitions but in the gap between private man and public persona.

Though such a gap is already present in Shakespeare (think of *Henry V*, or, even better, *Hamlet*) the idea of 'character' in our modern sense of personal individuality, and its associated sense of interior space, owes its origins more to the novel than to any other single source. The novel is, supremely, the art form of interiorized consciousness. Yet it is also arguable that the new personal sense of self was in part inspired by the new ways of reading the Bible created by the novel.

Theories of the origin of the novel are many and various. There were substantial prose narratives in both classical China and Japan, as well in the Roman world.[8] The story of Potiphar's wife (Gen. 39.7-20) was first told in an Egyptian story dating back at least as far as 1200 BCE. Whatever its precursors, however, the modern novel (like Protestantism) was undoubtedly a product of the printing press. It is perhaps significant that though the common word for the novel in both German and French (*roman*) connects it with earlier epic poetry (as in the fourteenth-century *Roman de la Rose*), in England, where the modern novel has its strongest roots, the name adopted, 'novel', stresses not its continuities with the past, but the newness of the form. Whether or not this is an accident of linguistic history, it reflects one of those momentous sea changes in reading that permanently altered the way in which books, whether sacred or secular, were understood and interpreted. It was probably not until the extraordinary success of Defoe's *Robinson Crusoe* in 1719 that people became aware of how the new art form was altering not merely standards

7.   Reeves, 'Bible and Literary Authorship', p. 17.
8.   *The Dream of the Red Chamber*, *The Story of Genji*, and *The Golden Ass* are all well-known examples.

of realism, but, less obviously, also the way in which other kinds of narrative were being read and understood.[9]

If Shakespeare and his fellow-dramatists had begun the exploration of character, they had worked almost invariably with aristocratic, and usually foreign, settings.[10] The novel continued this tradition, but in a middle-class and domestic context. Significantly it was the first art form created as much by women as by men, and what evidence we have of eighteenth-century readership suggests an overwhelmingly female audience. Hardly surprisingly, it was popular, low-status, and frequently denounced by moralists.

Nevertheless, as the eighteenth century progresses, we find that, increasingly, the Bible—and in particular the Old Testament—was ceasing to be read as though it spoke with a single omniscient dogmatic voice, and began instead to be read as novelistic dialogue, or even (in Bakhtin's terms) a heteroglossia, with a plurality of competing voices. At the same time, what had been universally accepted as an essentially polysemous narrative, with many threads of meaning, typological, anagogical, allegorical and moral, was being narrowed into a single thread of story, which was almost invariably interpreted as being 'historical'—and, needless to say, unreliable history at that.

For an early nineteenth-century commentator like Mrs Trimmer, however, the question of historicity could still be taken for granted. As with the mediaeval exegetes, what matters for her are not the 'facts' of history, but the *lessons* that it can teach us. Yet her way of phrasing what she evidently believes is an age-old truism shows unmistakably the subversive influence of the new art form:

> The Books that follow, as far as the BOOK OF ESTHER, are called the HISTORICAL BOOKS. The Histories they contain differ from all the other histories that ever were written, for they give an account of the ways of GOD; and explain *why* GOD *protected and rewarded* some persons and nations, and *why* he *punished* others; also, *what led* particular persons mentioned in Scripture to *do* certain things for which they were approved or condemned; whereas writers who compose histories in a common way, without being *inspired of God*, can only form guesses and conjectures

---

9. See Prickett, *Origins of Narrative*, ch. 3.

10. For Shakespeare's consistently aristocratic bias, see Erich Auerbach, *Mimesis* (Princeton: Princeton University Press, 1953). The obvious exceptions to this generality are Shakespeare's *The Merry Wives of Windsor*, Yarrington's *A Yorkshire Tragedy* and the anonymous *Arden of Faversham*.

concerning God's dealings with mankind, neither can they know what passed in the hearts of those they write about; such knowledge as this, belongs to *God* alone, whose ways are *unsearchable and past finding out*, and *to whom all hearts are open, all desires known!*[11]

God is here not so much Supreme Judge as Supreme Novelist; the biblical protagonists not types, but characters.

Nor is this shift of interest confined to Britain. For the French romantic, Chateaubriand, typology was similarly no longer adequate to convey the human qualities of biblical narrative. Like Mrs Trimmer, he has no thought of being original. His *Genius of Christianity* (1802) presents itself as being both traditional and conservative—but the result is unintentionally revolutionary. What mattered for Chateaubriand was the confluence of intellect and passion, in short, the delineation of character. For him, the Bible excels not merely in morals, but as literature. Indeed, without its aesthetic lead, modern literature could not exist:

> Christianity is, if we may so express it, a double religion. Its teaching has reference to the nature of intellectual being, and also to our own nature: it makes the mysteries of the Divinity and the mysteries of the human heart go hand-in-hand; and, by removing the veil that conceals the true God, it also exhibits man just as he is.

Such a religion must necessarily be more favourable to the delineation of *characters* than another which dives not into the secret of the passions. The fairer half of poetry, the dramatic, received no assistance from polytheism, for morals were separated from mythology.[12]

To see the impact of such character-driven, novelistic, criticism on traditional typological modes of biblical interpretation one need look no further than two commentaries on the story of Jacob and Esau, one from an early eighteenth-century volume, and an early nineteenth-century account of the same incident by Mrs Trimmer herself:

> This Mysterious History throughout, represents to us in all parts of it Jesus Christ, clothed in the outward appearance of a Sinner, as Jacob here was in that of Esau. It is also an admirable Figure of the Reprobation of the Jews, who desired nothing but the good things of the World; and of the Election of the Church, which (like David) desires but one thing of GOD, and requests but one Blessing.

11. Mrs (Sarah) Trimmer, *Help to the Unlearned in the Study of the Holy Scriptures* (London, 2nd edn, 1806), p. iii.

12. Trimmer, *Help to the Unlearned,* p. 232.

> We must have a care (as S. Paul saith) not to imitate Esau, who having sold his Birth-right to Jacob, and desiring afterwards, as being the Eldest, to receive the Blessing of his Father, was rejected, without being able to persuade his Father to revoke what he had pronounced in Favour of Jacob, notwithstanding his entreating it with many Tears. For as he had despised GOD, GOD also despised his Cries and Tears, as not proceeding from a sincere Repentance, nor from a true Change of Heart.[13]

This is typical typological exegesis. Somewhat improbably to modern sensibilities, Jacob's impersonation of the unfortunate Esau 'represents' Christ's incarnation in sinful flesh. Readers of Donne's *Holy Sonnet* XI, 'Spit in my face you Jewes...' will recall the similar parallel between Jacob and Christ in the sestet:

> And Jacob came cloth'd in vile harsh attire
> But to suplant, and with gainfull intent:
> God cloth'd himself in vile mans flesh, that so
> He might be weake enough to suffer woe.

So far from being one of Donne's more outrageous conceits, the figure was a standard one—even to the overt anti-semitism of the opening lines. The change between this and the second passage, by Mrs Trimmer, who also saw herself as a traditional exegete, could hardly be more startling. Here the search is still for 'meaning', but that word is conceived in quite different terms of author, character and plot:

> Jacob, in obedience to his mother, acts against his own conscience. Our Reason will show us that these are not things we should imitate in Isaac, Rebekah, and Jacob; therefore no remarks are made upon them by the sacred writer of their history. What we are particularly to observe here, is, that GOD made the faults of these three persons contribute to bring about his own good purposes. GOD knew beforehand what they would do; he also knew that Jacob, though he would do many wrong things, would keep from idol worship, and reverence his Creator, and bring up his family in the true religion; and that Esau on the contrary would marry among idolators, and depart from the right way; and GOD, possibly for this reason, ordained that Jacob rather than Esau should be the head of the great nation through which all the families of the earth should be blessed.[14]

---

13. Richard Blome (ed.), *History of the Old and New Testaments Extracted from the Sacred Scriptures, the Holy Fathers, and Other Ecclesiastical Writers* (London, 4th impression, 1712), p. 31. See also Prickett, *Origins of Narrative*, ch. 1.

14. Trimmer, *Help to the Unlearned*, pp. 32-33.

This is not typological but literary criticism. God is the supreme novelist, and our task is to work out the moral significance of the characters he has created. Yet one senses a certain unease. Mrs Trimmer has not had the advantage of reading her Bakhtin, knows nothing of heteroglossia, and has not read Chateaubriand, but she clearly suspects that this is not altogether the kind of morally improving narrative she was accustomed to producing in her own (numerous) religious tracts. Stripped of its typological gloss, the Bible is turning into a novel before her eyes, and she is not entirely sure it is the kind of novel she is going to approve of.

Such dangerous experiences are not unknown among readers of the Bible. For two thousand years people have found in it the mirror of their dominant art form. For the mediaeval world, largely illiterate and visual, the Bible offered a series of scenes to be painted on the walls of churches for instruction and edification. Later such 'scenes' could be presented on makeshift stages, or even on carts to be drawn around the streets of London, Coventry or Wakefield as part of the Corpus Christi rituals. Later still, for a newly Protestant Elizabethan London, the great 'drama' of God's Creation and Redemption of the world mirrored the complex action of the theatre, where sub-plot and main plot commented obliquely on one another, by imagery and juxtaposition.

Yet if the advent of the English eighteenth-century novel, and the new print culture of which it was a part, were to lead to our modern sense of characterization, the greatest study of biblical character was to come not from England, but from the unlikely context of twentieth-century Germany—where the novel had scarcely established a foothold until the beginning of the nineteenth century. Thomas Mann's massive tetralogy, *Joseph and his Brothers*, is essentially a study of biblical character-ization—not just of Joseph himself, and his brothers but of his father, his mother, and the entire context of the Canaanite and Egyptian worlds of the second millennium BCE. It is a world seen through twentieth-century eyes, drawing on the entire corpus of contemporary history, archaeology and anthropology of the ancient Near East. At its centre, of course, is the figure of Joseph himself, increasingly endowed with a 'modern' character and sensibility in contrast with a context where absolute rulers, child sacrifice and slavery were the norm. For Mann, Joseph is the first modern person—the man of vision and the type of the later artist.

The biblical context is no less significant. The novel was begun as early as 1926 and published between 1933 and 1943—the first two volumes in Berlin (1933 and 1934), the third in Vienna (1936), and the final one (for obvious reasons) in Stockholm (1943). From the start the narratives are animated by a tension between the mythological, even timeless, nature of the biblical material itself and the turbulent twentieth-century context in which the novels were written. At one level nothing could be further removed from the crises of German identity that shook the world during that decade than a historical novel about one of the most ancient stories of the Old Testament; but at another level, of course, as is always true of historical novels, the story as it took shape had everything to do with Mann's contemporary situation—both personal and political.

Certainly the Nazi censor responsible for reading the first volume in 1933, the writer Herbert Blank, saw its publication as a political act. 'It is simply not endurable', he wrote in his report on *The Tales of Jacob*, 'that, ten months after 30 January [the day Hitler became Chancellor], the emigrant Thomas Mann is able to retail in Germany a book full of Jewish tales.'[15] Mann had been marked down by the Nazis, immediately they came to power in 1933, as a 'liberal-reactionary'; he responded to their attacks by resigning from the Prussian Academy of Arts as a public act of protest against the new regime in the same year, and moved to Switzerland where he lived until 1939. At the outbreak of the Second World War he went to the United States, and in 1944, in a no less political gesture, became an American citizen.

If a novel about the book of Genesis, and what it meant to be a displaced and enslaved Israelite within a powerful and imperial high culture, had an immediate (indeed, prophetic) reference to the context of Nazi Germany, it is also true that this, arguably Mann's greatest work, arises uniquely from the German cultural tradition to which he was heir—and which, during the 1940s, he explicitly appropriated to himself. His famous claim in exile in California, *Wo ich bin ist die deutsche Kultur* ('Where I am is German culture'), has, I think rightly, been seen in its context as not so much a piece of personal arrogance as itself a 'necessary political act',[16] denying the competence of the crude and chauvinistic Nazi 'cultural' propaganda, and stressing the surviving life and continuity of an older German tradition of liberal culture. Yet the papal resonances of that

15. Joseph Wulf (*Literatur und Dichtung im Dritten Reich: Ein Dokumentation* [1966], p. 24), cited by R.J. Hollingdale in *Thomas Mann: A Critical Study* (London: Hart-Davis, 1971), p. 23.

16. T.J. Reed, *Thomas Mann: The Uses of Tradition* (Oxford: Clarendon Press, 1974), p. 1.

phrase[17] may also alert us to other levels, of a personal, rather than a political, imperialism. It is not so far from his 1916 statement to Ernst Bertram that he had long believed the tragedy of Germany to be 'symbolized and personified' by himself and his brother,[18] which, in turn, foreshadows Mann's later affirmation of a 'mystical union' with Goethe in the novel *Lotte in Weimar* (1939)—chronologically an interruption in the middle of the Joseph sequence. In short, however we are meant to take his claim to embody the cultural tradition of a whole nation,[19] it is hard to read it *simply* as a statement about the necessary exile of the German literary tradition during the Second World War. Mann stands unequivocally in the tradition of German romanticism, and it was a tradition that laid greater stress on the individuality and uniqueness of the artistic ego than perhaps any other. His claim, moreover, comes very close to Joseph's own to represent the Hebrew tradition, made first in Potiphar's house, and then subsequently in the Egyptian Court.

Yet Joseph's route towards fulfilment of this dynamic and self-conscious destiny is a long and complex one, and forms one reason, at least, for the massive length of the novel. Eliezer, Jacob's steward, is a semi-mythological figure, both in his name, which is the same as that of the servant of Abraham who had found Rebecca at the well, and in his own consciousness which does not fully distinguish between himself and his Eliezer-ancestors:

> the old man's ego was not quite clearly demarcated, that it opened at the back, as it were, and overflowed into spheres external to his own individuality both in space and time; embodying in his own experience events which, remembered and related in the clear light of day, ought actually to have been put into the third person... The conception of individuality belongs after all to the same category as that of unity and entirety, the whole and the all; and in the days of which I am writing the distinction between spirit in general and individual spirit possessed not nearly so much power of the mind as in our world of today... It is highly significant that in those days there were no words for conceptions dealing with personality and individuality, other than such external ones as confession, religion.[20]

17. *Ubi papem, ibi ecclesia* ('Where the Pope is, there is the Church').

18. Cited by Marcel Reich-Ranicki, *Thomas Mann and his Family* (trans. Ralph Manheim; London: Fontana, 1990), p. 4.

19. Reed, *Thomas Mann*, p. 340.

20. Thomas Mann, *Joseph and his Brothers* (trans. H.T. Lowe-Porter; London: Penguin, 1978), p. 78.

It is from Eliezer, as much as from his father, Jacob, that the young Joseph has learned his sense of the past. Not surprisingly, 'his ideas of time showed themselves to be hazy indeed; the past which he so lightly invoked being actually matter of remote and primeval distances'.[21] Even according to their own records, the gap between Abraham's departure from Ur and Joseph's time was some six hundred years—though, as Mann adds,

> six hundred years at that time and under that sky did not mean what they mean in our western history...the frame of Joseph's life, his ways and habits of thought were far more like his ancestors' than ours are like the crusaders.[22]

The point of this lengthy discussion of Joseph's mindset right at the start of the novel is to show both how (unlike his brothers) he is fascinated by his family history and traditions, and, at the same time, that his sense of that tradition, and his own place in it, is more mythological than it is historical. The idea of the blessing is, as it were, the dominant and organizing historical myth by which the other myths of origins are to be understood. The story of Joseph is that of the emergence from myth to historical self-consciousness.

This, surely, is also the meaning of the curious first chapter of the *Tales of Jacob*, entitled 'At the Well'. We first encounter the boy Joseph alone and half naked, contemplating beside his father Jacob's well. As is repeatedly made clear, the well is itself a symbol of the unfathomable depths of the past—both for Joseph, as he looks back upon the history of his tribe, and the legends of surrounding societies which have inevitably formed part of Hebrew mythology, and, at the same time for ourselves, as we try to understand the outlook of Jacob and his favourite son over a gulf of more than three thousand years. But Joseph, at the moment we encounter him, is not so much gazing into the deep well of the past, but into himself—what Henry James called 'the deep well of the unconscious'. He is not in love—and is probably too egotistical ever to be so in the sense that his father Jacob was with Rachel—but his state of contemplation has much in common with the condition of primary intuition which Schleiermacher describes as 'the highest flowering of religion'. For Jacob, like so many of the heroes of romantic and post-romantic novels, this state of self-conscious intuition was only to be reached through his sexual love for Rachel, his cousin, for whose sake he served his devious father-in-law 14

---

21. Mann, *Joseph and his Brothers*, p. 13.
22. Mann, *Joseph and his Brothers*, p. 78.

years. He had fled from his brother with only his life and the blessing. To become Israel, the father of the great people foretold in the dream at Bethel, he had first of all to learn to love something outside himself better than himself. His love for Rachel is at once his triumph and Joseph's immediate undoing, for from it stemmed Jacob's open favouritism towards Rachel's son and the consequent hatred of his half-brothers that was to send Joseph into the pit, and thence to the Midianite slavers and so to Egypt. All this is still in the future, however, and what we see in Joseph at this point is less a religious experience than, as it were, the readiness for it: the capacity for such intuitions as Schleiermacher describes, and the possession of what in Jacob's case is described as 'the copious flow of mythical association of ideas and their capacity to permeate the moment'.[23] It is significant how often in the conversation with his father that follows he refers to himself in the third person. As the inheritor of the blessing, he must learn to say 'I'; and if we turn from these first pages to the final volume, *Joseph the Provider*, we find that this is precisely what his experiences have taught him.

Indeed, it is surely significant that Joseph himself, with his supreme and cheerful assumption of his own divinely protected destiny, offers us one of Mann's most fully developed portraits of the artist in society.[24] No culture, neither ancient Egypt nor, certainly, Germany in the 1940s, is static, or an island unto itself. Not least among the prophetic roles of the artist is the task of giving voice, and even structure, to forces of change. Just as Luther, with his great sixteenth-century translation of the Bible had virtually created the modern German language, so Mann, symbolically in exile in the new world, sees himself as inheriting and renewing that process—once again in relation to the Bible.

As the Nazi censor seems dimly to have perceived from *The Tales of Jacob* as early as 1933, to make the Jew, stateless, nomadic, and infinitely adaptable, yet above all possessed of a unique vision, the type of the artist in society was a boldly polemical move. In that first volume Jacob/Israel has always a sense that his nomadic status is more than historical contingency, but a necessary attribute of his religion, for

> one served a God whose nature was not repose and abiding comfort, but a
> God of designs for the future, in whose will inscrutable, great, far-reaching
> things were in process of becoming, who, with His brooding will and His
> world-planning, was Himself only in process of becoming, and thus was a

23. Mann, *Joseph and his Brothers*, p. 57.
24. Hollingdale, *Thomas Mann*, p. 114.

> God of unrest, a God of cares, who must be sought for, for whom one must at all times keep oneself free, mobile and in readiness.[25]

This is still the God of the great promises to Abraham and to Isaac, but whose nature is now apparently protean: one not merely of change, but of dynamic evolution. Nor is this idea of a divine *entelechy* simply a metaphor: in Mann's God there is a consistent tension between a sense of mysterious divine purpose and an ironic assumption that he is no more than a reflection of the attributes historically attributed to him. Thus at times the narrative has all the conscious anthropomorphism of a lecture on the Higher Criticism. But this is, of course, deliberate. This study of character emerging from myth and primal participation could only be created from a post-critical consciousness. Similarly, Mann has no problems with the idea that the Joseph of the final volume is in the end *neither* Jewish *nor* German, but American. In his 1948 foreword to the English edition he writes:

> I have no objection if…critics say that the German of the 'Prelude in the Upper Circles' in Joseph the Provider 'is really not German any more'. Suffice it that it is speech, and suffice it that the entire opus is fundamentally a work of speech in whose polyphony sounds of the primitive Orient mingle with the most modern, with the accents of fictive scientific method, and that it takes pleasure in changing its linguistic masks as often as its hero changes his God-masks—the last of which looks remarkably American. For it is the mask of an American Hermes, a brilliant messenger of shrewdness, whose New Deal is unmistakably reflected in Joseph's magic administration of national economy.[26]

Joseph the Egyptian, re-invigorates the devastated land of Canaan; Mann the American sees himself re-invigorating the devastated land of Germany in ways neither could have imagined when they were unwillingly propelled upon their respective physical and spiritual expatriations. Beneath the obvious parallels lurk others—no less deliberate, one suspects. If the German of Mann's final volume is an 'Americanized' German, the parallel is with Luther's great re-creation of the language with his sixteenth-century translation of the Bible. To recreate a language is not merely to alter its words, but its concepts and its unconscious framework of thought. If (as is controversially arguable) Luther's German had laid the foundation

---

25. Hollingdale, *Thomas Mann*, p. 31.
26. Hollingdale, *Thomas Mann*, p. xiii. This is, of course, a quality lost to English translation, especially in the often hurried, infelicitous, and inaccurate translation of Lowe-Porter, which is all we have.

for the dogmatic, authoritarian, anti-semitic and Erastian outlook that was finally to destroy Germany, both physically and morally, in the twentieth century, the implication is that Mann's German is to lay the foundations of a more liberal, libertarian and open society.

Beneath that, even, is another, more complex, suggestion. Joseph, the dreamer, the administrator, the instigator of the first 'New Deal', is Mann's type of the artist, at once man of faith and secular sceptic. Mann's biblical character, and his identification with it, anticipates and articulates what Rorty later was to call the 'aesthetic turn' of twentieth-century thought. The roots of this idea lie, of course, not in modern American pragmatism, but in German Romantic thought—in the criticism of the Schlegels and in Schleiermacher's hermeneutics. We can see here why a novel such as *Joseph and his Brothers* could only emerge from a German context and not, despite the greater biblical influence of its literary culture, from the English-speaking world—though Mann's acknowledged 'Americanization' of his language might suggest that he is deliberately siting his novel at the confluence of the two literary traditions. Only there, perhaps, could a contemporary understanding of biblical meaning evolve. As so often in the past, biblical interpretation not merely mirrors the concerns and interests of its age, it strangely prefigures them, maintaining a dialogue now entering its fourth millennium.

JOSEPH THE PATRIARCH: REPRESENTATIONS OF JOSEPH
IN EARLY POST-BIBLICAL LITERATURE

Susan Docherty

Introduction

Of all the stories in the Hebrew Bible, it is perhaps the Joseph narrative in Genesis which has been appropriated most effectively and most enduringly.[1] From his prominence in mediaeval Islamic art and literature to his characterization in Mann's twentieth-century novel (discussed by Stephen Prickett in this collection), Joseph has been assured a rich and varied theological and cultural afterlife. This article is concerned with some of the earliest representations of Joseph, the interpretations found in the Jewish literature of the Inter-Testamental period. The number and variety of texts which retell or refer to the Joseph narrative testify to the great interest in his character and story among Jews as diverse as the members of the Qumran community and the Hellenistic Jewish philosopher Philo; several of the texts which were current in the period from approximately 250 BCE to 100 CE will be considered. In examining the aspects of the canonical narrative which each chooses to emphasize or downplay, particular attention will be given to their characterization of Joseph and to how the religious and cultural setting of the authors affected their exegesis of this narrative.

Many good reasons can be suggested for the continued popularity of the Joseph Story, but two are of particular relevance to this study. The first is the obvious appeal of these chapters of Genesis for later Jews, who took pride in the story of one of their ancestors rising to such an important position in the powerful Gentile land of Egypt. In particular, those Jews who

1. For a summary of the treatment of Joseph in biblical commentary, art and literature throughout the centuries, see A. Jacobs, 'Joseph the Patriarch', in D.L. Jeffrey (ed.), *A Dictionary of Biblical Tradition in English Literature* (Grand Rapids, MI: Eerdmans, 1992), pp. 414-16.

actually lived in Egypt, or in other parts of the Diaspora, may have found an important role model in Joseph, who was so successful in his adopted home, but who remained faithful to his Jewish heritage. The second important reason is the craft and complexity of the Genesis narrative which makes possible a wide range of interpretations and emphases. The character of Joseph stands out as one of the most multi-dimensional or ambiguous figures encountered within the pages of the Hebrew Scriptures. On a positive note, he was blessed by God throughout his time in Egypt (Gen. 39.2-5, 23; 41.51-52), refused to have intercourse with his master's wife (Gen. 39.7-12), was a successful administrator (Gen. 39.5-6, 22-23; 42.46-49), and his life story reveals God's providence in arranging for the people of Israel to find a home in Egypt during a time of prolonged famine (Gen. 45.5-8). There are, however, glimpses in the narrative of another side to Joseph: a lad somewhat spoiled by his father (Gen. 37.3), a youth who told tales on his brothers (Gen. 37.2) and boasted about his dreams of future greatness (Gen. 37.5-10), a man who intimidated and imprisoned his brothers when they turned up in Egypt (Gen. 42.7-24; 44.1-34) and even kept one of them bound as a hostage (Gen. 42.18-24). Almost all of the later interpretations of the Joseph narrative emphasize the positive and present Joseph as an idealised figure. However, the freedom and creativity with which later interpreters approached this rich biblical text offers interesting insights into their beliefs and concerns.

Inner-biblical Interpretation of the Joseph Story

Despite the very substantial treatment of Joseph in Genesis, there are in fact very few references to him elsewhere in the Hebrew Scriptures. Two passages, however, are germane to this enquiry. Psalm 105, dated by many commentators[2] to the third century BCE, reviews God's great deeds throughout history on behalf of Israel and includes a summary of the life of Joseph in vv. 16-22. Three features of the author's brief interpretation of the Joseph narrative are particularly striking. First, Joseph's sufferings on being sold into slavery in Egypt are exaggerated:

> His feet were hurt with fetters, his neck was put in a collar of iron (Ps. 105.18).

2. See, for example, M. Niehoff, *The Figure of Joseph in Post-Biblical Jewish Literature* (Leiden: E.J. Brill, 1992), p. 40.

Secondly, these sufferings are interpreted as being due to God testing Joseph (Ps. 105.19). Finally, the motif of Joseph's wisdom is introduced; not only did he rule over Pharaoh's house and possessions (Ps. 105.21), but he was also appointed by the king

> to instruct his princes at his pleasure, and to teach his elders wisdom (Ps. 105.22).

In this passage, then, it seems that Joseph's life and career are being depicted in terms of the Exodus, a central concern of Psalm 105. Aptowitzer[3] has drawn attention to the potential for Jewish commentators to interpret Joseph's life story as a prefiguring of Israel's destiny. Joseph, the favourite of his father, can be seen as representing the people of Israel, the beloved children of Yahweh. As he was mistreated by his brothers, taken to a foreign country and humiliated, so Israel has been enslaved in Egypt, and later invaded and exiled in Babylon. As Joseph subsequently attained rulership and power in Egypt, so the people of Israel hoped for future vindication and glory. The emphasis in Psalm 105 on the themes of Joseph's sufferings as a slave, his steadfastness under trial and his eventual success in Egypt serve therefore to remind the people of God's great deeds on their behalf in the past and to assure them that God can act to save even in the most desperate of situations.

In 1 Maccabees 2, Joseph is one of the figures cited by Mattathias in his farewell speech to his sons, in which he encouraged them to imitate Israel's righteous ancestors in remaining faithful to the law in difficult times:

> Joseph in the time of his distress kept the commandment, and became lord of Egypt (1 Macc. 2.53).

So Joseph's fidelity to the commandments of the Jewish law is praised, presumably a reference to his refusal to have intercourse with Potiphar's wife, and his powerful status as 'lord of Egypt' is also important. In commenting on this passage, Niehoff[4] has highlighted how this twofold stress on Joseph's religious devotion and his political achievement flow out of the Maccabaean context, characterized as it was by a mixture of zeal for the law and political ambition. For this author, Joseph was significant as a role model, both because of his observance of the law when tempted by Gentiles to abandon it and as a successful ruler in the political sphere.

---

3.   V. Aptowitzer, 'Aseneth, the Wife of Joseph: A Haggadic Literary-Historical Study', *HUCA* 1 (1924), pp. 239-306 (296).
4.   Niehoff, *Figure of Joseph*, p. 52.

Representations of Joseph in Hellenistic Jewish Texts

The Writings of Artapanus

Fragments of the work of Artapanus have been preserved in the writings of the Early Christian historian Eusebius. They provide an example of a very early interpretation of the Joseph narrative and demonstrate how it functioned as a source of pride and apologetic for later Jews living in Egypt. Artapanus's account of the Joseph narrative suggests that Joseph's brothers were jealous of his superior wisdom and understanding. To avoid mentioning the detail that Joseph arrived in Egypt as a slave, which might not have reflected well on his descendants, Artapanus explained that Joseph foresaw his brothers' plot against him and so persuaded some neighbouring Arabs to take him to Egypt (Eusebius, *P.E.* 9.23.1). After he arrived there, he became acquainted with the king, and so was appointed chief economic minister; nothing is said about his time as a servant and a prisoner before his exaltation to power. In his important position, he was able to reorganize Egyptian agriculture and create a more equitable system of land distribution. Joseph therefore was responsible for bringing about lasting benefits to Egyptian society, including the discovery of measurements. The implication of Artapanus's retelling of the story is that Egypt owes its prosperity as a nation to the intelligence of an Israelite.[5]

This representation of Joseph by Artapanus is wholly positive. His wisdom and intelligence are stressed, and he does nothing to provoke his brothers' jealousy. As noted by Gruen,[6] far from being a passive victim of a plot on his life, he is shrewd enough to arrange his escape to Egypt. There his administrative talents, as well as his virtue, ensure his rise to power. This depiction of Joseph would naturally have been very appealing to Jews living in Egypt. They could not only point to the popularity of their great ancestor with the people of Egypt but also claim him as the founder of the country's economic and social structure. Artapanus is the earliest witness to the great freedom taken by many Jewish interpreters in the early post-biblical period in their retelling of the Joseph narrative to suit their particular views, cultural setting and audience. Several of the

---

5. Collins has described the work of Artapanus as: 'the most elaborate example of "competitive historiography" which has survived from the Egyptian Diaspora'. See J.J. Collins, *Between Athens and Jerusalem* (New York: Crossroad, 1986), p. 38.

6. E.S. Gruen, *Heritage and Hellenism* (California: University of California Press, 1998), p. 88.

themes stressed in his work, particularly Joseph's innocence in the face of his brothers' hatred and an exaggeration of his influence and popularity as ruler of Egypt, recurred in later texts. Joseph's observance of the Jewish law is not central to Artapanus's presentation of the narrative, at least as it is reproduced in Eusebius. Joseph is presented as a shrewd and intelligent character, who is able to use his abilities to bring about his own success.

Joseph and Aseneth

Joseph and Aseneth, another extremely interesting text, demonstrates the continuing popularity of the Joseph story among Jews of the Diaspora. The unknown author wrote in Greek, and probably lived in Egypt where the narrative is set, as Egyptian idolatry is specifically condemned (e.g. 12.9).[7] Most commentators argue for a date of composition somewhere between 100 BCE (after the translation of the Septuagint, with which the author appears to have been familiar) and 115 CE (the time of the Jewish revolt under Trajan, after which the Jewish community in Egypt was substantially diminished).[8] The work is generally regarded as a long expansion, influenced by Hellenistic Romance novels,[9] of the brief statement in Genesis that Pharaoh arranged a marriage between Joseph and Aseneth, the daughter of Potiphera priest of On (Gen. 41.45). It falls into two distinct parts. Chapters 1–21 offer an account of how the wealthy and beautiful virgin Aseneth sees Joseph and immediately falls in love with him, converts to Judaism, and then marries Joseph, to the delight of her family and the Pharaoh. The second section, chs. 22–28, recounts how the Pharaoh's son and some of Joseph's brothers plot to kill Joseph and capture Aseneth, but are ultimately foiled in these attempts.

The work's focus on Aseneth suggests that the author was prompted at least in part by a desire to explain how Israel's revered and virtuous ancestor Joseph came to marry a Gentile woman, when intermarriage between

7.   An Egyptian provenance is suggested by Collins, *Between Athens and Jerusalem,* p. 89; C. Burchard, 'Joseph and Aseneth', in J.H. Charlesworth (ed.), *The Old Testament Pseudepigrapha* (New York: Doubleday, 1985), II, pp. 177-248 (187); and R.D. Chesnutt, *From Death to Life: Conversion in Joseph and Aseneth* (Sheffield: Sheffield Academic Press, 1995), p. 45.

8.   For a more detailed discussion of the work's date, see G. Bohak, *'Joseph and Aseneth' and the Jewish Temple in Hierapolis* (Atlanta: Scholars Press, 1996), p. 46; Chesnutt *From Death to Life,* pp. 80-85, and Collins, *Between Athens and Jerusalem,* p. 89. A date in the Ptolemaic Period seems most likely to me.

9.   Further detail about these influences can be found in H.C. Kee 'The Sociocultural Setting of *Joseph and Aseneth*', *NTS* 29 (1983), pp. 398-402.

Jews and Gentiles is so strongly condemned in the Hebrew Scriptures (e.g. Gen. 24.2-4, 37-41; 27.46; 28.1), and in later Jewish writings such as *The Book of Jubilees* and *The Biblical Antiquities* of *Pseudo-Philo*. The text itself states explicitly that association between Jewish men and Gentile women is against the ancestral laws, and leads inevitably to corruption and destruction (7.5). This difficulty is resolved by the story of Aseneth's conversion, and the emphasis on her virginity and outstanding beauty throughout the work also indicates her suitability as a wife for Joseph, despite her Egyptian origins.

The starting point for the presentation of Joseph in *Joseph and Aseneth* is his important role in Egypt during the years of plenty, as described in Genesis, but his status is enhanced beyond the picture given in the canonical text. The reaction of Pentephres, Aseneth's father, to the news that Joseph intends to call on him for refreshment during his tour of the area to gather surplus grain is instructive:

> And Pentephres heard this, and rejoiced exceedingly with great joy and said, 'Blessed (be) the Lord, the God of Joseph, because my lord Joseph thought me worthy to come to us'. And Pentephres called the (steward) of his house and said to him, 'Hurry and make my house ready and prepare a great dinner, because Joseph, the Powerful One of God, is coming to us today' (*Joseph and Aseneth* 3.3-4; cf. 4.7; 18.1-2).[10]

When Joseph arrived at the house, Pentephres and his whole family prostrated themselves before him (5.7), then led him in to sit upon a throne (7.1; cf. 20.1). The text thus stresses the honour in which Joseph was held by Aseneth's family and later describes their whole-hearted support for his marriage to their daughter (20.6-10). Perhaps the author wished to claim that Aseneth's marriage to Joseph was considered a privilege even among the Egyptian elite, the priestly aristocratic circles which were not particularly favourably disposed towards Jews at the time the work was written.[11]

A desire to draw attention to Joseph's status may also lie behind the detail that he was the one who approached Pharaoh to tell him that he wished to marry Aseneth (20.9; 21.2-3). In a subtle change from Gen. 41.45, a verse which might seem to imply that the Pharaoh imposed a Gentile bride on his subordinate, this author makes clear that Joseph was

---

10. All quotations from *Joseph and Aseneth* are taken from Burchard's translation of the longer text in Charlesworth (ed.), *Old Testament Pseudepigrapha*, II, pp. 202-47.

11. This point is further developed by H.C. Kee, who argues that the work was directed to a group of upper-middle-class Jews and converts, *Socio-Cultural Setting*, p. 410.

able to choose his own wife. While Joseph's position as second only to Pharaoh, with all the trappings of high office, is clear in the canonical text (Gen. 41.40-45; 45.8-9), *Joseph and Aseneth* goes further in actually describing Joseph as 'king of the whole land' (4.7; cf. 25.5; 29.9). Other Jewish texts also use the term 'king' of Joseph (Philo, *de Iosepho* 120; *T. Levi* 13.9; *Hist. Joseph* A verso line 26, A recto line 16; *Targ. On.* and *Ps.-Jon.*), but Joseph's power and status are certainly particularly emphasized in *Joseph and Aseneth*.

However, not only is Joseph made king of Egypt, but *Joseph and Aseneth* even seems to present him as a divine being. A particularly remarkable feature of this text is the god-like description of Joseph's appearance in ch. 5:

> Joseph entered, standing on Pharaoh's second chariot, and four horses, white as snow and with golden bridles, were harnessed (to it), and the entire chariot was manufactured from pure gold. And Joseph was dressed in an exquisite white tunic, and the robe which he had thrown round him was purple, made of linen interwoven with gold, and a golden crown (was) on his head, and around the crown were twelve chosen stones, and on top of the twelve stones were twelve golden rays. And a royal staff was in his left hand, and in his right hand he held outstretched an olive branch, and there was plenty of fruit on it, and in the fruits was a great wealth of oil (*Jos. Asen.* 5.5).

Fruits and oil are well-attested symbols of the peace and fertility given by the gods. The 12 precious stones and 12 golden rays have been interpreted as representative of the 12 tribes of Israel, or as having astrological symbolism,[12] but Dölger[13] has drawn attention to the fact that these were a traditional feature of depictions of the crown of the sun god Helios. The idea that Joseph is being presented in terms of the sun god receives further support when Aseneth refers to him as 'the sun from heaven' (6.2) and 'son of God' (6.3, 5; cf. 13.13; 18.11; 21.4; 23.10) after her first sighting of him:

> I...did not know that Joseph is (a) son of God. For who among men on earth will generate such beauty, and what womb of a woman will give birth to such light?... And where shall I flee and hide, because every hiding place he sees and nothing hidden escapes him, because of the great light that is inside him? (*Jos. Asen.* 6.3-4, 6).

12. Suggested by Burchard, '*Joseph and Aseneth*', p. 208.
13. Cited in Burchard, '*Joseph and Aseneth*', p. 208.

Usually in Jewish thought it is from God that nothing can be hidden. Significantly, the divine being or angel who later appears to Aseneth also looks

> in every respect similar to Joseph, by the robe and crown and royal staff (*Jos. Asen.* 14.9).

The designation of Joseph as 'the powerful one of God' (ὁ δυνατος του θεου) is frequent throughout the text (3.4; 4.7; 18.1, 2; 21.21; cf. the allusions to Joseph's power in Aseneth's prayers 11.6, 9; 12.13). Δυνατος became an important designation of God among Greek-speaking Jews. In short, there can be little doubt that contemporary depictions of Hellenistic gods have influenced this author's representation of Joseph. This raises interesting questions about the extent to which Jews in the Second Temple Period absorbed beliefs and imagery from the other religions with which they came into contact.[14]

Several of Joseph's virtues are extolled by Pentephres when describing him to Aseneth before his first visit to their house. In particular, he is praised for being god-fearing, self-controlled and a virgin (4.7). The theme of Joseph's chastity during the attempted seduction of Joseph by Potiphar's wife is important in other Hellenistic Jewish texts, particularly *The Jewish Antiquities* (discussed below). The frequent emphasis on Joseph's self-control (*Jos. Asen.* 4.7; 7.3-4; *Ant.* 2.184) and beauty (*Jos. Asen.* 6.3-4; 13.14; *Ant.* 2.41) may be due to the fact that these were characteristics much admired in Hellenistic circles. According to *Joseph and Aseneth*, Joseph did not have to deal only with the unsolicited attentions of his mistress, but he was continually being harassed by Egyptian women. His sustained virtue and faithfulness to the Jewish law under constant temptation is thereby stressed.

> For all the wives and the daughters of the noblemen and the satraps of the whole land of Egypt used to molest him (wanting) to sleep with him, and all the wives and the daughters of the Egyptians, when they saw Joseph, suffered badly because of his beauty. But Joseph despised them, and the messengers whom the women sent to him with gold and silver and valuable presents Joseph sent back with threats and insults, because Joseph said, 'I will not sin before (the) Lord God of my father Israel nor in the face of my father Jacob'. And the face of his father Jacob, Joseph always had before his eyes, and he remembered his father's commandments. For Jacob would

---

14. The identification of Joseph with the Egyptian god Sarapis by some Jews is the subject of a study by G. Mussies, 'The *Interpretatio Judaica* of Sarapis', in M.J. Vermaseren (ed.), *Studies in Hellenistic Religions* (Leiden: E.J. Brill, 1979), pp. 189-214.

> say to his son Joseph and all his sons, 'My children, guard strongly against
> associating with a strange woman, for association (with) her is destruction
> and corruption' (*Jos. Asen.* 7.3-5).

The legitimacy of mixed marriages is regarded by several commentators, including Philonenko,[15] as a major theme of the text, and was probably a live issue for the author's community. He uses his narrative to make clear that it would have been wrong for Joseph to have married Aseneth while she was still involved with the worship of idols and therefore a 'strange woman' (8.5-7), or to have had sexual intercourse with her before marriage (21.1).

Joseph is presented as remaining faithful to the Jewish food and purity laws, as well as to the commandments about fornication and intermarriage, presumably because the author wished his readers to imitate Joseph in all these areas. So we read that when Joseph arrived at the house of Pentephres to take some refreshment, a separate table was set for him, because:

> Joseph never ate with the Egyptians, for this was an abomination to him
> (*Jos. Asen.* 7.1).

It is noteworthy that while the idea that Joseph ate separately from the Egyptians is to be found in the book of Genesis (43.42), there the reason given for this is that it was an abomination for the *Egyptians* to eat with the Hebrews. When this author has done so much to emphasize the greatness of the position of Joseph and the honour in which he was held by even the wealthiest and most important in the land, it clearly would not have suited his purposes to imply that the Hebrews were despised by the Egyptians.

Joseph is also praised for his meekness and mercifulness (*Jos. Asen.* 8.8), presumably a reference to the servitude, false accusations and imprisonment which he endured, and then to his forgiving rather than vengeful treatment of his brothers. The theme of 'mercifulness' receives particular attention in *Joseph and Aseneth* and Joseph is a model for the author's insistence that those who worship God do not repay anyone evil for evil (28.5). The refusal to exact vengeance and the determination to treat even enemies with kindness and magnanimity is praised throughout the second part of the text (e.g. 28.7, 14; 29.3-6) and is a lesson taught also by the angel, who raises to life even the bees which wished to harm Aseneth (16.20-23). In this respect, too, Joseph resembles the forgiving God of Aseneth's prayers:

---

15. M. Philonenko, *Joseph et Aséneth* (Leiden: E.J. Brill, 1968).

What father is as sweet as you, Lord, and who (is) as quick in mercy as you, Lord, and who (is as) long suffering toward our sins as you, Lord? (*Jos. Asen.* 12.15; cf. 11.10-14, 18).

This theme of Joseph's lack of vengefulness is present also in Josephus (see particularly Judah's speech to Joseph after the arrest of Benjamin, *Ant.* 2.140-59) and *Pseudo-Philo* (8.10), and is prominent in several of the *Testaments of the Twelve Patriarchs* (e.g. *T. Sim.* 4.6-7; *T. Zeb.* 8.6; *T. Benj.* 3-4).

It is, then, the power and influence of Joseph, 'king' of Egypt, which most interested the author of *Joseph and Aseneth*, as it fascinated other Hellenistic Jewish commentators like Artapanus. Joseph's exalted status naturally functioned as a source of pride and encouragement to Jews living in Egypt many centuries later, perhaps especially if they were struggling to achieve acceptance and recognition in the Gentile society of their own time. Joseph is also presented as a model of faithfulness to the Jewish law in a Gentile environment. His marriage to a Gentile woman is justified by this story of her conversion to Judaism, an indication of the importance of this issue of intermarriage for the author's community. He also builds on the canonical narrative involving Potiphar's wife to emphasize Joseph's attractiveness to Egyptian women, and draws attention to the virtues of chastity and self-control. Above all, *Joseph and Aseneth* is uniquely significant because of its presentation of Joseph as more than a virtuous man, more than a powerful king: here he is represented as a 'son of God'.

Josephus's Jewish Antiquities

Book 2 of Josephus's 20-volume history of the Jewish people, the *Jewish Antiquities*, completed in 93–94 CE, includes a lengthy retelling of the Joseph narrative. Josephus was motivated by a desire to make the Hebrew Scriptures intelligible and attractive to an educated Gentile audience, so felt free to condense or omit narratives which did not suit this purpose, while expanding others with rhetorical features such as irony, drama and lengthy speeches. Feldman[16] has conducted a detailed investigation of Josephus's interpretation of the Hebrew Bible, arguing that he presents the major biblical characters as models of all those virtues which would have been most admired by his Gentile audience, virtues such as courage,

---

16. L.H. Feldman, 'Josephus' Portrait of Joseph', *RB 99/2* (1992), pp. 379-417, and *Josephus's Interpretation of the Bible* (California: University of California Press, 1998). See also T.W. Franxman, *Genesis and the 'Jewish Antiquities' of Flavius Josephus* (Rome: Biblical Institute Press, 1979).

temperance, justice and piety. It would be redundant to repeat here all the conclusions of Feldman and other commentators. Attention will be drawn only to the most significant features of the characterization of Joseph in the *Jewish Antiquities*, and to the ways in which Josephus's cultural setting and target audience have influenced his representation.

The significance of the Joseph narrative for Josephus is evident from the disproportionately lengthy treatment which he accords it. Several commentators[17] have inferred from this a belief on the part of Josephus that his own life paralleled in some respects that of his biblical namesake. It is probable that for Josephus, the correspondence between the life of Joseph and the experiences of the people of Israel (noted above in the introduction) took on a more personal note. His defence of his conduct during the Jewish war of 66–70 CE suggests that he felt that he was the undeserving victim of the jealousy of his 'brothers' or fellow-Jewish commanders and some sections of the people; partly because of their hostility towards him, he was, like Joseph, now living in a foreign land, where he had attained some success at the court of the emperor. His wholly positive presentation of the character of Joseph may perhaps, then, be influenced by a tendency to see something of himself in the biblical figure.

Josephus shares with many other interpreters the desire to emphasize Joseph's great virtue (see, for example, *Ant.* 2.23), and to offer explanations for the more dubious aspects of his conduct. No mention is made of anything which might have provoked his brothers' hatred of Joseph (such as his special coat, or his tale-bearing) and Reuben is made to state explicitly that Joseph had done his brothers no wrong (*Ant.* 2.26). Lest his readers should think that Joseph was indulging in boastfulness when he recounted his dreams to his family, Josephus adds the detail that he did so only because he wanted their help to understand the meaning of the dreams (*Ant.* 2.11). He directly contradicts Genesis in claiming that, far from rebuking his son,

> Jacob was delighted with the dream: grasping in his mind what it predicted and sagely and unerringly divining his import, he rejoiced at the great things it betokened (*Ant.* 2.15; cf. Gen. 37.10).[18]

17. See, for example, Feldman, *Josephus's Interpretation of the Bible*, p. 380, and Franxman, *Genesis and the 'Jewish Antiquities'*, p. 216.

18. All quotations from *The Jewish Antiquities* are taken from the translation by H.St.J. Thackeray in the Loeb Classical Library Series, IV (London: William Heinemann, 1930).

Likewise, Josephus is anxious to portray Joseph's treatment of his brothers on their arrival in Egypt as positively as possible:

> It was but to discover news of his father and what had become of him after his own departure that he so acted (*Ant.* 2.99; cf. 2.110).

The planting of the silver cup in Benjamin's sack is explained as a test to see whether his brothers would help or abandon him (*Ant.* 2.125). When he has revealed himself to his brothers in Egypt, Joseph openly declares his willingness to forgive them and to forget all about their attempts to harm him (*Ant.* 2.162).

Figure 29. *Coat of Many Colours* (1866, by Ford Madox Brown [1821–1893], Board of Trustees of the National Museums and Galleries on Merseyside [Walker Art Gallery, Liverpool]).

Josephus expands considerably on the biblical account of the attempted seduction by Joseph's mistress and uses this episode to focus attention on the virtues of Joseph's character. Her repeated efforts to tempt Joseph to have intercourse with her only serve to highlight his heroic chastity and self-control. He is even unmoved by her threat to accuse him falsely of assault, and repeatedly urges her to be faithful to her husband. Joseph is the kind of character who will remain steadfast even when greatly tempted,

> choosing to suffer unjustly and to endure even the severest penalty, rather than take advantage of the moment by an indulgence of which he was conscious that he would justly deserve to die (*Ant.* 2.51).

Joseph's status is as exalted in the *Jewish Antiquities* as in other texts of this period. First, Josephus claims that he was bought by the traders for the vast sum of 20 minas (*Ant.* 2.33), rather than 20 shekels of silver (Gen. 37.28), thereby increasing his value. Although sold into slavery, his master (named by Josephus as Pentephres) does not treat him as such, but

> held him in the highest esteem, gave him a liberal education, accorded him better fare than falls to the lot of a slave, and committed the charge of his household into his hands (*Ant.* 2.39).

Even in prison, his worth is recognized and he is treated accordingly:

> the keeper of the prison, noting his diligence and fidelity in the tasks committed to him, along with the dignity of his features, gave him some relief from his chains and rendered his cruel fate lighter and more tolerable, allowing him moreover rations superior to prisoners' fare (*Ant.* 2.61).

The fact that their ancestor had been a slave and a prisoner in Egypt may well have been a source of embarrassment to Hellenistic Jews, so Josephus and other commentators felt they needed to play down those aspects of the canonical text. Josephus would naturally rather emphasize the contribution of Joseph to Egypt, where he was hailed as the 'saviour' of the people (*Ant.* 2.94), entirely responsible for delivering the Egyptians in their time of famine, as they had taken no precautions themselves (*Ant.* 2.189).

Several features of Josephus's writing style would seem to demonstrate his desire to appeal to an educated Gentile audience. First, there is his creation of lengthy speeches, only loosely based on the canonical text, such as the dialogue between Joseph and his mistress when she tried to seduce him (*Ant.* 2.46-53; cf. Gen. 39.7-10), Reuben's attempt to persuade his brothers not to kill Joseph (*Ant.* 2.20-28; cf. Gen. 37.22) and Judah's plea to Joseph to spare Benjamin (*Ant.* 2.140-58). Such speeches are a very common rhetorical feature throughout Greek and Roman literature, and, as noted by Attridge,[19] Josephus's use of this device allows him to offer his insights into the motivation and point of view of the characters.

---

19. H.W. Attridge, *The Interpretation of Biblical History in the Antiquitates Judaicae of Flavius Josephus* (Missoula: Scholars Press, 1976), p. 40.

Josephus also introduces irony into his rewriting of the narrative: Joseph's master is, for example, said to be prouder than ever of his wife and her decorum after her false accusation of Joseph (*Ant.* 2.59). The dramatic potential of the narrative is highlighted by these ironical and rhetorical features, as well as by Josephus's interest in the inner thoughts and emotions of his characters (see *Ant.* 2.44 on the thinking of Joseph's mistress and 2.58 on why her husband should have believed her story about Joseph). Indeed, the extended treatment of this episode and his embroidery of the romantic and erotic features may have been influenced by the popularity at this time of Hellenistic romance novels.

The content as well as the style of the *Jewish Antiquities* is influenced by Josephus's purpose of presenting the Jewish people and their history in as attractive a manner as possible. It is possible, for example, that the emphasis on Joseph's loyalty to his master (*Ant.* 2.42), his obedience to his mistress (*Ant.* 2.43), and the way his organization of affairs in Egypt during the famine increased the loyalty of the people to their king, as well as Joseph's own reputation (*Ant.* 2.193) may be due to an apologetic desire to reassure Josephus's Gentile audience that pious Jews posed no revolutionary threat to society, despite the recent Jewish revolt against Rome in which the author himself had played a part. Also particularly interesting is Josephus's insistence that Joseph was more than willing to sell grain to the people of all nations who made their way to Egypt (cf. Gen. 42.6) because he

> held that all men, in virtue of their kinship, should receive succour from those in prosperity (*Ant.* 2.94; cf. 2.102).

He may well have been trying to answer those Gentile critics who regarded the Jews as being too insular.[20] Feldman has also argued that one of the features of Josephus's biblical interpretation is a tendency to downplay any sense of Jewish proselytizing, as this was viewed negatively by many of his contemporaries.[21] This may account for the lack of reference in the *Jewish Antiquities* to traditions about Aseneth's conversion.

The widespread popularity of Stoic philosophy is likely to lie behind Josephus's presentation of Joseph as a model of self-control, both when tempted by Potiphar's wife and when reunited with his brothers and his father. He urged his mistress to govern her passions (*Ant.* 2.43), for

---

20. For further expansion of this point, see Feldman, *Josephus' Interpretation of the Bible*, p. 355.

21. Feldman, *Josephus' Interpretation of the Bible*, pp. 343-44.

example, and, in *Jewish Antiquities*, Joseph's weeping when he reveals his identity to his brothers is not heard by the Egyptians (*Ant.* 2.160; cf. Gen. 45.2).[22] There are also hints about the qualities which he and his readers expected their rulers to display. In his plea on behalf of Benjamin, for example, Judah urges Joseph to act like the worthy governor he is and demonstrate magnanimity, clemency and generosity (*Ant.* 2.140-58). Joseph's career in Egypt is then summed up in the claim that he was:

> a man of admirable virtue, who directed all affairs by the dictates of reason and made but sparing use of his authority (*Ant.* 2.198).

The figure of Joseph is, then, extremely significant for Josephus, partly because he sees parallels between his own life and that of his biblical namesake, and partly because his was a story which appealed to Josephus's educated Gentile audience. Josephus draws out the full dramatic and romantic potential of the canonical narrative, adds his own rhetorical touches, and then uses the story to refute contemporary criticisms that the Jews were a rebellious and insular people. The Joseph of the *Jewish Antiquities* is a model of those virtues which Josephus held dear: chastity, self-control, steadfastness and patient endurance of whatever trials came his way. As a brother he is forgiving, and as a ruler he is magnanimous and efficient. This 'noble spirit' (*Ant.* 2.40), whose worth shone through even in periods of slavery and imprisonment, is indeed an ancestor in whom Hellenistic Jews like Josephus could take pride.

Representations of Joseph in Palestinian Jewish Texts

The Book of Jubilees
Jubilees is one of the earliest extant examples of the genre of Rewritten Bible, usually dated to the mid-second century BCE.[23] The work retells the history of Israel from creation to the time of Moses, demonstrating a great interest in chronology. It includes the mixture of summary, expansion and omission of biblical material, and high regard for non-biblical tradition,

---

22. The emphasis on Joseph's self-control is a prominent feature also of *4 Macc.*, as noted by J. Dochhorn and A.K. Petersen, 'Narratio Ioseph: A Coptic Joseph-Apocryphon', *JSJ* 30 (1999), pp.431-63 (441).

23. For a discussion of date, language and provenance, see G.W.E. Nickelsburg, 'The Bible Rewritten and Expanded', in M.E. Stone (ed.) *Jewish Writings of the Second Temple Period* (Philadelphia: Fortress Press; Assen: Van Gorcum, 1984), pp. 89-156 (101-103), or O.S. Wintermute, '*Jubilees*', in J.H. Charlesworth (ed.) *The Old Testament Pseudepigrapha* (Garden City, NY: Doubleday, pp. 35-142 (43-45).

which Alexander[24] has identified as key characteristics of this genre.

The scene is set in *Jubilees* for the Joseph narrative by the addition of an extra-biblical story, in which Jacob, together with his sons Levi, Judah and Joseph, roundly repels an attack by seven Amorite kings (*Jub.* 34.1-9). Prominence is given to Levi and/or Judah throughout *Jubilees* and in numerous other texts of the Inter-Testamental Period, and it is interesting to see Joseph included in this particular tradition. There is no scriptural warrant for any emphasis on his prowess as a warrior, but this passage serves the author as an early manifestation of Joseph's power, greatness and closeness to his father. As the story unfolds, the focus is on Joseph to such an extent that the other characters familiar from Genesis almost disappear from the scene. The author of *Jubilees* apparently did not share the interest of other texts in expanding on the personality and actions of Potiphar's wife (e.g. *Jewish Antiquities*), or Joseph's wife (e.g. *Joseph and Asenath*), or in giving attention to the differing roles of Joseph's brothers in the plot against him (e.g. *Test. XII Patr.*, *Narratio Ioseph*). Even the description of the role of the chief butler and the chief baker is reduced to a minimum and their dreams are not recounted in any detail (*Jub.* 39; cf. Gen. 40).

Texts of the Rewritten Bible genre attempt to resolve perceived difficulties and contradictions within the Hebrew Bible and to explain any passages which appeared unacceptable in the light of contemporary beliefs and practices.[25] There are several examples of this tendency to smooth out difficulties in the retelling of the Joseph narrative in *Jubilees*. The author offers an explanation for Joseph's apparently harsh treatment of his brothers when they came to Egypt and his planting of the silver cup on Benjamin.

> And Joseph thought of an idea by means of which he might learn their thoughts, whether they had thoughts of peace for one another. And he said to the man who was over his house, 'Fill all of their bags with food for them. And also return their money to them in the midst of their containers.

24. P.S. Alexander, 'Retelling the Old Testament', in D.A. Carson and H.G.M. Williamson (eds.), *It Is Written: Scripture Citing Scripture* (Cambridge: Cambridge University Press, 1988), pp. 99-118.

25. G. Vermes, 'Bible and Midrash: Early Old Testament Exegesis', in P.R. Ackroyd and C.F. Evans, *The Cambridge History of the Bible* (Cambridge: Cambridge University Press, 1970), I, pp. 129-31 remains a classic treatment of the types of problems with which early Jewish exegetes wrestled and their methods of dealing with them.

> And place my cup from which I drink, the silver cup, in the bag of the youngest one and send them off' (*Jub.* 42.25).[26]

As well as making clear Joseph's laudable motives for his action, this author (like Josephus and Philo) carefully avoids any mention of the detail that Joseph used his cup for divination (cf. 43.2, 10; cf. Gen. 44.5, 15). Similarly excised are the embarrassing references in Genesis to the fact that to eat with the Hebrews or to follow the Hebrews' occupation of shepherding were an abomination to the Egyptians (Gen. 43.32; 46.31-34; cf. *Jos. Asen.* 7.1). There is no mention of any feature of the canonical narrative which might reflect badly on Joseph: the tales he told about his brothers (Gen. 37.2), the special coat which marked him out as his father's favourite and contributed to the hatred felt towards him by his brothers (Gen. 37.3-4), his dreams of greatness which provoked the anger of his father and the jealousy of his brothers (Gen. 37.5-11) are all omitted in *Jubilees*. In this account, then, Joseph is presented as an entirely virtuous character, the undeserving victim of his brothers' plotting.

Although in *Jubilees* the episode of Potiphar's wife does not receive the extended treatment found in some other texts, there are several interesting features of the author's presentation of Joseph in the retelling of this incident:

> And Joseph was good-looking and very handsome. And the wife of his master lifted up her eyes and saw Joseph and desired him. And she begged him to lie with her. And he did not surrender himself but he remembered the Lord and the words which Jacob, his father, used to read, which were from the words of Abraham, that there is no man who (may) fornicate with a woman who has a husband (and) that there is a judgement of death which is decreed for him in heaven before the Lord Most High. And the sin is written (on high) concerning him in the eternal books always before the Lord. And Joseph remembered these words and he did not want to lie with her. And she begged him (for) one year. And he turned away and refused to listen to her. And she embraced him and seized him in the house so that she might force him to lie with her. And she shut the door of the house and seized him. And he left his garment in her hand and he broke the door and fled outside (away) from her presence (*Jub.* 39.5-9; cf. Gen. 39.6b-12).

So the length of time during which the woman tried to persuade Joseph to have intercourse with her is specified as a year. This precision fits in with this author's great interest in dating and chronology, but it also serves to

---

26. All quotations from *Jubilees* are taken from the translation by O.S. Wintermute, in Charlesworth (ed.), *Old Testament Pseudepigrapha*, II, pp. 35-142.

draw attention to Joseph's virtue and steadfastness during a long period of repeated temptation. In a subtle shift of emphasis from Genesis, Joseph's main reason for rejecting the advances of his mistress is presented not as concern about ingratitude to his master, but about the sin of fornication. Throughout *Jubilees*, the author shows a particular concern to condemn fornication and encourage strict adherence to the ancient Jewish Law. He also reinforces the idea of brotherly unity, perhaps indicating a belief that the Jews of his own day needed to be reminded about the benefits of remaining united. So Joseph revealed himself to his brothers only when he

> saw that the heart of all of them was in accord with one another for good (*Jub.* 43.14; cf. 46.1).

The theme of Joseph's popularity and success in Egypt is greatly developed in *Jubilees*. Joseph is said to have been loved by his master, Potiphar (39.10; cf. Gen. 39.17) and later his important position as second only to Pharaoh is highlighted by the inclusion of the detail that he went out daily to his judgement seat (*Jub.* 43.2). Nor does Joseph need to discuss with Pharaoh whereabouts in the country his father and brothers should settle. He is presented as being able to gift to his family the lands over which he rules on behalf of Pharaoh, and they receive not only Goshen, 'the best of the land of Egypt', but also Ramses and the neighbouring districts (45.6; cf. Gen. 46.31–47.6). The Joseph of *Jubilees* is the epitome of a righteous and beloved ruler.

> And Joseph ruled in all the land of Egypt and all of the judges and all of the servants of the Pharaoh and all of those who did the king's work loved him because he walked uprightly and he had no pompousness or arrogance or partiality, and there was no bribery because he ruled all the people of the land uprightly. And the land of Egypt was at peace before the Pharaoh on account of Joseph because the Lord was with him and gave him favour and mercy for all his family before all who knew him and those who heard witness of him. And the kingdom of the Pharaoh was upright. And there was no Satan and there was no evil (*Jub.* 40.8-9).

It is hardly surprising that a representation of Joseph as a Hebrew hero who was loved and respected by Gentiles because of his honesty and lack of arrogance should have been attractive to Jews who had experienced foreign domination in the very recent past. It is also possible to see in these verses a veiled critique of some of those in positions of power in the author's own time, although it is generally accepted[27] that the author of

---

27. See e.g. Wintermute, '*Jubilees*', pp. 44-45.

Jubilees viewed positively the contemporary Maccabaean rulers.

The representation of Joseph in *Jubilees* is, then, entirely positive. He appears completely innocent in the face of his brothers' desire to harm him and aspects of the canonical narrative which suggest a more ambiguous character are explained away or omitted. His virtues are emphasized, particularly his continued refusal to be tempted into the sin of fornication, and his great integrity as ruler in Egypt. His position in Egypt is exalted beyond the canonical text and the narrative also serves to highlight themes important to the author, such as the need to remain faithful to the Jewish Law and the importance of brotherly unity.

The Biblical Antiquities of Pseudo-Philo

Now extant only in Latin manuscripts, there is substantial scholarly agreement that *The Biblical Antiquities* was originally composed in Hebrew in Palestine, towards the end of the first century CE.[28] The work is generally accepted as an example of Rewritten Bible, covering the period from Adam to the death of Saul, although it is highly selective in its treatment of the Hebrew Scriptures, omitting large sections, and expanding other parts considerably with non-biblical material.

Perhaps because of his own historical circumstances, *Pseudo-Philo* was apparently particularly interested in the period of the Judges. Their trust in God and military successes when Israel's existence as a nation was under threat may well have been a model he believed the Jewish leaders of his time should imitate in the face of the contemporary dominance by Gentile powers.[29] This author is, then, less interested than others in the Joseph narrative, and summarizes it drastically. Eleven chapters of Genesis are outlined in only two verses:

> Now Jacob and his twelve sons lived in the land of Canaan. And these hated their brother Joseph, whom they delivered into Egypt to Potiphar, the

---

28. A full discussion of language, date and provenance can be found in H. Jacobson, *A Commentary on Pseudo-Philo's Liber Antiquitatem Biblicarum Vol. 1* (New York: Ktav, 1996), pp. 196-201; F.J. Murphy, *Pseudo-Philo: Rewriting the Bible* (New York/Oxford: Oxford University Press); or D.J. Harrington, '*Pseudo-Philo*', in J.H. Charlesworth (ed.), *The Old Testament Pseudepigrapha* (Garden City, NY: 1985), II, pp. 297-388 (298-300).

29. See Murphy, *Pseudo-Philo*, p. 264; cf. G.W.E. Nickelsburg, 'Good and Bad Leaders in Pseudo-Philo's *Liber Antiquitatem Biblicarum*', in G.W.E. Nickelsburg and J.J. Collins, *Ideal Figures in Ancient Judaism* (Ann Arbor, MI: Scholars Press, 1980), pp. 49-65 (61-64).

chief of Pharaoh's cooks, and he spent fourteen years with him. And after-ward the king of Egypt had a dream. And they told him about Joseph, and he explained to him the dreams. And after he explained to him the dreams, Pharaoh made him chief over all the land of Egypt. At that time there was a famine over all the land, as Joseph had discerned, and his brothers went down to buy food in Egypt because only in Egypt was there food. And Joseph recognised his brothers, but was not known by them. And he did not deal vengefully with them, and he sent and summoned his father from the land of Canaan; and he went down to him (*Biblical Antiquities* 8.9-10).[30]

Thus, no reasons are given for the brothers' hatred of Joseph, nor any details of their plot to kill him, the means of his arrival in Egypt, the overtures of his mistress, or his time in prison. Emphasis on the theme of divine providence, familiar both from the Genesis narrative and rewritings of the Joseph Story such as that of Josephus, is absent. Instead, the author highlights the fact that Joseph 'did not deal vengefully' with his brothers (8.10), an important feature, as noted above, of other representations of Joseph, such as *The Jewish Antiquities* and *Joseph and Aseneth*.

One very characteristic feature of *Pseudo-Philo*'s retelling of Scripture is his tendency to make connections between the episode being described and another passage. So, in condemning Samson's lust for the Philistine women, the author laments that he did not follow the example of Joseph, who 'was not willing to afflict his own seed' (43.5), presumably a refer-ence to his refusal to have intercourse with Potiphar's wife. Warnings against marrying Gentiles are frequent throughout the text (e.g. 9.1, 5; 21.1; 30.1; 44.7; cf. *Jub.*), so perhaps it is not surprising that there is no reference to the fact that Joseph did, in fact, marry an Egyptian woman.

The brief treatment of the Joseph Story in *The Biblical Antiquities* therefore suggests that the author felt that other Jewish heroes spoke more immediately than Joseph to the situation of his time. The narrative is, however, used to support his hostility towards intermarriage, and Joseph's lack of vengefulness is also praised.

Negative Characterizations of Joseph

Without exception, the works discussed above present Joseph in a wholly positive light, often going beyond the canonical text in emphasizing his

---

30. All quotations from *The Biblical Antiquities* are taken from the translation of Harrington, '*Pseudo-Philo*', in Charlesworth (ed.) *Old Testament Pseudepigrapha*, II, pp. 297-377.

virtuous character, his fidelity to the Jewish Law, or his great achievements as administrator and ruler in Egypt. The more questionable aspects of the biblical Joseph's character and behaviour have generally been smoothed out of these later rewritings. There are, however, two places in Jewish literature where an awareness of the ambivalent aspects of the biblical Joseph has been retained. The first of these is in the extensive writings of the first-century philosopher Philo, who gives two contrasting portraits of Joseph. One text, *De Iosepho*, is wholly positive and shares many features of interpretation with other Jewish texts, but the picture of Joseph given in his treatise on dreams, *De somniis*, is more negative. These varying treatments of the Joseph narrative probably indicate that Philo had different purposes in mind when he wrote each text.

In *De Iosepho*, Philo was particularly concerned with Joseph's exercise of power in Egypt. As Gruen explains:

> Philo's *de Iosepho* aimed above all to outline a model for the ideal statesman… Philo plainly took as his mission the idealization of Joseph, thus to present him as the epitome of statesmanly qualities. The dubious or questionable features that appear in Genesis are smoothed over or rationalized.[31]

As in so many Jewish writings, pride is taken in the idea that it was a Jew who saved the people of Egypt from famine, and Joseph's chaste behaviour is contrasted with what Philo regards as the licentiousness of Egypt (*Jos.* 42-53). In *De Somniis*, however, Joseph appears as a character somewhat flawed by pride and pomposity, as evidenced by his boasting about his dreams of greatness. Philo's characteristic allegorical exegesis is used to interpret Joseph's coat of many colours as representing a lack of stability of purpose. It would seem that one of Philo's intentions in writing this work was to point up his criticisms of the behaviour of some of the Roman politicians and rulers of his own time (cf. also his *Leg. Gai.* and *In Flacc.*).[32]

Finally in this connection, mention must be made of the rabbinic text *Genesis Rabbah*. In general, rabbinic commentators present Joseph as an idealized figure,[33] but in *Genesis Rabbah* it is noted that Joseph did wrong

---

31. Gruen, *Heritage and Hellenism*, p. 81.

32. This point is briefly discussed in Collins, *Between Athens and Jerusalem*, pp. 113-14; he argues against Goodenough's claim that Philo's portrayal of Joseph in *De somniis* was a veiled attack on Roman rule as a whole, as specific individuals are criticized rather than a general principle.

33. This generally positive treatment of Joseph is noted by Jacobs, 'Joseph the Patriarch', p. 416. For further detail on the treatment of Joseph in rabbinic sources, see

by taking advantage of the fact that he was his father's favourite son, and that the report he brought back about his brothers was false. His slavery and imprisonment in Egypt are therefore understood as his just punishment from God,[34] an interpretation that fits perfectly with the rabbinic view that any suffering must be a result of sin.

Conclusion

The texts surveyed here have amply demonstrated the great popularity of the Joseph narrative throughout the Inter-Testamental period among Jews of both Palestine and the Diaspora. Almost all of them idealize the figure of Joseph, as part of the general tendency of later works to smooth out any perceived difficulties in the canonical text and present the patriarchs in a most positive light. Joseph's virtue in refusing to accede to the desires of Potiphar's wife is frequently exaggerated, and great stress is put on his status as 'king' or 'lord' of Egypt. Naturally his success and exalted position were thought to reflect well on his Hebrew descendants. The various interpretations of the Joseph narrative reveal some of the concerns of the authors and the people for whom they were writing: for example, the issue of intermarriage with Gentiles, the continuing validity of the Jewish law and the need to promote unity are particularly prominent themes. The theological outlook of the authors also shines through these texts so that, for example, God's mercy is emphasized in *Joseph and Aseneth*, and a belief in God's righteousness affects the representation of Joseph in *Genesis Rabbah*.

A close study of these texts highlights the creativity and freedom with which later interpreters approached the Joseph narrative; from the shrewd administrator who arranged his own travel to Egypt presented by Artapanus, the 'son of God' encountered in *Joseph and Aseneth*, to the absence of any Egyptian wife in *Pseudo-Philo*. A Gentile audience is most clearly presupposed in the writings of Josephus; this is evident from his literary style and his emphasis on Joseph's beauty, virtue and generosity towards people of all races. Without overstating the differences between Palestinian and Hellenistic Jews,[35] it seems that in general more emphasis was

---

L. Ginzberg, *The Legends of the Jews*, Vols. II and V (Philadelphia: Jewish Publication Society of America, 1909 reprinted 1960).

34. This point is made by Dochhorn and Petersen, '*Narratio Ioseph*', p. 441; cf. Niehoff, *Figure of Joseph*, p. 124.

35. Several recent commentators have argued for a broad similarity of outlook

placed on Joseph's fidelity to the Jewish law in Hebrew texts such as *Jubilees* than in those of a Hellenistic provenance such as the writings of Artapanus and the *Jewish Antiquities*. These later representations of Joseph are united by their generally optimistic note; they proudly celebrate Joseph's prosperity and acceptance in a Gentile world, often experienced by Jews as hostile, and they encourage their readers to be confident that the virtuous will be rewarded in the end because God has been working for Israel's benefit in all the vicissitudes of their history.

between Judaean and Diaspora Judaism; see, for example, Collins, *Between Athens and Jerusalem*, p. 50.

HANS HOLBEIN'S *THE AMBASSADORS:*
BIBLICAL REFLECTIONS ON A RENAISSANCE MASTERPIECE

Larry J. Kreitzer

This short study is primarily concerned with Hans Holbein's painting *The Ambassadors* and some of the theological ideas that arise from a careful examination of it. To facilitate our consideration of Holbein's work the discussion will be framed by brief considerations of two of the most exalted passages within the letters of Paul, passages which over the centuries have stimulated our imaginations and challenged our perceptions of the wonder and majesty of God's grace. Thus we shall begin with the first of these Pauline texts, Col. 1.15-20, a passage which includes within it an important note about the work of Christ as an act of reconciliation. We shall then move on to Holbein's painting itself, noting three specific theological ideas which arise from a consideration of it. We shall conclude by briefly reflecting upon 2 Cor. 5.18-20, in which the image of ambassadorship is injected into Paul's teaching about the nature of the Christian faith.

Reconciliation and Restoration: Rethinking Colossians 1.15-20

The first of the Pauline passages is found in Colossians 1 where the apostle writes to the church in Colossae and chooses to include within his letter a short section of christological teaching. This section is generally regarded to be a pre-Pauline hymn, perhaps a song originally sung as part of the Early Church's worship. The hymn itself runs from 1.15-20, and in some translations of the Bible it is actually set out in verse; the translation offered by *The Jerusalem Bible* is a good example:

> [15] He is the image of the unseen God
>   and the firstborn of all creation,
> [16]for in him were created
>   all things in heaven and on earth:
>   everything visible and everything invisible,

Thrones, Dominations, Sovereignties, Powers—
all things were created through him and for him.
[17] Before anything else was created, he existed,
and he holds all things in unity.
[18] Now the Church is his body,
he is its head.
As he is the Beginning,
he was first to be born from the dead,
so that he should be first in every way;
[19] because God wanted all perfection
to be found in him
[20] and all things to be reconciled through him and for him,
everything in heaven and everything on earth,
when he made peace
by his death on the cross.

As we can readily see, the hymn makes mention of many of the central ideas and beliefs of Christian faith. We read of God's initiative in the action of creation and redemption, the headship of Christ over the Church, the in-dwelling of God in the person of Christ, the power of the Cross in effecting peace—all are included within this hymn of praise.[1] It is a veritable treasure trove, a theological mother lode, so to speak. We have struck a rich vein of thought here which could easily absorb our attentions for a whole series of sermons, bible studies and meditations, let alone the brief reflections offered here. The passage in Col. 1.15-20 is like a multi-faceted diamond, and we have space to concentrate on only one of the faces of this glittering gem here.

In v. 20 we read that God's desire in Christ is to have 'all things reconciled through him and for him'. It is this idea of reconciliation which I would like to explore, and even then I wish to narrow the focus some-what and concentrate on one particular dimension of that great Christian truth of reconciliation, a truth which, incidentally, is really only explored at any depth within the Pauline letters.[2] 'Reconciliation' language is

1. The secondary literature on the hymn is vast. One of the most interesting studies of the hymn is that offered by Paul Beasley-Murray, 'Colossians 1.15-20: An Early Christian Hymn Celebrating the Lordship of Christ', in Donald A. Hagner and Murray J. Harris (eds.), *Pauline Studies: Essays Presented to Professor F.F. Bruce on his 70th Birthday* (Grand Rapids, MI: Eerdmans, 1980), pp. 169-83.

2. See R.P. Martin, *Reconciliation: A Study of Paul's Theology* (London: Marshall, Morgan & Scott, 1981), for an excellent introduction to the issue. Also worth consulting on the matter is S.E. Porter, 'Peace, Reconciliation', in Gerald F. Hawthorne, Ralph P. Martin and Daniel G. Reid (eds.), *Dictionary of Paul and his Letters*

distinctively Pauline; it often comes as a surprise to discover that it is only in Paul's letters that the word 'reconciliation' (based on the Greek verbs καταλλάσσω and ἀποκαταλλάσσω)[3] is used. One of the most important ways that the Church has understood reconciliation over the years is to see it in terms of *restoration*. In short, 'to reconcile' means (among other things) 'to restore', 'to put back', or 'to return to its original state'. There are many examples of restoration that we can turn to that can give us insight into Paul's declaration about reconciliation, but within the bounds of this study I would like to use one that is particularly relevant. I speak, of course, of Holbein's remarkable painting known as *The Ambassadors*, a painting which is part of the collection of the National Gallery in London and one which has been recently restored.

Holbein's Masterpiece: Some Theological Reflections

Hans Holbein's *The Ambassadors* (Fig. 30) has been part of the National Gallery's collection since 1890, but was only returned to public display in April of 1996 after an absence of over three years (it was removed to the Gallery's conservation workshops in January of 1993).[4] The painting provides the opportunity for a fresh consideration of the Pauline ideas of reconciliation and restoration, and it is to the painting's contribution in these matters that we turn our attention.

The Subject Matter of the Painting: Portraying the Hope of Reconciliation

The Ambassadors is one of the best-known paintings of the German artist Hans Holbein the Younger (1497/8–1543). It is the largest surviving painting by the artist, measuring 207 cm × 209.5 cm in size. There are good grounds for claiming that the work is the first ever full-length, life-size portrait of two figures. In many ways the subject matter of the painting itself is a thought-provoking image of reconciliation, or perhaps to be more accurate, the *hope* of reconciliation.

(Leicester: Inter-Varsity Press, 1993), pp. 695-99.

3.   Stanley E. Porter, *καταλλα/σσω in Ancient Greek Literature, with Reference to the Pauline Writings* (Estudios de Filología Neotestamentaria, 5; Cordoba: Edi-ciones El Almendro, 1994), offers an impressive survey of the linguistic evidence.

4.   The story of the National Gallery's cleaning and restoration of the painting under the supervision of the Chief Conservator Martin Wyld is told in a fascinating BBC 2 documentary entitled *Restoring the Ambassadors* (1996). A videocassette of the 50-minute documentary is available from The National Gallery Publications Limited, 5/6 Pall Mall East, London SW1Y 5BA.

Figure 30. *The Ambassadors* (1553, by Hans Holbein,
The National Gallery, London).

The painting depicts two French diplomats (hence the title *The Ambassadors*), Jean de Dinteville on the left and Georges de Selve on the right. De Dinteville is resplendently dressed in a pink satin shirt and a black satin gown with velvet trim and a lynx-fur lining; de Selve wears a more modest brown damask robe, complete with a sable lining. The mosaic pavement is based on one found in Westminster Abbey. The two men stand before a brilliantly green damask curtain and have between them a table of two shelves, the top of which is draped in a richly patterned Turkish carpet of reds and blacks and yellows. The two shelves of the table contain a dazzling array of weird and wonderful objects which have been the subject of endless speculation. Just who are these two men, and what do they represent?[5]

5.   The National Gallery has published a lavishly illustrated book on the painting within their on-going Making and Meaning series; see Susan Foister, Ashok Roy and Martyn Wyld, *Holbein's Ambassadors* (Making and Meaning; London: National Gallery Publications Limited, 1997). An accompanying 30-minute video with the same title is also available. The video script is written by Susan Foister and Alexander Sturgis (who also narrates the film).

De Dinteville was appointed by King François I of France as the ambassador to England and served in the court of Henry VIII from 1532 to 1533 (he also served as the French ambassador on four other occasions). De Selve was the Bishop of Lavaur in the south-west of France, who visited his friend de Dinteville in London in the spring of 1533. This visit provided the opportunity for Holbein to paint the two of them together (it also allows us to date the work very precisely). Both of the ambassadors were fairly young for their positions in French society (de Dinteville was 29 and de Selve was 25), and both were men of enlightenment and vision. The painting belonged to the nobleman de Dinteville, and he probably commissioned Holbein to produce the work for his château in Polisy in France. The fact that this small village on the borders of Champagne and Burgundy is specifically identified on the globe which rests on the lower shelf of the table suggests the intended home of the painting itself. Holbein affixed his own name to the work, signing and dating it with the Latin inscription 'IOANNES HOLBEIN PINGEBAT 1533 ('Hans Holbein painted this in 1533') half-hidden in the shadows below de Dinteville's majestic robes. Derek Wilson, in his recent biography of Holbein, describes the painting thus:

> Holbein presents his sitters as they saw themselves and wished to be seen: men of culture, taste and intelligence; supporters of intellectual enquiry; patrons of the arts; men caught up in the exhilarating pursuit of knowledge. Yet there is more to the painting than this. It is a testament by Holbein and his patron to their shared concerns in the uncertain England of 1533.[6]

Thus, the date of 1533 is significant for it is a time of great stress and strain within the religious world of Europe, particularly in the Christian Church in England. King Henry VIII is engaged in a bitter and acrimonious dispute with the Papacy in Rome about the matter of his divorce of Queen Catherine of Aragon and marriage to Anne Boleyn (he had married her secretly in January of that year, flaunting both social convention and Papal injunction). Meanwhile, on the continent of Europe the social upheaval of the so-called Lutheran Reformation was well under way, causing immense rifts within the life of the Christian Church. The lute which we see in the painting on the lower shelf is often taken to be a symbol of this division, especially since it has a broken string as if to suggest that the music of harmony within the life of the Church can no

---

6. Derek Wilson, *Hans Holbein: Portrait of an Unknown Man* (London: Weidenfeld & Nicolson, 1996), p. 197.

longer be played. To the left of the lute is a pair of metal dividers, perhaps another visualization of the schism that seemed to threaten the Christian world at the time. To the right of the lute is a box of wooden flutes, another potential instrument upon which music of harmony could be played, but likewise defective insofar as one of the flutes is missing. Such temporal and earthly concerns stand in stark contrast to the seven objects displayed on the top shelf of the painting. Here, on the left, we see a beautifully coloured celestial globe, or astrolabe, giving the position of the stars. This turquoise blue astrolabe is surrounded by a number of mechanical gadgets and devices, all of which are designed to measure time and space in some way. Thus we have a polyhedral sundial, several quadrants, a cylindrical sundial, and, at the far right, the unusually shaped torquetum. In the words of Alexander Sturgis, these are

> intimations of worldly division (which) point perhaps to both the immutability of the universe and the passing of time which renders futile all earthly discord and disagreement.[7]

We see an additional hint of the hope of reconciliation in the shape of the books which lie open on the lower shelf. On the left side of the shelf, just below the globe, there is a textbook on mathematics written by a German from Nuremberg named Peter Apian. The name of the book was *Eyn Newe unnd wohlgegründte underweysung aller Kauffmanss Rechnung* ('A new and reliable instruction book of calculation for merchants') and it was first published in 1527. What is significant about it is that it is opened to a page containing a table on subdivision which begins with the ominous word *Dividirt* ('Divide'). This is deliberately contrasted with the book resting on the right side of the shelf, just below the lute. Close examination reveals this to be a copy of a German hymn book by Johannes Walther, first published in Wittenberg in 1524 and containing lyrics for spiritual songs by Martin Luther. Needless to say, this is quite an astonishing volume to be in the possession of a Catholic bishop of the time! The left side of the open book is Luther's German translation of the ancient hymn 'Veni Creator Spiritus' ('Come, Creator Spirit'); the right side is a song based on Luther's translation of the Ten Commandments. If ever there was a person committed to the reconciliation of Catholicism and the newly developing

---

7.   As narrated in the National Portrait Gallery video entitled *Making and Meaning: Holbein's Ambassadors*, written by Alexander Sturgis and Susan Foister (1997) produced by the National Gallery Audio Visual Unit. Distributed by National Gallery Publications Ltd, 5/6 Pall Mall East, London SW1Y 5BA.

Lutheranism, it is de Selve. He had been present at the Diet of Speyer in 1529 where attempts were made to reconcile the divisions of German Protestants and Catholics. As Alexander Sturgis goes on to state:

> De Selve, we know, both wrote and preached on the desirability for reconciliation between the two sides of the religious divide. The two hymns displayed, although written in German, are in fact simply translations of Catholic texts, and might therefore be intended to demonstrate the considerable common ground upon which men such as De Selve hoped that reconciliation might be founded.

The Painting's Preservation: The Painful Process of Restoration
Holbein's *The Ambassadors* is a powerfully executed painting consisting of oils and tempera on ten oak panels. As mentioned above, the work is once again on public view after having been in the restorer's studios of the National Gallery for over three years. Inevitably restoration of a work as old and as damaged as this painting was (it had been severely water damaged in several places) is difficult, even with the latest scientific and artistic tools being brought to bear in the process. For example, years of accumulated dirt and grime, not to mention layers of a yellowing varnish, had to be carefully and painstakingly removed from the painting centimetre by centimetre using a special solvent and cotton buds. Some 1,500 man-hours were dedicated to the restoration of this masterpiece, much of it done by Martin Wylde, the Chief Conservator of the National Gallery, working with the aid of magnifying goggles and specially designed microscopes. In order to restore the creator's original vision of his work of art such delicate processes are necessary, indeed essential, even though they are at times seemingly destructive and painful.

Such restoration has its counterpart in the spiritual realm, for it is often the case that an act of restoring broken relationships, true reconciliation, necessarily involves the stripping away of layers of hardness of heart. The accumulation of selfishness and insensitivity to others needs to be stripped away and removed before we are ever able to be reconciled with one another. The only way that we can begin to recapture the vivid colours of Holbein's painting, the soft contours of the robes with which the two principals of the painting are adorned, or to discover the artist's own signature in the lower left corner of the work (it had been all but lost due to the discoloration of the obscuring varnish), is to subject the work to a process of restoration. In similar fashion it is necessary for us as people to undergo the restoration process of God himself, in order that we can be found to bear the true image of the one who created us.

The Mysteries of the Work: The Hidden Christ as the Conqueror of Death
Two other points are worth noting about this painting of Holbein which
alerts us, and challenges us, to consider the restoring, the reconciling act of
God among us. The first concerns the rather unusual shape that appears in
the foreground between the two figures of de Dinteville and de Selve. At
first glance it is but a blob, a strange and inexplicable shape, perhaps some
blotched paint or a part of the water damage. However, when viewed from
one particular vantage point (just to the right of the painting, about one
metre from its base) the shape is quickly transformed into the shape of a
human skull. This is a classic example of a particular artistic technique
known as *anamorphosis*, the painting of objects in a distorted perspective
(Fig. 31 shows a picture of the image afforded by viewing from the necessary vantage point.)

Figure 31. *The Ambassadors* (skull), a detail.

It is not clear precisely how Holbein managed to produce this extraordinary object, nor what he was attempting to convey by means of it. However, the human skull is a long-standing symbol of human mortality, and
this is commonly regarded as the reason for its inclusion within the painting (which is otherwise done in a normal viewing perspective). It is as if
Holbein wants to suggest to the individual viewer that whatever one's
human achievements might be, whether one rises to the position of crown
ambassador or church bishop, mortality is a fact of life. Each of us must
die and surrender our life to God who is above all and who is responsible

for all. The message to the viewer is: *Memento mori!* Remember that you are mortal and must die. It is Holbein's equivalent of the classical idea of a *servus publicus*, a slave whose job it was to hold a laurel crown over the head of a victorious military general during a Roman triumph and whisper in the conqueror's ear the words: *hominem te esse memento* ('remember you are a man').[8]

To extend the idea and use it as a metaphor of human existence, we could say that we are reminded that at the centre of the painting which is our lives, if ever there is to be a restoration to God's original plan and purpose for us, there must be the spectre of death—a death to self, a mortification of our own desires and ambitions. Holbein lived in an age when the grim realities of death were all around; he himself fell victim to the plague in the autumn of 1543, just ten years after the completion of *The Ambassadors*.[9] He had already demonstrated an artistic interest in the subject of mortality with the popular series of woodcuts entitled *The Dance of Death* (1526).[10]

One other interesting facet arises from the restoration of Holbein's painting of *The Ambassadors*. In some ways it may be the most significant feature of all even though it is discreetly tucked away. In the upper-left-hand corner of the painting, all but obscured by the way in which the painting was framed and publicly displayed for centuries, is an absolutely astonishing insight, which is fitting as an expression of the artist's own hesitant Christian commitments, but also as a small window through which we glimpse the deepest of all theological truths. In this corner, we see a small, but unmistakable image of the crucified Christ (Fig. 32 shows

---

8.   For more on this aspect of Roman military triumph celebrations, see Robert Payne, *Rome Triumphant: How the Empire Celebrated its Victories* (New York: Barnes & Noble, 1962), pp. 41, 71; Larry J. Kreitzer, *Striking New Images: Roman Imperial Coinage and the New Testament World* (JSNTSup, 134; Sheffield: Sheffield Academic Press, 1996), pp. 133-34. Derek Wilson, *Hans Holbein*, p. 200, offers an alternative interpretation of the anamorphosis. He says: 'The anamorphosis is indeed a *memento mori*. It exhorts the beholder to keep his mortality ever before his eyes. But it also exhorts him 'Remember More'. Holbein, the humanist artist, emulates Erasmus, the humanist writer, who used the same kind of play on words in the title of his *Moriae Encomium, In Praise of Folly*'.

9.   Neither of the painting's two subjects were blessed with extreme longevity; Jean de Dinteville died in 1555 at the age of 52 and Georges de Selve died in 1541 at the age of 32.

10.   The series contained 41 illustrations and were composed while Holbein was living and working in Basel.

a detail of this section of the painting). It is as if Holbein wishes to make us aware of the fact that behind *every* act of restoration, *every* divine movement of reconciliation, stands the hidden Cross of Christ. We may not always see it, but it is there nonetheless, hovering over and energizing every act of reconciliation, human or divine, which takes place.

Figure 32. *The Ambassadors* (crucifix), a detail.

The painting thus juxtaposes the harsh realities of human mortality with the promises of resurrection hope made possible by the death of Jesus Christ on a cross. As some of the professionals most intimately connected with the conservation of the painting have put it:

> The whole painting then may be read as a meditation on Dinteville's melancholy and misery and on de Selve's despair at the condition of Europe. Standing on a floor which may allude to the cosmos, and placed between objects including astronomical instruments, perhaps arranged to simulate heaven and earth, and which certainly allude to a world of chaos, both men

think of the brevity of life and their end, but also of the hope of the life to come.[11]

Reconciliation and Ambassadorship: The Challenge of 2 Corinthians 5.18-20

The final point to emphasize within this short study concerns an image which Paul alludes to in the midst of one of his letters to the church in Corinth. In 2 Cor. 5.18-20 Paul adds to the foundational idea of reconciliation another image which helps to define his understanding of Christian mission—reconciliation is presented as part of the work of faithful ambassadors.[12] Thus, in 2 Cor. 5.18-19 Paul speaks of the redemptive actions of God through Christ in language that is very similar to the passage from Col. 1.15-20 with which we began our study. But he goes on in v. 5.20 to define his own Christian calling as a ministry of reconciliation and describes himself, and others, as ambassadors for Christ, ambassadors to whom this divine message has been entrusted. The translation of these verses provided by *The Jerusalem Bible* brings out the ambassadorial image quite well:

> [18]It is all God's work. It was God who reconciled us to himself through Christ and gave us the work of handing on this reconciliation. [19]In other words, God in Christ was reconciling the world to himself, not holding men's faults against them, and he has entrusted to us the news that they are reconciled. [20]So we are ambassadors for Christ; it is as though God were appealing through us, and the appeal that we make in Christ's name is: be reconciled to God.

Such a dynamic image of ambassadorship provides us with a new way of understanding what Christian reconciliation entails, what demands it makes upon those who are entrusted with ambassadorial responsibilities.[13]

---

11. Foister, Roy and Wyld, *Holbein's Ambassadors*, p. 57.

12. The most up-to-date treatment of the subject is Anthony Bash, *Ambassadors for Christ: An Exploration of Ambassadorial Language in the New Testament* (Wissenschaftliche Untersuchungen zum Neuen Testament, 92; Tübingen: J.C.B. Mohr [Paul Siebeck], 1997).

13. There is a particular difficulty in translating the 'ambassador' image in 5.20, namely, the fact that the Greek uses a verbal form (πρεσβεύομεν) rather than a noun construction (οἱ πρεσβεῖς) for the critical term concerned. Unfortunately, English does not use 'ambassador' as a verb in the way that Greek does. The closest an English translation can come to the sense of the Greek is to supply another verb to complement

It is a perspective with which Holbein might well have agreed, if the decision to present within his *The Ambassadors* a portrayal of a diplomat of a Catholic king together with a Catholic bishop (both of whom are surrounded by a host of objects suggestive of tensions with a developing Lutheran Protestantism) is anything to go by.

To return to the Pauline theme for a concluding thought: we could summarize by saying that for Paul to be an ambassador *for* Christ, an ambassador *of* Christ, means that reconciliation becomes one's aim, indeed, the very reason for existence. Ambassadorship and reconciliation are intimately connected in Paul's thought and the two ideas help to define what it means to be a follower of Christ. The Christian brief, the ministerial portfolio within the world, is that of effecting reconciliation wherever and whenever there is brokenness and division. Thus, to assist in the agonizing efforts of restoration, and that is part of what reconciliation involves, is a noble and sacred calling for all Christian believers. The Church's ever-present challenge is to be Christ's agents in the world whereby 'all things are *restored* in him'.

πρεσβεύομεν, and yield something like 'we *function* as ambassadors', or 'we *serve* as ambassadors'.

ON THE FRONTIER:
JUDITH AND ESTHER IN THE MYTH OF AMERICA

Margarita Stocker

As far as borders and boundaries are concerned, few have bulked so
largely in the modern Western imagination as the American frontier. It is
the location of that mythic film genre, the Western, and in the image of the
pioneers, a founding myth not only of the American imagination but of
American politics. In American politics the Bible has always played its
part, of course, from the first Puritan settlements of New England to the
contemporary political weight of the Moral Majority in the United States.
Less obvious, however, is why a heroine of the Old Testament Apocrypha
should have had a significant role in American culture. In the book of
Judith, the heroine preserves the Israelites from destruction by the Assyr-
ians, when she kills their general, Holofernes. The book is effectively a
biblical epic of 'love and war' and nationalism. Probably the most popular
and seminal novelist of his time, author of the profoundly American
Leatherstocking series of novels, James Fenimore Cooper recalled her in
The Deerslayer (1841), the first of the series. The finest American novelist
of the nineteenth century, Nathaniel Hawthorne, evoked her in his most
ambitious work, *The Marble Faun* (1859). The first American film director
of note, working in the fledgling industry which would become America's
most dominating cultural vehicle, D.W. Griffith filmed her story as *Judith
of Bethulia* (1913). This was the first of his trademark epics, even though it
is practically unknown by comparison to the classic *Birth of a Nation*.
More: this was the first ever full-length Hollywood motion picture. This
striking history among the more monumental instances of the American
imagination must prompt the question, why Judith? The reasons run deep,
just as the apocryphal heroine herself was a unique figure.

Figure 33. *Judith and Maidservant with the Head of Holofernes* (c. 1625
by Artemisia Gentileschi [1597–c. 1651], The Detroit Institute
of Arts/Bridgeman Art Library).

The first part of the answer is to be found in the cultural history bequeathed
to Americans from Britain and Europe. As I have shown elsewhere,
Judith's icon has been very much more ubiquitous, and significant, in
Western culture than hitherto suspected.[1] So much so, indeed, that tracing
its history illuminated Western concepts of sex, death, violence and power.
She was a femme fatale of a uniquely formidable kind, since God himself
had elected her into this role as the instrument of his vengeance. Unlike

---

1.   M. Stocker, *Judith, Sexual Warrior: Women and Power in Western Culture*
(New Haven and London: Yale University Press, 1998), discusses her history from
mediaeval times to the present.

other fatal females, she was a sacred heroine, and consequently resistant to the conventional misogynist stereotypes of such women in Western culture. Much of her iconographic history over the centuries has reflected our culture's difficulty in accommodating itself to this recalcitrant icon of female dominance. As a result, many versions of her story—whether in the visual arts, literature, drama, opera or film—have been not merely adaptations, but active distortions of the original, in which vested interests have sought to moderate or mitigate her challenge to various ingrained Western attitudes. Evidently, as a mankiller, she was sexually challenging; and as a sacred heroine, morally challenging. Most importantly for the United States, however, she was politically challenging as well.

In the Reformation past that lingered among the Puritans in colonial America, the apocryphal heroine had symbolized Protestant doctrine, Protestant revolt and Protestant zeal. As the assassin of the enemy general who had menaced the ancient Israelites, she was for a century the most important and inspiring model for Protestants at war. One aspect of her diverse political history was thus as heroine of radicals, whether in mass movements or individually, as assassins of the great and powerful. For the young American state, the most significant European event was the French Revolution, with which of course it had close ideological and political associations. And in the Revolution there had been a Judith, invoking the already long history of her icon in French politics. In 1793 a young woman named Charlotte Corday, directly instigated by the example of the apocryphal heroine, had assassinated the foremost revolutionary demagogue, and was ever after celebrated as a second Judith.[2] By the nineteenth century, both the French and the English antecedents had coloured Judith's icon for Americans. The more active their political consciousness, the more significant she was. As a figure for radicalism, she could be brought to have a role in the nation's perceptions of itself.

Judith and Esther in Hawthorne's The Marble Faun *and* The Scarlet Letter
In Hawthorne's novel, *The Marble Faun,* it is Judith's religious and sexual significances that are important to his complex and dark allegory. That will not concern us here, because it has been discussed elsewhere.[3] Rather, the significance of Hawthorne's Judith for the American national myth resides in her pairing with contrasting female figures. In *The Marble Faun,*

2. Stocker, *Judith, Sexual Warrior*, pp. 111-19.
3. Stocker, *Judith, Sexual Warrior*, pp. 169-72.

Judith herself has two incarnations. She is the subject of disturbing paintings by the artist heroine, Miriam, herself a dark European beauty. 'She had attempted the story of Judith, which we see represented by the old masters so often, and in such various styles'. In fact Miriam's interest in biblical femmes fatales is excessive, since she repeatedly depicts both Judith and her canonical analogue, Jael—the great murderesses, as Hawthorne reminds us insistently. He does so because of Miriam's mysterious past and guilty future, which turn upon murder. In her paintings, 'Over and over again, there was the idea of woman acting the part of a revengeful mischief towards man'. It is curious that Hawthorne, an author of great religious interests, should seem to forget Judith's sacred context and ascribe her homicide to sexual vengeance. She becomes an instance of sexual pathology.

The painting of Judith is described in detail: grisly, bloody, grotesque. What Hawthorne wishes to convey is not only the vengeful potency of Judith, with which Miriam identifies, and the similar experience of her own psyche. He wishes also to convey that this is unacceptable, not only as homicide, but because the perpetrator herself becomes a victim of it. 'The head of Holofernes…being fairly cut off, was screwing its eyes upward and twirling its features into a diabolical grin of triumphant malice, which it flung right in Judith's face',[4] shocking his murderess. Miriam always begins the paintings with high passionate fervour, but usually ends by converting them to bathos. In this way Hawthorne implies his spiritual point, that even if Miriam's homicide were as easily exculpated as Judith's—her situation had been coercive—nevertheless it does her more damage than her victim. She lives in guilt, fear and misery. By driving her to a damning act, he, not she, is the victor in their struggle.

Underscoring this, Hawthorne has her paint also Beatrice Cenci, a famed Italian parricide whose portrait was a cult object for American tourists in Italy. She herself had been celebrated in her day as a tragic victim of the full rigour of the law, since popular opinion had seen her action as the excusable manslaughter of a cruel father. Because of that, she had been represented as a Judith, justified in murder.[5] This, however, is not Hawthorne's view: Cenci, like Judith's other avatars in Miriam's studio, represents the artist's own infection by evil.

---

4. Nathaniel Hawthorne, *The Marble Faun* (New York: NEL, 1961), p. 39.
5. Stocker, *Judith, Sexual Warrior*, pp. 110-11.

This is why Judith has two incarnations in the narrative, both as Miriam's obsessive subject and as Miriam herself. Before her lover recognizes one of her paintings as a self-portrait, he sees it as Judith: a beauty who 'might ripen to be what Judith was, when she vanquished Holofernes with her beauty, and slew him for too much adoring it'.[6] All of Hawthorne's animadversions to Judith portray hers not as a patriotic or religious homicide, but a sex-murder. Ironically, even Miriam's lover, Donatello, is named by Hawthorne after the celebrated Italian artist, whose sculpture of Judith slaying Holofernes is renowned (see Fig. 34). The sexualization and criminalization of Judith's icon becomes a way of estranging us from them, and of suggesting that women are subject to criminal passions. Pressed upon by guilt and fear, both lovers are dramatized and tainted by their symbolic envelope, in what is seen as Judith's crime. Theirs is an antique, European experience of evil, which a biblical comparison helps to characterize as almost primeval.

By contrast to the dark Miriam, Hawthorne introduces another artist, a young American named Hilda: Anglo-Saxon not Mediterranean, American not European, not a Catholic but a white Anglo-Saxon Protestant, of the ethnic group drawn from the first settlers. Belonging not to the Old World but to the dominant class in the New, Hilda is innocence itself. As Miriam says, 'Hilda, your innocence is like a sharp steel sword!'[7] Implicit in that it is a contrast to the heavy war sword of Holofernes, which Judith had used to decapitate him. In previous representations of her icon, the sword had often been used as a symbol of the virtue of Justice. Here, however, Hawthorne's revisionist use of Judith has suggested that hers was a more savage phenomenon: his insistent repetition that Judith was a 'Jewess' discriminates her from the Christian ethic. That is embodied in Hilda's pure American Protestantism, a virtue symbolized by a sword of steel. Her profoundly decorous and respectable character seems also to suggest Hawthorne's idea of true womanhood, as opposed to the deviant Miriam. Similarly, the American icon of Justice with which she is associated politicizes the contrast. The contrast of Hilda with Miriam-Judith implies the younger, fresher, cleaner virtues of the new nation, America. Judith's Old World, Old Law context comes to define the American spirit by contrast.

6. Hawthorne, *Marble Faun*, p. 43.
7. Hawthorne, *Marble Faun*, p. 55.

Figure 34. *Judith and Holofernes* (sculpture by Donatello [c. 1368–1466],
1457 [bronze] Palazzo Vecchio [Palazzo della Signoria],
Florence/Bridgeman Art Library).

That is not to say that Hawthorne's view of America is simplistic. His
The Scarlet Letter (1850) explored the bigotry of colonial New England,
in which his own ancestors had been deeply and shamefully implicated.
There, too, a significant biblical name contributed to the characterization
of the heroine and her situation. Named after the biblical Esther, secretly a
Jewess married to a pagan emperor, Hester is an anomaly in her own

community. Wearing a badge of shame, she is an outcast for the sin of adultery. Like Esther, she holds an explosive secret, since the father of her illegitimate child is the local minister, an apparently saintly man idolized by the community. Their sanctimoniousness, severity and bigotry are all hazarded to exposure by the truth. This is why Hawthorne gives the sinner the forename of a biblical heroine, who had delivered the Israelites from persecution. Certainly in his Victorian universe, she is a sinner and has seduced a man of God. But the consequences of their sin so fundamentally disturb the unChristian Christianity of their community that there is a kind of medicine in it. The moral paradox of that situation is expressed, symbolically, by the naming of a 'fallen woman' as God's instrument. This is the Esther of a New England locked into pharasaical attitudes, a New World not yet New enough. Truly to be the Promised Land that its founders had dreamed of, America had to progress beyond the Puritan mindset. That is the implication of Hawthorne's introductory chapter, which explicitly ruminates upon the guilt of his ancestor: suggesting that America has not yet wholly unburdened herself of the narrow-minded tyrannies of its Puritan past. In fact, Hawthorne says that he will 'take shame upon myself' for his ancestors' sins of cruelty and persecution.[8] The legalized massacre of the Salem witch-hunts is the Hawthorne family's own relic of national guilt.

This introductory chapter is set in England, where Hawthorne lived for a time, and it is from the Old Country that he ruminates upon his own, the new. This serves to emphasize the Americanness of the story he will tell. More important, though, it implies that the Puritan settlers carried some form of sinfulness with them from the Old Country to America, polluting a hitherto virgin territory. Like the Hawthorne family guilt, the colony inherited the sins of the fathers. Hester Prynne is a fallen mother, and her daughter leaves the colony, an émigré while her mother is an outcast. Genealogy and heritage become a matter of what can be included or excluded in the national consciousness. And that is represented by women, distanced as Other by shame or exportation. Finally, Hester is tolerated but not of them. Whereas in *The Marble Faun* the young New Englander could be contrasted to European corruption, here it is something the new country cannot escape. That is because Italy, unlike England, was not the ethnic and religious progenitor of New England.

---

8.   Nathaniel Hawthorne, *The Scarlet Letter* (Harmondsworth: Penguin, 1970).

In symbolic nomenclature, there is in fact a subterranean connection between Hawthorne's two novels. From earliest times, Esther and Judith had been paired in Christian doctrine and art, because both had been the saviours of their nation.[9] During the nineteenth century, however, the parallel between the two icons had transmogrified into a contrast. The bourgeois moralism of the times could not accept Judith's seductive and homicidal aspects as compatible either with Christian doctrine or with current sexual morality. Indeed, her sexual reputation was such that in contemporary English idiom 'a Judy' was the name for a common or loose woman.

It is in that context that Hawthorne portrayed his fallen, bohemian artist as a Judith. Thus in England, George Meredith's 'fallen woman' in *One of Our Conquerors* would be named Judith, and she goes so far as to invoke her apocryphal predecessor as the antecedent for her unhappy social situation, in which 'respectable women' and insolent men treat her with contempt. Moreover, it was precisely in a society whose literature was required to observe a coy unspecificity about sexual matters that such symbolic forenames conveyed so much important information. One way of eroticizing or of classifying a female character was, among other things, to name her Judith.

Esther's implications had—except for Hawthorne, who was iconoclastic in this respect—travelled in the reverse direction. Having softened the character of her husband, the emperor, and influenced him to spare her people, she was a model of the best kind of Victorian wife: ornamental, pious, compassionate, an improving domestic influence upon her husband. This last point was the most important. In this century, American women in particular were becoming politically vocal. By the 1850s they were already demanding the vote. For them, Esther could signify the kind of woman who both contributed to the virtues and dignity of the home and exerted a beneficial political influence. When Elizabeth Cady Stanton led a team of educated women in a project to translate and comment on the Bible, they regarded their work as a landmark in the struggle for women's social and political emancipation.[10] Their commentary celebrates Esther as a model for the virtues, dignity and good sense of married women. In this, they were intentionally appealing not only to their own feminist convictions but also to an image of women which chimed with current social mores. Esther was an idealized version of the good, strong, virtuous but

9. Stocker, *Judith, Sexual Warrior*, pp. 12-13.
10. *The Woman's Bible* (New York: European Publishing, 1895, 1898).

certainly *domesticated* woman. In no way did she offend nineteenth-century moralism or the belief that a woman's rightful place was in the home; this was no militant, turbulent suffragette, who trespassed on the public arena of men. Rather she did what was accepted as natural, which was to influence her husband behind the scenes. At a time when women were being more demanding, this was a role model which did not disturb fundamental social values; it is not surprising that men often found it acceptable.

It was, then, at best fortuitous that Judith's icon had sunk so low. In the Apocrypha, she had challenged and rebuked the elders of her city, the political and religious authorities; she had invoked vengeance for the maidens of Israel, raped by their enemies; she had killed the Assyrian leader 'by the hand of a woman' (Jdt. 16.6). Long before Freud declared her castratory, it was obvious that here was a heroine who had, in fact, traduced shibboleths and assassinated patriarchy. In that light, she had become not Esther's dominant sister but her opposite.

Nineteenth-century mores welcomed Esther as an improved version of 'the angel in the house', a royal wife who could reassure women of their new dignity in that role; whereas Judith the widow had become the unmarriageable woman. She was the outcast, the termagant who shadowed the feminist. As Esther was idealized, Judith was demonized.

This contrast was particularly appealing to contemporary novelists because of the ruling paradigm of womanhood: the contrast of wife with prostitute, respectable with fallen, which tended to characterize women along a single, sexual faultline. When Fenimore Cooper sorted his women characters according to the paradigm of iconic pairs, he went rather further along the misogynist road than most novelists of the time. Certainly, he offered Judith and Esther as sisters, quite literally. In doing so, however, he did not simply posit two opposing paradigms of the mysterious sex, one good and one bad: but depicted a pair in which neither offered much to the male. From a psychosexual point of view, all of Cooper's novels are curious, but *The Deerslayer* is the most disturbed.

Judith in Cooper's The Deerslayer

The first of his hugely successful Leatherstocking Novels, *The Deerslayer*[11] is a founding text of the American myth of self-definition.

---

11. Fenimore Cooper, *The Deerslayer* (New York: Signet, 1963).

Cooper's success was not owing to outstanding literary skills: his writing can be verbose, repetitive and turgid. Rather, what the Leatherstocking series offered its enthusiastic public was an apparently authentic evocation of the early American wilderness, its frontiersmen, its settlers, its rogues, its Indian tribes and its colonial wars. In Cooper's novels these became a beguiling evocation of the 'virgin territory' and infant convulsions that brought into being the American nation. To a young country—the opening of the novel reminds its readers how young—Cooper offered adventurous accounts of her genesis in the previous century. His purpose is self-consciously mythic, and his readers accepted the lineaments of that national myth.

In this novel, the events of the narrative take place at the edge of 'civilization', in the wilderness beyond the settlements and the local, colonial British garrison. Here, on the frontier, friendly and hostile Indian tribes complicate the natural challenges and dangers of the wilderness; and a colonial war is about to break out along the border with Canada. The hero, with the mythic appellations Deerslayer and Hawkeye, is a young frontiersman of courage, stamina and quite astounding virtue. He is pious, ethical, gallant and chivalrous. Explicitly, he is the embodiment of integrity and truth: his primary characteristics are 'plain-dealing and frankness', 'truth and fair-dealing', indeed an actual inability ever to tell an untruth, in any circumstances, even if it were to save his own life. As yet inexperienced and untried at the beginning of the novel, this frontiersman will become the hero of the whole series, a totemic figure of vigorous American manhood: he is, in effect, the spirit of independence that will characterize the American Revolution that is yet to come.

At another level, however, Deerslayer is a mythic projection of his author. Like Deerslayer, the author professed himself the voice of 'fearless truth' in politics. Cooper's class was the old, privileged, affluent stratum of white Anglo-Saxon Protestants. They had played a part in the Revolution. Inevitably, his family had political and diplomatic interests and connections, and Cooper himself became increasingly embroiled in active politics. His mentor was the Frenchman who was a hero of the American Revolution, Lafayette, and his own contact with France familiarized him with its political bequest to America.

In the 1830s Cooper had been a Democrat, without any of the egalitarian convictions that that might suggest, for he was very much of his class. In 1838 he had published *The American Democrat*, a highly personal statement of his convictions about the historical and natural character of the United States as a political entity.[12] Perhaps its most salient point, for him at least, is the distinction he draws between democracy and the nature of demagogy. True democracy is characterized by truth, 'the frankness of freemen', as opposed to the lies of demagogues. He emphasizes repeatedly that in America, the tyranny of public opinion, misled by the wrong sort of politician, can be just as dangerous as the tyranny of old monarchies in Europe. America had cast off the British monarchy, and must not now resubmit itself to another kind of domination. Cooper's is the voice of a gentrified oligarchy suspicious of the masses. The enemy of the state is the fickleness, ignorance and malleability of 'public opinion'.

Against this, Deerslayer is the idealized icon of true American individualism. Unlike a demagogue, he always speaks the truth, without fear or favour. His 'plain-dealing' is the ideal opposed to the mob. And as an American should, Cooper implies, he thinks for himself. In many long disquisitions, Deerslayer attacks popular prejudices and insists that he himself always judges as he finds. That is what both Deerslayer and Cooper say, often and at length, as is Cooper's wont. In fact, however, Deerslayer's attitudes seem unlikely to perturb received opinions on anything much.

He unreservedly accepts the authority of Christianity in all things, although sectarian differences do not interest him. In the same way, *The American Democrat* had vigorously reasserted the theocratic impulse behind the original colonizers, and Cooper insisted that God's revelation and doctrine must never be contradicted in politics. Race is also an important issue in the novel, and not only because of its historical setting; Cooper has his eyes on the contemporary Indian wars as well. On Indians, Deerslayer's opinions are offered as necessarily definitive, precisely because, unlike most white men, he has lived with and absorbed the skills of an Indian tribe, the Delawares. He likes good Indians and detests bad ones, rebutting the assertions of his colleague, Hurry, that all Indians are simply animals. Yet he is in no doubt that the difference between white and red skins is crucial. The key point, in this respect, is his attitude to miscegenation, which he finds wholly unacceptable. Offered his life in exchange for marrying a woman of the Huron tribe, he will not do it. Like many such crises in the novel, this is a test designed to prove Deerslayer's heroic integrity. Implied in them all, moreover, is that he is a role model for all right-thinking Americans, if they are true to their revolutionary heritage.

12. G. Dekker and L. Johnston (eds.), *The American Democrat* (Harmondsworth: Penguin, 1969). See especially pp. 70, 170, 205.

His attitude to women is conventional for his times. He thinks that they are soft whereas men are hard, and creatures of feeling, vulnerable to transports of excessive emotion, easily frightened, and open to seduction by unscrupulous men. He is both protective and given to lecturing them on their female characteristics. His verbosity on all matters is inevitable, however, for he is the voice of America's true self.

According to D.H. Lawrence, in his groundbreaking study of the American classics,[13] Deerslayer is paradigmatic of a white American myth, which is at once committed to the idea of 'Liberty', and yet imprisoned within a rigid Puritan selfhood. Lawrence regarded this individualism as a precarious, timorous construction, which sustained itself only by denying human instincts. Those instincts are represented (sexually) by women and (racially) by Indians and blacks. When Deerslayer condemns miscegenation, it is an instance of self-repression, the repression which is the only way he can secure his psychic independence and strength. Lawrence's analysis is perceptive.

As the mythic incarnation of American manhood, Deerslayer represents a mental apartheid, which he expresses in mitigating terms as a matter of recognizing that whites have one set of racial 'gifts' while Indians have another. That boundary founds his identity upon separation from racial and sexual Others, despite his admiration for and homosocial intimacy with the Delawares. He is presented as a presexual character, attractive to some women but not himself attracted. In so far as he is in love with anyone, it is his Indian friend Serpent. Since, however, Serpent's very name encodes a homosexual temptation in the wilderness—the American Garden of Eden—the internalized law against homosexuality prevents any course other than homosocial sublimation in Deerslayer's attitude to his friend. As an instance of our hero's compassionate character, Cooper has him lecture Serpent to the effect that he must treat his bride kindly, unlike many Indian men; there seems to be both sublimation and racial patronage at work in this exchange.

The romantic plots in the novels play out a process of repression. In *The Deerslayer* that process is particularly evident and uneasy. That becomes even more pronounced if one is familiar with the way in which the book of Judith has been, over many centuries, repeatedly adapted and imitated. In the nineteenth century, it became even more common to use the story and its symbols in disguise. The apocryphal heroine does make an explicit

---

13. D.H. Lawrence, *Studies in Classic American Literature* (Harmondsworth: Penguin, 1971), pp. 66-68.

appearance in the novel, and does so at its narrative crisis. In fact, though, the significance of the book of Judith is much more extensive in Cooper's novel. *The Deerslayer* is in fact an outgrowth of the apocryphal story, and almost entirely dependent upon it. Two of the central characters, its key incidents and its overall plot all derive from Judith's story. That crucial fact is invisible unless you are privy to the history of her icon. It is the more astonishing because a modern reader, particularly, is most unlikely to associate a frontier adventure story with a biblical female myth. What strikes Cooper's readers is the evocation of the frontier. What strikes the student of Judith is that he has imported her story into a celebration of iconic American manhood. The covert source of the novel is, in effect, the repressed Other in her most challenging iconic guise.

It is probable, however, that at least some of Cooper's contemporary readers were more alert to the biblical narrative behind this. This was not only because of her icon's residence in political consciousness. Certainly Hawthorne expected his American readers to be familiar with the biblical story, and it was generally well known, quite apart from its political associations in the United States. Moreover, *The Deerslayer* is insistent in its emphasis upon the significance of the Bible to its events.

As the frontier war begins along the borders of New England, a lonely outpost is in danger from hostile Indians. Built on piles in a lake, 'Muskrat Castle' is the abode of the Hutter family, a widowed father and his two daughters, Judith and Hetty. Before she died, their mother frequently instructed them in the Bible, and particularly in the book of Job. Their friend, a trapper named Hurry, comes to their aid, in company with the hunter Deerstalker and Serpent. There are various encounters with the hostile Indians, including an attack on the 'castle' in which Hutter is scalped whilst still alive, and then left to die. Meanwhile, the besieged have taken refuge on Hutter's houseboat, known as 'the Ark'. By this time. although pursued by Hurry, Judith has fallen in love with Deerslayer. Hetty is in love with Hurry. When Judith rejects Hurry's proposal, he abandons the women. The story reaches its climax when, having captured Deerslayer, the Indians torture him as a prelude to killing him. Both of the women try to intervene to save him. Hetty, who is 'feeble-minded', is treated kindly by the Indians and immune from harm, because they consider her mental condition a sacred affliction. As she has on a previous occasion, Hetty goes to their camp, Bible in hand, to expound its precepts to them and to beg mercy. When this fails, Judith appears on the same errand. She has a taste for finery which is anomalous on the frontier and somewhat above her social station, and she has deliberately dressed in her finest brocade to impress the Indians. She claims that she is a woman of great importance in the British colony, and demands Deerslayer's release before her soldiers punish the Indians. Challenged by the chief, she confirms her status by reference to Hetty's Bible, implying that the book of Judith is about her. This stratagem is exposed, however, when the retarded Hetty reveals that she is simply Judith Hutter, as the chief suspected. Judith's own local fame does not help her in this; the Indians have heard of her because she is widely celebrated as extraordinarily beautiful. Finally, however, because Hurry has alerted the nearest garrison, the Indian camp is overrun by the British, and Hetty dies of a stray bullet. Judith is not only in love with Deerslayer, but has lost her family, home and financial support: for all these reasons she proposes to him. He, however, rejects her, because, Cooper affirms, he does not love her. However, it is possible that he would have thought about her desperate situation, we assume, were it not for one thing. Much pursued by the officers of the garrison, Judith has acquired a 'loose' reputation. (She has in fact been seduced by an officer, Warley, much to her own remorse.) Deerslayer admits that because of this he would not marry her. Reunited with Warley, who is recalled to England, Judith thereafter lives in a house on his estate as a 'kept woman'. Meanwhile, Deerslayer goes on to establish his mythic renown.

As traditionally in American national myth, the 'wilderness' is at one level a prelapsarian paradise, the paradisal portrayal of the lakeland wilderness. The many invocations of religious doctrine and dissent, and the overt biblical allusions, all serve not only to convey Cooper's religious convictions but also to support their political associations. In particular, they are the context for his rewriting of biblical narrative. That focuses on the iconic pair, Judith and Hetty (Esther), both of whom explicitly discuss the biblical provenance of their Christian names. Hetty/Esther is simple, sweet, domesticated, loving, and pious. She is the domestic angel reduced to literal imbecility. Her death is treated like a martyrdom, and contrasted with Judith's squalid fate.

Judith is the elder, and dominant, not merely because of Hetty's disability. At the opening of the novel, she is the subject of a long conversation between Hurry and Deerslayer, when it is established that she is unusual and even unique. Like her mythic original, she is astoundingly beautiful: Cooper emphasizes this repeatedly, as does Deerslayer: 'her personal charms so universally produced' their effect. We are meant to conclude that in the truly incomparable nature of her beauty she is exactly like the original, whom God made irresistible. Her character is equally striking. Like her original, she is bold and fearless; more, she is a frontierswoman, practised with a rifle. She also precisely mimics the original's remarkable combination of gifts, beauty and brains. Judith Hutter has 'Speech and looks [that] go hand in hand... Such a gal, in a month, might spoil the stoutest warrior in the colony'. These thoughts are straight from the Apocrypha: 'There is not such a woman from one end of the earth to the other, both for beauty of face, and wisdom of words', and the Assyrian warriors fear her power to deceive (Jdt. 10.19; 11.21). The original's eloquence is imitated in her impressive speech to the Indian chief, where, Cooper tells us, her avoidance of direct lies permits Deerslayer to translate her words into the Indian language without qualm. In this deployment of evasion and ambiguity she directly imitates the biblical heroine's deception of Holofernes.

Moreover, here one of Deerslayer's own attributes locks into the book of Judith. There, as centuries of Christian commentary had pointed out, the character Achior embodied Truth and truth-telling. In this episode of the novel, Deerslayer's central attribute is what permits Judith to play Judith. In other words, the story of Judith becomes simply an episode in the greater history of Deerslayer. It is absorbed into a founding masculine American myth.

Except that this displacement of the feminine, whether as the passionate and turbulent Judith or the infantilized domestic Esther, belies the whole foundation of the novel. It does not simply characterise its Judith after the original. The relations between the central characters all distribute themselves as in the book of Judith. Judith's pursuer, Hurry, is a boastful and uncouth equivalent of the military braggadoccio, and this—like his predatory and unchivalrous behaviour and his barbaric attitudes, is fetched from Holofernes, the vain general. Judith's officer-lover is a lecher fetched from the same place. Just as rewritings of the Judith story often make Achior her true lover, so Deerslayer is her love-object Achior.

Overall, the novel's plot also derives directly from the Apocrypha. The frontier war echoes the similarly colonial conflict in the original, and the besieged 'castle' is a wilderness version of the fortified city which Judith defends. Just as commentaries described that city as the Church, so the castle has an Ark, which symbolized precisely that—a wilderness ark, more inclusive than any sect or denomination, and thus in The American Way. Judith does not actually kill any Indians, but she knocks one off the ark and escapes others by her skill and stamina in handling a canoe. When the crisis occurs, she explicitly imitates the Book of Judith by formulating a secret plan, using Hetty in place of Judith's maid, as her ally, imitating Judith's careful toilette and richest costume, demanding to see only the enemy leader, and addressing him boldly, craftily and beguilingly. Like her original, she refuses offers of marriage—in this case, Hurry's—and also like her, ends in a kind of hermetic seclusion.

Figure 35. *Judith with the Head of Holofernes*, Giovanni Antonio Pellegrini (c. 1710, The Barber Institute of Fine Arts, The University of Birmingham).

There are two signal differences, however. This is Judith in a nineteenth-century guise, as a fickle flirt and fallen woman, a fact which here out-weighs any other character attribute. In the original, the chaste and modest heroine adopted a fine dress only to seduce Holofernes, whereas finery is Judith Hutter's abiding weakness. Hurry tells her that he will be kind enough to overlook her reputation if she will marry him, but Judith has always despised him. What may strike us as the key element in this episode is the truth of Hurry's observation, that having lost their father the women need a man's protection and material support. Yet in Judith's two attempts to obtain Deerslayer as a husband, this crucial point is never mentioned. What Cooper offers as Judith's motive is her love for him. The fact is that, as she leaves with the soldiers for the protection of the garrison, Judith has to find a man to support her. That she does, that he has already seduced her in any case, and that he is rich, are all eminently practical considerations. What Cooper does not mention is that she does not appear to have any alternatives. The only one offered in the narrative is Hurry, who is close to being a villain, since he represents the rogue element in the American nation. For Cooper, though, Judith's fate is the pretext for a meditation on the general propensity of humankind to sin. For him, her initial seduction was the wrongdoing from which the rest followed.

So much so, indeed, that the gender-alignment of virtue and vice in the Book of Judith is here re-aligned. Cooper has run that narrative so close, that we should not be surprised that he even translates the two blows which Judith needs to decapitate Holofernes. Holofernes is fragmented here among the male characters. Hurry has his barbarism and desire for Judith, Warley has his military profession, the Indian chief has his power over Judith's nearest and dearest, and the ruthless brute, Hutter, is scalped in an echo of Holofernes' beheading. But whereas the original needed two blows to kill her would-be ravisher, this Judith makes two abortive attempts to propose to Deerslayer. The crisis of gender relations is reversed from feminine victory in the Apocrypha to feminine defeat and abasement in the novel.

But this is only the culmination of Cooper's narrative strategy throughout, which is to reverse the narrative of the Book of Judith. This Judith is the same, and does all the same things, and fails utterly in her objectives. The original story is the repressed Other of this self-consciously mythic novel. Simultaneously, *Deerslayer* explodes the most authoritative legend of female power, and erects upon its ruins the masculine myth of America.

If this Judith is the 'Wild Rose', as she is called by Serpent, it is a form of wildness that Deerslayer does not want in his wilderness. That is the untamed beauty that he loves. His mythic bond with it would be compromised by her, a naturalized bond that is effectively made the white American's claim to own it. In that women have no direct share: in *The American Democrat* Cooper dismisses the idea of women's suffrage out of hand. He will not discuss it, because for him it is by natural law impossible. Moreover, he affirms, 'Manhood' is the key to the American constitution. Politically as well as sexually and mythically, the Book of Judith is the repressed Other of *The Deerslayer*.

The narrative's rejection of domesticity for the white man is complete: Hetty dies, Judith is rejected, and her seducer will not marry her because she is socially beneath him. Even her father is a widower. Worse, it transpires that in fact he is not her father. Her mother had been a fallen woman too, reduced to marrying far beneath her station when her lover abandoned her. A congenital imbecility, in Hetty's case, and a congenital immorality, in Judith's case, are seen to descend in the female line. Knowing now her illegitimacy, her daughter laments that now the only name she has is 'Judith'. We can hardly miss the mythic constitution conferred by that: she is an archetype of what the novel is repudiating. The original's victory over a hostile patriarchy is displaced and minimized as her 'father's' death, scalped, but not by her. And then it turns out that he is not her father anyway, but a one-time pirate as well as a blackguard. This lawless context and her illegitimacy signal that this Judith cannot be part of the bringing of 'civilization' (as Cooper describes it at the very beginning) to a virgin land. That is why she is expelled from it, and Deerslayer proof against sexual enticement. His frigidity is America's strength.

Similarly, the sexual and racial threats to that autonomy and hegemony are identified. This is achieved even when Judith is apparently praised: 'such another as is not to be found atween this and the sea; Judith is as full of wit, and talk, and cunning, as an old Indian orator'. The claims of both sexual and racial Others are repudiated, by and for the 'true' and 'honest' rights of Deerslayer.

In contrast to that Americanness, Judith's seducer is a British aristocrat, and it is to Britain that she returns with him: to the corrupt, old class, old world where she belongs. Even there, her curiously indefinite social status on the American frontier has been exchanged only for social ostracism, a hypocritically hidden mistress. What she says about her social invisibility and degradation is, in fact, echoed by the fallen Judith in George Meredith's English novel. His Judith complains, 'when men get women on the slope to their perdition...they do as much as murder.... Judith! damnable name... I did something in scripture... Judith could again'. [14] Judith Hutter says, If all men had...honest tongues...there would be less wrong done in

---

14. George Meredith, *One of Our Conquerors* (1891; London: Chapman and Hall, 1910), pp. 339-41.

the world', because of their 'baseness and deception... I get warm when I think of all the wrong that men do'. Both fallen women feel at once victimised and vengeful.

But Judith Hutter's claim to be the victim of men is not supported in this novel: Deerslayer reads a lecture on female virtue to Hetty, and Mrs Hutter had warned her daughters against her own sin. The failing in Judith is innate, as is her unfeminine boldness. Similarly, her appeal to the Old Testament authority when in the Huron camp had been exposed as a false claim to status and power. The rejection of her sexual menace becomes, mythically, part of the American overthrow of the Mother Country and its rule.

Not only in this respect, Judith Hutter's characterization as a 'daughter' is highly significant. Familial relations are important in a novel which focuses on origins—racial, social and national. Cooper's construction of American identity in this novel is an account of origins, both as a rendering of American history and as a formative idealization of the American psyche. The founding event of the nation was of course the Revolution, an oedipal rising against the colonists' own homeland. The oedipal character of the Revolution was reflected in classic American literature, which American critics have suggested manifests an incomplete, oedipal response to both eroticism and mortality.[15] As I have suggested, the Book of Judith is a counter-cultural myth in direct opposition to the Oedipus myth.[16] If Oedipus's is the revolt against patriarchy of the Son, Judith's is the revolt of the Daughter. And hers is counter-cultural also in its altruism, because by her revolt she does not obtain power herself, and indeed rejects all honours and advantages. More, the feminine opposite to the oedipal myth of masculine identity is underlined by her refusal to marry again. She remains a feminine Otherness with its own autonomy. Whether in sexual identity, moral probity, or political power, Judith's myth is not only the rival to Oedipus's, but hostile to it. In his, he can inherit the very power he has challenged. But. like that power, he would not wish to allow the same privilege to Judith, because the power is patriarchal. It is the Law of the Father, wrested from him. As son moves to patriarch, as America moves from colonial son to republic, the revolt of the daughter must be repudiated and expunged.

---

15. See for instance Leslie Fiedler, *Love and Death in the American Novel* (Harmondsworth: Penguin, rev. edn, 1984).

16. Stocker, *Judith, Sexual Warrior*, pp. 21-23 *et passim*.

Prominent American women of the leading Revolutionary class had not been entirely content with the new constitution of the nation. It may be that Judith's icon was in fact suggested to Cooper's mind by the fame of Judith Sargent Murray, daughter of the politician Withrop S. Murray, who was a feminist patriot and 'daughter of the revolution'. She herself had been a writer preoccupied with the formation of the national character.[17] In Cooper's Judith Hutter, an oedipal construction of American identity is brought into direct and extended conflict with its mythic opposite, by inverting the apocryphal story. A self-conscious myth of origins for the dominant culture demands the exclusion of a counter-cultural myth which is all too close to it. Once knowingly illegitimate, Cooper's Judith is 'reduced' to her mythic identity: 'I am Judith, and Judith only'; 'If I am a bird of fine feathers, I have also my name'—but it is one of shame and disinheritance.

Ratifying America as the justified rebel son, as legitimate nationhood, involved repudiating illegitimacy as descending through the female line. The line runs from the fallen, absent mother to the fallen, illegitimate daughter, who in the Indian camp admits she is not the British Queen, but does lay false claim to power. A kind of imposter and unwanted immigrant, reared by a pirate, she is re-exported to Britain, where she can live out her decadent destiny. Against her shadow, we are meant to recognize the consequently defined, definitive figure of Deerslayer as national legitimacy and independence.

Judith in Griffith's Judith of Bethulia

By the end of the century, America had experienced its own Civil War. It was a confrontation of the modernized North with the still largely rural South, a confrontation of two different aspects of America. From the defeated South came the film-maker D.W. Griffith, whose cinematic ambitions lay in epic. After the epic *Judith of Bethulia* would follow both another biblical epic, *Intolerance*, and the national epic *Birth of A Nation*. But he went to Judith first. Adapted from the successful American play of 1904 by Thomas Aldrich, her story offered both the intimate scenes and the broad spectacle which Griffith could so strikingly combine.

One of the techniques which he developed for this purpose was the intercutting which so struck Karl Brown that it inspired a determination to work for him.

17. Judith Sargent Murray, *The Gleaner* (1798).

His highest objective, as nearly as I could grasp it, was to photograph thought. He could do it. In *Judith of Bethulia* there was a scene in which Judith stands over the sleeping figure of Holofernes, sword in hand. She raises the sword, then falters. Pity and mercy have weakened her to a point of helpless irresolution. Then she thinks, and the screen is filled with the mangled bodies of those, her own people, slain by this same Holofernes. Then her face becomes filled with hate as she summons all her strength to bring that sword whistling down upon the neck of what is no longer a man but a blood-reeking monster.[18]

At this thematic crisis, the intercutting does more than render palpable what Judith's commitment to her own people is based upon: a patriotic altruism. It ensures that she is exculpated from the inhumanity of a cold-blooded murder, even as we watch her strike.

Since this Judith has actually fallen in love with Holofernes, the inter-cutting dramatizes the conflict between private inclination and an altruistic commitment which overrides it, at great personal cost. Holofernes has tempted her also with power and riches, but it is her love for him which is the stumbling block. What the scene confirms is her self-sacrifice for her country, the integrity of her motive, and the humanity in her homicide. Unlike most versions of the event, Griffith's preserves a direct linkage between the murder and politics. And the linkage is strengthened by emotional power, both of Judith's loss and of her commitment to the Israelite nation. It is also the only version of the story in which a Judith in love with Holofernes is not hopelessly compromised by that fact, person-ally, morally and politically. Even were Griffith's not a fine film, this scene alone is a unique achievement.

Although Judith remains profoundly unhappy afterwards, the final epi-sodes in Bethulia maintain her sense that there was no alternative. Nation comes before personal considerations, as it would not for Holofernes. Since the essential point of the original Judith's triumph as a deliverer is that she did the only thing that could be done, and she alone could have done it, the stress upon this fact is highly effective. Alternating between private pain and full acknowledgement of her people's joy, the actress Blanche Sweet's face becomes a beautiful icon of patriotism.

That was an important attribute of Griffith, too, who was a loyal son of the South, committed to what he saw as its old chivalric values. His father, of whom he was inordinately proud, had been a distinguished general in

18. Karl Brown, *Adventures with D.W. Griffith* (New York: Signet, 1973), p. 21.

the Civil War, who, according to his son, was wounded five times.[19] In the previous year, Woodrow Wilson had been elected President, on a platform of the 'New Freedom', especially for the small businessman and the farmer. Wilson appealed to the agrarian Southerner in Griffith. The lost pastoral world of the Old South, and the war that had ruined her, were what, I suggest, attracted him to Judith's epic. Judith the obscure widow, who rose to greatness, is like the 'little people' whom Wilson promised to free from bureaucratic constraints. So are her Israelites, whom she liberates from oppression by the conqueror. In contrast, Judith the wealthy widow is the best of her people, like a Southern belle in the old style. Griffith had grown up in a matriarchy, and had no problems with that idea. For him Judith's distinctive character and exceptional femininity embodied the ornaments and values of the South.

Similarly, its pastoral ethos is evoked in the opening scene, where a young Israelite woos his sweetheart as she draws water from a well outside the city, a scene rudely interrupted by the invasion of Holofernes' soldiers. This is the rape of the Edenic agrarian South by the militarily superior North, and this city is like her besieged cities. As the South had, but the Bethulians in the Apocrypha had not, Griffith's defenders mount a furious, desperate and heroic resistance. Also like the South, they are doomed to defeat by an enemy immeasurably more powerful in men and material. Except that, in this biblical world where right can overcome might, Griffith can rewrite history. His Judith saves his antebellum world. For the audience, it is Griffith's demonstration of higher American values, which must be resuscitated after the war. As distinct from the barbaric values of the industrialized North and its Holofernean army, he suggests, these are the softening virtues of civilization.

To this end, the myth's elevation of femininity is actually stressed rather than feared. Holofernes is the epitome of brute masculine power. Whether barking orders, beating his subordinates, or wooing Judith, he is also above doing anything himself. All of his activities are conducted from his couch, and with this the whole spectrum of his power becomes identified. In this, Griffith is brilliantly capitalizing on a technical difficulty. In order to disguise the difference in height between the short actor Henry Walthall and the tall actress Sweet, he tends to keep Holofernes seated or recumbent. That establishes a sinister contrast between his personal inactivity and the wide scope of his power to destroy. His ennui is, indeed, so pro-

19. For Griffith's account of his background, see J. Hart (ed.), *The Man Who Invented Hollywood: The Autobiography of D.W.Griffith* (Louisville, KY: 1972).

nounced that the unavailing attempts of subordinates and dancing girls to keep him amused, or to deflect his anger, are positively comic. By this means, their terror of him is emphasized, the emotional sterility of megalomania is moralized, and the power of Judith to bring bewitching novelty into his world is enhanced. Her statuesque quality contrasts with the gyrations of his disregarded concubines, for this is a Southern lady. Sweet was for Griffith an instance of an ideal, what he called 'the spiritual type of woman', according to the actress Lillian Gish.[20]

Holofernes' power, as identified with his luxurious couch, prepares for the beheading scene, since that is where he has fallen asleep. In most representations of the murder scene the bed sexualizes it; but here the couch has accrued so many other associations that its sexual element does not deface its symbolism of power: despotism, coercion and psychotic brutality. Implied in the murder is the disempowering of everything the couch represented: power without responsibility or mercy.

It is the civilization represented by femininity which can humanize power, and America. In *Intolerance*, the theme of man's inhumanity to man again takes a woman as the central focus for the ideals of compassion and pacifism. This film developed out of a project, *The Woman and the Law*, which survived as the film's modern plot strand and its subtitle. Anticipating this iconic role for true American femininity, *Judith of Bethulia* turns upon the fact of Judith's childlessness. This had, indeed, been an issue in Aldrich's play, which reflected a contemporary idealization of motherhood as woman's vocation: no longer simply a private function, but a higher duty to the race.[21]

The enemy Holofernes thus becomes for Aldrich 'Slayer of babes upon the mother-breast'. But his Judith, having committed an act that offends against the mother-milk of human kindness, is inconsolable. The hand that killed Holofernes was by rights 'soft and gentle', 'Moulded to press a babe

20. Lillian Gish, *The Movies, Mr. Griffith and Me* (London: Columbus, 1988), p. 85. The brief consideration given to this film by B. Babington and P.W. Evans, *Biblical Epics: Sacred Narrative in the Hollywood Cinema* (Manchester and New York: Manchester University Press, 1993), pp. 43-44, is intelligent but, I think, misguided. It is true that Judith is denied fecundity and sexual fulfilment, but these features are important elements of the Apocryphal original. See M. Stocker, 'Biblical Story and the Heroine', in M. Warner (ed.), *The Bible as Rhetoric: Studies in Biblical Persuasion and Credibility* (London: Routledge, 1990), pp. 81-104. The film looks rather different to their view, if considered in the light of Judithic traditions and Griffith's goals.

21. Stocker, *Judith, Sexual Warrior*, pp. 184-85.

against her breast!' She begs her people to regard her as dead, a lost female relation: 'some beloved wife or child/ Or sister that died long and long ago!' This is the retribution visited upon her for denying her own nature as a woman, which is to give life rather than take it. Pursued by her pining lover Achior, she repudiates men in general: 'Let no one born of woman follow me!'[22] Her grief, shame and loneliness thus remake the story as what Aldrich terms a 'Tragedy'. By making his Judith repudiate men in general, and lament her barrenness, Aldrich had suggested that she was unnatural. An anomaly among women, she delineated by contrast the normality and life-giving character of the Ideal Mother—'an apple-pie Mom'—a domesticated archetype. Aldrich's Judith was, again, an effortfully dispelled Other.

That, however, did not suit Griffith's quite different purpose. He actually wished to generalize and politicize Judith's significance. When adapting Aldrich, Griffith greatly amplified the theme of motherhood. In an early scene, Judith comforts a starving mother and baby. Called 'Little Mother in Israel', she is played by Lillian Gish, Griffith's preferred choice for fragile heroines in a wicked world. Unable to be a mother, Judith sublimates her vocation as deliverer of her people. Stronger than Gish, one of those whom she protects, Judith becomes the Mother of Israel. She is a sublime version not simply of Southern matriarchy but of national humanity. Allegorically and ideally, she symbolizes what America can be if softened and fully civilized. Capitalist and industrialized, it must nevertheless not only prosper economically and exert power wisely, but protect the weak, and foster communality. For Griffith, America as a whole had not yet attained that maturity.

However, the political significance of his film was taken out of his own hands, and decisively diverted, by the advent of war in Europe. Griffith was summoned to Britain, and the film was released in 1914 as Allied propaganda. In the new circumstances, the Israelites had become the Allies, Holofernes the German, and Judith's American specificity was absorbed into an international context. Whereas Cooper's Judith had been deliberately suppressed as the Other America, Griffith's was obliterated by history itself.

22. Thomas B. Aldrich, *Judith of Bethulia: A Tragedy* (Boston and New York: Houghton, Mifflin, 1904), pp. 79, 83-84, 98.

Conclusion

There is, however, a much greater irony about the way in which monumental works of American culture have suppressed Judith's iconic significance, while simultaneously recognizing it. In the Apocrypha, and in the European revolutions, what she signified was freedom: above all, a spiritual freedom from which all other liberating impulses flowed. European painters, such as Bloemart and Sirani and Parmigianino, had all emphasized her triumph over evil and tyranny by using the symbolism of torches to light her display of the tyrant's head to the people of the City of God. In Parmigianino's version, indeed, she is herself the torchbearer, and strikingly similar to the Statue of Liberty. Designed by a Frenchman to represent the similarly Revolutionary Land of the Free, that statue affects to welcome the weak, the humble and the oppressed—whom Judith the 'weak and feeble woman' figured—to a new world of paradisal opportunity. What American culture seems to have forgotten, even when religious writers are at work, is that Judith signifies the spiritual version of American individualism. In the Apocrypha as now, what she immutably represents is the capacity of each individual to be, like her, a hero of the spirit. We may take that to mean, using the title of a film by a black American, 'Do the Right Thing'. Whatever it costs.

LETHAL WOMAN 2: REFLECTIONS ON DELILAH
AND HER INCARNATION AS LIZ HURLEY

J. Cheryl Exum

In a recent book, *Plotted, Shot and Painted*, I examine cultural representations of biblical women in literature, music and particularly in the visual
arts of painting and film, asking how these women's 'stories' are altered,
expanded or invented—and to what ends.[1] One of the women to whom I
devote considerable attention is Delilah, a literary creation who has entered into our cultural consciousness in a way few other biblical characters
have. Most people know her as a temptress and seductress, even if they do
not associate her with the biblical story, and many remember her as the
woman who betrays Samson by cutting his hair, which robs him of his
strength (which is in the Bible), and, what is more, a woman who uses sex
to get Samson to tell her what she wants to know (which is not in the
Bible). It is indeed noteworthy that Delilah is so well known, given the
fact that she has such a small role, a mere 18 verses, in the whole Bible.
    How is it that a minor biblical character has become so famous—or
infamous—in popular culture? I suggest it is because, although the Bible
tells us next to nothing about Delilah, the story of Samson and Delilah has
two themes that have captured people's imaginations over the centuries:
that of a man betrayed by the woman he loves, and that of a man tempted
to break faith with his god-given destiny by a woman. These are powerful
themes, and it is understandable that people would want to hear more
about them than the Bible tells us. And so we have numerous retellings of
the story that supply many more details. In all of them that I know of, the
woman is a snare; she causes the man's downfall, and it is because he
cannot resist her. This is the age-old stereotype of the lethal woman—the
woman who is irresistible and deadly. Delilah is so fascinating, I think,

1. J. Cheryl Exum, *Plotted, Shot and Painted: Cultural Representations of
Biblical Women* (JSOTSup, 215; Gender, Culture, Theory, 3; Sheffield: Sheffield Academic Press, 1996).

because, in popular thinking, she so well fits the stereotype. She is the embodiment of the *femme fatale*—the woman who is sexually alluring, at once both fascinating and frightening, and ultimately fatal to a man.

As I was finishing *Plotted, Shot and Painted*, a new cinematic version of *Samson and Delilah* was announced from Turner Pictures; unfortunately, the film was released too late for me to include it in my study of Delilah. This 1996 *Samson and Delilah* stars Liz Hurley as Delilah and Eric Thal as Samson and is directed by Nicolas Roeg, the acclaimed director of such memorable films as *Walkabout* (1970), *Don't Look Now* (1973*), The Man Who Fell to Earth* (1976) and *Bad Timing* (1980), among others. When I saw the film, I could not help making comparisons between it and Cecil B. DeMille's 1949 Hollywood spectacle, *Samson and Delilah* (with Hedy Lamarr as Delilah and Victor Mature as Samson), to which I devoted considerable attention in the book. DeMille's is a masterpiece of biblical film making (it gets better after repeated viewings); the 1949 film sparkles in spite of its age, with memorable dialogue and impressive overacting. Roeg's, sadly, does not succeed, in spite of some of the impressive hall-marks of the director—the quick cuts, the flashbacks that take us inside the character's head, and the innovative cinematography. Roeg is let down by the screenplay. It lacks coherence, and is at times simply confusing or silly. More important, it ignores the prime dictum, 'show, don't tell!', and relies upon an all-too-often didactic narratorial voice-over to carry the story rather than making demands on the actors.[2] Not that the actors are particularly convincing, or even interesting. Dennis Hopper is miscast as the Philistine General Tariq, whose boredom with the company in ancient Gaza could easily be mistaken for boredom with the role, while Eric Thal is a rather insipid Samson, confused about the meaning of his life (but, then, Victor Mature was also insipid, though not troubled by existential doubts). But it is Liz Hurley, as Delilah, who is most ineffectual, giving us a character who is unsympathetic and boring at the same time.

Hurley's Delilah left me very disappointed and wondering at the lack of imagination in casting such a one-dimensional stereotypical femme fatale as the Delilah of the 1990s. So when Martin O'Kane invited me to give an audio-visual presentation on Delilah,[3] I took the opportunity to consider

---

2.　The voice-over narration draws attention to the textuality of the film, as if to say, 'This is the Bible you're watching!'

3.　At the 2000 annual meeting of the Catholic Biblical Association of Great Britain, jointly sponsored by the Bible and Arts Programme, Newman College. I take

the new cinematic Delilah in the light of the biblical Delilah and, especially, of my favorite Delilah, Hedy Lamarr. The presentation relied heavily on visual materials, especially slides and film clips, and it drew on the chapter about Delilah in *Plotted, Shot and Painted* for many of its insights. Since I cannot reproduce the visual component here and I do not wish to repeat too much from my earlier discussion, I offer the present article as a supplement to the analysis in *Plotted, Shot and Painted*. I shall focus here on the two cinematic Delilahs, analyzing them in terms of three questions raised by gaps in the biblical story that retellings typically attempt to answer: Who is Delilah? Why did she betray Samson? What happened to her afterwards?

The Biblical Delilah
It might be helpful at the outset to note what the Bible does and does not have to say about Delilah. It could hardly be said to begin at the beginning:

> After this he loved a woman in the valley of Sorek, whose name was Delilah. The rulers of the Philistines came to her and said to her, 'Entice him, and see by what means his strength is great, and by what means we may overpower him and bind him in order to humiliate him; and we will each give you eleven hundred pieces of silver' (Judg. 16.4-5).

The Bible goes on to tell us that she accepted the bribe to discover the secret of Samson's strength, but it does not tell us why. Instead of explaining *why* she did it, the Bible goes into great detail about *how* she did it. Three times she asks Samson the secret of his strength, and he makes up a phony story: he could be bound with fresh bowstrings that have not been dried, with new ropes that have not been used, by weaving his hair into the web on her loom. Three times Delilah tries to weaken him by doing these very things. The fourth time, she accuses him of not loving her enough to share his secret with her, and this ploy works. He tells her that the source of his strength is his long hair. So while he is asleep, Delilah gives him history's most famous haircut. He loses his strength; the Philistines seize him, blind him, and take him as their prisoner to grind at the mill in the prison house.

That is basically the whole story. So why did Delilah betray Samson? It is not much of an answer to say that she could not resist the temptation of

this opportunity to acknowledge the invaluable technical assistance of Keith Mears, of the University of Sheffield.

a large sum of money. At least that answer has failed to satisfy readers over the centuries. The Bible tells us that Samson loved her but it neglects to mention whether or not she loved him. Did she—even a little? Obviously not enough to refuse to betray him at any price, but that does not mean she felt no affection toward him. The silence concerning Delilah's feelings leaves us sufficiently in the dark for later retellings of the story to fill it in very different ways. Another thing the Bible neglects to tell us is what happens to Delilah in the end. We know what happens to Samson: he is brought to the Philistine temple, where he prays to God to restore his strength, and he pulls down the temple, killing himself along with his enemies. But what about Delilah? The Bible does not even bother to mention Delilah again after the betrayal. Was she one of the spectators killed when the temple came crashing down? We'd like to know.

Who Is Delilah?

Most versions of the doxa answer the question, who is Delilah, by making her a Philistine and a harlot. Although neither identification is explicitly made in the Bible, there is nothing in the Bible to discourage us from drawing such conclusions. By telling us so little, the Bible invites us to fill in the gaps with our preconceptions and familiar stereotypes. In particular, the process that results in typecasting Delilah as a Philistine prostitute can be understood as what happens when readers automatically adopt the Bible's prejudices against Philistines and against foreign women.[4] Moreover, identifying Delilah as a Philistine points to a reluctance on the part of readers to consider that Samson might have been betrayed by one of his own people. Making her a harlot helps to explain why she betrays him: a harlot, a woman with loose morals, is the kind of woman who would betray a man (I am speaking here of cultural stereotypes). Heaven forbid a woman would betray a man if she really loved him!

---

4.   The Philistines are enemies, and foreign women are an enticement to Israelite men, who find it difficult to resist them. The reason for this assumed irresistibility, at least in part, has to do with their foreignness: the foreign woman is different, mysterious—and her mystery is intriguing; with her, a man doesn't know for sure *what* might happen. Playing with her is like playing with fire, but the challenge of playing without getting burned can be exciting. We have here, I think, an early version of the stereotype of the lethal woman—the woman whose sexuality is all the more desirable because it is forbidden. As Samson tells his mother in DeMille's epic, 'Forbidden figs are sweeter'.

Whereas the biblical Delilah is not identified in terms of any family connections, both the 1949 film and the 1996 one give Delilah a background that relates her to other characters. In Roeg's *Samson and Delilah*, Delilah is a Philistine, the cousin of the king of Gaza. This makes her a member of the royal court and explains how she will become involved in a political plot to capture Samson even before she meets him. While not a 'common' harlot, she is a 'loose woman'. In her second of numerous brief scenes, General Tariq calls Delilah a loose woman, to which she sultrily replies, 'And if I weren't, I'd find that remark offensive, General'. The general is stroking her arm as they discuss how to please a woman like her, woodenly mouthing the soap-opera dialogue of Allan Scott's script. We discover later that, contrary to the impression they give, Delilah and the general are not lovers.[5] 'Loose' suggests 'unscrupulous', so that we will not be surprised at her willingness to have sex with Samson, or at her willingness to betray him. The scene serves to tell us that Delilah's interest in Samson is aroused by reports of his exploits even before she has seen him. In considering whether any man could meet her sexual expectations, she proposes, 'Except perhaps this Israelite hero'.[6]

In DeMille's *Samson and Delilah*, Delilah is also a Philistine. She does not, however, initially have any connection with the court or Gaza. She lives in Timnah and is the younger sister of Samson's bride, whom he abandons after she betrays the secret of his riddle to her countrymen. Although at one point in the 1949 film (in a scene I will discuss in more detail below) Samson calls her 'the great courtesan of Gaza', she is not a 'loose woman'. And in spite of being 'the woman that rules the ruler of the five cities', she and the ruler, or Saran, as he is called (played by George Sanders), have no sex scenes. They never even kiss, in contrast to Liz Hurley and Dennis Hopper. DeMille's Delilah is in love with Samson from the very beginning of the film, when she vainly tries to steal him

---

5.   There is no such character as the general in the biblical story; his prominent role in the film is at Delilah's expense, for he is the real source of interest in an otherwise uninspired royal court. He is also the one, besides, eventually, Samson, who perceives the divine purpose behind Samson's capture. In his tacit recognition of the power of Samson's god, he resembles DeMille's Delilah, who prays to that god for help (see below). This is only one of Delilah's functions in DeMille's film that the general assumes in Roeg's (others include the idea of how to capture Samson and a visit to Samson in prison, which sets Samson on the path to self-discovery).

6.   For some viewers the prostitute image may be reinforced by Liz Hurley's resemblance to Barbara Hershey as the Magdalene in *The Last Temptation of Christ*.

away from her sister (a young, golden-haired Angela Landsbury), and all she ever wants is him ('You're the only thing in the world I want', she tells him early in the film, and 'You're all I want', she says when she finally succeeds in seducing him).

Why Does Delilah Betray Samson?

Casting Delilah as a 'loose woman', as Roeg does, provides a partial answer to the question, Why does Delilah agree to betray Samson for money? An unscrupulous woman can be bought for betrayal as well as for sex. I suspect the portrayal is also meant to make her seem sexier by making her uncommonly sexually experienced. A self-acknowledged man-eater, she has appetites only a he-man like Samson could satisfy. Making Delilah a Philistine, as both DeMille's and Roeg's films do, provides her with other, even stronger reasons to betray Samson—patriotism or religious duty. It is thus somewhat surprising that patriotism and religion play such a small role in both films.

Roeg's film does a poor job of supplying Delilah with credible motivation for betraying Samson. On the one hand, she does it for the money. Liz is a thoroughly modern Delilah, who believes, 'A girl must look to her future'. But she is also sexually excited by the prospect of seducing such a splendid specimen of masculinity. Significantly, the plan proposed for defeating Samson depends precisely on the mysterious fascination of the lethal woman, the excitement tinged with danger, or, as the Philistine general, played by Dennis Hopper, puts it, 'the allure of strange flesh'.

King: They say their god gives him his strength.
General Tariq: I'm just a simple soldier, Majesty, not a priest.
King: Your plan hardly indicates a military cast of mind.
General Tariq: A soldier can only deal with what he knows, and what we know of Samson is he prefers our women to his own. The allure of strange flesh is strong with him.
King's son: This scheme is preposterous. What certainty do you have that this Samson will take the bait you offer?
King: (*laughs*) Ha, ha, ha. Wouldn't you if she was offered to you?
Son: What are we, panderers? This is no way to neutralize an enemy.
General Tariq: There is no general on this earth could devise a better plan to lay his enemy low than to capture him by that part of his body in which he is the weakest.
King: The fish will take the bait, but will the bait agree to the fish?

Delilah:	In fishing there's only one certainty: you can never be sure of your catch. There's always the danger that the fish may escape with the bait. Is that not so, General? (*He gestures in deference.*)
King:	Very well, agreed. Delilah?
Delilah:	I'll be proud to serve my people—in return for a financial consideration.
King:	Ah, yes, your loyalty to the throne is measured in silver. I'm offended but not surprised. How much?
Delilah:	Eleven hundred pieces of silver—from everyone in this chamber.

During this discussion, the camera keeps cutting to Liz Hurley, who smiles and does her best to appear detached, amused and sexy. But she has no depth, and her presence in the film is largely ornamental. She sits passively as the king, his son and the general debate the plan to capture Samson with 'the allure of strange flesh'. Unlike the biblical account, which tells us Samson loved Delilah and then that the Philistines approach her with a bribe (suggesting a temporal, causal connection), in the film Delilah agrees to betray Samson before we are told, by means of a voice-over, that he 'truly loved her as a man loves a woman'. She agrees to serve as 'bait', for they know that Samson will bite, being like any other man in his inability to resist the femme fatale. Will she be able to resist him? Her provocative response, 'in fishing there's always the danger that the fish will get away with the catch', seems to suggest that Delilah could fall for Samson's charms.[7]

Although the jacket to my video of Roeg's *Samson and Delilah* says that Delilah is torn between her love for Samson and loyalty to her people,[8] this is not borne out in the film, where she volunteers to serve her people

---

7.   Possibly an echo of the way DeMille concludes the corresponding scene? See below. Later in the film, after Samson has been captured and Delilah has requested he be brought to the temple to entertain his captors, she confesses to the general that she now knows 'the pain of feeling'.

8.   A theme especially well developed in John Milton's *Samson Agonistes*. Milton explores a range of motives for Delilah's betrayal of Samson, including curiosity, woman's nature, jealousy, patriotism, religious duty, and even love. Milton has Delilah explain that, after much soul searching, she put her patriotic and religious duty above her love for Samson. Her defense of her deed is really quite credible. She says that her love for Samson played an important role in her decision: she was afraid he might someday leave her for another woman, but also afraid for his safety. Moreover, she says she was assured that no real harm would come to him. Milton, of course, does not intend for us to believe her.

'in return for a financial consideration'. That her patriotism has its limits comes as no surprise to the king: 'Ah, yes, your loyalty to the throne is measured in silver. I'm offended but not surprised'. The money will make her self-sufficient, which seems to be her overriding motive (again, a very modern intervention: she wants to have the means to leave Gaza when the king dies and his inept son succeeds him). But we are *meant* to believe that it is not only the money, that she is sexually excited by the assignment. Between the scene discussed above, in which she is identified as a 'loose woman', and this one, she has seen Samson. He just happened to be nearby as she was strolling along the river bank, and he rushed in to rescue her by killing a lion that just happened to pounce out of nowhere to threaten her.[9] They exchanged meaningful looks, but no words, before he bolted over the hills. In recounting the adventure back at the court, she remarks, 'A woman would die for a man like that', but it is a throw-away line, for her fascination with Samson is not sufficiently developed to be convincing.

Figure 36. *Eric Thal and Liz Hurley as Samson and Delilah*

9. Both films show Samson killing a lion, for this part of the biblical story is necessary to prepare the audience for his riddle and its answer (What is sweeter than honey? What is stronger than a lion?). Both films have Delilah witness the event, though an important factor in the biblical account is its secrecy. In DeMille's film, Delilah accompanies Samson on a lion hunt.

Hedy Lamarr as Delilah is anything but passive and superficial in Cecil B. DeMille's classic, *Samson and Delilah*. She is in complete control of the film. Even the betrayal is her idea, unlike the biblical account and Roeg's version, where the Philistine rulers come up with the plan to use Delilah to capture Samson. Although the film script could hardly dispense with such a memorable biblical detail as the 1100 pieces of silver from each of the Philistine lords, the payment Delilah asks for appears to be an afterthought. Initially she asks only for the Saran's favor. When he replies, 'But you have that. Is that all you want?', she pauses for a moment, as if thinking (and perhaps intuiting that her generous offer was too transparent), says, 'No', and then, when one of the Philistine lords interrupts to suggest 'some little bauble', she lights upon the idea of silver—1100 pieces from each of the Philistine lords. Here, too, her offer to capture Samson also depends on the allure of the femme fatale: 'Perhaps he'll fall before a woman. Even Samson's strength must have a weakness. There isn't a man in the world who will not share his secrets with some woman'.[10] She makes a condition, however. Though she wants to see Samson captured, she does not want him harmed: 'No drop of his blood shall be shed, no blade shall touch his skin'.

A major difference between this scene and the corresponding one in Roeg's film is that DeMille's audience already knows that Delilah is hopelessly in love with Samson (and not simply sexually excited at the prospect of seducing a man she has heard of only through rumor and seen only once). The Saran is not quite convinced that Delilah's devotion is really to him, and he voices as well the audience's doubts: 'A man who could stop the heart of a lion might stir the heart of a woman'. The line is more poetic and its imagery better fitted to the story than 'in fishing there's always the danger that the fish will get away with the catch'.[11] Moreover, having the Saran voice this risk rather than Delilah gives it more credibility, for DeMille uses the Saran to make occasional astute and prophetic observations—a less intrusive and more effective way of offering authorial comments than Roeg's narrator, who has a penchant for preaching the biblical story at us.

10. The Philistine lords embellish the stereotype of the femme fatale presented here. They chip in, 'More men have been trapped by smiles than by ropes' and 'Bring in a woman and she'll bring on trouble'.

11. In spite of the fact that the film later has the general explain that 'our gods have the tail of fish because our ancestors were seafaring people'.

So, if she loves him, why does Delilah offer to betray Samson? DeMille gives us a complex, multi-layered Delilah, with a full range of emotions: love, desire for revenge, hate, jealousy. She says she blames Samson for the deaths of her father and sister, which occurred at his wedding feast, after the Philistines cheated to obtain the answer to his riddle (actually Delilah is more responsible for their deaths than Samson is, since *she* put the Philistines up to it, in hopes of preventing Samson's marriage to her sister so that she might marry him herself—definitely a complex character). But her real motive—and there is never any doubt about this—is love, a love so obsessive it must destroy and be destroyed by the object of its desire in order to obtain it.[12]

Figure 37. *Victor Mature and Hedy Lamarr as Samson and Delilah*

Delilah's love for Samson is 'a fire to make all other loves seem like ice', and, like fire, it is all consuming. This is especially clear in the events leading up to the haircut scene. Miriam, the wholesome girl-next-door from Samson's own tribe of Dan, who has loved him since his youth, arrives on the scene to bring Samson back to help his people (the wholesome girl-next-door provides a safe but uninteresting alternative to the femme fatale, who threatens to tempt the hero away from his calling).

12. This will be underscored in the finale.

To prevent Samson from leaving, Delilah drugs him and cuts his hair (in the Bible she does it while he sleeps). After he is taken prisoner and hears about the payment she will receive, he declares, 'Your arms were quicksand. Your kiss was death. The name Delilah will be an everlasting curse on the lips of men'. She retorts:

> I could have loved you with a fire to make all other loves seem like ice. I would have gone with you to Egypt, left everything behind, lived only for you. But one call from that milk-faced Danite lily and you run whining at her heels. No man leaves Delilah.

Although Delilah has the fury of a woman scorned, she does not forget the promise she secured from the Saran that 'no drop of his blood shall be shed; no blade shall touch his skin', and she repeats it to the soldiers. Only later does she discover that Samson has been blinded, which follows the letter but not the spirit of the agreement.

Roeg's version of what motivates Delilah to betray Samson is very different. Unlike both the Bible and DeMille's version, Samson is awake when Delilah cuts his hair; indeed, they have a chat about it beforehand. The film seeks to give the impression that Delilah loves Samson, that it pains her to betray him. So we see her delaying, apparently not wanting to make her move, and then cutting his hair simply because 'when power is given, how can it not be used?' Samson is suddenly painfully robbed of his strength, in contrast to the biblical account, which tells us he did not know that his strength had left him.

Samson: (*wakes up*) Why have you been crying, my only love, have you not slept?

Delilah: I've been watching over you.

S: And you were sad?

D: My heart is heavier than all the iron in our land.

S: Why?

D: When you were sleeping, I held the power of life or death in my hands. (*He takes hold of her hand in which she holds a razor.*)

S: The life or death of the man you love. But you did not cut.

D: No, I did not. (*He kisses her hand with the razor in it.*)

D: But now.

S: Now?

D: Now I must.

S: Put that away.

D: When power is given, how can it not be used?

S: Because love is stronger still.

D: Oh yes, love. Love. (*She cuts.*)

The conflict is between power and love. A whole night passes while Samson sleeps, and Delilah does not cut his hair. In their corny conversation, Samson says this is because love is stronger than power. Apparently it isn't. So is this a judgment on the strength of her love? Something about her action seems so, well, arbitrary. Is this simply the way a 'loose woman' behaves?

A later scene between Delilah and Naomi (the wholesome girl-next-door of this film, who has loved Samson for as long as she can remember) addresses this issue, though it does not resolve it. Naomi has come to Gaza to see Delilah in order to beg to be allowed to see Samson. To Naomi's repeated refrain, 'you hated him so much', Delilah responds with a flurry of explanations: 'They paid me well', 'He'd become too dangerous', 'I loved him too well'. (I loved him too well?)[13] There is, however, no continuity with her earlier explanation, no mention of power given that must be used. During this exchange, the camera cuts from Delilah, watching from the window, to the sight of Samson being taken to the temple,[14] a sight that obviously distresses Delilah. Delilah becomes agitated with her servant, which suggests that Naomi's accusation is getting to her (while at the same time showing the thoughtless and insensitive way she treats the attendants who wait upon her). But I suspect we are meant to believe Delilah does love Samson; she has been moping around the palace for several scenes, and she looks somewhat relieved when she perceives that Samson was never in love with Naomi (showing how self-centered she is). Naomi's response to Delilah's claim to have loved Samson too well is probably the most appropriate line of dialogue in the film: 'This is not love'. And, indeed, Liz Hurley, in contrast to Hedy Lamarr, is not convincing as a woman in love. Not to me, anyway. The fault is not entirely hers; the screenplay does not offer much to work with.

13. Is this an attempt to claim the kind of obsessive love DeMille's Delilah has for Samson?

14. The editing is somewhat confusing here. Naomi comes to beg to see Samson. There is then a scene in which Delilah requests that Samson be taken to the temple to entertain his captors, followed by a scene between her and the general, in which he asks her why she seeks to humiliate Samson more and she says, in one of her many illogical explanations, 'even though I sold him, he's still mine'. Then her audience with Naomi continues, as Samson is brought to the temple. Perhaps her explanation is a jealous reaction to Naomi. Perhaps it is Delilah's way of showing Samson belongs to her, not to another. It can be compared to the (more intelligible) response of DeMille's Delilah who tells Miriam when she comes to the temple arena to beg for Samson's life, 'I'd rather see him dead than in your arms'.

What Happens to Delilah after the Betrayal?

As I mentioned above, in the biblical story Delilah simply drops out of the picture after the betrayal; nothing is said about her being among the spectators when Samson pulls down the temple of Dagon. This is a rather significant gap, and many versions of the doxa fill it by placing her there, which has the advantage of satisfying the need to see the woman punished. Both films have Delilah die with Samson in the temple, but under vastly different circumstances.

DeMille makes the story of Samson and Delilah into a love story for all time. His Delilah is sorry for what she has done, Samson forgives her, and they are reconciled in the end. DeMille both redeems his lethal woman, by showing her change of heart, and punishes her, by killing her off in the film's dramatic finale. By praying to Samson's god to help her to help him, Delilah effectively converts, and she ends up being God's instrument in Samson's final victory over the Philistines. It is Delilah, and not a young boy as in the Bible, who leads Samson to the two columns that support the temple—the pillars he will push down, causing the temple to collapse, killing all the spectators. As they die together in a brilliant cinematic resolution, she and he are redeemed together: he, through his new-found faithfulness to his god, and she, through him.

DeMille has Delilah enable Samson to fulfill his destiny as God's instrument against the Philistines. Interestingly, Roeg tells us this in a voice-over at the end of the film, but he does not show us how she does it, apart, of course, from being responsible for his capture and his being brought to the temple for the Philistines' amusement. Although Delilah dies along with everyone else when Samson pulls down the temple, there is no reconciliation between Samson and Delilah, no love story here. Delilah agrees to allow wholesome-girl-next-door Naomi to go to the temple to see Samson, but, in return, Naomi must do something for Delilah. Because he is going to destroy the temple, Samson tells Naomi to leave. She begs for a kiss first. Delilah then leans over and kisses Samson in her place. Perhaps we are supposed to think that wanting to kiss Samson is a sign of Delilah's love for him. Perhaps we are supposed to be moved. But I find this a cruel thing to do to a blind man who is about to die. Her act not only reveals, once again, her self-centered shallowness but, more important in my view, serves to underscore the woman's treachery. Delilah's last act is to deceive Samson yet again! Unlike Hedy Lamarr, Liz Hurley is a Delilah with no redeeming qualities. I would have expected a 1990s Delilah to challenge the stereotype of the lethal woman more than a

1950s one, but this is not the case. The 1990s Delilah simply perpetuates the stereotype at its worst. Roeg, at the film's end, acknowledges Delilah's important function by having his omniscient and irritating narrator explain in a voice-over that 'it was through the Philistine woman, Delilah, that Samson finally came to the faith which began the liberation that the Lord God of Israel had promised'.[15] But without redeeming the woman.

Coming to Terms with the *Femme Fatale*

Redeemed or not, Delilah of the cinema is a lethal woman, whose desirability has lead to Samson's undoing. What, we might well ask, is it about the lethal woman that makes her so fascinating and enduring as a cultural stereotype?[16] She is, I think, fascinating to men and women for different reasons. But she is lethal only to men. If a woman is desirable and dangerous, who is doing the desiring and who is endangered? Men (I am talking about cultural stereotypes here, and not individual cases; this is, moreover, a heterosexist stereotype). The stereotype of the mysterious, sexually alluring, dangerous woman is about woman as mysterious, sexually alluring and dangerous to men. This is a man's view of women—not a woman's view—and, as such, it tells us more about the men responsible for it than about women. The stereotype is really about the mysterious, powerful attraction a man feels toward a woman and his unconscious fear that somehow he might get hurt. Instead of saying, 'I'm afraid of her', the man says, 'She's dangerous'. Instead of saying, 'I desire her', he says, 'She's seductive'. In other words, rather than admitting his desire and his fear, the man projects them onto the woman, thus producing the desirable, dangerous woman.[17]

The lethal woman, desirable but deadly, is a reminder—to men—of the danger of desire. Desire can make a man reckless. It can get him into trouble. Surrender yourself to a woman? The moral of the biblical story is: 'Don't do it!' Samson yielded, and look what happened to him. If even an apparently invincible strong man like Samson can be undone by a woman, how much more so should the ordinary man be on his guard.

---

15. This line is a good example of how long-winded and sermonic, bordering on the sanctimonious, the film's narrator is.

16. For a fuller discussion, see Exum, *Plotted, Shot, and Painted*, pp. 219-35.

17. Karen Horney, *Feminine Psychology* (London: Routledge & Kegan Paul, 1967), pp. 135-39.

It follows that the more a man knows about the temptress, the better prepared he is to deal with her. Like many other retellings of the story of Samson and Delilah, these cinematic versions can be viewed as attempts to tame, or master, the lethal woman by supplying knowledge about her that produces a sense of security. Who was Delilah? Why did she betray Samson? What happened to her afterwards? Answering these questions about Delilah is a way of accounting for what the lethal woman is really like—and so, of minimizing both her attraction and the danger she poses (for example, disparaging her by making her a prostitute, or by showing that a bad woman will be punished in the end).

Whereas retellings of the story of Samson and Delilah answer these questions in different ways, they remain true to the biblical account in one respect: they make Samson the hero of the story. He is on the 'right' side, the side of truth, freedom, God, and the law of the father. Delilah, the lethal woman, is on the wrong side. She is foreign, she sleeps with the enemy, and, as activator of his desire, she is a snare for the hero ('I'll never be free of you, Delilah', says Samson in DeMille's film). What about Delilah's desire? Can the woman ever win? Not in the Bible. And to judge from my most recent example, Nicolas Roeg's 1996 film, not in Hollywood either. Roeg's *Samson and Delilah* perpetuates the age-old cultural stereotype of woman as seductive, fickle, untrustworthy and deceptive. From the Bible to Hollywood, it looks like the lethal woman is here to stay. Ever since Samson, men have been unable to resist her and, like Delilah, women will play her for the power she has over men.

Cinematic Gender Performance

Like any representation, the femme fatale is never fully under the control of its creators. We can recognize the lethal woman for the stereotype it is and for what, within its limits, it reveals about men. I like DeMille's version of the story of Samson and Delilah because I think it does this, and because the director and the actors seem to be having fun with the stereotype. One particular scene in the movie illustrates this better than any other. It is the scene where Delilah has set out to discover the secret of Samson's strength, and Samson, who has become an outlaw, comes to rob her tent, not knowing whose tent it is. The setting is at night, tall palm trees are outlined against a star-studded dark blue sky, and soft music is playing. The tent is lavishly furnished. When he sees the form of a woman behind a diaphanous curtain, Samson tells her not to cry out. She says:

'I won't; are you afraid?' He pauses for a moment, as if considering the question carefully, and responds: 'Of a woman—Yes'.

Throughout the scene, Hedy Lamarr plays to the camera. She wears a gorgeous two piece, tight-fitting, clinging silver lamé outfit that reveals her bare midriff, and she uses her body provocatively, offering herself to Victor Mature in bold moves, swinging around on the poles that support the tent so that she constantly interposes her body in front of whatever object he lays his hands upon to plunder. He claims he is not stealing but collecting what rightfully belongs to his people: 'These are taxes. Your Saran taxes us, I tax the Philistines'. At one point, as he is stuffing some costly garments into a bag, she sashays in front of him and says, 'What pretty Danite girl will wear these taxes?' As he looks up to answer her, he stops mid-sentence, and runs his eyes up and down her, as if stunned for the first time by her beauty. Whereas she has been the object of the spectator's gaze for some time, she now becomes quite evidently the object of Samson's gaze. The scene draws our attention to the danger that the woman represents and the man's inability to resist her by having Samson recognize that he is the object of 'the oldest trick in the world: a silk trap baited with a woman'. And it underscores the femme fatale's power that comes from the knowledge that 'men always respond'.

Samson: The woman that rules the ruler of the five cities must have great wealth. Where's the rest of it?

Delilah: Not far away. (*Swings herself on top of a large chest that Samson is about to open.*) I will hide nothing from you.

S: The oldest trick in the world—a silk trap baited with a woman. (*He lifts her up and casts her onto a fur rug. She turns to look at him provocatively.*)

D: You know a better bait, Samson? Men always respond.

S: Of all the women in Gaza, why did the Saran send you?

D: I asked to come.

S: Why?

D: I knew you'd yield to any other woman.

S: And you came here to save me?

D: No, I came to betray you.

S: By the four winds, you have courage, Delilah.

D: (*Holds up a silver plate beside her face and rubs it against her cheek.*): Don't overlook this. It's a gift from the Saran.

S: You could bind a man tighter than the Saran's chains.

D: Could I bind you?

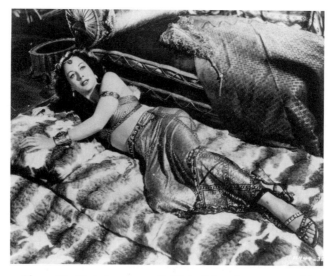

Figure 38. *Hedy Lamarr as Delilah. 'Men always respond.'*

In this scene, the mechanisms of the femme fatale construct are laid bare—the man's desire for the woman ('Men always respond'), and his fear of being undone by her ('Are you afraid?' 'Of a woman—Yes'). So, too, are the mechanisms for masking male anxiety, investigation of the woman and fetishism.[18] The film investigates Delilah by exploring her past and her motivation for betraying Samson, here brought to the fore when she tells him she has come to betray him.[19] It fetishizes her by transforming her physical beauty into something satisfying in itself.[20] Throughout the film, and especially in this scene, the camera angles, the lighting, the close-ups of Lamarr's face, her provocative costume all remind us that she is the object of the look for the theater audience as well as for Samson.

DeMille cast Victor Mature and Hedy Lamarr in the title roles of his *Samson and Delilah* because, he claimed, 'they embody in the public mind the essence of maleness and femininity'.[21] By situating the essence of conventional masculinity and femininity (interestingly paired as 'maleness'

18. See Laura Mulvey, *Visual and Other Pleasures* (London: Macmillan, 1989), pp. 14-26.

19. Like the biblical Delilah, she makes no secret of her intention.

20. Mulvey, *Visual and Other Pleasures*, p. 21.

21. Cited in Derek Elley, *The Epic Film: Myth and History* (London: Routledge & Kegan Paul, 1984), p. 36.

and 'femininity') 'in the public mind', the comment implicitly acknowledges the constructedness of gender, and, indeed, what Victor Mature and
Hedy Lamarr give us is a splendid performance of gender roles calculated
to fit the expectations of 1950s audiences (with the ancient 'oriental'
setting providing a pretext for some liberties). Victor Mature is imperson-
ating a macho man, and Hedy Lamarr infuses the role of vamp with an
'excess of femininity'.[22] It may be camp,[23] but it is not just camp,[24] for
there is a subversive aspect to their self-conscious projection of masculinity and femininity as spectacle.[25] This is the scene—and the only point in
the film—where Delilah is called 'the great courtesan of Gaza', confirming
her reputation as sexual siren. Lamarr knows we are watching and she is
confident of the effect her performance will have on the audience. Men
always respond, and women may enjoy seeing how confident she is that
she can use her sexuality to get what she wants. And we know it is all a
grand illusion. The gender role playing is exhibited so clearly and with
such exaggeratedness that one cannot take it seriously. The 1949 film
gives us spectacle and entertainment. One problem with the 1996 film is

22. The term is Mary Ann Doane's (*The Desire to Desire: The Woman's Film of
the 1940s* [Houndmills: Macmillan, 1987]), p. 25; see her discussion of femininity as
masquerade, pp. 17-43.

23. Susan Sontag labels Victor Mature as camp because of his 'exaggerated he-
man-ness' ('Notes on "Camp"', in Sontag, *Against Interpretation* [New York: Dell
Publishing Co., 1966], pp. 275-304 [279]).

24. See Babington and Evans' defense of Victor Mature, in Bruce Babington and
Peter William Evans, *Biblical Epics: Sacred Narrative in the Hollywood Cinema*
(Manchester: Manchester University Press, 1993), pp. 227-37. Their title of this 'coda'
to their book suggests their estimation of Mature: 'Victor Agonistes; or, Justice Done
to an Unconsidered Star'.

25. Their overt performances of masculinity and femininity destabilize the
distinctions between the natural and the artificial and open a space for a radical critique
of traditional constructions of sex, gender and desire within the heterosexual matrix;
see Judith Butler, *Gender Trouble: Feminism and the Subversion of Identity* (New
York: Routledge, 1990), pp. 43-57, 128-41. In this essay I have been generalizing
about conventional masculinity and femininity for the purposes of analyzing the *femme
fatale*, since the stereotype relies on these same generalizations. One of the pleasures of
DeMille's film is the subversiveness of the gender performance, and much remains to
be said about the flexibility of the spectator's subject positioning and multiple cross-
gender positions of identification, pleasure, desire, and fantasy; see Babington and
Evans, *Biblical Epics*, pp. 227-37; Jackie Stacey, *Star Gazing: Hollywood Cinema and
Female Spectatorship* (London: Routledge, 1994), pp. 24-48.

that it seems to take itself too seriously.[26] What are we to make of Eric Thal's confused he-man and Liz Hurley's over-sexed liberated woman retrojected into the ancient world?

Hedy Lamarr is such a strong screen presence and Delilah is such a complex character in DeMille's script that we want to *know* what motivates her and what happens to her afterwards. With Liz Hurley, it is hard to care. As I noted above, Hurley's presence is largely ornamental. It is Samson who frets about his destiny, Samson who develops as a character who finally discovers his mission when it is thrust upon him. In contrast to DeMille's film, where Hedy Lamarr receives top billing over Victor Mature and Delilah is the main interest, Roeg's film is not really about Delilah at all; it should have been entitled *Samson*, not *Samson and Delilah*. But because in the culturally circulating doxa Samson and Delilah are famous lovers, her role must be foregrounded.[27] Hurley is there to provide a 1990s compulsory sex interest, and she and Thal have a lengthy sex scene to convince us that they are no ordinary lovers in their passion.

Hurley has a number of other, brief appearances on screen, but mainly as decoration, as a reminder that she is a character in the story. Like the biblical Delilah, she is primarily a function. Like the biblical Delilah, her motivation remains a subject of speculation. I do not think the ambiguity is intentional so much as the result of wooden acting and inept scripting. What little character development there is is entirely unflattering: 'loose', self-centered, unloving, shallow, wishy-washy. Considering the limitations

26. The seriousness is underscored by the tendency of the film's narrator to moralize and preach a biblical message that is problematic in itself (the xenophobia of Judges; the Israelites as the worshippers of the true god and the Philistines caricatured as evil, etc.) and (one hopes) not meaningful for a modern audience.

27. We might ask, why the need to make the story of Samson and Delilah into a love story? And we could answer that a romantic interest is an important ingredient of a film (or, for that matter, a tale), or that, especially in the case of DeMille, the director has a famous star he wants to showcase. But there seems to be as well—and the doxa bears this out—a need on the part of readers to make this story into a love story, a need which may arise from our concern with knowing (including sexual knowledge and knowledge of the other), which picks up on a theme already in the biblical account. On the relation of knowledge, power, and sex in the story of Samson and Delilah, see J. Cheryl Exum, *Fragmented Women: Feminist (Sub)versions of Biblical Narratives* (Sheffield: Sheffield Academic Press; Valley Forge, PA: Trinity Press International, 1993), pp. 77-84; Mieke Bal, *Lethal Love: Feminist Literary Readings of Biblical Love Stories* (Bloomington: Indiana University Press, 1987), pp. 37-67.

imposed by the values of classical Hollywood cinema and by the rough contours of the biblical story, it is strange that a cultural Delilah fifty years older could go so much further toward giving us a strong, intelligent, interesting, complex (and even subversive) Delilah than a Delilah of the 90s, in the wake of feminism (or should I say a backlash?). I'm holding out for a version of the story in which, if she cannot win, at least the woman isn't a loser.[28]

28. If Martin Scorcese could make Judas into an interesting character and a hero of sorts in *The Last Temptation of Christ*, why not a heroic Delilah? A possible scenario (following the rough contours of the biblical story): Delilah is an Israelite. She and Samson know he has a mission to deliver Israel from the Philistines, but he scorns it in favor of whiling away the hours with her. She tries therefore to break off the relationship, protesting she doesn't love him any more, but always without success. Finally, in an effort to prove to him that she doesn't love him, so that he will leave her and fulfill his destiny, she makes a bargain to turn him over to the Philistines, stipulating that 'no drop of his blood shall be shed'. She, of course, will be instrumental in his final victory in the temple. Or a version against the grain of the biblical story: Delilah is a Philistine, and the film does not privilege the Israelite point of view. The Philistines are no better or worse than the Israelites, and Delilah and Samson are caught up in national rivalries. Some of the motives for the betrayal presented, and rejected, by Milton could be developed here. Roeg's film makes a gesture in this direction with its development of Samson's marriage to a woman from Timnah, in which she and her family are treated sympathetically. Similarly, DeMille: after Delilah learns the secret of Samson's strength, and just before Miriam appears on the scene (incidentally, she is accompanied by a young Saul), Delilah invites Samson to come with her to Egypt, so that 'we'll not be Danite and Philistine there, only Samson and Delilah'.

HEROES OF THE PROMISED LAND: TRANSLATING AMERICAN
FRONTIER MYTHS INTO BIBLICAL EPICS

Joy Sisley

Translation Criticism and the Biblical Epic

In an advertising trailer for *Abraham* in the *Turner Pictures* Old Testament
mini-series, a male voice sonorously announces over edited clips of the
film:

> In the time of Pharaohs and slaves, of Sodom and Gomorra, one man led his
> people on a journey that would demand undeniable faith, untold courage,
> and the ultimate sacrifice…an extraordinary presentation of biblical epic for
> all times and all audiences. Abraham is an exciting and realistic portrait of a
> timeless story. Abraham is a story for the ages, the ultimate journey, the
> ultimate adventure. Abraham will prove as timeless as the story itself…

Promoted with splendid hyperbole, the *Turner Pictures* Old Testament
epic mini-series is presented as an apotheosis of history and narrative.[1]
Narrative as History. The Narrative from which all other narratives take
their inspiration. The extravagance of the promotional material is matched
by the excessive naturalism of the series' cinematic image and the narrative realism of each episode. The historicizing of biblical narrative in the
Turner Pictures series is a common characteristic of recent adaptations for
television. Less spectacular and more intimate than their cinematic pre-
decessors, these adaptations present us with an immediate problem of
interpretive excess. But unlike the biblical epics of early cinema, this

---

1. A Lube Production (USA) in association with Lux Vide BetaFilm (Germany)
and Rai Uno (Italy) © Turner Pictures 1994–1996. The series is distributed by Turner
Home Entertainment, Atlanta, GA 30303, USA, and is available as the *TNT Bible
Collection* through Gateway Films/Vision Video at http.//www.visionvideo.com. The
series consists of *Abraham, Jacob, Joseph, Moses, Samson and Delilah*, and *David*.
The films run from 94 to 200 minutes and star well-known British and American
actors.

excess is not borne of the genre's aesthetic and spectacular extravagance. The naive realism of the biblical epics' televisual cousins has a closer affinity to the romantic historicism of the nineteenth-century French illustrator, Gustave Doré, whose compositions set the style for biblical illustration for well over a century.[2] In the case of television production, the question of excess is linked to an intellectual tradition of historical criticism which has introduced a particular brand of translative literalism to the genre.

The trailer's description of *Abraham* as a realistic portrait functions as an important metaphor for translation that is reiterated in the frequently repeated aim of film and television adaptation to bring Bible stories to life. The Vision Video catalogue in which *Abraham* is advertised is exemplary: *Jesus* (1979), produced by John Heyman and filmed in Israel, is described as 'so true-to-life that you'll feel like you're in first-century Palestine'. The *Visual Bible*'s word-for-word rendering of the *Gospel of Matthew* is presented as an eye-witness account in which 'the centuries melt away, and we are intimately involved in the life of Jesus'. Typically, these films or videos are advertised as 'stories which will come alive for audiences of all ages', where the temporal distance of the original stories is magically erased. As metaphors for historical realism, the promotional statements aim to treat the narratives as history; they create a privileged spectatorial position for the ideal viewer within the story space itself ('be there', 'travel the dusty roads') that implies an omniscient perspective within the narrative. These claims not only remind us that the Bible is above all a *translated* book but also raise questions about what these modern translations share with their written originals. Significantly, as historical drama, films like the *Turner Pictures* Old Testament series imply the existence of real historical characters and events behind the biblical stories—patriarchs whose epic acts of belief and courage afford them the standing of heroes. Recent biblical approaches, however, have taken issue with the literalism of historical criticism just as archaeology has failed to provide substantiating evidence for the existence of Old Testament patriarchs as historical figures.[3] Moreover, to take the implication of a common

---

2.　See G. Goethals, 'The Imaged Word: Aesthetics, Fidelity, and New Media Translations', in P.A. Soukup and R. Hodgson (eds.), *Fidelity and Translation: Communicating the Bible in New Media* (Franklin, WI: Sheed & Ward, 1999), pp. 133-72.

3.　For two publications that deal with the historicity of Old Testament writing, see J. Romer, *Testament: The Bible and History* (London: Michael O'Mara Books

historical referent for the films and the Old Testament stories at face value is to overlook the narrative excesses of both texts. One should not be misled by the rhetoric of transparency embedded in these televisual translations. As a translative strategy historical drama has other functions than to transport the modern reader to the scene of the story. Historical reconstruction shares a common goal with literal translation in its desire to bridge the gap between the supposed world of the original text and that of the modern reader and to disguise the interpretive work of translating.

The task of revealing that interpretive work shares the descriptive and analytic procedures of those biblical commentators who have adopted a cultural approach to the Bible.[4] This approach in modern biblical criticism is interested in the cultural (by which is usually meant textual and inter-textual) contexts of the Bible and its expression in art, literature, music or film. But whereas one of the characteristics of this approach is to blur or transgress boundaries[5] between the original works and their interpretations or rewritings, my treatment of television productions such as the *Turner Pictures* Old Testament series as translation regards such transgressive attempts with a measure of doubt. The question of these productions' referential ground and their interpretive limits returns to haunt us in more complex and demanding forms, for it is precisely in the interstices between ancient and modern and attempts to mask their cultural differences that the ideologies of translation are most effective. An analysis of the translative strategies of historical drama attempts to hold at bay the interpretive excesses of the films studied here by asking the question, how do they function as translation? How does historical reconstruction cross the boundaries of time to give contemporary coherence and significance to the ancient biblical stories?

Current approaches in Translation Studies address a much broader spectrum of questions than simply those which concern themselves with faithfulness to an original text. Translations are treated as autonomous texts in the host culture rather than more or less fair copies of an original. Nowadays, it is commonly accepted that translators work within institutional and systemic constraints such as patronage, publishers, poetics and

Limited, 1988), and T.L. Thompson, *The Bible in History: How Writers Create a Past* (London: Pimlico, 2000).

4.   See for example Bal, *Reading Rembrandt*; Exum, *Plotted, Shot, and Painted*; Exum and Moore (eds.), *Biblical Studies, Cultural Studies*; Kreitzer, *Old Testament in Fiction and Film*.

5.   Exum and Moore, *Biblical Studies, Cultural Studies*.

language; they rewrite or manipulate their source texts to suit the political, ideological, or cultural needs of their readers. Translation criticism asks questions about what translations reveal about the culture within which they circulate, how social and political inequities between source and target cultures are manifested, and how those power relations are perpetuated, challenged or undermined through the processes of translation. Disclosing contemporary and local horizons of interest in translation means that, far from being a transparent and faithful reflection of another text, translation is an active, open process, intimately connected with the pursuit of interests in the target culture.[6] It is with such questions in mind that I have been looking at animated and live action historical reconstructions of biblical narrative. My main interest is in how representations of the supposed historical and geographical contexts of biblical narrative bridge the gap between the time frame of the Bible and its contemporary reception. The construction of a historical imagination both in the advertising rhetoric of video catalogues and programme trailers and in the visual and narrative modes of story-telling in the videos themselves is central to the question of how biblical antiquity is negotiated in these narratives.

The promotional language that frames these audio-visual translations seems to play a central role in constructing a particular conception of historical reality which is calculated to abolish the temporal distance of the original and iron out the cultural specificities of contemporary interpretations. In doing so, the advertising establishes a sense of continuity from the past tense of the original text to the present of its reception. For example, the way in which *The Revolutionary, Parts I and II* is advertised by Vision Video illustrates how the elision of past and present works on the film or television screen.

> These fast-paced films on Jesus, made in high definition technology, show his life and teaching in a way never seen before. The main events from the Gospel sources are presented with careful attention to details and the original historical and cultural context. Originally shown in state-of-the-art virtual reality theatres, these riveting and acclaimed presentations are now offered in letterbox format.[7]

---

6.   See S. Bassnett and A. Lefevere, *Constructing Cultures: Essays on Literary Translation* (Clevedon, Philadelphia, Toronto, Sydney, Johannesburg: Multilingual Matters, 1998).

7.   Excerpt from Vision Video's advertisement for *The Revolutionary*, Parts I and II.

There are several significant ideas implied by this statement. First, there is a concept of narrative time expressed as a dimension of screen time—*these fast paced films*. Screen (or text) time, the pace at which the story unfolds is contrasted with story time, the original historical time of the Gospel narratives. The contrast makes explicit the difference between the world as it was then and the viewer's experience of it now *in a way never seen before*. Secondly, the screen time of the film is described in spatial rather than chronological terms. This is reinforced by two metaphors for the film's realism: the high definition technology and the virtual reality of its original presentation. Thus time and space are conflated for the viewer who is primed by the film's promotion for an experience of the past historical in the present. But the claims made by producers, promoters and distributors of these productions for their historical accuracy and inter-pretive fidelity are in many senses a masquerade. Although historical reconstruction may purport to provide a window on the past that may have been validated by archaeological research or historical biblical criticism, they also, and more particularly, provide a narrative on the present. As Marie Wyke notes in her introduction to her book on cinema and history, history in film is a useful device to speak of the present time while also being a discourse about the past.[8] The historiography of films that aim to bring the Bible to life is a fiction in two senses of the word: as a reconstruction of the past it is necessarily narrative but through its rhetorical and narrative devices it also invites viewers to collude in the imaginative projection of the present onto the past without exceptional regard for what it was really like, say, when Moses led the children of Israel out of Egypt into the wilderness. The imaginative historical spaces created in these films are entirely conceptions of the technologies of film production such as framing, lighting and focus. In films, as in painting therefore, looking becomes an essential feature of interpretation.

The ways in which any of these films represents its characters as historical figures also contributes to the verisimilitude of the characters as they are translated onto the screen. Quite a variety of approaches has been used, but for the purposes of the present discussion I will focus on the *Turner Pictures* portrayal of *Moses*, *Samson* and *Abraham*. The Turner series is particularly interesting because, while it presents its central characters as epic heroes in fairly conventional ways (at least insofar

---

8.   M. Wyke, *Projecting the Past: Ancient Rome, Cinema and History* (New York and London: Routledge, 1997), pp. 8-13.

as epic cinema is concerned), it also makes extensive use of the iconography and narrative themes of Hollywood Westerns. Genre shifts are an inevitable consequence of translating from one medium to another and constitute one of the principle transformations of the Bible. These transformations have an important effect on what the Bible is and what it means for its viewers. In the case of the Turner series, genre choice is a significant factor in creating the particular historical imagination of stories. The series achieves a doubling of the hermeneutic flow described by Larry Kreitzer by appropriating Epic and Western generic conventions.[9] While Hollywood Westerns construct a vision of America as the Promised Land in biblical terms, the series reconstructs a vision of the biblical Promised Land in terms of Western iconography. The series uses these genres to construct plausible worlds through which the broader social or cultural themes of their narrative are worked out.[10] To study the construction of a historical imagination in the Turner series, therefore, requires attending to the ways in which its narrative and visual conventions give coherence and significance to the biblical stories it translates.

Although directed by different cinema directors, the films in the Turner series exhibit a stylistic and thematic unity that is due not only to costume design and Moroccan film locations but also to their common use of Epic and Western cinematic themes and iconography. The choice is hardly surprising given the conventionally established affinity of Epic and Western genres to issues of national and moral identity that constitute the central thematic core of the series.[11] Far from the literal reconstruction of biblical history ostensibly offered by their cinematographic realism, the films rework the preoccupation of Americans with their own national and moral boundaries within the frame of an epic account of the establishment

9. See Kreitzer, *Old Testament in Fiction and Film.*

10. See S. Neale, 'Questions of Genre', in Barry Keith Grant (ed.), *Film Genre Reader II* (Austin: University of Texas, 1995), pp. 3-22 (p. 5).

11. E. Buscombe (ed.), *The BFI Companion to the Western* (London: Andrew Deutsch/BFI Publishing, 1998); J.L. Koosed and T. Linafelt, 'How the West Was Not One: Delilah Deconstructs the Western', *Semeia* 74 (1996), pp 167-82; on the references to Deuterocanonic laws about housebuilding in *Unforgiven*, see D. Pye, 'The Western (Genre and Movies)', in Barry Keith Grant (ed.), *Film Genre Reader II* (Austin: University of Texas Press, 1995), pp, 65-95; on narrative themes in *The Searchers* which are based on accounts in the book of Numbers of the 40 years the Israelites spent wandering in the wilderness after their escape from Egypt.and on the affinity between epic and Western cinema, see Elley, *Epic Film.*

of a nation of Israel across several centuries (in which, incidentally, the landscape and dress style do not change). The series reflects an identifiably American rather than biblical historical sensibility that relies on presenting certain forms of human struggle as universal through a selective and allegorical interpretation of Old Testament narratives. In this context, the combination of Epic and Western is central to the series' historical imagination because it offers the possibility of creating biblical heroes modelled on epic lines and placing them in a Promised Land modelled on Western lines.

Landscape of the Promised Land

The heroes' development in the Turner series is intimately connected to their discovery and defence of the Promised Land. The landscape, therefore, becomes a central trope in the narrative development of each film. The wide open spaces, the stark juxtaposition of fertile, cultivated land and desert, and the receding perspective of the filmic frame and deep focus of the cinematography offer far more than a mimetic representation of the geography of ancient biblical lands. They symbolize the conception of an Israelite national identity that has both historic and modern resonances. Consequently, the wilderness, represented as an inhospitable and hostile territory in contrast to the land flowing with milk and honey, is a central element of the narrative, the principal frame in which each of the stories unfolds and the hero fulfils his destiny. In order to understand the hero, then, it is important to appreciate the symbolic function of the landscape and the significance of the series' use of Hollywood Western iconography.

The narrativization of the Promised Land in Hollywood Westerns is played out in the frontier thesis of American literature and film. The frontier, according to Eric Heyne is a textual or metaphorical border rather than a physical geographic one. It consists of four terms: *desert* and *garden, margin* and *range*.[12] These terms represent the four poles of two figurative axes.

12. E. Heyne, 'The Lasting Frontier: Reinventing America', in E. Heyne (ed.), *Desert, Garden, Margin, Range: Literature on the American Frontier* (New York: Twayne Publishers; and Toronto: Maxwell MacMillan, 1992), pp. 3-15.

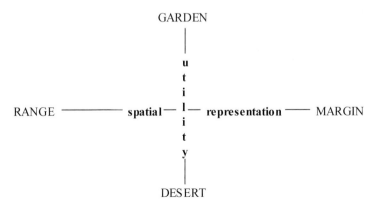

Figure 39. *The Frontier Thesis*

On the *desert/garden* axis of utility, land that had not been populated by whites was usually characterized in terms of its potential availability for economic exploration via farming, mining and ranching. Any land that was potentially viable was seen as a garden. It represented settlement and wealth as opposed to the wilderness, or desert, which remained a place of danger and deprivation. The wilderness, however, has not always been seen as hostile and dangerous territory. It has also been a positive symbolic force as a place of individual growth and development. According to American frontier biographer Frederick Jackson Turner (1861–1932), the wilderness nurtured individualism and helped promote American democracy. It symbolized a space in which the true moral qualities of free choice and self-willed confinement could be developed.

Cutting across the *desert/garden* axis is the *margin/range* opposition which functions as a spatial representation. On this axis, the frontier represents both a border to be crossed to reach places and the places themselves. As a margin, the frontier is constantly moving. As a boundary it demarcates the line between garden and wilderness, between the domesticated and the uncivilized, unmapped, emptiness. The frontier-as-margin functions in opposition to the frontier-as-range. The range is always a relatively empty space. It is, as Eric Heyne argues, the place Americans go to test social conventions against the old standard of nature, to take measure of their civilization.[13]

The antinomies of wilderness and Promised Land, through which the themes of national identity are worked out, tie the Turner series explicitly to the discourses of the Hollywood Western. In *Moses*, the dramatic

---

13. Heyne, *Lasting Frontier*, p. 6.

confrontations between the rebellious, stubborn Hebrews and God's promise (represented by a fertile landscape shown always panoramically from the mountain top or in swooping aerial photography) is framed by stereotypically Western shots of the Hebrew caravan winding its way through the barren landscape. In this film, the wilderness represents exile, while the fertile land represents settlement and a moral and social order. The frontier is a border to be crossed, and its crossing represents the ultimate emancipation of the Hebrew slaves. The scene in which the Hebrews have their first sight of the Promised Land is emblematic of this theme. The scene opens with a camera move from a close up of barren sand and gravel to a panoramic shot of a verdant valley. As the camera rises to a view of the valley over the gathered Hebrews' shoulders, comments can be heard such as '...green as far as the eye can see', 'It's so beautiful', 'There is the Promised Land. Moses, we should never have doubted you'. The music rises with the camera move in a soaring crescendo. The stark juxtaposition between barren wasteland and verdant garden is repeated in an identical camera movement in the final scenes when a dying Moses climbs the mountain to take a last view of the Promised Land from which he is barred.

More important in these scenes, however, is the film's representation of the moral boundary to be crossed by the Hebrews. In the first of the scenes mentioned, an entirely unbiblical exchange between Moses, Eliaph and Zarak (one of the ringleaders of grumblers and trouble-makers) makes the film's politics of independence explicit:

> Eliaph   When will the Lord appear to lead us forward?
> Moses   He won't.
> Zarak   What?...are we expected simply to walk into Canaan and occupy it?
> Moses.   How else will it be delivered into our hands?
> Eliaph   Surely, the Lord will do it for us.
> Moses   We must act for ourselves, Eliaph, if we are to be a free people.

Moses repeats this theme in his farewell speech to Joshua:

> The land of Canaan is only promised, Joshua. Every inch will be a struggle. You must now build a new Israel based upon the love of the law, not blind obedience to it.

In *Moses,* the wilderness is a testing ground for the Hebrew's moral and political self-determination. The second part of *Moses* is devoted to the Israelites' wandering in the desert after they have crossed over the Red Sea and Pharaoh's armies have been destroyed. This enables the narrative to develop the theme of law and community that has been described as a central generic theme of the Hollywood Western. For example, Koosed and Linafelt argue in their analysis of the film *Unforgiven* that:

> The classic Western is less about escaping the constricting aspects of law and culture (i.e. The East), as is often supposed, than it is about establishing an even stricter code of law and conduct. The fact that the setting is the wide open, lawless, western territories only serves to accent the necessity for strict enforcement.[14]

The Israelites wander in the desert for 40 years until they have learned to be free, or to symbolically throw off their habitual dependence on an Egyptian order, imposed by their former slave masters, and internalize the stricter code of law given by God. In a scripted addition to the account in Exodus of Jethro's visit to Moses, the liberal democratic ideology underpinning the film's theme of freedom is spelled out. To his (biblical) advice that Moses appoint other Israelite leaders to help him adjudicate people's disputes, Jethro adds:

> Have you traded an Egyptian slave owner for a task master in the heavens? Laws are not sufficient by themselves. The people must learn how to follow the Law without Moses or any leader. They must learn to want to follow the Law without fear of any whip on their backs or their souls. To follow the Law because they are free not to. When they have learned that they will truly be free, until then they are still slaves.

The speech mirrors the tensions of the frontier thesis of Hollywood Westerns, in which civil society represented by an urban, industrialized, institutionally ordered society of the American East coast (portrayed by the Egyptians) is opposed to a struggle to establish a utopian social order based on concepts of community and solidarity made tangible by the homestead and the town that are inevitably threatened by the lawlessness of the Wild West. *Moses* reworks this confrontation in a number of important ways. In the second part of the film, the confrontation between order and anarchy is characterized as a conflict within its own community between the factions who want to return to the relative comforts of Egypt and those who want to press on to the Promised Land. The confrontation is twice resolved by violent and fatal argument between the factions. The Israelites' gradual internalization of their own sense of social order is portrayed visually by scenes of increasing domestic organization each time camp is pitched so that, finally, the encampment resembles a small,

---

14. Koosed and Linafelt, 'How the West Was Not One', pp. 167-82 (169).

orderly town dominated by the tabernacle (house of God) on the hill. This moral order is represented in visual spaces such as the one created by the tabernacle, an enclosure constructed out of poles and curtains, and the spaces between the Hebrews' tents. Whereas in earlier scenes, their tents are pitched in a disordered fashion in a landscape dominated by stones and boulders, once an emergent moral order is established, the tents are pitched on flat ground, in neat lines, with wide 'streets' between them.

In *Samson and Delilah*, the antinomy of garden and wilderness is used in a somewhat different way. In this episode what is at stake is a defence of the Israelite's moral ownership of the Promised Land. The Philistines, who ride out of the desert like marauding Indians in the early captivity Westerns swooping down on their defenceless victims, pose an external threat to the order and integrity of Israelite social and political identity. *Samson and Delilah* is about the moral right of ownership conferred through their status as the Chosen People. In this film, the frontier between garden and wilderness is in some scenes very sharply marked, a line drawn literally by the vegetation. As a demarcation of political and moral boundaries this frontier serves to characterize the Philistines as the evil oppressors through an association of the desert with immorality, brutality and pantheistic barbarism and of the garden with an emergent moral modernity and monotheistic order.

The Israelites live on the margin where the green marks the limits and the tenuous boundaries of the Promised Land. For the Israelites, the desert is a place of destruction, where the line between garden and desert is sharply drawn to represent the Israelites as chosen and the Philistines as oppressors. The boundaries of the margin are more blurred in Samson's personal narrative as he moves back and forth between the Israelites and the Philistines, alternately betrayed by one then the other. The permeability of the boundary here reflects the ambiguity of Samson's character as he works out his destiny. If the desert is enobling in *Moses* because it is close to nature, in *Samson* it is portrayed in opposite terms as the farthest remove from civilization.

The characterization of garden and wilderness in these films is central to the formation of heroes' characters and the narrative's dramatic conclusion. In *Moses*, the quest for a national identity based on the moral qualities of free will and self-determination is distilled in Moses' character. Moses' spiritual journey from Pharaoh's court where he is the ridiculed and stammering adopted child of Pharaoh's daughter, the gradual politicization of his Hebrew identity, and eventually his assumption of moral leadership are crystalized by his stay in Moab. In these scenes, the wilderness is represented as the *range* in classic Western style right down to the last details of their plot lines: a stranger (Moses) appears in a lonely homestead; the stranger defends the homestead from some external threat; a romantic liaison develops between the stranger and one of the women in the homestead; the stranger leaves again—alone. In the film, Jethro's and his three daughters' livelihood depends on a mixed economy of pastoralism, cultivation and weaving. The *mis-en-scène* of this section creates a backdrop for the development of Moses' character through his interaction with other characters. Moses appears at Jethro's dwelling out of the harsh glare of the desert sun. But his budding romance with Zipporah is shot in the cool green of Jethro's olive groves. The scene is shot through a filter, giving the frame misty edges. Later on, when Moses takes over the care of Jethro's sheep, the olive grove is replaced by scrub-land. But this time the sun's glare is excluded. As Moses sets off for his unexpected encounter with God in the burning bush, the landscape is lit by the morning sun casting long shadows across the film frame and illuminating the smoke blowing from the family homestead's hearth. Finally, following his encounter with the burning bush, Moses runs out into the empty spaces of the hills surrounding Jethro's farm, to come to terms with his divine mission. In these scenes, the margin-as-range is represented as a romanticized and charmed place. The desert is a place of refuge, a space where Moses discovers and assumes his heroic identity. In true Hollywood Western form, Zipporah represents the civilizing influence of the wilderness on Moses the outlaw. The landscape is portrayed here as a romantic and feminizing space. As this part of the story develops, Moses begins to discover his destiny as a Hebrew so that, by the time God speaks to him out of the burning bush, the expansiveness of the landscape has come to represent the magnitude of God's promise. Moses moves through this landscape with a familiarity and ease that speaks of his destiny as a great leader.

For Samson, the landscape as margin is a place of dis-ease. Samson's first encounter with Delilah encapsulates this trope. Samson has fled into the wilderness to escape the pressures of his family and townspeople. As he fishes in the river, he sees Delilah camped by the riverside. Delilah's presence is a ruse to lure Samson into the Philistine's trap. Samson falls for this. But as he stalks Delilah, he sees a lion stalking the campsite. Samson springs to the rescue overpowering the lion and killing it. The scene takes place on the riverbank where desert and oasis meet, where

grass and palm trees grow out of the sand dunes. Metaphorically the space
is an ambiguous one filled with the burning flames of desire and revenge.
Not for Samson the surety of knowing how he will fulfil his destiny. He
doesn't work this out until the final scenes of the film when he discovers
how to harness his strength with his faith in God. Whenever Samson runs
away from home and from the demands of his people to lead them in
rebellion against the Philistines, the wilderness he escapes to is represented as a verdant, alluring place. His first encounter with Delilah occurs
on the banks of a river bordered by greenery and palm trees and rimmed
by the ever-present desert. The lands of his father-in-law are lushly
cultivated (like those of the Israelites). Unlike the *Moses* film, these spaces
are represented as neither romantic nor feminizing. Our hero, Samson is
not to be civilized by this touch. Samson secures nothing from these
spaces except betrayal which in turn fuels his lust for revenge. In *Samson
and Delilah* the struggle for a utopian social order is underpinned by the
politics of revenge. But finally, the land reclaims its own as in the last
scene when Samson's body is reclaimed for burial. The high angle of the
final shots framing the funeral cortège re-establishes the garden rimmed
now by a desert that no longer harbours the threat of marauding Philistines
riding bare-back on their horses.

Heroes of the Promised Land

While the representations of landscape and metaphorical tropes of the
frontier are taken from the Western, the depiction of the central character
of each of these films is closer to the construction of an epic hero rather
than that of the Westerner. There is a remarkable consistency in the representation of the central characters of the Turner series. Not only are each
of the heroes great and wise men, they are also troubled, tormented
characters. They are therefore in many ways, more complex than many of
the heroes of Hollywood Westerns. Unlike the Westerner who is a man of
action that does what a man has to do in order to establish law and order
on the frontier, the Turner heroes have to make moral and physical
choices. If, as Derek Elley argues, epic heroism involves characters that
are 'supra (or sometimes super) human, waging an allegorical struggle on
their own plane…surrounded by…secondary characters who act on them
morally',[15] then we must look for the development of their heroism not
only to the landscape that shapes their moral and political identity but also

---

15. Elley, *Epic Film*, p. 16.

to the relation between the central and secondary characters. The heroes of this biblical series are interesting because of their reluctance to accept a destiny that has been imposed on them by a God who has singled them out as leaders of his chosen people. Their reluctance is formulaic, so one example is sufficient; this time from *Abraham*. Abram (played by Richard Harris), who at the beginning of the film has more material possessions than he could wish for, is filled with a strange kind of longing that he cannot place. One day, after nearly drowning in a flash flood, he hears the voice of God promising that he will make a great nation of Abram and his descendants. Abram goes to his father to seek his blessing on his quest for the land that God has promised. The scene is set in an inner courtyard. Abram, his brother, and his father discuss Abram's departure.

Father   Who knows this God?

Abram   I don't know father. Perhaps many. In their hearts.

Brother   Oh, I see. A god to be worshipped in ignorance.

Abram   Not so, brother. It is simply that I don't know him. Yet. But in time.

Brother   In time. But now he's telling you to pack up everything and everyone and leave for who knows where. No. It's insane. I refuse to follow this brother of mine.

Father   You have changed Abram. I can see it. (*Cutaway to scene with Sarah and other women.*)

Brother   If Abram and his men leave, we are at risk. And you, brother, are in greater danger. Out there. Alone. Your people will be like sheep among jackals.

Abram   I feel that I am protected

Brother   Those nameless gods again. (*Father orders Abram's brother to leave the room.*)

Father   Abram. You're my son. You owe me obedience. Instead you listen to this unknown god. A nameless god who whispers into your ear and bids you to leave your father's house. To break your heart and mine. What kind of god is this?

Abram   (*In a whisper*) I don't know father. (*Hesitantly*) But I...I have... heard his voice. It spoke to me above the silence of all the other gods.

Father   You despise the gods who have given you protection?... You renounce all our gods because you found a new god?

Abram   (*Long silence*) I cannot stay father. As much as it grieves me the thought of leaving you. (*stammering*) I felt...I...I've heard him call me.

This recurring motif bears the hallmarks of a Protestant redemption narrative. Our hero is filled with an unidentifiable desire, usually experienced as a lack; he has an epiphanal moment of clarity in which the one true God calls to him; he takes his first step on the long and difficult road to salvation. The chosen people function as his alter ego. They represent the inner struggle he has with his own destiny or the pull between the course of action decided by humans and the course of action determined by God. On this plane, the hero's allegorical struggle assumes universal proportions in its portrayal of Western philosophical individualism. The historical consciousness of this narrative is entirely modern in its representation of epic heroism. It reflects what John McWilliams Jr has described as American poet Walt Whitman's transformation of the epic hero:

> Whitman [is convinced]...that the self's visionary power has replaced battle bravery as the essence of modern heroism...For Whitman, heroism is revealed in perceptions rather than actions...[he] insists on extending his experience and his heroic perceptions to all men, (sic) not merely to Americans, because New World culture has made universal heroism possible.[16]

This particular portrayal of heroism transforms the Turner series into an epic of democracy. Moses' exchange with his father-in-law, Jethro, after his epiphany at the scene of the burning bush, reiterates the scene in *Abraham* of our hero's dawning vision as he sets forth to found or save a nation. In this case it is Moses who doubts the call. Jethro challenges him and Moses runs out into the night. Later he returns. Zipporah is waiting for him.

Moses	Did I see God?
Zipporah	Only you can answer that Moses.
Moses	If I go back to Egypt as the voice commanded they may kill me.
Zipporah	Not if God is with you. Not if he is sending *you* to free your people.
Moses	Can't even talk in the presence of Pharaoh. Can't talk.
Zipporah	It is a true call. You must answer it.
Moses	They may kill your husband.
Zipporah	I will trust in God. Will you?

Similarly, Samson's moment occurs towards the end of the film when he is blind and imprisoned. His earlier acts of battle bravery amount to no more than a stereotypical display of physical strength that serves the pursuit of his own desires, not the interests of his people.

---

16. J.P. McWilliams, Jr, *The American Epic: Transforming a Genre, 1770–1860* (Cambridge: Cambridge University Press, 1989).

America as the Promised Land

While it presents a universalizing conception of history, this series' historical imagination betrays the specificities of its own cultural context which contributes, in great part, to viewers' recognition of their relation to the ancient texts. The combined generic representations of landscape and heroism invite an allegorical reading of the series. The iconographic and narrative allusions to the Hollywood Western's representation of American landscape bind the biblical narratives to a vision of the founding of America as the divine will of providence. The parameters of an emergent Israelite national identity in the series is displaced onto a particular conception of American identity that reflects a conservative Protestant politics and morality. The history of Israelite national and cultural identity is explored within the same exclusive limits of the classical Hollywood Westerns, exclusive that is of women, indigenous Indian populations, Irish immigrants and the descendants of African slaves.

The series' historiography and its translation strategy thus fulfil the same function. If the literalism of the series' historiography functions as a translation strategy designed to establish a transparent relationship between the ancient narratives and their contemporary interpretation, the generic representation of time and space is crucial to the series' reality effect designed to suppress an awareness of cultural difference between ancient and modern. In attempting to bridge the gap between ancient and modern the series implicates its viewers in a particular conception of history. As Vivian Sobchack notes of the narrative representation of history in the Hollywood epic:

> The importance of the genre is not that it narrates and dramatizes historical events accurately according to the detailed stories of academic historians but rather that it opens a temporal field that creates the *general* possibility of recognising oneself as a *historical subject* of a particular kind.[17]

The phenomenological aspects of narrative time in the Turner epics are therefore bound up with how viewers symbolically make sense of their social experience, a process that is concerned with the central philosophical question of 'how to comprehend ourselves in time'.[18]

---

17. V. Sobchak, 'Surge and Splendor: A Phenomenology of the Hollywood Historical Epic', in Barry K. Grant, *Film Genre Reader II* (Austin: University of Texas Press, 1995), pp. 280-307 (286).

18. Sobchack, 'Surge and Splendor', p. 283.

The importance of the Turner series' universalizing narrative conventions lies in its imaginative construction of Old Testament history to fabricate an American subjective identity. The epic heroes in this series are modelled on an American romantic tradition of historical fiction in which fictionality and historicity are blurred and which attempts to make American history coincide with biblical history in its view of America as the Promised Land.[19] It thus enables an exploration of American political and moral identities which is bound up with the mythical invention of America as the Promised Land through the literature and film of the past two and a half centuries. In their study of biblical epics Bruce Babington and Peter Evans draw attention to, but do not develop, the thematic importance of the Promised Land in the epics' complex narrative construction of American identity in relation both to Jewish immigration to the USA and American involvement in geopolitical events of the twentieth century and especially the Middle East.[20] Emily Budick traces a similar tendency with respect to the social realities of American writers from the eighteenth century to the present.[21] While parallelisms between these realities and their creative reconstruction do not constitute any kind of history, it is important to bear in mind that the *Turner Pictures* epics as historical narratives belong to a literary and cultural tradition that has deep roots in the American psyche.

If in the Turner series the theme of the Promised Land provides a biblical parallel for the founding myths of America, then the frontier thesis provides a parallel for an American concept of democracy that is projected onto a world stage and justifies its defence of democracy. This leaves us with the interesting possibility of reading allegorically into the Turner heroes' reluctance the United States' own ambivalent and reluctant assumption of their international role as peace keepers and defenders of democracy. In these terms, the historicity of the Turner series coincides with the United States' vision of its geopolitical role since Vietnam. An allegorical reading would seem to endorse the argument that as translation the series rewrites biblical narratives to suit the political, ideological or cultural needs of its viewers. It also supports one of the principal

---

19. For a discussion of this tradition, see E.M. Budick, *Fiction and Historical Consciousness in the American Romance Tradition* (New Haven and London: Yale University Press, 1993).

20. Babington and Evans, *Biblical Epics*, pp. 36-41.

21. For a relevant discussion of the construction of identity in American literature, see Budick, *Fiction and Historical Consciousness*, and McWilliams, *American Epic*.

arguments of modern historiography that history tell us more about the writer's understanding of the past than the past itself, that the world a writer reflects is the one she knows.[22] The significance of the Turner series has very little to do with the literary and cultural worlds in which the biblical stories originally circulated. The ways in which these stories are translated into the contemporary context of American television would seem to have more to do with their appropriation in the ongoing mythologizing of America as the Promised Land. It is significant, therefore, that the generic forms in American cinema most closely associated with historical actuality have been appropriated as translation models, for the history thus represented lends moral credence to a particular vision of the founding of America and the maintenance of its political and moral frontiers.

---

22. For a discussion about modern historiography and biblical history, see Thompson, *Bible in History.*

JESUS, MARY AND JOSEPH!
(HOLY) FAMILY VALUES IN FILM

Gaye Ortiz

There is much material written, and many more apocryphal stories told, about the Holy Family—after all, it is held up by the Catholic Church as a model for family life, which in turn is 'the original form of, and the preparation for, all social relationships'.[1] But when we take an in-depth look, what do we find? At the very least, an atypical family consisting of a young woman who has become pregnant through a very unusual method, not too dissimilar to the virgin birth stories of ancient goddess religions; her husband, who is not the biological father but, according to some accounts (Epiphanius, *Protevangelium*) is more of an elderly protector who set an example for Catholic fathers as 'the leader of the Holy Family';[2] and a child who, again similar to mythological heroes, has superhuman powers and is destined for greatness. Feminists have claimed that Mary is an impossible role model for women; Joseph disappears from the scene fairly quickly, so that all we are left with is legend; and Jesus is a precocious child who grows up to display a tense, if not downright aggressive, attitude towards his mother and family. As Feuerbach might say, this is a dysfunctional family!

An Approach to Film

In recent years there have been a number of interesting films about the family—very recently we have seen the award-winning *American Beauty* and the cross-cultural family in *East Is East*. In order to explore ways of

---

1. Ernst Troeltsch cited in Ferdinand Mount, *The Subversive Family* (London: Jonathan Cape, 1982), p. 21.
2. C. Rengers, 'A Year of St Joseph' http.//catholic.net.80/RCC/periodicals/homiletic/april96/, p. 1.

seeing filmic representations of the family, which could throw up questions we might have about the relevance of the family today, the following four elements of theological and cultural analysis are helpful:

Reflection—Reflection is necessary as we feel films before we begin to understand them or to articulate the ideas coming from them. Larry Kreitzer employs the term 'reversing the hermeneutical flow' in his studies on the interaction of film with the Bible.[3] David Graham explains that 'the use of the film medium in religious discussion may make us reflect upon our theological ideas or religious praxis'.[4]

Narrative—Film tells a story above all. There has been an ongoing debate about whether film is myth, parable or even the modern-day equivalent of the morality play.[5] Investigating the type of story—the genre—and the way it is told, particularly in reference to its cultural milieu, can lead us to insights about the story. Film tells its story through visual images, adding to—and sometimes distracting from—the meaning we make.

'Reading' film—How do we know what a film 'means'? There can never be a single reading of a film—in fact there are as many readings as there are viewers—but I find useful the framework given by Stephen Brie and David Toreville[6] in which they propose that a dominant or preferred reading is one that coincides with the encoded meaning given through the production process, while an oppositional reading rejects and critiques this dominant construction; a negotiated reading falls somewhere in between. This kind of approach is helpful when exploring some of the cultural influences on film, as well as in understanding any changes between the period it was made and the expectations and cultural assumptions the audience may have.

Analogy—Analogy is defined by David Tracy as 'a language of ordered relationships articulating similarity-in-difference'.[7] I will employ analogy

3. Kreitzer, *New Testament in Fiction and Film*, and *Old Testament in Fiction and Film: On Reversing the Hermeutical Flow*.

4. C. Marsh and G. Ortiz (eds.), *Explorations in Theology and Film* (Oxford: Blackwell, 1997), p. 38.

5. Peter Malone, *The Film* (Melbourne: Chevalier, 1971, p. 104), quotes from Anthony Schillaci, *Movies and Morals* (New York: Sheed and Ward, 1968), in which the modern film is likened to plays like *Everyman*.

6. S. Brie and D. Torevell, 'Moral Ambiguity and Contradiction in Dead Poet's Society', in C. Marsh and G. Ortiz (eds.), *Explorations in Theology and Film* (Oxford: Blackwell, 1997), pp. 167-80.

7. David Tracy, *The Analogical Imagination* (New York: Crossroad, 1987), p. 408.

here, when reflecting upon the events in a film and comparing them to events in the Bible. Karl Rahner said that reality not merely has analogies but *is* analogy through and through.[8] The Christ event has constantly been the subject of theological and cultural reinterpretation, and, through the religious films I will discuss below, analogy can help in connecting this event and its cast of biblical characters to filmic characters from adventure and science fiction genres. Analogy is never perfect, and sometimes it is the breakdown in similarity which feeds our reflections.

In tracing the characters who make up the Holy Family, I will point out how Jesus, Mary and Joseph are portrayed in two particular films from the religious film genre, Pasolini's *The Gospel according to St Matthew* (1964) and George Stevens's *The Greatest Story Ever Told* (1965). This contrast and comparison will also engage in dialogue with some of the issues thrown up by the Gospels of Matthew and Luke, in order to articulate the identity of this family and the values it seems to promote. I will then go on to analogize these portrayals with three films which might be categorized as 'secular', *Superman* (Richard Donner 1978), and *The Terminator* and *Terminator 2: Judgment Day* (James Cameron, 1984 and 1991). These films contain variations on the Holy Family theme, but in exploring the values they present we are challenged to find some common ground with the biblical (both textual and filmic) representations.

Characterization in Film

> The notion of the person is basic to our making sense of the external world.[9]

Interpreting characters in film, whether fictional or not, can hinge upon our ability to make connections between the person we see and the schema of 'the person' as defined in contemporary Western cultures. When David Bordwell asks 'what is a person', he lists the following categories:

1) a human body; 2) perceptual activity; 3) thoughts, including beliefs; 4) feelings or emotions; 5) traits or qualities; 6) capacity for self-impelled actions, such as communication, goal-formation and achievement.[10]

8.   Tracy, *Analogical Imagination*, p. 412.
9.   David Bordwell, *Making Meaning* (London: Harvard University Press, 1991), p. 151.
10.   Bordwell, *Making Meaning*, p. 152.

Once we are able to build up a picture of such a person, we begin to ascribe semantic meaning to her as well, so that 'what a character is or has can be translated into what the character means'.[11] In his discussion, Bordwell is primarily concerned with the art of film criticism, pointing out that critics do not believe that characters are 'real people'. There is more to film-making, in other words, than believing what we see with our eyes.

The authors of *Savior on the Silver Screen*[12] add to this line of thought when proposing a set of criteria that we can use in viewing films within the Christ film genre. They point out that every film is a commercial venture—the goal of making money is inseparable from the film itself. But they also suggest that a 'broader set of values' can be discerned in a film 'despite or because of the profit motive that was involved in the preparation of the film'.[13] They also propose that films can say something about the audience, when we ask questions like: What in the film appeals to you? What does the film evoke in you that causes you to examine the vast inventory of your beliefs about God, Jesus, the Church…? What are some of the characteristics of our own image of these characters, and does the film reinforce, revise or even replace those characteristics?[14]

Religious Film Genre—Considerations

Derek Elley in his book on the epic film says that film-makers suffer from 'an excess of reverence' which 'fetters the imaginations of scriptwriters'.[15] Peter Malone, priest, film critic and President of the International Catholic Organisation for Cinema, has asked whether religious films are really religious. He says that traditionally this genre has not been too successful at the box office, and suggests four reasons why. First, film-makers are mainly 'cashing in on the word of God' and (as in the case of *Salome*) were interested in a loose Hollywood treatment of a few sensational Bible verses which featured Rita Hayworth![16] This accusation links to Malone's second point, that film-makers lack judgement about the issues of importance in the Bible—the fictitious scene in *Ben-Hur* where Jesus gives the

---

11. Bordwell, *Making Meaning*, p. 154.

12. R. Stern, C. Jefford and G. Debona, *Savior on the Silver Screen* (New York: Paulist, 1999).

13. Stern, Jefford and Debona, *Savior on the Silver Screen*, p. 22.

14. Stern, Jefford and Debona, *Savior on the Silver Screen*, p. 22.

15. Elley, *Epic Film*, p. 43.

16. Elley, *Epic Film*, p. 141.

title character a drink of water is more impressive than the Sermon on the Mount scene.

Thirdly, Malone says that discretion and taste are often lacking in these films. He uses the example of the over-the-top Hollywood treatment of the crossing of the Red Sea in *The Ten Commandments*, a film which got the following put-down from *Time* magazine: '[the film is] roughly comparable to an eight-foot chorus girl—pretty well put together, but much too big and much too flashy'.[17] We must also remember the star-studded cast of *The Greatest Story Ever Told* (including John Wayne as the centurion who drawled, 'Surely this was the Son of Gawd').

Malone's main criticism, however, is that film-makers do not seem to know how to read the Bible. The 'religious message, as it was written down', is held hostage to a determination to portray things literally through trick photography and special effects. Even Pasolini is guilty of a literalist technique because he treats Matthew's Gospel as a chronological biography.[18] Elley also makes this point, saying that as of 1984 he had seen no film which managed to 'humanise the biblical text yet maintain its epic stature'.[19]

With regard to cinematic treatments of Mary, Babington and Evans point out that only in the iconoclastic images from film-makers Scorsese and Pasolini do we not find the iconic Mother, 'an absolute of asexual purity and self-sacrifice'.[20] They state that in most biblical films Mary—and other female characters—are perceived from the male angle, and the biological and emotional relationship between her and Jesus constrains her from breaking free of patriarchal conceptions of women.

Add to this the notion of 'holiness' (as in the title of the Holy Family) and it is no wonder that it comes as a welcome relief to see the mother in

---

17. As quoted by William Telford, in Marsh and Ortiz (eds.), *Explorations*, p. 117. Telford also weighs in with the problems of portraying Jesus in film, citing the dilemma of choosing a well-known or unknown actor, so as not to be saddled with the audience's preconceptions, with what Babington and Evans call the 'star-texts of meanings from previous films' (Babington and Evans, *Biblical Epics*, p. 53). Other constraints include Jesus: hard man or wimp, divine or human, inoffensive or blasphemous (see Telford, in Marsh and Ortiz (eds.), *Explorations*, pp. 127ff).

18. Malone, *Film*, p. 143.

19. Elley, *Epic Film*, p. 43. He comments as well on the influence that Renaissance and the Old Masters artistic legacy has had on the portrayal of the Christ, emphasizing tradition over innovation.

20. Babington and Evans, *Biblical Epics*, p. 108.

The Life of Brian, who slaps her crying new-born as the Magi reclaim their gifts and rush off to the correct manger. *The Life of Brian* is an antidote to the over-emphasis on reverence in most religious films. I would like to get around this problem by focusing instead on family values as they might be read in the films of Pasolini and Stevens—they are values, which, by definition, help a family to sustain belief in its mutually constructed reality.

David Morgan points to the interplay between biology and culture which is at the heart of family relationships as well as to the tremendous shift in society that today informs and problematizes our notions of the term 'family'. He suggests that the role of religion in family life has been to support family values, which have to do with positing the family as a 'central institution within society, endorsing the principles of fidelity and the fulfillment of familial obligations'.[21] Analyzing the family, let alone what comprises family values, is not the task I have set for myself—I would rather let film draw out our ideas and insights in the light of our own knowledge and experience.

The Greatest Story Ever Told

This film is one of the great American epics, following Cecil B. DeMille and Nicholas Ray. George Stevens aimed to present a historically accurate picture of the time of Christ. It is also said to be an attempt to put the Christ story into context with the Hebrew Scriptures and in particular the writings of the prophets. This can be seen in the early section of the film, which portrays the Holy Family in exile in Egypt. Travellers bring the news that Herod is dead, and instinctively the reaction of the parents is to go home. The family then travels to Nazareth in the midst of unrest, only to be met on the road with rows of crucified Jews.

Several observations may be made about sequence of events surrounding the family and how Jesus, Mary and Joseph are characterized. First, Joseph in the Egyptian exile scene is shown intoning from a scroll of the Scriptures, 'For unto us a child is born, unto us a son is given...' He is reading this to Mary who is holding the child, and we see that Jesus is still quite a young baby—probably not yet able to walk. Joseph comes across as a learned man who recognizes the import of what he is reading; in fact earlier in the film, when the Magi come to visit, both Joseph and Mary are

---

21. David Morgan, 'Family', in P. Clarke and A. Linzey (eds.), *Dictionary of Ethics, Theology and Society* (London: Routledge, 1996), pp. 371-75 (372).

heard in voice-overs, which signify their thoughts: 'He shall be great and called son of the most high'. This signals to us that the parents are remembering and reflecting upon what the angel has told them about the child and what was told to them by Simeon at the Temple.

Even the baby seems to have a gravity beyond his years—as Stern observes, 'Jesus seems to be the most gnostic in this film, seeming to know beforehand the whole trajectory of his life, discerning the significance of crosses even as an infant'.[22] The characters seem weighed down with the portentousness of the whole situation in which they find themselves, and their slow entry into Nazareth is accompanied by a myriad of anguished prayers which, although visually linked to the ruthless crackdown on the populace, foreshadow the fate of Jesus.

Gerald Forshey in *American Religious and Biblical Spectaculars* (1992) comments that Stevens uses the Gospel accounts interchangeably in order to tell the story in its most familiar form, and makes his characters into symbols 'in order to present a universal Christ…even his family is played as a symbol'.[23] Forshey quotes from a *Boston Globe* review of the film, in which it says 'Dorothy McGuire plays the Virgin Mary—more as a symbol than as a woman, who never ages, never speaks, and merely shows on her face the sorrows of the mother of Jesus'.[24]

The Holy Family is also overshadowed—or even overwhelmed, as is almost everyone in this film—by the scenery. Stevens thought the American Southwestern landscape would be a dramatic fictional counterpart to Palestine, but the sweeping vistas tend to make the characters small and almost insignificant. Stern says that 'Mary and Joseph are mere specks as they make their way across the desert'.[25] Forshey points out that the scenes recall the 'big-sky' Hollywood Westerns, and that 'when the Holy Family return from their Egyptian exile, their presence [is] barely discernible at the very bottom of the frame, the remainder of the image filled with billowy clouds proclaiming the infinity of the universe'.[26]

We might say, then, that *The Greatest Story Ever Told* is focusing on the big picture, and that a dominant or preferred reading of the film may

22. Stern, Jefford and Debona, *Savior on the Silver Screen*, p. 145.

23. G. Forshey, *American Religious and Biblical Spectaculars* (London: Praeger, 1992), p. 96.

24. Forshey, *American Religious*, p. 119.

25. Stern, Jefford and Debona, *Savior on the Silver Screen*, p. 146.

26. Forshey, *American Religious*, p. 141.

suggest that the characters are there for mainly a symbolic purpose, we can pull out from it very few indications of 'family values', apart from a clear dedication of the parents to the child and their awareness of his destiny: or, to use Morgan's terms, fidelity and obligation. The Gospels speak of the 'marvel' and 'wonder' with which Mary and Joseph received the predictions about their son, but it is an excessively reverential or even majestic air that may come through to us in Stevens's characters.

The Gospel According To Saint Matthew

Made the year before *The Greatest Story Ever Told*, this Italian film could not be a greater contrast to the Hollywood epic. Critics have labelled it 'rough-hewn', primitive, neorealist—closer to a passion play than a film. Its characters are played by non-professional actors—including Pasolini's mother as the aged Mary—and it was filmed in black and white in the southern Italian countryside.[27]

Also by contrast, it relies solely upon one Gospel for its dialogue. Not everything in Matthew's Gospel is included, however (the genealogy is missing, for example). The film begins abruptly with a close-up of Mary's face, directly gazing at Joseph as he discovers she is pregnant. The reaction shot from Joseph, Stern says, shows the 'biting reality' of the scene which is 'often glossed over by those who interpret Matthew's gospel'; his look needs 'no words to explain his emotional turmoil, a feeling that no words can adequately explain or demystify'.[28] This scene is without any sound, the silence contributing to a rather appropriate dream-like quality, as Joseph quickly leaves Mary and sits down near a field where children play and falls asleep. He wakes to the angel telling him that the child is conceived of the Holy Ghost and to take Mary as his wife.

The dreams of Joseph play a vital part in making sense of the narrative, both for him and for us. Stern remarks that Joseph's dream 'becomes the way he makes sense of the mysterious event and so gives the audience a way to interpret their own experience of the gospel'.[29] In fact, Joseph

---

27. Stern, Jefford and Debona, *Savior on the Silver Screen*, p. 98, make the observation that 'Pasolini seems more interested in creating a sense of the people with whom Jesus likely would have interacted'.

28. Stern, Jefford and Debona, *Savior on the Silver Screen*, p. 104.

29. Stern, Jefford and Debona, *Savior on the Silver Screen*, p. 121. Peter Fraser, *Images of the Passion* (Trowbridge: Flicks, 1998), p. 71, states that this film cannot be

seems to sleep quite a lot due to the film's compressed action and editing! To compare the representation of this Holy Family with Stevens's family, one can examine Joseph's second dream, when he is told to take the family into exile. As in the Gospel, the story precedes the slaughter of the innocents, Herod's death and Joseph's third dream calling the family back from exile.[30]

The image of the Holy Family in this section of the film is quite different from Stevens's film, and there is considerable emotion emanating from the facial expressions of Mary and Joseph. When Joseph decides to return from exile, it is not because a traveller tells him while he recites Scriptures, but because he is told by the angel to do so. He then scans the surrounding landscape, and catches Mary's eye while she is spreading out the washing; her face is luminous and expectant, and there is a real connection being made between the two characters. But the crowning moment of this scene is the toddler Jesus, playing with other children and wearing a mini-Roman toga. He is animated and seems to be a happy and well-fed but ordinary child. He heads for his father, who stretches out his arms, clearly besotted with the child.

Even in the hardship of exile, this seems to be a family whose members have emotional ties to one another, who communicate with one another on a level that does not need portentous pronouncements. Mary is not a porcelain-doll icon, but a young woman whose eyes are full of meaning. This film gives Joseph one of his meatiest film roles of the genre, and (despite his tendency to narcolepsy!) he is neither a martyr to his calling from God nor a decrepit old man whose role is only as a guardian to the Madonna and Child. The natural quality of the actors gives an air of normality, and as Fraser suggests, 'there is no one single incarnational moment in the film but an ever-growing incarnational presence';[31] it is Pasolini's 'optimistic humanism' which points to 'the divinity inherent in all humanity'.[32]

---

systematically explained on the thematic level because it primarily operates on the experiential level.

30. Fraser, *Images of the Passion*, p. 74, comments that the scene of the massacre is a 'visual montage' filling a gap in Matthew's account, which simply quotes Jeremiah rather than describing the attack and then narrates the family's return from Egypt. He says that Pasolini's intent is to 'underline for emotional effect what Matthew suppresses'.

31. Fraser, *Images of the Passion*, p. 77.

32. Fraser, *Images of the Passion*, p. 76.

Science Fiction—Considerations of the Genre

Fraser remarks that 'Passion narratives in film are remarkably common'.[33] In part this is because the Western tradition's stories of 'saviour-warriors' developed from ancient mythological characters as described by Joseph Campbell in his classic study, *The Hero with a Thousand Faces* (1988).[34] Further, he says that in such 'seemingly secular vehicles as *The Karate Kid, The Terminator* and *Batman*...we find echoes of the same heroic motifs grounded in the primary Christian model of redemption'.[35]

And where we find a saviour figure we sometimes find his 'holy' family, often bemused, confused or bewildered when confronted with their offspring's heroic destiny. Here, I will confine my explorations to the science fiction genre, which has been defined as being based on a 'sense of wonder'. Stephen May in *Stardust and Ashes* (1998) quotes Damon Knight:

> We live on a minute island of known things. Our undiminished wonder at the mystery, which surrounds us, is what makes us human. In science fiction we can approach that mystery, not in small, everyday symbols but in the big ones of space and time.[36]

Superman

May discusses the dominant science fiction treatment of aliens as saviours—not only 'bringers of hope and the saving knowledge', but also morally better than those of us on Earth.[37] This is certainly the message we get in the opening sequence of *Superman*, the 1978 film of the classic comic book hero starring Christopher Reeve. We are introduced to impending eco-disaster on the Planet Krypton, and Jor-El, a learned and morally superior man of his own advanced race, is making plans to send his son out into the cosmos to escape the apocalypse. This scenario recalls the adventures of another baby hero, Moses, floated down the river to be rescued and cared for by a surrogate parent.

33. Fraser, *Images of the Passion*, p. 10.
34. J. Campbell, *The Hero with a Thousand Faces* (Princeton: Princeton University Press, 1988).
35. Fraser, *Images of the Passion*, p. 10.
36. S. May, *Stardust and Ashes* (London: SPCK, 1998), p. 13.
37. May, *Stardust and Ashes,* p. 93.

What we see in *Superman* are parents who are aware of their son's tremendous gifts and talents, and who are making a sacrifice to save him. The speech that Jor-El makes is poignant and leaves us in no doubt of the love they have for their son: 'You will travel far but we will never leave you, even in the face of our deaths. The richness of our lives will be yours'. The mystical imparting of the father's qualities and experiences culminates in the phrase 'The son becomes the father and the father the son', and during the child's trip through space he is tutored in the history of his new home, with the one proviso: 'It is forbidden for you to interfere with human history'.

We know of course that although Christian theology would feel at home with the phrase 'The son becomes the father and the father the son', the point of Christ made human is entirely *meant* to change human history. Still, we can find symmetry in the care of the father for the son, the imparting of love and strength in order to equip him on earth.

The adoptive parent, someone who takes on the care of a child and who grows to love him, is introduced through the characters of Mr and Mrs Kent. These characters are a real contrast to the child's heavenly parents, and are as plain and simple as the mid-western cornfields, which they farm. Like the barren wives in the scriptures Mrs Kent has for years prayed for 'the good Lord to see fit to give us a child'. This miraculous child, who arrives in a spectacular fashion, is the answer to her prayers. Her husband is reluctant but after the boy saves his life he accepts him as his son, albeit a very extraordinary son.

The Kents bring the child up to live an ordinary life on the farm; they realize his tremendous strength but they do not exploit it or ignore it. Rather, they give him love, security and support. In a later scene, the teenage Clark asks his father why he can't 'show off' doing things he is capable of—asking 'is a bird showing off when it flies?' Mr Kent tells Clark that he is here 'for a reason, I don't know whose reason, whatever the reason'. In this uncertainty Mr Kent is quite the opposite not just from Clark's true father Jor-El, but also from Stevens's Joseph, obviously an adoptive father who sees very clearly in the Scriptures the reason why the child has come to earth. Mr Kent, like Joseph, disappears from the scene before his adoptive son grows up. Just in case you don't remember—Clark Kent goes on to become an ordinary news reporter, but contrary to his father's warning, he does interfere in the earth's history to save the woman he loves.

The Terminator

Finally, the production of a story that deals with a 'holy' family, spanning seven years and two films—*The Terminator* and *Terminator 2: Judgement Day*, both directed by James Cameron. The most significant feature of this story is the strong mother character, Sarah Connor, who along with her son John is the co-redeemer of the human race. Fighting against world domination by the machines, Sarah first encounters the future when a machine comes back in time; its task is to kill the mother-to-be of the human hero leading the resistance against the cyborgs. If it can eliminate him by going into the past to prevent his birth, the machines can subdue all human resistance in the future.

Time travel is another well-known science fiction motif, and of course is evocative of the notion in Christian theology of the sending of the pre-existent Word into a particular time and place on earth. Sarah escapes from the Terminator, with the help of a human warrior named Kyle. He is a fellow-fighter and friend of John Connor, and, like the Terminator, has also travelled back in time. He tells Sarah about her son, professing his willingness to 'die for John Connor', but more importantly he hails her as a 'legend' and brings her a message from the future: 'Thank you Sarah, for your courage through the dark years'.[38] As with the announcement to Mary in the Gospels, Sarah is struck with wonder at the thought of being the mother of a man destined for a special role, that of saving the human race. But unlike Mary, Sarah at first mocks and rejects the prediction, saying, 'I didn't ask for this honour, I don't want it—any of it'. But by the end of the first film, she is preparing for the birth of her son by going out into the desert; the last scene shows Sarah recording her thoughts—perhaps like Mary, keeping these things and pondering them in her heart—so that he will know one day the story of his birth. Like Mary, she can see the consequences of her acceptance of motherhood stretching into the future to all generations. Kyle is destined to be the father of John Connor, and, however short-lived, his love for and belief in Sarah are matched by his willing sacrifice in coming back through time to warn her about the Terminator—he knows he cannot go back into the future and may meet a violent death, but he comes to Sarah so that the future of humanity will be assured. He may not be a father in the conventional sense—impregnating a

---

38. *Terminator 2: Judgment Day* (James Cameron, 1991).

woman from the past and then dying before the child is born—but he is ready to protect his child in whatever way he can.

Terminator 2: Judgement Day brings us up to date with the story several years on; John is a young boy on the verge of his teenage years, rebellious and rash. His behaviour is the result of being fostered out to homes while Sarah is incarcerated in a mental institution due to her terrorist activities against technological 'big business'. She has accepted her role as the mother of a saviour figure by also attempting to avert the very circumstances which will require her son in the future to take on the saviour role.

Sarah has transformed herself into a warrior, but her son has not understood her determination to prevent the nightmare vision of annihilation that we will see in this clip. After she has escaped from the mental hospital, she goes out into the desert with her son and the cyborg that has come back from the future to protect him. They uncover hidden caches of weapons that will help them in destroying the technology, which will soon lead to the creation of Terminator robotics. John begins to form an affectionate bond with the cyborg, and Sarah finds new and ironic insights into the qualities of fatherhood.

Of all the would-be fathers who came and went over the years, this thing, this machine, was the only one who measured up. In an insane world, it was the sanest choice.[39]

These are Sarah's thoughts, but upon which values is she basing her observations? The cyborg gives John what the boy needs, protection and attention, without end. He will always be there for the boy, instead of offering excuses or being too busy to spend time with him. Again, although not a biological link, the relationship is one of support, trust and ultimately love (although technically the cyborg does not arrive with the capacity for emotion, but certainly departs with it). We could again identify these family values in terms of fidelity and obligation.

Conclusion

What do these films, particularly the two belonging to the religious film genre, say about family values? The fact is of course that the Nativity stories are widely recognized by biblical scholars as sections of the Gospels to which a literalist meaning has been assigned by many Christians. These stories are intertwined with and central to the celebration of the

---

39. *Terminator 2: Judgment Day* (James Cameron, 1991).

Christmas event in Christian worship and practice. The fact that the Holy Family has been held up by the Church as the ideal model for family life makes it very difficult to examine critically the interface between the Gospel accounts and the Church teaching that has grown up around them. Certainly, to observe the Stevens and Pasolini films with a view to extracting information about family values is to recognize a literalist and idealized reading of the Holy Family, which clings on to the popular Church image despite the anomalous profile of the family (as described in the introduction).

In the context of this article, two studies on the family are particularly relevant. William Goode, in his book *The Family* (1982), lists the factors or family values which help children in both tribal and industrial societies to socialize effectively. The most important are: warmth, nurturance and affection; identification of the child with the parent; consistency; and giving freedom to the child.[40]

Vergote and Tamayo found that their studies on parental figures[41] and the functions they fulfill with respect to their child produced differentiated but complementary factors: while the mother's character consists primarily of qualities of availability and tenderness, and only secondarily of authority, the father is characterized primarily by a sense of law and authority, and secondarily by availability or receptivity. But they conclude that contemporary society is seeing a shift away from the paternal kinds of authority traditionally associated with the family—a less authoritarian approach is called for in a situation where the father is 'more directly the one who gives the law, but…is less supported and authenticated by universally recognised values'.[42] This shift can also be noted in recent changing perceptions of God, whose characterization is shown in Vergote and Tamayo's study to be profoundly affected by our perceptions of our own fathers.

Using this assertion to construct an oppositional reading to the films we have examined here, perhaps the stern, authoritarian father figure—whether it be Joseph in *The Greatest Story Ever Told*, who refers to the patriarchal Scriptures while reflecting upon the future of his son, or the wise Jor-El in *Superman* who passes on his legacy to the child hurtling

---

40. W. Goode, *The Family* (Englewood: Prentice–Hall, 1982), p. 87.

41. A. Vergote and A. Tomayo, *The Parental Figures and the Representation of God* (Paris: Mouton, 1981), p. 272.

42. Vergote and Tomayo, *Parental Figures*, p. 272.

through space to Earth—is a character that is not so familiar or attractive to today's audiences. Those types of characters belong to another era, perhaps, when men had all the answers and were looked up to for leadership, guidance and paternal protection. The trend in our society, when so much about the family is changing, may be instead to welcome the father figure whose protection comes not out of patriarchal authority but out of nurture and affection, and the mother figure that is not merely a passive Madonna. Families today might instead value an active engagement in the process of parenting which we see in Pasolini's Joseph and which is matched by the unconventional but no less loving parental unit of Sarah and the cyborg—in short, families which contain 'values that enhance the condition of being human'.[43]

43. B. Berger and P. Berger, *The War over the Family* (London: Hutchinson, 1983), p. 187.

A Voice Crying in the Wilderness:
The Biblical Hero in Opera with Specific
Reference to John the Baptist

Anthony Axe

Introduction

The arts have been instrumental in giving fresh insight into the nature of biblical characters and influential in the way they are generally perceived. Perhaps painting has been the most influential in this respect but of its nature opera, too, is an excellent medium for developing and conveying character. In opera all the aesthetic media—music, poetry, drama, dance and the visual arts—work together simultaneously to the same end, complementing and reinforcing one another. The visual arts in set and costume design enable us to see the director's idea of what the character and the environment in which he operates look like.[1] The literary arts represented by the libretto, the poetic text through which the characters communicate with the audience, give a verbal description of the character and convey his thoughts about himself and others' thoughts about him. And, most importantly, we have the music which takes us beyond what language and the visual arts can express, creating an immediate emotional response which puts the listener in direct communication with the characters and situations presented on the stage. This article represents a preliminary investigation into opera's contribution to the fleshing-out of biblical characters. The main section of the paper deals with the operatic treatment of John the Baptist, chiefly because there are three operas that use his character as an essential part of their plot; no other biblical character has been given such attention by opera composers and librettists. Each opera deals with John the Baptist in a different way; collectively, they provide us

---

1. I use the masculine pronoun for character throughout this article, since I am dealing here almost exclusively with the male character in opera.

with excellent examples of how opera can deepen our understanding of the idea of character in the bible.

Surprisingly, given the interest in the subject matter, there are not many operas which concern themselves with biblical plots, let alone with biblical characters, and the reason for this is not difficult to ascertain. Censorship and public opinion thought the theatre an unfit medium for religious expression. Religious subjects were considered to be unsuitable material for entertainment in such a scandalous place as the theatre, with its legendary loose women, stage door Johnnies and immoral goings-on. Civic authorities were draconian with regard to opera and throughout the nineteenth century every new work had to pass the scrutiny of the censor before it was given the go-ahead for public performance. There was no end of religious oratorios which were, of their nature, given in concert form without scenery or costumes, where the members of the audience had to use their own imagination to conjure up the world of the bible and where each performance was imbued with a pseudo-religious veneer. But the representation on the stage of someone else's creation to do with a biblical subject was taboo. Pagan or non-Christian religions did not come into conflict with the censor, so Bellini, for example, could get away with showing the illicit love of a Druid priestess in *Norma* (1831). Religion or religious practice was regarded as a positive element in opera. Meyerbeer had no problem with *Les Huguenots* (1836) nor had Verdi with the almost mandatory religious scenes in his operas because religious belief in the context of political events or moral argument was the subject.[2]

Opera was invented and developed in Christian Europe and the religious sensibilities of the public had to be taken into account. During the late Renaissance, opera characters were often allegorical representations of ostensibly pagan virtues which concealed Christian concerns.[3] For the same reason, the first operas which dared to base their plot on a biblical subject took a story from the Old Testament rather than the New. Not only did this provide a good story and supply the spectacle, without which no nineteenth-century opera worth its salt would be complete, it also avoided giving offence to the mainly Christian public by avoiding New Testament characters. With Old Testament subjects, visually exciting scenes abound:

---

2.   For example, *I Lombardi* (1843), *Giovanna d'Arco* (1845), *Jérusalem* (1847), *Stiffelio* (1850), *Il Trovatore* (1853).

3.   In the opening and closing scenes of Cavalli's *La Calisto*, for example, Nature, Eternity and Destiny discuss whether Calisto, having been seduced by Jupiter and tormented by Juno, is worthy to take her place in the heavens.

Philistine temples can be pulled down, the occasional orgy can be included and the chorus spiced up in the exotic costume of ancient civilizations. In comparison, Jesus' life of its very nature offers little spectacle. The miracles were, on the whole, private affairs with God preferring to communicate through a human being and not by interfering dramatically with the workings of nature.

So the first biblical operas mined the Old Testament for their plots. Moses was a favourite and both Rossini and Schoenberg composed operas based on him, *Mosè in Egitto* (1818) and *Moses und Aaron* (concert performance 1954, full production 1959). Verdi produced *Nabucco* (1842) which deals with the Babylonian exile but in which there is no biblical character as such except the pagan Nebuchadnezzar. Saint-Saëns chose the story of Samson versus the Philistines for his biblical epic opera *Samson et Dalila* (1877). The Danish composer Carl Nielsen lighted upon the antagonism between Saul and David for his opera, *Saul and David* (1902). The New Testament is represented by only three works: Richard Strauss used the John the Baptist story for his opera *Salome* (1905) as did Massenet in *Hérodiade* (1881) and the still-living composer, Menotti, wrote the television opera *Amahl and the Night Visitors* (TV production 1951, stage production 1952) using the story of the Magi at the birth of Christ (Mt. 2.1-18). Recently a new opera which dares to use Jesus himself as its central character has been produced to critical acclaim and much discussion, *The Last Supper* (2000) by Harrison Birtwistle. This short catalogue contains every extant opera which has an overt biblical story as its subject.

When composers dared to present biblical characters in their works, the concerns of opera rather than those of Scripture were the motivating force. The essential material of opera plots shows little variation, love and/or the betrayal of love being the composer's prime concern. The resulting drama usually takes the form of a passionate love affair set against the vast canvas of some biblical event, the latter providing only the spectacle opera audiences crave. These operas, generally speaking, are not meant to increase understanding of the biblical stories or characters. This concern with operatic rather than biblical values usually results in the focus of the plot being shifted from the theological issues of the biblical account to the often fictitious love affair between the biblical hero and the woman to whom he is attracted. It is worth noting that every biblical opera has been written by a man which has resulted in the woman in the story being the more interesting character.

Samson et Dalilah and Parsifal

This is typified in *Samson et Dalila*, where Samson has been allotted the task of freeing the Israelites from Philistine captivity (Judg. 13–16). Now already we have a distortion of the historical and biblical 'facts' which have been sacrificed on the altar of operatic necessity. Instead of a territorial war being conducted between the Israelites and the Philistines for control of the Shephelah, we have a Babylonian exile situation where the Israelites are enslaved to them. At the beginning of the opera the Hebrews are lamenting their fate when Samson appears and stirringly encourages them to put their trust in God.

> Samson: It is the voice of the Lord who speaks through my mouth... Have you forgotten him, he who in his might once espoused your cause? He who, full of forgiveness, so often caused his oracles to speak for you, and rekindled your faith at the fire of his miracles? He who through the Sea was able to cleave a passage for our fathers fleeing a shameful slavery?
>
> The Hebrews: Those times are gone when the God of our fathers protected his children, harkened to their prayers!
>
> Samson: Miserable wretches, be quiet! Your lack of faith is a blasphemy.[4]

There is no doubt that Samson is a powerful character in the opera but the biblical Samson is characterized as an action hero rather than an orator or prophet. But, in a way, the comment is redundant—who remembers this bit from the opera anyway? What the listener does remember is the seductive aria sung by Delilah which expresses at the same time the allure yet the treachery of love alongside the attraction and danger of female sexuality. Saint-Saëns provides music which accentuates the sensuality of an already extremely sensuous text.

> Delilah: My heart opens to your voice as the flowers open to dawn's kisses! But, O my beloved, the better to dry my tears, let your voice speak once more! Tell me that you are coming back to Delilah for ever! Remind me once again of the promises of bygone days, those promises I loved! Ah! Answer my tenderness, fill me with ecstasy!
>
> Samson: Delilah! Delilah! I love you![5]

4. Libretto taken from the 1992 recording CDS 7544702, English translation EMI Records Ltd, 1963.

5. Libretto taken from the 1992 EMI recording CDS 7544702, English translation EMI Records Ltd, 1963.

In this instance, the biblical hero tries to keep his virtue and his mind set on God's commission, which results in his turning out to be quite boring dramatically. The woman, on the other hand, uses every ounce of her female allure and sexuality to seduce him, with the upshot that she gets all the best tunes and turns out to be by far the more complex character.

The question should be asked at this juncture whether or not an opera like *Samson et Dalila* adds to our understanding of the biblical characters it presents. There is an inherent danger in embroidering a biblical character with characteristics not evident in the original biblical account. If there is no biblical reference point then anything can be said of that character and, as has happened so often in opera, a different character results from this free treatment. That Samson becomes a Prophet rather than a Judge in the biblical sense is one fundamental distortion. But perhaps the feature of this particular story that has made most impact on the reader is that through his being besotted by a woman, Samson lost all that he stood for. That woman saps man's strength and diverts his mind from his God-given mission is a familiar theme in the arts. Saint Saëns' opera presents this fatal flaw in Samson's character

But there are operas which take a biblical character and put him or her in disguise, as it were. These operas treat characters as biblical types transferred to a different time and place from their biblical originals, but in which they are still recognizable from the Bible. One of the more subtle examples of character substitution is the eponymous character of Wagner's *Parsifal* (1882). The argument rages, and has raged for over a century, as to whether this Wagner opera is based on Christian themes or not.[6] Is the central character, Parsifal, Jesus and does the story involve specifically Christian concerns? Nowadays it is fashionable to shy away from or deconstruct any Christian influence there might be in the arts but it seems inescapable that Parsifal is a type of Christ and the concerns of the opera—sin, repentance, forgiveness and redemption—are, when juxtaposed in this way, specifically Christian. But in order to present this overtly religious work without it running into problems from the censor or the public, Wagner saw it as a form of liturgy which ingeniously bridged the gap between the church and the theatre. It was the opera which opened his newly built theatre in Bayreuth, the Festspielhaus, designed specifically to present his own operas. He called *Parsifal*, therefore, not an opera but a *Bühnenweihfestspiel*, a *festival play for the consecration of a stage*,

---

6.   L. Beckett, *Parsifal* (Cambridge: Cambridge University Press), pp. 103-28.

and the stage set for the Hall of the Grail at the premiere was inspired by the interior of Sienna Cathedral. Until quite recently it was the custom not to applaud at a performance of *Parsifal*. After all, one wouldn't applaud after a religious service in a cathedral.

Parsifal is a true hero. He saves the religious order, the Knights of the Grail, from destruction; he heals Amfortas the type of sexual sinner; he destroys utterly the evil power in the opera and brings salvation to all. At the start of the opera, Parsifal is depicted as the 'pure fool', a designation which immediately recalls St Paul's theme of being a fool for Christ (1 Cor. 4.10). The plot of the opera is concerned with the brotherhood of the Knights of the Grail whose task it is to guard two sacred artefacts associated with Christ's passion. The first is the holy grail, the cup used by Jesus at the last supper and which next day was utilized to collect his blood at the Crucifixion. The second artefact is the sacred spear with which the soldier pierced Jesus' side at the Crucifixion. The spear has been stolen by a disgruntled would-be knight, Klingsor, who now makes it his business to lure the pure knights into sin by means of his succubus-like flower maidens. Amfortas, the king and leader of the Grail Knights, having been seduced, was wounded by the sacred spear itself wielded by the evil Klingsor. The Brotherhood of the Grail has since been deteriorating but hope is kept alive by the prophecy that the 'pure fool', the only one who can put things right again, will appear one day and reverse its fortunes.

There are two pseudo-Eucharist scenes in the opera but perhaps the most Christ-like incident occurs towards the end, after Parsifal has gained knowledge through pity. After many years of wandering, he has found his way back to the Castle of the Grail and it is Good Friday. There Kundry, the woman who laughed at Jesus on the cross and who is thus in need of redemption, Magdalen-like, washes Parsifal's feet, pours ointment onto them from a phial, and dries them with her hair while the old Grail knight, Gurnemanz, anoints him as king. In Wagner's operas the stage directions are as important as the words sung:

> (*Kundry bathes Parsifal's feet with humble zeal. He watches her in silent wonder.*)
> Parsifal: You wash my feet, now bathe my head, O friend!
> (*Gurnemanz scoops his hand in the spring and sprinkles Parsifal's head.*)
> Gurnemanz: May this purity bless you, pure one! Thus may the load of all
>   guilt be washed away!
> (*While Gurnemanz solemnly sprinkles the water, Kundry draws from her bosom a golden phial and pours part of its contents over Parsifal's feet, which she dries with her hastily unbound hair.*)

Parsifal: You have anointed my feet, let Titurel's knight anoint my head.
(*During the following, Gurnemanz empties the phial over Parsifal's head,
gently strokes it and then folds his hands upon it.*)
Gurnemanz: Thus was it promised to us; thus do I bless your head, as king to
                greet you. Pure of heart! Pitying sufferer, enlightened healer!
                As you have endured the sufferings of the redeemed, lift the last
                burden from his head!
(*Unperceived, Parsifal scoops up water from the spring.*)[7]

The phrases Gurnemanz heaps on Parsifal: *Pure of heart! Pitying sufferer,
enlightened healer!* are usually reserved for Jesus. This opera has to be
taken more seriously than more traditional operas like *Samson et Dalila* in
that it does not rely on biblical spectacle for its effect but attempts to
expound on New Testament teaching. It treats the biblical text in the way a
sermon would deal with it, examining the text and bringing out theological
implications not obvious in the original. The biblical character's 'academic' thoughts are revealed in this way and we learn more about his
intellectual life. Here we are on rather safer ground than when the composer creates 'facts' to make the character more interesting on stage.
Theology can be said to come from what the character said or did but new
scenarios are in reality just fiction.

It may appear that opera is only able to express character through the
words sung. Every composer, almost without exception, begins to compose the music after he has received the libretto. Music is written to suit
words and rarely vice versa. Even in an opera such as Richard Strauss'
Salome, where Oscar Wilde's play has been used almost verbatim (in
translation, of course), the libretto is a selection of what the dramatists,
both librettist and composer, wished to use in order to create and define
their characters. The music is most often employed to impart extra meaning to the words by creating mood, emotion and colour. Thus a sung
sentence can mean different things depending on how it has been set to
music, the latter revealing subtext and hidden agenda in the libretto.
Wagner was quite exceptional in that he wrote both the words and music
for his operas and the creative process was a unity.

John the Baptist as Biblical Hero
Looking at the character of John the Baptist enables us to examine in some
detail how opera has treated the biblical hero. There are three operas in

---

7.   Libretto taken from the 1973 Decca recording 417 143-2, English translation
Lionel Salter, 1970.

which he appears, each one developing the character in an entirely different way from the other two, using or misusing in varying degrees information gleaned from the Gospels. The New Testament accounts of the Baptist depict him as an Old Testament prophet type, dressed in a camel hair garment tied by a leather belt, leading an ascetic life in the desert (Mt. 3.1-4; Mk 1.4-6). He is described as a messenger who prepares the way of the Lord (Mt. 3.3; Mk 1.3; Lk. 3.4). The people regard him as a genuine prophet (Mt. 14.5) yet he is accused of being possessed by a demon (Mt. 11.18; Lk. 7.33). He has disciples (Mt. 14.12; Mk 6.29; Lk. 7.18-24) and his ministry is so like that of Jesus that many believed Jesus to be John reincarnated (Mt. 14.2; Mk 6.14; Lk. 9.7). John is unafraid of those in authority (Mt. 3.7) and hurls insults at the Pharisees and Sadducees, calling them a brood of vipers, warning them of the wrath to come and encouraging them to bear fruit that befits repentance (Mt. 3.8).

Figure 40. *Salome Receives the Head of St John the Baptist* (1607–10 by Michelangelo Merisi da Caravaggio [1571–1610], The National Gallery, London/Bridgeman Art Library).

But John has his vulnerable side too evinced by his uncertainty about the identity of Jesus (Mt. 11.2f, Lk. 7.18-20). He is arrested and executed at the request of Herod's wife, Herodias, whom he accused of adultery for marrying her husband's brother and hence she held a grudge against him (Mk 6.17-19). Herod listens to John's preaching, is puzzled by it yet heard him 'gladly' and saw in him a righteous and holy man but was afraid of him and kept him from harm (Mk 6.20). He baptized people, preaching *a baptism of repentance for the forgiveness of sins* (Lk. 3.3) which is *good news* (Lk. 3.18). The most notorious piece of biblical information concerning John is that Herodias's daughter, Salome, danced for Herod who impetuously offered her anything she desired as a reward. Her mother, Herodias, persuaded her to ask for John's head on a platter, which was duly delivered (Mt. 14.6-11; Mk 6.21-28). John's body was then buried by his disciples (Mt. 14.12; Mk 6.29). In John's Gospel, the Baptist is mysticized. He was sent from God to bear witness to the light (Jn 1.6-8) and acclaims Jesus as *the Lamb of God who takes away the sins of the world* (Jn 1.29) and declares him to be the Son of God (Jn 1.34).

As with any of the arts, opera is subject to fashion and innovation, and the three operas under scrutiny exhibit their differences in the depiction of John the Baptist chiefly because of these two factors.

Hérodiade

The first opera to consider is *Hérodiade* by the French composer Jules Massenet. Note the title is not 'John the Baptist' but 'Hérodiade', that is, Herodias, Herod's wife. To all intents and purposes, Massenet need not have read the New Testament accounts with regard to John the Baptist because, although the opera uses the biblical characters famous from the accounts, the plot has nothing to do with the preaching or life of the saint. If all our information about John the Baptist came from this opera, then we would know a completely different character from the one we are acquainted with in the biblical text. *Hérodiade* is a good example of how an opera, because the character of the biblical celebrity is so altered, is unable to 'fill in the gaps' and make the historical person more real to us. Massenet's John the Baptist is a more rounded character than the biblical John the Baptist, but he is just not the same person.

Hérodiade received its premiere in Brussels in 1881 but was not seen in Paris until 1884. Massenet's librettists, Angelo Zanardini and Paul Milliet, used a short story with the same title written by Flaubert in 1877 as their source for the libretto. Surprisingly, and crucial to the understanding of the plot, is that Salome, unlike the dancing siren at the court of Herod Antipas, is a pure, simple, homeless girl knowing nothing of court life, who is in Jerusalem searching for the mother who abandoned her in childhood. Her mother is Herodias, a piece of information kept secret until the final dénouement, and so neither Herod nor Herodias has any idea who Salome is until just before the end of the opera. The musical idiom is typically French of the late nineteenth century and has nothing remotely biblical about it except for the spurious orientalism of the various dances.

It is a spectacular opera with plenty of work for the chorus which masquerades variously in the set pieces as merchants, slaves, courtiers, Jewish citizens and Roman soldiers. The nineteenth-century French taste for ballet in opera is catered for in dances for priestesses, female Babylonians, female Egyptians, female Phoenicians and female Gauls. The centre of interest in the opera is the love between John the Baptist and Salome, the latter being the vulnerable homeless girl mentioned earlier, who is hopelessly in love with John. This is totally non-biblical, of course, the New Testament story being that Salome danced at the court of Herod and at her mother Herodias's request, asked Herod for the head of John the Baptist. Here she is a groupie of John the Baptist who, she says, *is sweet, is good; his words are serene*, again hardly the character we know from the Gospels who was acerbic, badgering and urgent in his mission.

After a substantial amount of time spent on biblical and historical posturing, Massenet at last introduces us to John the Baptist through the eyes of Herodias.[8] She demands that Herod do something about the man she has just seen in the desert who insulted her. Her description of John matches in spirit that of the Gospels (Mt. 3.1, 4, 7, 10, 12; Mk 1.6). A terrifying prophetic figure accosted her, reminding her that her iniquities must be punished. Herod is startled when his wife demands John's head, a mere nod on the part of the composer in the direction John's fate in the Bible (Mk 6.2-6). His execution is merely reported at the end of the opera, clearing the way for the far more dramatic event of Salome's suicide.

> Hérodiade: Avenge me a supreme offence! From you, from you alone I
> expect my vengeance. I went this morning into the desert, and
> an almost naked man with a menacing look and a rough voice
> loomed up in the middle of the path! As when a storm wind
> rises, his voice, invoking destiny, pursues me, troubling me and

---

8.   There is a link here with Wagner's *Parsifal*. In Christian legend Herodias evolved into the female equivalent of the Wandering Jew, seeking atonement for her sins. Wagner based the enigmatic Kundry in *Parsifal* on this legendary character.

outraging me. 'Tremble,' he said, 'tremble, Jezebel! What cala-
mities have you caused! You must account to heaven! Go, the
anger of the prophet has called to the nations; soon you will
bow your head before their curses!'

Herod:	Who is this man?
Hérodiade:	It is John! It is the infamous apostle who preaches baptism and the new faith!
Herod:	What can I do? What do you want of me?
Hérodiade:	I must have his head!
Herod:	Gods![9]

The conversation between Herod and his wife, punctuated both gram-
matically and musically with an excess of exclamation marks, develops
into a domestic squabble in which Herodias recognizes Herod's fear of
John when he remarks that John is strong, revered everywhere and loved
by the Jews, consoling them in their misery. Of course, John's message
was anything but consoling to the Jewish authorities (Mt. 3.7-12) so even
his message has been altered for the purposes of the plot. The conversation
is interrupted by the appearance of John himself and, surprisingly, he is a
tenor. Tenors are romantic heroes in opera, not apocalyptic preachers. But
of course, the main interest in John, for Massenet, is that he is the object of
Salome's affections and, operatically speaking, a soprano cannot be in
love with a baritone—their voices would not blend well in the love duets!
John denounces Herodias as a Jezebel in tones that are hectoring rather
than biblically terrifying. But again we note the terror of Herod.

Herod, Hérodiade:	Ah! It is him again!
John:	Jezebel! No pity! Strike then! No one will ever have pity on your suffering! Woe upon you!
Herod:	Ah! He pursues her within my palace! It is he! Oh, what terror! His voice strikes terror in me. Fellow! Cease your threats. Fear my wrath.
John:	Calm your wrath. Be gone! Do not talk of being offended. You whom the Lord already weighs in the balance![10]

As the royal couple flee into the palace, Salome appears on the scene. It is
obvious from the change in the tone of the music, from hyper-dramatic to
hyper-romantic, that she is in love with John. It is a pure idealized love

9.   Libretto taken from the 1995 EMI recording CDS 7243 5 55378 2 9, English
translation Hugh Graham.

10.   Libretto taken from the 1995 EMI recording CDS 7243 5 55378 2 9, English
translation Hugh Graham.

(something to remember when examining Strauss' opera on the same theme) but he is determined to protect his virtue and tells her that their destinies are entirely different and they must go their separate ways.

Salome: John! I see you once more!

John: Child, what do you want of me?

Salome: What I want, John, is to tell you that I love you and that I am yours!...that I love you and that my whole being hangs on the sound of your voice!

John: Salome, what are you saying?

Salome: I belong to you, I love you. Away from you I was suffering, and see, I am healed! I belong under your gaze; my face is bathed in tears, and my heart trembles with happiness!

John: What can your shining light wish for in the shadows of my life? What would become of your newly-blossoming youth on my stony path? For you, it is the time when the rashest desires invite kisses on hungry lips; for you it is the season for love![11]

Salome now, instead of kisses, is given a sermon in return but the message is couched in terms of the French Second Empire rather than the Roman Empire:

John: Do you not hear the sacred hymns which rise up and the vows of mystic souls as they spread their golden wings? Child, behold this dawn, new faith is about to be born. Child, behold this dawn of faith and immortality.[12]

However, Salome hears what she wants to hear and her response is not what John intended. 'Ah! I hear you', she says, but then reveals that she hasn't been listening:

I adore you! The flash of your eyes brighter than the dawn illumines the heavens! I love you! I adore you! I am yours![13]

What's a man to do, particularly if he's a biblical operatic hero?

An important theme in the opera is Herod's obsession with Salome, whom he has seen earlier in the market place. With regard to John, he intends to use him to advance the revolt against the Romans. But in the

---

11. Libretto taken from the 1995 EMI recording CDS 7243 5 55378 2 9, English translation Hugh Graham.

12. Libretto taken from the 1995 EMI recording CDS 7243 5 55378 2 9, English translation Hugh Graham.

13. Libretto taken from the 1995 EMI recording CDS 7243 5 55378 2 9, English translation Hugh Graham.

closing spectacular scene of Act II, a powerful confrontation between Herod and the Roman Proconsul results in the latter, in a somewhat unlikely outburst, declaring religious freedom for all. John appears and proclaims the superiority of spiritual over temporal power, thus Herod's plans for using John to get rid of the Romans is doubly undermined. However, lest we forget John's real significance, the beginning of Act III shows Phanuel, a Chaldean astrologer at Herod's court, ruminating on John's character. His description accords well with what we think we know about John. What is John? he asks.

> Is he a man? Is he a god? His voice rolls like thunder; he says you will find, if you seek, powers will crumble into dust! People, gird up your loins! And the lowly, as he passes, seem to await a signal, and kings hide their face in the folds of their royal mantle![14]

John the Baptist in that passage is allotted the ambiguous aspect of Jesus' identity, whether he is human or divine (Mk 8.27-30). He is also credited with some of his preaching too, namely, the destiny of earthly glory, principally that of Jerusalem (Mt. 24.2), the admonition to the people to gird up their loins (Lk. 12.35) and the advice that if they wish to find, then they must seek (Mt. 7.7).

In the following scene we learn that John has been arrested because Herod wants to placate the Romans and the Pharisees who fear for their power over the people. The Jewish authorities' hatred of John is presented in a scene set, improbably, in the Temple. This operatic version of the Herodian Temple has no barriers and courts excluding various degrees of ritual impurity. On the contrary, it seems open to all including dancing girls, a Roman Proconsul who addresses the worshippers, Herod the King and, of course, priests. These last implore Herod to do away once and for all with the Baptist. Their pleas are taken from the Gospel accounts of the Passion when the priests demand that Jesus be executed. John is even described as being Galilean so that Herod, being ruler of Galilee, has to take the fatal decision to execute John. Obviously John wasn't interesting enough on his own so he has been practically deified by the composer. He is now a false messiah whom Herod will attempt to use for his own political purposes. If John complies he will be allowed to live.

At this point John is brought in and what we now witness is a copy of the trial of Jesus as seen in the Gospels (Mt. 26.57, 59-68, 27.11-26;

14. Libretto taken from the 1995 EMI recording CDS 7243 5 55378 2 9, English translation Hugh Graham.

Mk 14.53, 55-65; 15.1-15; Lk. 22.66–23.1-5, 13-25). The crowd notes his humility and majesty evident in Jesus' Gospel conversations with both Caiaphas and Pilate. Herod, in the opera a Pontius Pilate look-alike, questions him. John's message is that of the angels at the birth of Christ, 'Peace to men of good will' (Lk. 2.14). When John declares that he preaches freedom the priests note this as evidence of treason towards Caesar, reminiscent of their, 'We have no king but Caesar!' in the Passion narratives (Jn 19.15). Herod, again taking the place of Pilate, wants to release John, not because he is innocent as in the Gospels but because he is mad. In an aside, Herod asks John if he will be his ally in subverting Roman rule and John refuses. His fate is now sealed. The priests call for his crucifixion, not beheading, Herodias accuses him of blasphemy and the crowd adds its cries for crucifixion. John in this opera has become Jesus.

Herod:	Fellow, what is your name?
John:	I am John, son of Zechariah.
Herod:	So is it true that by your prophecy the people are stirred up?
John:	I have said: peace to men of good will!
Herod:	What arms have you, to establish your creed? What arms?…
John:	I have only one weapon: the word!
Herod:	So, then, what is your goal?
John:	My goal? Freedom!
Crowd:	Freedom! Freedom!
Priests, Hérodiade, Herod, Vitellius:	He insults Caesar! Death to him! Torture!
Herod:	Truly this man cannot be condemned: he is a madman! (*quietly, to John*) Thanks to me the crowd is volatile; one word!… Would you serve my plans and my hatred?
John:	God does not lower his gaze to the plotting of kings!
Priests:	He insults Caesar; death to him! Torture! Majesty, would you allow this insult? He has disregarded our law! Death to him! Put him on the cross, and if he is to live let his God deliver him! death to the blasphemer!
Hérodiade:	Death to the blasphemer! Crucify this false Messiah! Death to him! Death to him![15]

Salome now reveals publicly that she is in love with John, and Herod's jealousy seals the Baptist's fate. Act IV takes place in a vault in the temple

15. Libretto taken from the 1995 EMI recording CDS 7243 5 55378 2 9, English translation Hugh Graham.

serving as John's prison. He sings the standard farewell-to-life aria but some interesting theological points are included. John calls himself the Son of God and also admits to himself that he loves Salome. Jesus' doubts came when he was on the Cross and had to do with his feeling that God had forsaken him. The sign of God's forsaking John is that he has sent this profane love for Salome to deflect him from his divine mission.

> John: I have no regrets for the prison of earthly life; escaping humanity, I go, calm and tranquil, to be wrapped round with eternity! I have no regrets and yet, oh, frailty! I think of that child whose radiant features are always before my eyes, whose memory weighs me down! O Lord, if I am thy son, tell me: why dost thou suffer love to come and shake my faith? And if I come out of this struggle, bruised and vanquished, tell me who has allowed it. Whose fault is this downfall? Memory which weighs me down... Lord, am I thy son?[16]

The following scene is a banquet where Salome is pleading for the life of John the Baptist, quite the reverse of the biblical account where she insistently demands his execution. Even Herodias is moved at this point but it is too late. The executioner appears with a bloodied sword. But there is a shock awaiting us at the end. Salome runs to stab Herodias who cries, *'Spare me, I am your mother!'* This news is too much for Salome who turns the dagger on herself and dies.

The critics were not complimentary about the opera after its Paris premiere. Camille Saint-Saëns, the composer of *Samson et Dalila*, who was acting at that time as music critic for a Parisian journal wrote with more than a pinch of irony:

> Help, Flaubert! Help me, all of you who have been charmed by this strange type of lascivious adolescence and unconscious cruelty called Salome, the very flower of evil grown in the shadow of the Temple, enigmatic and fascinating. Come and explain to me how Salome is changed into a Mary Magdalen, or rather do not explain. I do not seek to understand, and I will not busy myself with the eccentricities of a poem that escapes my feeble intellect.

Another critic found the characters of all the personages 'denatured', thought Salome had been turned into a kind of Hebraic grisette, and the prophet John into a simpleton who is finally ensnared by the hussy's wiles.

---

16. Libretto taken from the 1995 EMI recording CDS 7243 5 55378 2 9, English translation Hugh Graham.

The entire opera is fictional, having very little to do with the biblical John the Baptist. Massenet's Salome does not live at court. She is not the seductive dancer with a hold over Herod that the Gospels would have us believe. Instead she is a homeless lost individual whose life finds its only purpose in pursuing an impossible love. The main plot of the opera is an examination of John's relationship with Salome, a relationship of which the New Testament accounts are entirely ignorant. In fact the interesting relationship in the Bible is between Salome and her mother, Herodias. It is because her mother wants John dead that Salome asks Herod for his head. In *Hérodiade*, Salome goes all out to preserve his life.

Salome

Massenet's *Hérodiade* is about as far from the biblical story of John the Baptist as is possible without losing touch with it altogether. *Salome*, in contrast, is altogether more faithful to the character of John found in the Gospels. In 1903 Richard Strauss saw Oscar Wilde's play, *Salome*,[17] and recognized immediately the operatic possibilities of its poetic language and vivid imagery. The inherent musical quality of the language was also recognized by Wilde himself who wrote that it contained 'refrains whose recurring motifs make it like a piece of music and bind it together as a ballad',[18] a description that would be just as applicable to Strauss's method of composition. Because of the musicality of the original play, Strauss was able to use it, after making extensive cuts for the sake of conciseness, almost word for word for the libretto of *Salome*.[19] The opera, like the play, is louche, violent and erotic. The music, produced in 1906, sounds much more modern than that of Massenet, yet is firmly grounded in the same romantic tradition. Its chromaticism reflects vividly the decadence and voluptuousness of Herod's court and the work is a heady concoction of religion, sex and murder.

The entire action takes place at the court of Herod where John, called in this opera by the Hebrew equivalent Jokanaan, is already imprisoned when the opera begins. His prison is a cistern in the middle of the courtyard of

17. Oscar Wilde, *Salomé*, translated from the original French version by Lord Alfred Douglas, in *The Works of Oscar Wilde* (London: Spring Books, 1963).

18. Oscar Wilde, *De Profundis* (letter to Lord Alfred Douglas from Reading Gaol, January–March 1897), in Rupert Hart-Davis (ed.), *The Letters of Oscar Wilde* (London: Hart-Davis, 1962).

19. See N. Del Mar, *Richard Strauss* (London: Barrie & Rockliff, 1965), I, pp. 241-46.

Herod's palace so even when not on stage his presence is felt constantly in the midst of the action. And this time John is a baritone! The stentorian tones that this type of voice can produce are needed to convey the seriousness of the Baptist's message, which is first heard issuing from the depths of the cistern where he has been imprisoned. The choice of prison invites comparison with the Old Testament prophet Jeremiah who was also kept in a cistern and railed against the establishment (Jer. 38.6). Already the opera widens our perspective on John the Baptist in that we can now compare him with one of the great Old Testament prophets. John the baritone's words are strictly biblical, gleaned from John the Baptist's preaching in the gospels (Lk. 3.16) and the prophecies of Isaiah (Isa. 35.5-7).

> John: (*from the cistern*) After me shall come another mightier than I. I am not worthy so much as to unloose the latchet of his shoes. When he comes, the solitary places shall be glad. When he comes, the eyes of the blind shall see the day, and the ears of the deaf shall be opened.[20]

When Salome first hears his voice, her obsession with him begins its dreadful course towards their mutual destruction. The opera *Salome* presents the Gospel story of John's beheading as the confrontation between two obsessed human beings: John is obsessed with his mission and with the adultery of Herodias and Salome's non-biblical sexual obsession with John is distilled into the obsession to 'kiss his mouth'. It begins when she hears the voice of John emanating from the cistern, and she asks that he be brought out so that she can have a closer look at him. John is led in, his obsession becoming increasingly obvious as he continues to spout invective against Herodias, detailing at length the catalogue of her abominations. He does not notice Salome until she stands directly in front of him. Herein lies another theme of the opera. Far from being a prospective lover of Salome, John fails totally to see her as a person in her own right and knows her only as the daughter of a vice-ridden mother. Her origins as daughter of Herodias count for everything, her individuality for nothing. His refusal to see her only increases Salome's desperation that she be noticed and desired by him. John asks:

> Who is this woman who is looking at me? ... I know not who she is. I do not wish to know who she is.

---

20. Libretto taken from the 1962 Decca recording 414 414-2, English translation from Oscar Wilde's *Salomé*.

Salome proudly gives her full title:

> I am Salome, daughter of Herodias, Princess of Judaea.

Then John repulses her because of her mother's reputation:

> Back, daughter of Babylon!... Thy mother hath filled the earth with the wine of her iniquities.[21]

But Salome, already well into her obsession, does not hear the insults. Only the beauty of his voice registers with her and here we have the first instance of borrowed imagery from the Song of Solomon, 'The voice of my beloved!' (Song 2.8, 14). Beautiful is the last epithet that springs to mind when describing John's voice as it thunders invective from his subterranean prison. Furthermore, it would be difficult to think of anything less attractive than this unwashed stinking man from the desert, dressed in an old camel skin, with breath reeking from eating locusts and reeking even more from spending time in the cistern. But Salome sees him through the rose-coloured spectacles of her obsession and instantly desires him, desiring to touch his body. The discrepancy between what she sees and what is actually there could not be greater.

> Salome: Jokanaan, I am amorous of thy body! Thy body is white like the lilies of a field that the mower hath never mowed. Thy body is white like the snows that lie on the mountains of Judaea. The roses in the garden of the Queen of Arabia are not so white as the body. Neither the roses in the garden of the Queen of Arabia, nor the feet of the dawn when they light on the leaves, nor the breast of the moon when she lies on the breast of the sea...there is nothing in the world so white as thy body. Let me touch thy body.
>
> John: Back, daughter of Babylon! By woman came evil into the world. Speak not to me. I will not listen to thee. I listen but to the voice of the Lord God.[22]

John regards himself as inviolable and consecrated to his mission so, having been repulsed, Salome for a short while sees him as he really is and tells him his body is hideous. But then the process is repeated as she turns her attention to his hair. But the more he rejects her, the more she desires him and finally she realizes that the fulfilment of her desire lies in kissing his mouth. This idea, too, is taken from the beginning of the Song of

21. Libretto taken from the 1962 Decca recording 414 414-2, English translation from Oscar Wilde's *Salomé*.

22. Libretto taken from the 1962 Decca recording 414 414-2, English translation from Oscar Wilde's *Salomé*.

Solomon: *O that you would kiss me with the kisses of your mouth!* (Song 1.2). In describing John's body, his hair and his mouth, Salome draws her imagery not from the Gospel accounts but freely from the Song of Songs (see for example, Song 2.1 *roses*, 2.2 *lilies*). John parries her sexual flattery and attempts to preach the word of God to her but really does not know how to cope with her insistence on kissing his mouth. So, of his own accord he retreats to the cistern defeated.

John: Art thou not afraid, daughter of Herodias?
Salome: Let me kiss thy mouth.
John: Daughter of adultery, there is but one who can save thee. So seek him. He is in a boat on the Sea of Galilee, and he talketh with his disciples. Kneel down on the shore of the sea, and call to him by his name. When he cometh to thee (and to all who call on him he cometh), bow thyself at his feet and ask of him the remission of thy sins.
Salome: Let me kiss thy mouth.
John: Cursed be thou! Daughter of an incestuous mother, be thou accursed!
Salome: Let me kiss thy mouth, Jokanaan.
John: I will not look at thee, thou art accursed, Salome, thou art accursed. Thou art accursed.
(*He goes down into the cistern.*)[23]

This scene is a good illustration of how the music deepens the meaning of the words. Each protagonist is singing in a different key. John's music, reflecting the certainty of his calling, is firmly grounded in the stable key of C major and sounds sturdily hymn-like whereas Salome's music is in the unstable region of C sharp minor. During the argument John's rock-like music degenerates as it is drawn into Salome's slippery and elusive musical environment, suggesting that he is losing control of the situation.[24] He now physically disappears from the scene for a long time and the emphasis shifts to Salome's relationship with Herod.

A short interlude follows where the Jews ask that Herod hand John over to them and during the course of the conversation John's nature is considerably developed, employing ideas found in the Gospels. *He is a*

23. Libretto taken from the 1962 Decca recording 414 414-2, English translation from Oscar Wilde's *Salomé*.

24. For further discussion of this and other aspects of the way the music works in symbiosis with the libretto, see Derrick Puffett, 'Salome as Music Drama', in D. Puffett (ed.), *Richard Strauss: 'Salome'* (Cambridge: Cambridge University Press, 1989), pp. 58-87.

holy man...a man who has seen God (Mk 6.20). The Jews have heard it said *that Jokanaan himself is the prophet Elijah* (Mk 1.6). At this point Salome takes control of the situation and sets out to seduce Herod, an easy task because he is obsessed with her. She manipulates him, by performing the Dance of the Seven Veils, into ordering the execution of John, and she is as persistent in obtaining John's head as she was on kissing his mouth. Again in the opera there is close adherence to the biblical story, Herod offering Salome half his kingdom (Mk 6.23) and she insisting that the head be served on a platter (Mk 6.25).

The arm of the executioner appears out of the cistern bearing the silver charger on which lies the head of John the Baptist. Salome seizes it exultantly and expresses her triumphant determination to kiss his mouth. He is now in her power but, in a way, he has been removed from it.

> (*A huge black arm, the arm of the executioner, comes forth from the cistern, bearing on a silver shield the head of Jokanaan. Salome seizes it.*)
> Salome: Ah! Thou wouldst not suffer me to kiss thy mouth, Jokanaan. Well, I will kiss it now. I will bite it with my teeth as one bites a ripe fruit. Yes, I will kiss thy mouth.[25]

Then follows a passage in which Salome exults at the victory of her desire over John's reluctance to have anything to do with her. In a particularly ghoulish passage she tells the head how ugly it is and that its fate will be unspeakable. Then the tone changes as her obsession with John takes over and, to the strains of the most meltingly erotic, beautiful and achingly despairing orchestral accompaniment, she once more sings the praises of his beauty, her words recalling again the Song of Solomon (Song 1.15; 4.1):

> Ah! Jokanaan, Jokanaan, thou wert beautiful. Thy body...was a garden full of doves and silver lilies.

She realizes that the sole object of her desire has been put beyond her reach forever. The vision of Salome drooling over the John the Baptist's severed head fills Herod with disgust and he orders the lights to be quenched. In the darkness Salome, at last, kisses the mouth of the Baptist. But what she tastes there is not the bitter taste of death but the bitter taste of love and she triumphantly declares that at last she has fulfilled her ambition, her obsession, and has kissed his mouth. The opera seems to be

---

25. Libretto taken from the 1962 Decca recording 414 414-2, English translation from Oscar Wilde's *Salomé*.

resolved, but the chord which should form part of the resolving cadence is unexpectedly one of the most discordant sounds ever heard in the opera house. Herod orders his guards to kill Salome and she is promptly dispatched.

> Salome: Ah! I have kissed thy mouth, Jokanaan. Ah! I have kissed thy mouth. There was a bitter taste on thy lips. Was it the taste of blood? No! But perchance it is the taste of love... They say that love hath a bitter taste... But what of that? What of that? I have kissed thy mouth, Jokanaan. I have kissed thy mouth.[26]

John the Baptist and Salome are dead and Herod finds his situation worse than before. Nothing is resolved.

Strauss's opera is unique in presenting a picture of John the Baptist which increases our awareness of his prophetic role. In it he appropriates the words of the two great prophets of the Old Testament, Isaiah and Jeremiah, inviting the listener to make a comparison between them and himself. Furthermore, we are encouraged to flesh out the Gospel picture of John and consider his attractiveness by use of the sensual and beautiful imagery of the Song of Solomon. The music and setting supply the detailed picture of the exotic, ancient oriental court of Herod missing from the prosaic Gospel accounts; the human emotions of the protagonists are delineated in a way that would have been foreign to the evangelists. In the Gospel accounts the story is presented in a straightforward manner, little attention being given to what motivates the characters to behave as they do. In Richard Strauss's *Salome* each principal character is imbued with all-too-human motivations for their outrageous actions. John the Baptist, in particular, is shown to adopt his heroic stance because of deep commitment to his mission and his utter conviction that he is on the side of God.

Die Meistersinger von Nürnberg

Finally an opera which can be regarded as the apotheosis of John the Baptist, Wagner's *Die Meistersinger von Nürnberg*. This is not ostensibly about John the Baptist but the entire action takes place on the eve and day of his feast, Midsummer's Day. The plot is set in mediaeval Nuremberg where music is under the strict control of the Guild of Mastersingers. A young knight, Walther, has fallen in love with Eva, the daughter of one of the principal burghers but her father has offered her as the prize for the

---

26. Libretto taken from the 1962 Decca recording 414 414-2, English translation from Oscar Wilde's *Salomé*.

winner of the song contest, held annually on the feast of John the Baptist. The plot concerns the efforts of the young knight to compose and sing an original song which will satisfy the Mastersingers and win the competition. Wagner always wrote his own libretto and so the music and words of this opera are inseparable, conceived as an artistic unity.

That the setting of the opera on the feast of John the Baptist is important is indicated by the opening chorus which is sung in St Catherine's Church in Nuremberg. It is basically a chorale after the style of Bach, the words of which form a summary of the theology concerning John the Baptist. Although there are points in common with the Gospel accounts of John the Baptist, notably Jesus coming for baptism by John (Mt. 3.13-15; Mk 1.9), the historical and biblical character has passed into the devotional and theological lives of ordinary Christians as they pray that the Baptist will be there to meet them when they cross the heavenly Jordan from this life into the next.

> Congregation When the Saviour came to thee,
> willingly accepted thy baptism,
> offered himself up to a sacrificial death,
> he gave the covenant for our salvation
> that we might consecrate ourselves through
> his baptism so as to be worthy of his sacrifice.
> Noble Baptist! Christ's precursor!
> Receive us graciously there at the River Jordan.[27]

Act II is set on Midsummer's Eve, the eve of St John's Day and, as the curtain rises, we see a group of apprentices singing of the occasion. Here *Johannistag* is equated with Midsummer Day and midsummer madness.

> Apprentices Johannistag! Johannistag!
> Flowers and ribbons in plenty!
> Every man woos as he wishes…
> Hurrah! Hurrah! Johannistag![28]

The conjunction of the feast of John the Baptist and Midsummer's Day imparts a certain licence which encourages unorthodox behaviour, a far cry from the Baptist's biblical call to repentance. So all-pervasive among the population is this madness that a riot ensues which closes Act II.

---

27. Libretto taken from the 1971 EMI recording CDS 7 49683 2, English translation by Peter Branscombe.

28. Libretto taken from the 1971 EMI recording CDS 7 49683 2, English translation by Peter Branscombe.

The principal character in this delightful comedy is a middle-aged widower and shoemaker, Hans Sachs, a character based on the historical person who wrote a famous chorale extolling the Reformation.[29] The name, Hans, is an affectionate diminutive for Johannes or John. The shaker and mover of this opera is therefore named after John the Baptist. At the start of Act III it is the morning of St John's Day. Hans Sachs is reading in his workshop and is interrupted by his apprentice, David, who is due to become a journeyman and so sings his test piece to show that he is ready to graduate. It is a song about John the Baptist but contains a legend about a woman from Nuremberg who went all the way to the River Jordan to be baptized by John only to return home and find, on the banks of Nuremberg's own river, a man called Hans—another John. This reminds the apprentice that St John's Day is also his master's name day and so he gives him a present.

> David   'On Jordan's bank St. John did stand
> to baptise all the peoples of the world:
> a woman came from a distant land,
> from Nuremberg she had hastened;
> her little son she carried to the river's bank,
> received there baptism and name;
> but when they then took their homeward way
> and got back to Nuremberg again,
> in German land it soon transpired
> that the person who on the Jordan's bank was named John, was
> called Hans on the River Peignitz.' Hans! Hans! Sir! Master! It's
> your name day! No! How can one forget something like that! Here!
> Here, the flowers are for you, the ribbons,—and what else is there
> now? Yes, here! Look, Master! A splendid cake! Wouldn't you like
> to try the sausage too?[30]

Scene 2 of Act III is the culmination of the St John's Day celebrations and the setting for the song competition. The scene is spectacular as the craftsmen's guilds process with their floats and standards, with the Mastersingers arriving by boat and the citizens of Nuremberg all assembling in the meadows to celebrate the feast day of their patron saint, John the Baptist, appropriately by the river. The opera transforms him into a local industry. The apprentices eventually call the crowd to order but at that

29. Hans Sachs was 28 when he first read Luther's writings and in 1523 he wrote the poem *Die Wittembergisch Nachtigall* in his honour.

30. Libretto taken from the 1971 EMI recording CDS 7 49683 2, English translation by Peter Branscombe.

moment Hans Sachs arrives and the crowd greet him with his own composition, the hymn to the Reformation, 'Wach auf, es nahet gen den Tag' (Awake! The dawn is drawing near).

> The Crowd   Awake! The dawn is drawing near; I hear a blissful nightingale singing in the green grove,
> its voice rings through hill and valley;
> night is sinking in the west, the day arises in the east,
> the ardent red glow of morning
> approaches through the gloomy clouds.[31]

Conclusion

Opera plays its part, as do the other fine arts, in offering the listener new and fresh insights into biblical characters. In general, the writers of the New Testament were not so much interested in developing character as in expounding theological principles and so we need the imagination of practitioners in the arts to make these ancient characters more human and more alive for us. Opera presents John the Baptist as a tenor in love, a baritone in trouble and even voiceless yet vividly present in the lives of ordinary people. It tells us nothing about John the Baptist that we cannot glean from the Bible but it invites us to elaborate on his humanity and those aspects of his humanity that have a universal ring across the centuries and to which anyone can easily relate.

Does opera enable us to see biblical characters more clearly and does it bring what they stand for into sharper focus? In Strauss' opera, Salome is certainly not interested in John's message which is only vital and immediate to John himself. Complaining of his lack of interest in her, she herself is not really interested in John the person, but only in his body. The person obsessed shows little interest in the true nature of their obsession, falling instead for their own construct of that person. Salome's perspective is certainly not shared by the Gospel writers. The French composer, Massenet, was interested in the Baptist's message from the point of view of plot; for him it was a source of revolution and of bringing the people together. It first attracted the gentle Salome of *Hérodiade* but she is interested more in John the man than John the prophet. She really is in love with his spirit, unlike Strauss' Salome who lusts after his body. Wagner with *Die Meistersinger* is, by contrast, only interested in the message and

---

31. Libretto taken from the 1971 EMI recording CDS 7 49683 2, English translation by Peter Branscombe.

what it means for the people of Nuremberg. The person of John does not really enter into it, in the same way as the person of Christ frequently does not enter into popular religion or abstract theology. But John's message has given the people their patron saint and his work in connection with Jesus has given them their religious devotion.

A multitude of current approaches to the Bible explore how art, literature and film can be used as a means of interpreting the biblical text. Little is done on music and almost none on opera, and the reasons for this are not so difficult to discern. First of all very few operas exist which are based on a biblical theme so there is much less material up for discussion. But more importantly, a painting, sculpture, work of literature or film is a finished product and it is durable in the form in which the artist intended. Once it goes on show to the public it is not going to change through the years. Caravaggio's painting of John the Baptist (Fig. 40), for example, is the same today as it was on the day when he completed it and will always be exactly as he wanted it. So what could be said of it in Caravaggio's time is just as valid today. More insight may be revealed with the passing of time but any valid critical comment is always based on the original work.

With opera, criticism is of an entirely different sort because what is being discussed is never the same. It is true that the words and music were finished for all time after the composer had dotted his last crotchet but there is always the element of interpretation to consider which makes every production, if not every performance, a different work of art. Operas are ephemeral. One director's production of *Salome* can almost be an entirely different piece from that of another director. Using the same words and music, the same opera in fact, John the Baptist can be presented as a bigoted and unsympathetic prophet, a revolutionary leader or a victim of human passion. Three different John the Baptists can be obtained from the same work of art. In a sense, an opera does not exist until it is performed, unless it is being interpreted by someone other than the artist who produced the work. And in every production there are many artists involved who interpret and embellish the composer's original vision. The conductor interprets the music, the director puts his or her stamp on the whole piece, the designer overlays his or her vision on the look of the production and each singer creates his or her own role. For this reason productions rather than operas are the subject of discussion.

In addition, the individual's reaction to any one performance is the same as his or her reaction to any work of art. We bring our own experience and emotional baggage with us, so when we attend an opera performance our response to it is largely personal and highly subjective. When reading the biblical text our imagination fleshes out the perfunctory characterization we find there. In an opera written by a great composer, the imagination of others helps us make a rounded character from the two-dimensional biblical original.

A new opera is not a common occurrence these days and religious subjects are not fashionable in our modern world so the chances of opera on a religious subject appearing would seem to be extremely unlikely. Yet a biblical opera, commissioned by Glyndebourne from the contemporary composer Harrison Birtwistle, received its premiere recently at the Berlin Deutsche Staatsoper.[32] The subject of the opera was the biblical hero par excellence, Jesus, and his encounter with the apostles at the Last Supper. Nowadays our moral sensibilities are dulled and so Jesus can be shown on the stage without fear of the censor's red pencil or public outrage. The composer himself set down the aims of the opera thus: *What really interests me about The Last Supper is that it is about a group of ordinary men—some of them fishermen, 'the salt of the earth'—caught up in something extraordinary.*

This comment presents in a nutshell how opera can bring biblical characters to life for us. He sees the apostles as 'ordinary men' whose lives were fundamentally changed by circumstances, an occurrence most people experience at some time in their lives. The apostles, biblical characters all, biblical heroes some, in this way become more familiar, less remote and therefore more congenial to us. Opera with a biblical theme, it seems, is not dead but alive and well as it adapts itself to a new millennium.

RECOMMENDED RECORDINGS

Samson et Dalila, EMI CDS7 54470-2 (2 CDs), L'Opéra Bastille Ch. & O, Myun-Whun Chung, 1992. *Samson*—P. Domingo, *Dalila*—K. Meier.
Parsifal, Decca 417 143-2 (4 CDs), VPO, Solti, 1973. *Parsifal*—R. Kollo, *Gurnemanz*—G. Frick, *Kundry*—C. Ludwig.
Hérodiade, EMI Dig. CDC5 55378-2 (3 CDs), O du Capitol Toulouse, Plasson, 1995. *John*—B. Heppner, *Salome*—C. Studer.

---

32. *The Last Supper*, music by Harrison Birtwistle, libretto by Robin Blaser, Premiere 2000.

Salome, Decca 414 414-2 (2 CDs), VPO, Solti, 1962. *Jokanaan*—E. Waechter, *Salome*—B. Nilsson.

Die Meistersinger von Nürnberg, EMI CMS5 67086-2 (4 CDs), 1971. BPO, Karajan. *Walther*—R. Kollo, *Hans Sachs*—T. Adam, *Eva*—H. Donath, *David*—P. Schreier, *Magdalena*—R. Hesse.

BIBLIOGRAPHY

Abrams, Judith Z., *Judaism and Disability* (Washington, DC: Gallandet University Press, 1998).

Ainsworth, Maryan W., and Keith Christiansen (eds.), *From Van Eyck to Bruegel* (New York: Metropolitan Museum of Art, 1998).

Aldrich, Thomas B., *Judith of Bethulia: A Tragedy* (Boston and New York: Houghton, Mifflin, 1904).

Alexander, P.S., 'Retelling the Old Testament', in D.A. Carson and H.G.M. Williamson (eds.), *It Is Written: Scripture Citing Scripture* (Cambridge: Cambridge University Press, 1988), pp. 99-118.

Allen, T.W., and E.E. Sikes, *The Homeric Hymns* (London: Macmillan, 1904).

Amis, K., *Rudyard Kipling* (London: Thames and Hudson, 1975).

Amishai-Maisel, Ziva, *Depiction and Interpretation: The Influence of the Holocaust on the Visual Arts* (Oxford: Pergamon Press, 1993).

Andrews, Lew, *Story and Space in Renaissance Art: The Rebirth of Continuous Narrative* (Cambridge: Cambridge University Press, 1995).

Apel, W., *Gregorian Chant* (Bloomington, IN: Indiana University Press, 1958).

Apter-Gabriel, Ruth (ed.), *Chagall: Dreams and Drama* (Jerusalem: Israel Museum, 1993).

Aptowitzer, V., 'Aseneth, the Wife of Joseph: A Haggadic Literary-Historical Study', *HUCA* 1 (1924), pp. 239-306.

Ariès, Philippe, *Centuries of Childhood* (London: Cape, 1962).

Art Treasures of England: The Regional Collections (Catalogue of 1998 exhibitions; London: The Royal Academy of Arts, 1998).

Attridge, H., *The Interpretation of Biblical History in the Antiquitates Judaicae of Flavius Josephus* (Missoula: Scholars Press, 1976).

—*Scenes from the Drama of European Literature* (trans. R. Mannheim; New York, 1959).

Auerbach, Erich, *Mimesis* (Princeton: Princeton University Press, 1953).

Baal-Teshuva, Jacob, *Marc Chagall* (Köln: Taschen, 1998).

Babington, Bruce, and Peter William Evans, *Biblical Epics: Sacred Narrative in the Hollywood Cinema* (Manchester: Manchester University Press, 1993).

Backhouse, Janet, *The Illuminated Page: Ten Centuries of Manuscript Painting in the British Library* (London: The British Library, 1997).

Bal, Mieke, *Lethal Love: Feminist Literary Readings of Biblical Love Stories* (Bloomington: Indiana University Press, 1987).

—*Reading Rembrandt: Beyond the Word Image Opposition* (Cambridge: Cambridge University Press, 1991).

Barkan, Elazar, and Marie-Denise Shelton (eds.), *Borders, Boundaries, Diasporas* (Stanford, CA: Stanford University Press, 1998).

Barrett, G.S., *The Earliest Christian Hymn* (London: James Clarke, 1897).

Bash, Anthony, *Ambassadors for Christ: An Exploration of Ambassadorial Language in the New Testament* (Wissenschaftliche Untersuchungen zum Neuen Testament, 92; Tübingen: J.C.B. Mohr [Paul Siebeck], 1997).

Basil of Seleucia, *Oration 7 (PG* 85.110).

Bassnett, S., and A. Lefevere, *Constructing Cultures: Essays on Literary Translation* (Clevedon, Philadelphia, Toronto, Sydney, Johannesburg: Multilingual Matters, 1998).

Bayen, Bruno, *La Fuite en Égypte* (Paris: L'Arche, 1999).

Bazley, Basil M., 'Freemasonry in Kipling's Works', *The Kipling Journal* 16 (1949), pp. 13-14, and *The Kipling Journal* 17 (1950), pp. 7-11.

Beasley-Murray, Paul, 'Colossians 1.15-20: An Early Christian Hymn Celebrating the Lordship of Christ', in Donald A. Hagner and Murray J. Harris (eds.), *Pauline Studies: Essays Presented to Professor F.F. Bruce on his 70th Birthday* (Grand Rapids, MI: Eerdmans, 1980), pp. 169-83.

Beckett, L., *Parsifal* (Cambridge: Cambridge University Press, 1996).

Beckett, Wendy, *The Gaze of Love: Meditations on Art* (London: Marshall Pickering, 1996).

Benham, H., *Latin Church Music in England 1460–1575* (London: Barrie & Jenkins, 1977).

Berdini, Paolo, *The Religious Art of Jacopo Bassano: Painting as Visual Exegesis* (Cambridge: Cambridge University Press, 1997).

Berger, B., and P. Berger, *The War over the Family* (London: Hutchinson, 1983).

Bernidaki-Aldous, Eleftheria A., *Blindness in a Culture of Light* (Frankfurt: Peter Lang, 1990).

Bible: Authorized King James Version (with an Introduction and Notes by Robert Carroll and Stephen Prickett; Oxford World's Classics; Oxford and New York: Oxford University Press, 1997).

Billson, Anne, *My Name Is Michael Caine: A Life in Film* (London: Muller, 1991).

Bischel, M.A., 'Hymns, Early Christian', *ABD* 3 (1992), p. 351.

Bloch, Ernst, *Atheism in Christianity: The Religion of the Exodus and the Kingdom* (New York: Heider, 1972).

Blome, Richard (ed.), *History of the Old and New Testaments Extracted from the Sacred Scriptures, the Holy Fathers, and Other Ecclesiastical Writers* (London, 4th impression, 1712).

Bohak, G., *'Joseph and Aseneth' and the Jewish Temple in Hierapolis* (Atlanta: Scholars Press, 1996).

Bojarski, Edmund A., 'A Conversation with Kipling on Conrad', *The Kipling Journal* 34 (1934), pp. 12-15.

Bordwell, David, *Making Meaning* (London: Harvard University Press, 1991).

Brémond, Henri, *A Literary History of Religious Thought in France*. III. *The Triumph of Mysticism* (London: SPCK, 1936).

Brie, S., and D. Toreville, 'Moral Ambiguity and Contradiction in Dead Poet's Society', in C. Marsh and G. Ortiz (eds.), *Explorations in Theology and Film* (Oxford: Basil Blackwell, 1997), pp??

Brock, S., 'Sarah and the Aqedah', *Le Muséon* 87 (1974), pp. 67-77.

Brooks, Cleanth Jr, and Robert Penn Warren, *Understanding Fiction* (New York: Appleton-Century-Crofts, 1943).

Brosh, Na'ama, and Rachel Milstein (eds.), *Biblical Stories in Islamic Painting* (Jerusalem: Israel Museum, 1991).

Brown, Karl, *Adventures with D.W. Griffith* (New York: Signet, 1973).

Brown, Raymond E., *The Birth of the Messiah* (New York: Doubleday, 1993).

Brueggeman, Walter, *The Bible and Post-Modern Imagination: Texts under Negotiation* (London: SCM Press, 1993).

—*Cadences of Home. Preaching among Exiles* (Louisville, KY: Westminster John Knox Press, 1997).

Budick, E.M., *Fiction and Historical Consciousness in the American Romance Tradition* (New Haven and London: Yale University Press, 1993).

Burchard, C., 'Joseph and Aseneth', in J.H. Charlesworth (ed.), *The Old Testament Pseudepigrapha* (New York: Doubleday, 1985), II, pp. 177-248.

Buscombe, E. (ed.), *The BFI Companion to the Western* (London: Andrew Deutsch/BFI Publishing, 1998).

Butler, Judith, *Gender Trouble: Feminism and the Subversion of Identity* (New York: Routledge, 1990).

Caine, Michael, *Acting in Film* (New York: Applause Theatre Book Publishers, 1990).

Calkins, Robert G., *Illuminated Books of the Middle Ages* (London: Thames and Hudson, 1983).

Campbell, J., *The Hero with a Thousand Faces* (Princeton: Princeton University Press, 1988).

Carli, Enzo, *Duccio's Maestà* (Florence: Istituto Fotocromo Italiano, 1998).

Carrington, Charles, *Rudyard Kipling: His Life and Work* (London: Macmillan, 1955).

Carroll, Robert P., 'Biblical Translation', in Adrian Hastings (ed.), *The Oxford Companion to Christian Thought* (Oxford: Oxford University Press, 2000).

—'Exile! What Exile? Deportation and the Discourses of Diaspora', in Lester L. Grabbe (ed.), *Leading Captivity Captive* (European Seminar in Historical Methodology 2; JSOTSup, 278; Sheffield: Sheffield Academic Press, 1998), pp. 62-79.

—'The Hebrew Bible as Literature—a Misprision?', *Studia Theologica* 47 (1993), pp. 77-90.

—'Lower Case Bibles: Commodity Culture and the Bible', in J. Cheryl Exum and Stephen D. Moore (eds.), *Biblical Studies/Cultural Studies* (The Third Sheffield Colloquium; JSOTSup, 266; Sheffield: Sheffield Academic Press, 1998), pp. 46-69.

—'The Reader and the Text', in A.D.H. Mayes (ed.), *Text in Context* (Oxford: Oxford University Press, 2000), pp. 3-34.

—*Wolf in the Sheepfold: The Bible as Problematic for Theology* (London: SCM Press, 1997; original edition SPCK, 1991).

Chadd, D. (trans. and ed.), *John Sheppard*: I: *Responsorial Music* (Early English Church Music, 17; London: Stainer & Bell, 1977).

Chesnutt, R.D., *From Death to Life: Conversion in Joseph and Aseneth* (Sheffield: Sheffield Academic Press, 1995).

Ciasca, A. (ed.), *Sacrorum Bibliorum: Fragmenta Copto-Sahidica*, I (Rome: Musei Borgiani, 1885).

Cohen, Morton, *Rudyard Kipling to Rider Haggard: The Record of a Friendship* (Rutherford: Farleigh Dickinson University Press, 1965).

Cohen, P., *Ramban on the Torah* (Massachusetts: Rubin, 1985).

Collins, J.J., *Between Athens and Jerusalem* (New York: Crossroad, 1986).

Cook, N., *Kipling's Myths of Love & Death* (London: Macmillan, 1989).

Cook, Richard, 'Rudyard Kipling and George Orwell', *Modern Fiction Studies* 7 (1961–62), pp. 125-35.

Cooper, J.F., *The Deerslayer* (New York: Signet, 1963).

Cornell, Louis L., *Kipling in India* (London: Macmillan, 1966).

Courtauld, S.A., 'Kipling's Literary Allusions', *The Kipling Journal* 25 (1933), pp. 7-20.

Cox, H.H. (ed.), *The Calov Bible of J.S. Bach* (Ann Arbor, MI: UMI Research Press, 1985).

Creach, Jerome F.D., *Yahweh as Refuge and the Editing of the Hebrew Psalter* (JSOTSup, 217; Sheffield: Sheffield Academic Press, 1996).

Crook, Nora, *Kipling's Myths of Love & Death* (London: Macmillan, 1989).

Curzon, David, *Modern Poems on the Bible: An Anthology* (Philadelphia: Jewish Publication Society, 1994).

D'Espagne, J., *Shibboleth: or the Reformation of several places in the Translation of the French and English Bible* (London, 1655).

Daniel, K.W., *Francis Poulenc: His Artistic Development and Musical Style* (Studies in Musicology, 52; Ann Arbor, MI: UMI Research Press, 1980, 1982).

David, H.T., and A. Mendel (eds.), *The Bach Reader: A Life of Johann Sebastian Bach in Letters and Documents* (New York: W.W. Norton, 1945).

Davies, Philip R., 'Exile? What Exile? Whose Exile?', in Lester L. Grabbe (ed.), *Leading Captivity Captive* (European Seminar in Historical Methodology 2; JSOTSup, 278; Sheffield: Sheffield Academic Press, 1998), pp. 128-38.

—*In Search of 'Ancient Israel'* (JSOTSup, 148; Sheffield: Sheffield Academic Press, 1992).

de Hamal, Christopher, *A History of Illuminated Manuscripts* (London: Guild Publishing, 1986).

—*A History of Illuminated Manuscripts* (London: Phaidon, 2nd edn, 1994).

Dekker, G., and L. Johnston (eds.), *The American Democrat* (Harmondsworth: Penguin, 1969).

Del Mar, N., *Richard Strauss*, I (London: Barrie & Rockliff, 1965).

Derbes, Anne, *Picturing the Passion in Late Medieval Italy: Narrative Painting, Franciscan Ideologies and the Levant* (Cambridge: Cambridge University Press, 1998).

Doane, Mary Ann, *The Desire to Desire: The Woman's Film of the 1940s* (Houndmills: Macmillan, 1987).

Dobrée, Bonamy, *Rudyard Kipling: Realist and Fabulist* (Oxford: Oxford University Press, 1967).

Dochhorn, J., and A.K. Petersen, '*Narratio Ioseph*: A Coptic Joseph-Apocryphon', *JSJ* 30 (1999), pp. 431-63.

Doe, P., 'Latin Polyphony under Henry VIII', *Proceedings of the (Royal) Musical Association* 95 (1968–69), pp. 81-95.

Donoghue, Denis, *The Practice of Reading* (New Haven and London: Yale University Press, 1998).

Doré, Gustave, *La Bible* (Paris: Ars Mundi edition, 1998).

Douglas, Mary, *Leviticus as Literature* (Oxford: Oxford University Press, 1999).

Du Buisson, Mesnil, *Les Peintures de la Synagogue de Doura-Europos* (Rome, 1939).

Duchet-Suchaux, Gaston, and Michel Pastoureau, *The Bible and the Saints* (Flammarion Iconographic Guides; Paris: Flammarion Press, 1994).

Duquesne, Jacques, *La Bible et ses Peintures* (Paris: Fixot, 1989).

Elley, Derek, *The Epic Film: Myth and History* (London: Routledge & Kegan Paul, 1984).

Elliot, J.K. (ed.), *The Apocryphal Jesus: Legends of the Early Church* (Oxford: Oxford University Press, 1996).

—*The Apocryphal New Testament: A Collection of Apocryphal Christian Literature in an English Translation based on M.R. James* (Oxford: Clarendon, 1993).

Ellis, Marc H., *A Reflection on the Jewish Exile and the New Diaspora* (Liverpool: Friends of Sabeel UK, 1998).

Erickson, Kathleen Powers, *At Eternity's Gate. The Spiritual Vision of Vincent van Gogh* (Grand Rapids, MI: Eerdmans, 1998).

Erickson, Richard J., 'Divine Injustice? Matthew's Narrative Strategy and the Slaughter of the Innocents (Matthew 2.13-23)', *JSNT* 64 (1996), pp. 5-27.

Eriksen, Thomas H., *Ethnicity & Nationalism: Anthropological Perspectives* (London: Pluto, 1993).

Exum, J. Cheryl, *Fragmented Women: Feminist (Sub)versions of Biblical Narratives* (Sheffield: Sheffield Academic Press; Valley Forge, PA, 1993).

—*Plotted, Shot and Painted: Cultural Representations of Biblical Women* (JSOTSup, 215; Gender, Culture, Theory, 3; Sheffield: Sheffield Academic Press, 1996).

Exum, J. Cheryl, and Stephen D. Moore (eds.), *Biblical Studies/Cultural Studies* (The Third Sheffield Colloquium; JSOTSup, 266; Sheffield: Sheffield Academic Press, 1998).

Fakhry, A., *The Necroplis of El Bagawat in Kharga Oasis* (Paris: Services des Antiquités de l'Egypte, 1951).

Farrar, Frederic W., *The Life of Christ as Represented in Art* (London: A. & C. Black, 1894).

Farrell, Gabriel, *The Story of Blindness* (London: Oxford University Press, 1956).

Feldman L.H., *Josephus' Interpretation of the Bible* (California: University of California Press, 1998).

—'Josephus' Portrait of Joseph', *RB* 99/2 (1992), pp. 379-417.

Fiedler, Leslie, *Love and Death in the American Novel* (Harmondsworth: Penguin, rev. edn, 1984).

Fischer, E., *J.S. Bach*, EMI 1989, CDH7630392.

Foister, Susan, Ashok Roy and Martyn Wyld, *Holbein's Ambassadors* (Making and Meaning; London: National Gallery Publications Limited, 1997).

Forestier, Sylvie, *Marc Chagall: Die großen Gemälde der Biblischen Botschaft* (Stuttgart: Belser Verlag, 1992).

—*Marc Chagall 1887–1985* (Nice: Musée National Message Biblique Marc Chagall, 1998).

Forshey, G., *American Religious and Biblical Spectaculars* (London: Praeger, 1992).

Fowl, S.E., *The Story of Christ in the Ethics of Paul: An Analysis of the Function of the Hymnic Material in the Pauline Corpus* (JSNTSup, 36; Sheffield: JSOT Press, 1990).

Franxman, T.W., *Genesis and the 'Jewish Antiquities' of Flavius Josephus* (Rome: Biblical Institute Press, 1979).

Fraser, Peter, *Images of the Passion* (Trowbridge: Flicks, 1998).

Freedberg, David, *The Power of Images: Studies in the History and Theory of Response* (Chicago: The University of Chicago Press, 1989).

Freire, Paulo, *The Pedagogy of the Oppressed* (London: Sheed & Ward, 1972).

—*The Politics of Education* (London: Macmillan, 1985).

Fussell, Paul Jr, 'Irony, Freemasonry, and Humane Ethics in Kipling's "The Man Who Would Be King"', *English Literary History* 25 (1958), pp. 216-33.

Ginzberg, L., *The Legends of the Jews*, II and V (Philadelphia: Jewish Publication Society of America, 1909 reprinted 1960).

Gish, Lillian, *The Movies, Mr. Griffith and Me* (London: Columbus, 1988).

Gledhill, John, *Power and Its Disguises: Anthropological Perspectives on Politics* (London: Pluto, 1994).

Goethals, G., 'The Imaged Word: Aesthetics, Fidelity, and New Media Translations', in P.A. Soukup and R. Hodgson (eds.), *Fidelity and Translation: Communicating the Bible in New Media* (Franklin, WI: Sheed & Ward, 1999), pp. 133-72.

Gombrich, E.H., *The Story of Art* (London: Phaidon Press, 16th edn, 1995 [1950]).

Goode, W., *The Family* (Englewood: Prentice–Hall, 1982).

Goodenough E., *Jewish Symbols in the Greco-Roman Period* 10 (Princeton: Princeton University Press, 1953–68).

Gould, G., 25 August 1959, Salzburg Concert, Sony 1994, SMK53474.

Grabbe, Lester L. (ed.), *Leading Captivity Captive* (European Seminar in Historical Methodology 2; JSOTSup, 278; Sheffield: Sheffield Academic Press, 1998).

Grafton, Anthony, April Shelford and Nancy Siraisi (eds.), *New Worlds, Ancient Texts: The Power of Tradition and the Shock of Discovery* (Cambridge, MA and London: The Belknap Press of Harvard University Press, 1992).

Graham, William A., *Beyond the Written Word: Oral Aspects of Scripture in the History of Religion* (Cambridge: Cambridge University Press, 1987).

Grant, Michael, and John Hazel, *Who's Who in Classical Mythology* (London: Routledge, 1996).

Green, Roger Lancelyn (ed.), *Kipling: The Critical Heritage* (London: Routledge & Kegan Paul, 1971).

Greenslade, S.L. (ed.), *The Cambridge History of the Bible*. III. *The West from the Reformation to the Present Day* (Cambridge: Cambridge University Press, 1963).

Gregory of Nyssa, *On the Son of God and the Holy Spirit PG* 46.573.

Grenfell, B.P., and A.S. Hunt, '1786. Christian Hymn with Musical Notation', in *The Oxyrhynchus Papyri*, XV (Egyptian Exploration Society Graeco-Roman Memoirs; London: Egypt Exploration Society, 1922), pp. 21-25.

Grobel, Laurence, *The Hustons* (London: Bloomsbury, 1990).

Grubb, Nancy, *The Life of Christ in Art* (New York: Abbeville, 1996).

Gruen, E.S., *Heritage and Hellenism* (California: University of California Press, 1998).

Gundry, Robert H., *Matthew* (Grand Rapids: Eerdmans, 1994).

Guthrie, D., *New Testament Introduction* (Downers Grove, IL: Inter-Varsity Press, rev. edn, 1970)

—*The Pastoral Epistles: An Introduction and Commentary* (TNTC; Leicester: Inter-Varsity Press; Grand Rapids: Eerdmans, rev. edn, 1990).

Habermas, Jürgen, *Knowledge and Human Interests* (London: Heinemann Educational, 1978).

—*The Theory of Communicative Action* (2 vols; Boston: Beacon Press, 1984, 1987).

Hagen, Rose-Marie, and Rainer Hagen, *Pieter Bruegel* (Cologne: Taschen, 1994).

Hall, S. (ed.), *Melito* (Oxford: Clarendon Press, 1979).

Hare, Douglas R.A., *Matthew* (Interpretation Series; Louisville: John Knox Press, 1993).

Harrington, D.J., *Pseudo-Philo*, in J.H. Charlesworth, *The Old Testament Pseudepigrapha* (Garden City, NY: Doubleday, 1985), II, pp. 297-388.

Harris, Richard, *A Gallery of Reflections: The Nativity of Christ* (Oxford: Lion Publishing, 1995).

Harrison, F.L., *Music in Medieval Britain* (Buren, The Netherlands: Fritz Knuf, 1980).

Harrison, J.F.C., *The Second Coming: Popular Millenarianism, 1780–1850* (London: Routledge & Kegan Paul, 1979).

Harrison, James, *Rudyard Kipling* (Twayne's English Author Series, 339; Boston: Twayne Publishers, 1982).

Hart, J. (ed.), *The Man Who Invented Hollywood: The Autobiography of D.W. Griffith* (Louisville, KY: 1972).

Harthan, John, *Books of Hours and their Owners* (London: Thames and Hudson, 1978).

—*The History of the Illustrated Book* (London: Thames and Hudson, 1997).

Harvey, Paul, *The Oxford Companion to Classical Literature* (Oxford: Oxford University Press, 1986 edn).

Hastings, Adrian (ed.), *The Oxford Companion to Christian Thought* (Oxford: Oxford University Press, 2000).

Hawthorne, Nathaniel, *The Marble Faun* (New York: NEL, 1961).

—*The Scarlet Letter* (Harmondsworth: Penguin, 1970).

Hell, H., *Francis Poulenc* (trans. E. Lockspeiser; London: John Calder, 1959 [French original: Paris: Librairie Plon, 1958]).

Henderson, I., 'Ancient Greek Music', in E. Wellesz (ed.), *The New Oxford History of Music*. I. *Ancient and Oriental Music* (London: Oxford University Press, 1957), pp. 336-403.

Hengel, M., *The Cross of the Son of God: containing The Son of God, Crucifixion, The Atonement* (trans. J. Bowden; London: SCM Press, 1986).

Heyne, E., 'The Lasting Frontier: Reinventing America', in E. Heyne (ed.), *Desert, Garden, Margin, Range: Literature on the American Frontier* (New York: Twayne Publishers; and Toronto: Maxwell MacMillan, 1992), pp. 3-15.

Hill, Christopher, *The English Bible and the Seventeenth-Century Revolution* (London: Allen Lane, 1993).

Hill, Edmonia, 'The Young Kipling', in Harold Orel (ed.), *Kipling: Interviews & Recollections, Volume 1* (London: Macmillan, 1983), p. 99.

Hofman, M., and J. Morehen (eds.), *Latin Music in British Sources c1485–c1610* (EECM Sup. vol. II; London: Stainer & Bell, 1987).

Hofmann K., 'Preface', in K. Ameln (ed.), *Johann Sebastian Bach Motetten Motets BWV 225–230* (Kassel: Bärenreiter-Verlag, 1995), pp. 2, 4.

Horney, Karen, *Feminine Psychology* (London: Routledge & Kegan Paul, 1967).

Howsam, Leslie, *Cheap Bibles: Nineteenth Century Publishing and the British and Foreign Bible Society* (Cambridge: Cambridge University Press, 1993).

Hughes, A., *Medieval Manuscripts for Mass and Office: A Guide to their Organization and Terminology* (Toronto: University of Toronto Press, 1982).

Hull, John M., *Hellenistic Magic and the Synoptic Tradition* (London: SCM Press, 1974).

—*On Sight and Insight: a Journey into the World of Blindness* (Oxford: One World, 1998).

Huston, John, *An Open Book* (London: Columbus Books, 1988).

Imberciadori, J.V., *The Collegiate Church of San Gimignano* (Poggibonsi, Tuscany: Nencini, 1998).

Jacobs, A., 'Joseph the Patriarch', in D.L. Jeffrey (ed.), *A Dictionary of Biblical Tradition in English Literature* (Grand Rapids, MI: Eerdmans, 1992).

Jacobson, H., *A Commentary on Pseudo-Philo's Liber Antiquitatem Biblicarum Vols. 1 and 2* (New York: Ktav, 1996), pp. 196-201.

Jaffrey, Saeed, *Saeed: An Actor's Journey* (London: Constable, 1998).

Jastrow, M., *Dictionary of the Targumim, the Talmud Babli and Jerusalmi, and the Midrashic Literature* (New York: The Judaica Press, 1982).

Jeffrey, David Lyle (ed.), *A Dictionary of Biblical Tradition in English Literature* (Grand Rapids: Eerdmans, 1993).

Jensen, R., 'The Offering of Isaac in Jewish and Christian Tradition', *Biblical Interpretation* 2 (1994), p. 105.

—'Mark 7: 22-26: The Blind Man from Bethsaida', *NTS* 25 (1978), pp. 370-83.

Johnson, E.S., 'Mark 10.46-52: Blind Bartimaeus', *CBQ* 40 (1978), pp. 191-204.

Josephus, *The Jewish Antiquities* (trans. H.St.J. Thackeray in the Loeb Classical Library Series, IV; London: William Heinemann Ltd, 1930).

Kael, Pauline, *When the Lights Go Down* (London: Boyars, 1980).

Kee, H.C., 'The Socio-Cultural Setting of *Joseph and Aseneth*', *NTS* 29 (1983), pp. 398-402.

Kemp, Sandra, *Kipling's Hidden Narratives* (Oxford: Basil Blackwell, 1988).

Kent, D., 'Shackled Imagination—Literary Illusions about Blindness', *Journal of Visual Impairment & Blindness*, 83, 3 (1989), pp. 145-50.

Kimnack, Wilson (ed.), *Jonathan Edwards: Sermons and Discourses 1720–23* (Yale University Press, 1992).

Kipling, R., *Wee Willie Winkie and Other Stories* (1888). A facsimile of the original volume was published in Frome, Somerset, by The R.S. Surtees Society in 1988.

Knight, G.W. III, *The Faithful Sayings in the Pastoral Letters* (Kampen: Kok, 1968).

König, Eberhard, *Caravaggio* (Cologne: Könemann, 1997).

Koosed, J.L., and T. Linafelt, 'How the West Was Not One: Delilah Deconstructs the Western', *Semeia* 74 (1996), pp. 167-82.

Koudelka, Josef, *Exiles* (London: Thames and Hudson, 1997).

Kraeling, C.H., *The Synagogue: The Excavations of Dura-Europos Final Report VIII, Part 1* (New Haven: Yale University Press, 1956).

Kreitzer, Larry J., *Film and Fiction in the Old Testament: On Reversing the Hermeneutical Flow* (The Biblical Seminar, 24; Sheffield: Sheffield Academic Press, 1994).

—*The New Testament in Fiction and Film: On Reversing the Hermeneutical Flow* (Sheffield: Sheffield Academic Press, 1993).

—*Striking New Images: Roman Imperial Coinage and the New Testament World* (JSNTSup, 134; Sheffield: Sheffield Academic Press, 1996).

Lampe, G.W.H., and K.G. Woollcombe (eds.), *Essays on Typology* (London: SCM Press, 1957).

Landfield, Alvin, and Franz R. Epting, *Personal Construct Psychology, Clinical and Personality Assessment* (London: Human Sciences Press, 1986).

Langdon, Helen, *Caravaggio: A Life* (London: Chatto and Windus, 1998).

Lawrence, D.H., *Studies in Classic American Literature* (Harmondsworth: Penguin, 1971).

Le Huray, P., *Music and the Reformation in England 1549–1660* (Cambridge Studies in Music; Cambridge: Cambridge University Press, repr. with corrections 1978 [London: Herbert Jenkins, 1967]).

Leaver, R.A., *J.S. Bach and Scripture: Glosses from the Calov Bible Commentary* (St Louis: Concordia, 1985).

Levine, P., *Leviticus* (The JPS Torah Guide; New York: Schocken Books, 1989).

Lewis, C.S., *Selected Literary Essays* (Cambridge: Cambridge University Press, 1969).

Lieu, J.M., 'Blindness in the Johannine Tradition', *NTS* 34 (1988), pp. 83-95.

Lincoln, Frances, *The First Christmas* (London: The National Gallery, 1992).

Long, A.A., and D.N. Sedley, *The Hellenistic Philosophers* (2 vols.; Cambridge: Cambridge University Press, 1977).

Luz, Ulrich, *The Theology of the Gospel of Matthew* (Cambridge: Cambridge University Press, 1996).

Lyon, John, 'Half-Written Tales: Kipling and Conrad', in Phillip Mallett (ed.), *Kipling Considered* (London: Macmillan, 1989), pp. 115-34.

Machlis, J., *Introduction to Contemporary Music* (New York: W.W. Norton, 2nd edn, 1979 [1961]).

MacIntyre, Alasdair, *After Virtue: A Study in Moral Theory* (London: Duckworth, 2nd edn, 1985).

MacMunn, G.F., 'Kipling's Use of the Old Testament', *The Kipling Journal* 32 (1934), pp. 110-19.

Madsen, Axel, *John Huston* (London: Robson Books, 1979).

Magee, Bryan, *On Blindness: Letters between Bryan Magee and Martin Milligan* (Oxford: Oxford University Press, 1995).

Mallett, Phillip (ed.), *Kipling Considered* (London: Macmillan, 1989).

Malone, Peter, *The Film* (Melbourne: Chevalier, 1971).

Mann, Thomas, *Joseph and his Brothers* (trans. H.T. Lowe-Porter; London: Penguin, 1978).

Marsh, C., and G. Ortiz (eds.), *Explorations in Theology and Film* (Oxford: Basil Blackwell, 1997).

Martin, R.P., 'Aspects of Worship in the New Testament Church', *Vox Evangelica* 2 (1963), pp. 6-32.

—*Reconciliation: A Study of Paul's Theology* (London: Marshall, Morgan & Scott, 1981).

Mason, Philip, *Kipling: The Glass, the Shadow and the Fire* (London: Jonathan Cape, 1975).

May, S., *Stardust and Ashes* (London: SPCK, 1998).

Mayes, A.D.H. (ed.), *Text in Context* (Oxford: Oxford University Press), 2000.

McClure, John A., *Kipling and Conrad: The Colonial Fiction* (Cambridge, MA: Harvard University Press, 1981).

McKinnon, J., 'On the Question of Psalmody in the Ancient Synagogue', in I. Fenlon (ed.), *Early Music History: Studies in Medieval and Early Modern Music*, VI (ed. I. Fenlon; Cambridge: Cambridge University Press, 1986), pp. 159-91.

McKinnon, J. (ed.), *Music in Early Christian Literature* (Cambridge Studies in the Literature of Music; Cambridge: Cambridge University Press, 1987).

McWilliams, J.P. Jr, *The American Epic: Transforming a Genre, 1770–1860* (Cambridge: Cambridge University Press, 1989).

Mellers, W., *Francis Poulenc* (Oxford: Oxford University Press, 1993).

—*Man and his Music: The Story of Musical Experience in the West: Romanticism and the Twentieth Century*, IV (London: Barrie & Jenkins, repr. 1977 [London: Barrie & Rockliff, 1962]).

Meredith, George, *One of Our Conquerors* (1891; London: Chapman and Hall, 1910).

Merleau-Ponty, Maurice, *The Phenomenology of Perception* (London: Routledge, 1962).

Milgrom, J., *Leviticus* (New York: Doubleday, 1991).

—'Two Biblical Hebrew Priestly Terms: *Sheqetz* and *Tame*', *MAARAV* 6 (1992), pp. 107-16.

Miller, James E. *The Western Paradise: Greek and Hebrew Traditions* (San Francisco: International Scholars Publications, 1997).

Miller, Malcolm, *Chartres Cathedral* (Andover, Hampshire: Pitkin, 1996).

Minnis, A.J., *Mediaeval Theory of Authorship* (London: Scolar, 1984).

Mintz, Ian, *Hurban: Responses to Catastrophe in Hebrew Literature* (New York: Columbia University Press, 1984).

Morgan, David, 'Family', in P. Clarke and A. Linzey (eds.), *Dictionary of Ethics, Theology and Society* (London: Routledge, 1996), pp. 371-75.

Mormando, Franco, 'An Early Renaissance Guide for the Perplexed: Bernardino of Siena's *De inspirationibus*', in John C. Hawley (ed.), *Through a Glass Darkly: Essays in the Religious Imagination* (New York: Fordham University Press, 1996), pp. 24-49.

Mount, Ferdinand, *The Subversive Family* (London: Jonathan Cape, 1982).

Mountford, J.F., 'Greek Music in the Papyri and Inscriptions', in J.U. Powell and E.A. Barber (eds.), *New Chapters in the History of Greek Literature* (Second Series; Oxford: Clarendon Press, 1929), pp. 146-83.

Muir, Kenneth, 'Kipling and Eliot', *Notes & Queries* 1 (1954), pp. 400-401.

Mulvey, Laura, *Visual and Other Pleasures* (London: Macmillan, 1989).

Murphy, F.J., *Pseudo-Philo: Rewriting the Bible* (New York/Oxford: Oxford University Press).

Murray, C., 'Art and the Early Church', *JTS* 28 (1977), pp. 313-45.

Murray, Dom Gregory, *The Choral Chants of the Mass* (The Society of St Gregory, 7; Bristol: Burleigh Press, 1947).

Murray, Judith Sargent, *The Gleaner* (1798).

Murray, Peter, and Linda Murray, *The Oxford Companion to Christian Art and Architecture* (Oxford: Oxford University Press, 1996).

Mussies, G., 'The *Interpretatio Judaica* of Sarapis', in M.J. Vermaseren (ed.), *Studies in Hellenistic Religions* (Leiden: E.J. Brill, 1979), pp. 189-214.

Neale, S., 'Questions of Genre', in Barry Keith Grant (ed.), *Film Genre Reader II* (Austin: University of Texas, 1995), p. 5.

Neusner, Jacob, *Understanding Seeking Faith: Essays on the Case in Judaism* (Atlanta: Scholars Press, 1986).

Nickelsburg, G.W.E., 'The Bible Rewritten and Expanded', in M.E. Stone (ed.), *Jewish Writings of the Second Temple Period* (Philadelphia: Fortress Press; Assen: Van Gorcum, 1984), pp. 89-156.

—'Good and Bad Leaders in Pseudo-Philo's *Liber Antiquitatem Biblicarum*', in G.W.E. Nickelsburg and J.J. Collins (eds.), *Ideal Figures in Ancient Judaism* (Ann Arbor, MI: Scholars Press, 1980), pp. 49-65.

Niehoff, M., *The Figure of Joseph in Post-biblical Jewish Literature* (Leiden: E.J. Brill, 1992).

Noakes, Susan, 'Gracious Words: Luke's Jesus and the Reading of Sacred Poetry at the Beginning of the Christian Era', in Jonathan Boyarin (ed.), *The Ethnography of Reading* (Berkeley: University of California Press, 1993).

Norden, E., *Agnostos Theos: Untersuchungen zur Formengeschichte religiöser Rede* (Stuttgart: Teubner, 1913; repr. Darmstadt: Wissenschaftliche Buchgesellschaft, 1956).

O'Kane, Martin, 'The Biblical King David and his Artistic and Literary Afterlives', *Biblical Interpretation* 6 (1998) pp. 313-47.

Origen, *Homilies on Genesis 8* (*PG* 12.208-09).

Orwell, George, 'Inside the Whale', in Orwell, *Inside the Whale and Other Essays* (Harmondsworth: Penguin Books, 1962), pp. 9-50.

—'Rudyard Kipling', in Andrew Rutherford (ed.), *Kipling's Mind and Art* (London: Oliver & Boyd, 1964), p. 72.

Paffard, Mark, *Kipling's Indian Fiction* (London: Macmillan, 1989).

Page, Norman, *A Kipling Companion* (London: Macmillan, 1984).

Pailin, David A., *A Gentle Touch: From a Theology of Handicap to a Theology of Human Being* (London: SPCK, 1992).

Parker, John, *Sean Connery* (London: Victor Gollancz, 1993).

Paulson, William R, *Enlightenment, Romanticism and the Blind in France* (Princeton: Princeton University Press, 1987).

Payne, Robert, *Rome Triumphant: How the Empire Celebrated its Victories* (New York: Barnes & Noble, 1962).

Pêcheux, Michel, *Language, Semantics and Ideology: Stating the Obvious* (London: Macmillan, 1982).

Pelikan, Jaroslav (ed.), *Luther's Works: Lectures on Genesis* (St Louis, MO, 1964).

Philonenko, M., *Joseph et Aseneth* (Leiden: E.J. Brill, 1968).

Pinney, Thomas (ed.), *The Letters of Rudyard Kipling, Volume 1: 1872–1889* (London: Macmillan, 1990).

—*Something of Myself and Other Biographical Writings* (Cambridge: Cambridge University Press, 1990).

Pöhlmann, E. (ed.), *Denkmäler altgriechischer Musik: Sammlung, Übertragung und Erläuterung aller Fragmente und Fälshchungen* (Nürnberg: Verlag Hans Carl, 1970).

Pollak, Oliver B., 'The Man Who Would Be King', *The Kipling Journal* 46 (September 1979), pp. 10-13.

Porter, Stanley E., Καταλλάσσω *in Ancient Greek Literature, with Reference to the Pauline Writings* (Estudios de Filología Neotestamentaria, 5; Cordoba: Ediciones El Almendro, 1994).

—'Pauline Authorship and the Pastoral Epistles: Implications for Canon', *BBR* 5 (1995), pp. 105-23;

—'Peace, Reconciliation', in Gerald F. Hawthorne, Ralph P. Martin and Daniel G. Reid (eds.), *Dictionary of Paul and his Letters* (Leicester: Inter-Varsity Press, 1993), pp. 695-99.

Porter, W.J., 'Sacred Music at the Turn of the Millennia', in S.E. Porter *et al.* (eds.), *Faith in the Millennium* (Roehampton Institute London Papers, 7; JSNTSup; Sheffield: Sheffield Academic Press [in preparation]).

Poulenc, F., *Entretiens avec Claude Rostand* (Paris: R. Julliard, 1954).

—*My Friends and Myself* (conversations assembled by S. Audel; trans. J. Harding; London: Dennis Dobson, 1978; French original: Geneva and Paris: La Palatine, 1963).

Powell, M.A., *The Gospels* (Philadelphia: Fortress Press, 1998)

Prigent, P., *Le Judaisme et l'Image* (Tübingen: Mohr, 1991).

Puffett, Derrick, 'Salome as Music Drama', in D. Puffett (ed.), *Richard Strauss: 'Salome'* (Cambridge: Cambridge University Press, 1989).

Pui-Lan, Kwok, *Discovering the Bible in the Non-Biblical World* (Maryknoll: Orbis, 1995).

Pye, D., 'The Western (Genre and Movies)', in Barry Keith Grant (ed.), *Film Genre Reader II* (Austin: University of Texas Press, 1995), pp??

Ragusa, I., and R.B. Green (eds.), *Meditations on the Life of Christ* (trans. I. Ragusa; Princeton, NJ, 1961).

Reed, T.J., *Thomas Mann: The Uses of Tradition* (Oxford: Clarendon Press, 1974).

Reeves, Marjorie, 'The Bible and Literary Authorship in the Middle Ages', in Stephen Prickett (ed.), *Reading the Text: Biblical Criticism and Literary Theory* (Oxford: Basil Blackwell, 1991), p. 16.

Reich-Ranicki, Marcel, *Thomas Mann and his Family* (trans. Ralph Manheim; London: Fontana, 1990).

Reinach, T., *La musique greque* (Editions d'aujourd'hui; Paris: Payot, 1926).

Restoring the Ambassadors (video; London: The National Gallery, 1996).

Reventlow, Henning Graf, *The Authority of the Bible and the Rise of the Modern World* (London: SCM Press, 1984).

Rhymer, Joseph, *The Illustrated Life of Jesus Christ* (London: Bloomsbury, 1994).

Ricketts, Harry, *The Unforgiving Minute: A Life of Rudyard Kipling* (London: Chatto & Windus, 1998).

Ricoeur, Paul, *Interpretation Theory: Discourse and the Surplus of Meaning* (Forth Worth: Texas Christian University, 1976).

Romer, J., *Testament: The Bible and History* (London: Michael O'Mara Books Limited, 1988).

Rutherford, Andrew (ed.), *Kipling's Mind and Art* (London: Oliver & Boyd, 1964).

Ryken, Leland, James C. Wilhoit and Tremper Longman III (eds.), *Dictionary of Biblical Imagery* (Downers Grove, IL and Leicester, England: Intervarsity Press, 1998).

Sacks, Oliver, *Awakenings* (London: Duckworth, 1973).

—*A Leg to Stand On* (London: Duckworth, 1984).

—*Seeing Voices: A Journey into the World of the Deaf* (London: Picador, 1991).

Santoni, Eric, *La Vie de Jésus* (Paris: Editions Hermé, 1990).

Sarna, N.M., *Genesis* (The JPS Torah Guide; New York: Schocken Books, 1989).

Sawyer, J., 'Root Meanings in Hebrew', *JSS* 12/1 (1967).

Schillaci, Anthony, *Movies and Morals* (New York: Sheed and Ward, 1968).

Scholder, Klaus, *The Birth of Modern Critical Theology: Origins and Problems of Biblical Criticism in the Seventeenth Century* (London: SCM Press; Philadelphia: Trinity Press International, 1990).

Schweitzer, A., *J.S. Bach* (2 vols.; trans. E. Newman; Leipzig: Breitkopf & Härtel, 1911).

Scott, James M. (ed.), *Exile: Old Testament, Jewish, and Christian Conceptions* (SJSJ, 56; Leiden: E.J. Brill, 1997).

Senior, Donald, *What Are They Saying about Matthew?* (New York: Paulist Press, 1996).

Smith, J.A., 'The Ancient Synagogue, the Early Church and Singing', *Music & Letters* 65.1 (1984), pp. 1-16.

Snaith, N.E. (ed.), *Leviticus and Numbers* (London: Nelson, 1967).

Sobchak, V., 'Surge and Splendor: A Phenomenology of the Hollywood Historical Epic', in Barry K. Grant, *Film Genre Reader II* (Austin: University of Texas Press, 1995), pp. 280-307.

Sontag, Susan, *Against Interpretation* (New York: Dell Publishing Co., 1966).

Stacey, Jackie, *Star Gazing: Hollywood Cinema and Female Spectatorship* (London: Routledge, 1994).

Stepanov, Alexander, *Lucas Cranach the Elder* (Bournemouth: Parkstone, 1997).

Stern, R., C. Jefford and G. Debona, *Savior on the Silver Screen* (New York: Paulist Press, 1999).

Stewart, J.I.M., *Rudyard Kipling* (New York: Dodd, Mead & Company, 1966).

Stock, Augustine, *The Method and Message of Matthew* (Collegeville, MN: The Liturgical Press, 1994).

Stocker, M., 'Biblical Story and the Heroine', in M. Warner (ed.), *The Bible as Rhetoric: Studies in Biblical Persuasion and Credibility* (London: Routledge, 1990), pp. 81-104.

—*Judith, Sexual Warrior: Women and Power in Western Culture* (New Haven and London: Yale University Press, 1998).

Sturgis, Alexander, and Susan Foister, *Making and Meaning: Holbein's Ambassadors* (video; London: The National Portrait Gallery, 1997).

Sugirtharajah, R.S., *Voices from the Margin: Interpreting the Bible in the Third World* (London: SPCK, 1995).

Sukenik, E., *The Ancient Synagogue of Beith Alpha* (Jerusalem, 1932).

Taylor, Charles, *Sources of the Self: The Making of the Modern Identity* (Cambridge: Cambridge University Press, 1989).

Terry, C.S., 'Johann Sebastian Bach', in E. Blom (ed.), *Grove's Dictionary of Music and Muscians* (10 vols.; New York: St Martin's Press, 5th edn, 1954), I, p. 306.

Thomas, Anabel, *Illustrated Dictionary of Narrative Painting* (London: National Gallery Publications, 1994).

Thompson, George, *The First Philosophers* (London: Lawrence and Wishart, 1955).

Thompson, T.L., *The Bible in History: How Writers Create a Past* (London: Pimlico, 2000).

Tompkins, J.M.S., *The Art of Rudyard Kipling* (London: Methuen & Co., 1959).

Torito, Marco, *Pinacoteca Nazionale di Siena* (Genova: Sagep Editrice, 1993 edn).

Tracy, David, *The Analogical Imagination* (New York: Crossroad, 1987).

Trimmer, Mrs (Sarah), *Help to the Unlearned in the Study of the Holy Scriptures* (London, 2nd edn, 1806).

Turner Pictures Old Testament Mini-series, A Lube Production (USA) in association with Lux Vide BetaFilm (Germany) and Rai Uno (Italy) © Turner Pictures 1994–1996. The series is distributed by Turner Home Entertainment, Atlanta, GA 30303, USA and is available as the *TNT Bible Collection* through Gateway Films/Vision Video at http.//www.vision video.com

Underwood, F.A., 'The Indian Railway Library', *The Kipling Journal* 46 (March 1979), pp. 6-15, and *The Kipling Journal* 46 (June 1979), pp. 10-17.

Usherwood, Nicholas, *The Bible in 20th Century Art* (London: Pagoda, 1987).

Van Woerden, I., 'The Iconography of the Sacrifice of Abraham', *VC* 15 (1961), pp. 214-55.

Verdi, Richard (ed.), *Art Treasures of England. The Regional Collections*. Catalogue of 1998 exhibition (London: The Royal Academy of Arts, 1998).

Vergote, A., and A. Tomayo, *The Parental Figures and the Representation of God* (Paris: Mouton, 1981).

Vermes, G., 'Bible and Midrash: Early Old Testament Exegesis', in P.R. Ackroyd and C.F. Evans (eds.), *The Cambridge History of the Bible* (Cambridge: Cambridge University Press,1970), I, pp. 129-31.

Viertel, Peter, *Dangerous Friends* (Middlesex: Penguin Books, 1992).

Wagner-Lam, A., and G.W. Oliver, 'Folklore of Blindness', *Journal of Visual Impairment and Blindness* 88, 3 (1994), pp. 367-276.

Wainwright Elizabeth, 'The Gospel of Matthew', in Elisabeth Schüssler Fiorenza (ed.), *Searching the Scripture: A Feminist Commentary* (London: SCM Press, 1995), pp. 635-77.

Wallman, Jane, 'Disability as Hermeneutic: Towards a Theology of Community' (unpublished PhD thesis, University of Birmingham, School of Education, 2000).

Walsh, Eugene A., *The Priesthood in the Writings of the French School* (Washington, DC: Catholic University of America Press, 1949).

Weiss, Z., and E. Netzer, *Promise and Redemption: A Synagogue Mosaic from Sephhoris* (Jerusalem: The Israel Museum, 1996).

Wellesz, E., *A History of Byzantine Music and Hymnography* (Oxford: Clarendon Press, 1961, 2nd rev. edn, 1961, repr. 1998).

Werner, E., 'Music', in G.A. Buttrick (ed.), *The Interpreter's Dictionary of the Bible* (4 vols.; Nashville, TN: Abingdon Press, 1962), III, pp. 457-69.

West, M.L., 'Analecta Musica', *ZPE* 92 (1992), pp. 1-54.

—*Ancient Greek Music* (Oxford: Clarendon Press, 1992).

—'Texts with Musical Notation', in M.W. Haslam *et al.* (eds.), *Oxyrhynchus Papyri*, LXV (Egypt Exploration Society Graeco-Roman Memoirs, 85; London: Egypt Exploration Society, 1998), pp. 81-102.

Whitehead, A.N., *Process and Reality: An Essay in Cosmology* (The Gifford Lectures in Edinburgh 1927–28; New York and London: The Free Press [1929], paperback 1979).

Wilde, Oscar, *De Profundis* (letter to Lord Alfred Douglas from Reading Gaol, January– March 1897), in Rupert Hart-Davis (ed.), *The Letters of Oscar Wilde* (London: Hart-Davis, 1962).

—*Salomé* (trans. Lord Alfred Douglas), in Oscar Wilde, *The Works of Oscar Wilde* (London: Spring Books, 1963).

Wilkinson, John, *Interpretation and Community* (London: Macmillan, 1963).

Williamson, H.S., 'Masonic References in the Works of Rudyard Kipling', *The Kipling Journal* 31 (1934), pp. 76-92.

Wilson, Angus, *The Strange Ride of Rudyard Kipling: His Life and Works* (Harmondsworth: Penguin Books, 1979).

Wilson, Carolyn C., *Italian Paintings XIV—XVI Centuries in the Museum of Fine Arts, Houston* (The Museum of Fine Arts, Houston, in association with Rice University Press; London: Merrell Holberton, 1996).

Wilson, Derek, *Hans Holbein: Portrait of an Unknown Man* (London: Weidenfeld & Nicolson, 1996).

Wilson, Edmund, 'The Kipling That Nobody Read', in Andrew Rutherford (ed.), *Kipling's Mind and Art* (London: Oliver & Boyd, 1964).

Wintermute, O.S., *Jubilees*, in J.H. Charlesworth (ed.), *The Old Testament Pseudepigrapha* (Garden City, NY: Doubleday, 1985), II, pp. 35-142.

Woman's Bible (New York: European Publishing, 1895, 1898).

Wright, Susan, *The Bible in Art* (New York: Smithmark, 1996).

Wulf, Joseph (*Literatur und Dichtung im Dritten Reich: Ein Dokumentation* [1966], p. 24), cited by R.J. Hollingdale in *Thomas Mann: A Critical Study* (London: Hart-Davis, 1971), p. 23.

Wyke, M., *Projecting the Past: Ancient Rome, Cinema and History* (New York and London: Routledge, 1997).

Yule, Andrew, *Sean Connery: Neither Shaken Nor Stirred* (London: Little, Brown and Company, 1993).

INDEXES

INDEX OF REFERENCES

OLD TESTAMENT

NEW TESTAMENT

OTHER ANCIENT REFERENCES

INDEX OF AUTHORS

JOURNAL FOR THE STUDY OF THE OLD TESTAMENT
SUPPLEMENT SERIES